SOUTH AFRICA
AND THE INTERNATIONAL MEDIA
1972–1979

SOUTH AFRICA
AND THE
INTERNATIONAL MEDIA
1972–1979

A Struggle for Representation

JAMES SANDERS

FRANK CASS
LONDON • PORTLAND, OR

First published in 2000 in Great Britain by
FRANK CASS PUBLISHERS
Newbury House, 900 Eastern Avenue
London IG2 7HH

and in the United States of America by
FRANK CASS PUBLISHERS
c/o ISBS, 5804 N.E. Hassalo Street
Portland, Oregon 97213-3644

Website: www.frankcass.com

British Library Cataloguing in Publication Data

Sanders, James
South Africa and the international media, 1972–1979: a
struggle for representation
1. Mass media – South Africa – History 2. South Africa – In
mass media 3. South Africa – Foreign public opinion, British
4. South Africa – Foreign public opinion, American
I. Title
302.2'3'0968

ISBN 0-7146-4979-1 (cloth)
ISBN 0-7146-8041-9 (paper)

Library of Congress Cataloging-in-Publication Data

Sanders, James, 1963–
South Africa and the international media, 1972–1979: a struggle
for representation / James Sanders.
p. cm.
Based on the author's doctoral dissertation.
Includes bibliographical references (p.) and index.
ISBN 0-7146-4979-1. – ISBN 0-7146-8041-9 (pbk.)
1. South Africa–In mass media. 2. Mass media–Political aspects–
South Africa. 3. Anti-apartheid movements–South Africa. 4. South
Africa–Race relations–Political aspects. 5. South Africa–
Politics and government–1961–1978. I. Title.
P96.S68S26 1999
070.4'49968–dc21   99-39575
                                                                    CIP

Typeset by Vitaset, Paddock Wood, Kent
Printed in Great Britain by
MPG Books Ltd, Bodmin, Cornwall

Contents

Illustrations

Foreword

This scholarly book has an interest which goes far beyond its special time and place. The problems of media coverage of South Africa in the 1970s are themselves important and dramatic, at a time when the southern part of the continent was surging back into the headlines as a potential new Vietnam and a frontier of the Cold War. But the three main media stories which this book dissects – the exposure of low black wages, the South African intervention in Angola and the Soweto uprising – also provide general insights into the problems of journalists operating in foreign countries, and present a kind of caricature of the limitations and shortcomings of the media in providing their 'first draft of history'. In these pages any student of journalism can find many of the recurring snags and pitfalls which lurk on the road towards truthful reporting, including ideological and racist assumptions, dependence on very limited sources, and particularly the elaborate disinformation which governments can so easily provide. The remarkable story of South Africa's information network, set up by Dr Eschel Rhoodie, the Goebbels of the Pretoria government, shows how easily a well-financed propaganda offensive could buy both favourable comment and reporting in the western world. But the author's accounts of how misleading news stories came to be published are scrupulously dispassionate and fair, backed up by painstaking sources. They avoid any simplifications and conspiracy theories which bedevil many of the left-wing critiques of the media; but they leave readers to make their own deductions about the shortcomings of journalism.

Each of the three major case-histories focuses on quite different kinds of coverage. The exposure of the low wages paid by British companies in South Africa, conducted by Adam Raphael in the *Guardian* in 1973–74 and recounted in Chapter 5, was an outstanding example of investigatory reporting from Britain at a time when it was at a peak, backed up by strong editorial support – at the cost of some loss of advertising – and leading to a parliamentary investigation which succeeded dramatically in improving wages and changing company attitudes. But it also spotlighted the basic argument about the role of capitalist enterprises in confronting an authoritarian and racist regime: should they seek to alleviate the hardships of employees, or should they get out altogether through disinvestment, and thus deny the regime any economic support from overseas, and precipitate an economic crisis which would force it to change the system? And the campaign against low wages itself had a basic limitation which emerges clearly in this account: for it was essentially paternalist in its conception, based on the assumption that black workers were the passive victims of apartheid, dependent on the decisions of white masters, and unable themselves to play a decisive role in their liberation from the system.

The coverage of the Soweto uprising in 1976, dealt with in Chapter 7, shows another aspect of journalistic paternalism: for the reporting of the students' revolt revealed the previous lack of black reporters who were alone able to understand the rebellion which was largely unforeseen by white editors and journalists. After Soweto it fell on the shoulders of black journalists, as the black editor Percy Qoboza later put it, 'to keep South Africa and the outside world informed about what was going on'. And the realisation that young black rebels were challenging apartheid through their own efforts, as James Sanders emphasises, 'forced South African liberals to face the contradictions of their position'. The fear that an African revolt would threaten the whole future of whites in South Africa, expressed among others by Alan Paton, gave way to the acknowledgement by the media overseas that Africans were making apartheid unworkable. 'The representation of African agency,' as Sanders writes, 'far from instilling panic or philosophical angst in the commentaries of the international media, demonstrated the scale of resistance to the apartheid system.'

The other case-history, about the revelation of South Africa's invasion of Angola in 1975–76, dealt within Chapter 6, has a broader significance as a classic example of cold-war reporting, when the confrontations in Southern Africa were being seen as a parallel to the Vietnam war. But the different interpretations which the author describes are not straightforward issues between left-wing and right-wing journalists, and they show all the confusions and accidents which characterise most field reporting. The discovery that South African troops were in Angola was made by two reporters sympathetic to the anti-communist leader Jonas Savimbi, Fred Bridgland of Reuters and Michael Nicholson of Independent Television News; Reuters were nervous about stating categorically that South Africans were fighting inside Angola, so 'the overall effect of Bridgland's story was not clarity but confusion'; while Nicholson's TV report, which gave only brief snatched footage of two white faces, was not convincing enough to have much immediate impact. When Tony Hodges filed a report on the South African presence for the *Observer* in London it was not put on the front page. The cruder Cold War element in the Angolan story overwhelmed the more significant fact that South Africa had entered the war. 'While the majority of the observers of the Angolan war became distracted by the Cold War implications', as Sanders describes, 'only the vigilant few concentrated on the South African presence.'

The three case-histories are only part of the author's dissection of the role of the media which, as he says, 'reveals at least as much about the international media as it does about South Africa'. He shows how heavily foreign correspondents – until recently all white – depended on a tiny group of sources, and one newspaper, the *Rand Daily Mail*; while a single stringer could often write for several newspapers under different by-lines. He suggests how the comforts and privileges of the correspondents, and their fear of being deported, could easily discourage them from more adventurous reporting of the black opposition. And he describes the limitations of the anti-apartheid movement abroad as an effective lobby; and how it had many similarities with the anti-slave trade in the eighteenth and nineteenth centuries. But he also shows how important the role of individual journalists could be, particularly the protégés of Laurence Gandar, the crusading editor of the *Rand Daily Mail* from 1957 and 1966.

For many readers without specialist knowledge of South Africa this book spotlights more general questions about the difficulties of fair reporting. By rigorously looking back at news reports in the light of the pressures at the time, and the facts as they later emerged, it provides a model for the most useful area of media studies, which can enable both journalists and historians to assess the accuracy of contemporary reporting and its qualifications as 'the first draft of history'.

Anthony Sampson
July 1999

Acknowledgements

This book originated as a doctoral dissertation written under the supervision of Professor Shula Marks. I remain particularly grateful for her critical guidance, imagination and encouragement. At the heart of my thesis were the extensive interviews I conducted with more than 140 journalists, anti-apartheid campaigners and South African propagandists. These sources provided endless challenges and essential insights. Although I would like to thank all the interviewees who found the time to talk with me, particular thanks go to Stanley Uys, Benjamin Pogrund, Denis Herbstein, Adam Raphael, J.D.F. Jones, Anthony Sampson, Len Clarke, Mike Popham, William Raynor, Barbara Rogers, Ethel de Kaiser, Antony Thomas, Larry Heinzerling, Michael Kaufman, Karen Rothmyer, David Beresford, John Carlin, Chris Munnion, Mervyn Rees, Nat Serache and Gabu Tugwana.

My research in South Africa and the United States of America was made much easier by the friendship and kindness of Stephen, Gerlind and Lisa Bayliss, David Ferguson, Miranda and S.K. Pyne, Daniel Rosenberg and D.C. Lord. I consulted numerous libraries in both countries but special reference should be made to the Africa News archive in Durham, North Carolina, the Cullen Library, University of the Witwatersrand and the Cory Library, Rhodes University, Grahamstown. In Britain, my research benefitted from lengthy discussions with Ralph Smith, Shaun Milton, Geoffrey Godbert, Nick Holt and Ralph Tittley. My reading of the press reports of the 1970s would have been far more laborious without the cuttings assembled by the Royal Institute of International Affairs. The research was supported by grants and scholarships from the School of Oriental and African Studies, the University of London Central Research Fund and the Institute of Commonwealth Studies, which awarded me a Postgraduate Fellowship for the year 1995–96.

In any study of the media, the need for accurate reporting and balanced analysis is essential. It is simply not good enough to preach one thing while practising another. I have attempted to be scrupulously fair with my sources but in any book containing this degree of detail some errors are inevitable. I will be grateful for any corrections.

My final thanks, however, go to my parents, John and Diana Sanders, my wife, Amrit, and my daughter, Isidore, who tolerated my long absences from home and provided a welcome release from the vagaries of South African propaganda.

James Sanders
Evesham
June 1999

Abbreviations

A-AI	African-American Institute
A-AM	Anti-Apartheid Movement
ABC	American Broadcasting Company
ACOA	American Committee on Africa
AFP	Agence France Presse
AI	Amnesty International
AIM	Accuracy in Media
ANC	African National Congress
AP	Associated Press
ATV	Anglia Television
BBC	British Broadcasting Corporation
BCM	Black Consciousness Movement
BFI	British Film Institute
BOSS	Bureau of State Security
CBS	Columbia Broadcasting System
CCSA	Christian Concern for Southern Africa
CFS	Committee for Fairness in Sport
CIA	Central Intelligence Agency
CIS	Counter-Information Services
CNA	Central News Agency
CPGB	Communist Party of Great Britain
EEC	European Economic Community
FAA	Foreign Affairs Association
FBI	Federal Bureau of Investigation
FCA	Foreign Correspondents' Association
FCO	Foreign & Commonwealth Office
FNLA	National Front for the Liberation of Angola
GEC	General Electric Company
IBA	Independent Broadcasting Authority
IBM	International Business Machines
IDAF	International Defence and Aid Fund
INC	Indian National Congress
ITN	Independent Television News

LWT	London Weekend Television
MIT	Massachusetts Institute of Technology
MPLA	Popular Movement for the Liberation of Angola
NAFF	National Association For Freedom
NBC	National Broadcasting Company
NP	National Party
OAU	Organisation of African Unity
OFNS	Observer Foreign News Service
PAC	Pan-Africanist Congress
PLO	Palestine Liberation Organisation
RIIA	Royal Institute of International Affairs
RTZ	Rio Tinto-Zinc
SAAN	South African Associated Newspapers
SABC	South African Broadcasting Corporation
SAC	South Africa Committee
SACP	South African Communist Party
SADF	South African Defence Force
SAF	The South Africa Foundation
SAIRR	South African Institute of Race Relations
SANA	Southern African News Agency
SAPA	South African Press Association
SASO	South African Students Organisation
SDECE	Service de Documentation Extérieure et Contre-Espionage
SIS	British Secret Intelligence Services
STST	Stop the Seventy Tour
SWAPO	South-West Africa People's Organisation
TTP	To The Point
TTPI	To The Point International
TUC	Trades Union Council
UBJ	Union of Black Journalists
UDF	United Democratic Front
UKSATA	United Kingdom–South Africa Trade Association
UN	United Nations
UNESCO	United Nations Educational, Scientific and Cultural Organisation
UNITA	National Union for the Total Liberation of Angola
UNP	University of Natal, Pietermaritzburg
UPI	United Press International
UPITN	United Press International Television News
WASA	Writers Association of South Africa
WCC	World Council of Churches

1

Representation and Refraction

Because of the pressures of space, of the constant need to compress and synthesize, what really happened is not always what we wrote about, even if our facts were indisputable, not because of an intent to deceive, but because we are compelled to deal in essentials ... I have always been struck by the fact that reporters, relaxing and drinking together, are always swapping stories about what happened and that these stories are funnier, truer and more revealing than anything they write for their media.[1]

The fault, I know, lies with my own feebleness of wit, yet sometimes I suspect that social scientists live in a world beyond the reach of ordinary mortals, a world organized in perfect patterns of behavior, peopled by ideal types, and governed by correlation coefficients that exclude everything but the most standard of deviations. Such a world can never be joined with the messiness of history.[2]

At the beginning of the 1970s, 'the only apparent blips on white South Africa's rosy horizon ... were nagging inflation and the growing irritant of an international sports boycott'.[3] By the end of the decade, South Africa had experienced a resurgence of industrial unrest, the fall of the Portuguese empire, the collapse of the policy of détente with sub-Saharan Africa, the Soweto uprising, the Information scandal and the imposition of a mandatory arms embargo by the United Nations. The 'blips' which had irritated the country in 1970 had grown into a full-blown economic crisis and a global anti-apartheid campaign for disinvestment.[4] Great Britain and the United States of America had also experienced a dramatic decade. Great Britain's post-war political consensus collapsed during the mid-1970s in political acrimony. In the United States, President Nixon resigned in 1974 following the Watergate scandal; meanwhile the United States experienced the global repercussions of their strategic defeat in Vietnam. Although British and US relations with South Africa had been consciously low key in the period between the early 1960s and 1974, the fall of the

Portuguese empire exposed the significance of the region to Western policy-makers. In response, Britain and the United States developed a form of 'domino theory' for southern Africa which suggested that, following the independence of Angola and Mozambique, the crisis in Rhodesia/Zimbabwe would need to be resolved before the future of South West Africa/Namibia could be negotiated. Finally, the problem of apartheid in South Africa could be addressed.[5]

The role of the South African government was considered to be a crucial component in the Rhodesia/Zimbabwe crisis by British and American politicians. South African–US relations became more complex following the debacle in Angola (1975–76). For a short period, US Secretary of State, Henry Kissinger, developed a version of his famous 'shuttle diplomacy' in order to address the problems of southern Africa, but the election of Democrat President Jimmy Carter in November 1976 ushered in a new period of tension between the two countries.[6] The American focus on South African human rights was reduced following the United Nations vote in favour of a mandatory arms embargo (October 1977). During 1978 and 1979, relations between the two countries were uncomfortable but not critical.[7] The minority Labour government elected in Britain in 1974 called a second general election in the same year but only managed to win a tiny parliamentary majority. By 1977, the Labour administration was dependent upon support from the Liberal Party in order to remain in office and, although a number of Labour politicians expressed support for the anti-apartheid cause, the Labour government continued to perceive Rhodesia as the central problem for Britain. In addition, many members of the British 'establishment' remained sympathetic to the South African cause.[8] Significantly, the Labour government was not prepared to introduce any new diplomatic initiatives for the southern African region without full US support and leadership.[9] In both Great Britain and the United States, Conservative and Republican politicians, who were far less critical of South Africa, were waiting in the wings. The election of Margaret Thatcher in 1979 and President Ronald Reagan in 1980 closed the window of opportunity which had existed during the previous half-decade for international action against the Republic.

Throughout the 1970s, the South African government engaged in an extensive campaign of propaganda and disinformation in order to counter the work of the global anti-apartheid movements. The central aspect of its campaign was a determined attempt to reinforce links between South Africa and the West. On one level, this led the South African state to demonstrate its willingness to assist the United States and Britain in finding a resolution to the problem of Rhodesia.[10] On another level, the campaign concentrated upon establishing connections between South Africa and the emerging 'New Right' in Britain and the US. At its most dramatic, it also involved covert attempts to buy influence in both Washington DC and the global media. This defensive propaganda campaign was later exposed by the South African domestic English-language press, in what became known as 'Muldergate' or the 'Information scandal'. It eventually led to the downfall of South Africa's State President and ex-Prime Minister, John Vorster, the Minister of Plural Relations and Development and Information, Cornelius Mulder, the head of the Bureau of State Security (BOSS), Hendrik van den Bergh, and the Secretary for Information, Eschel Rhoodie.

Although the British and American governments may not have viewed it as such, the South African state was engaged in a 'war of representation' during the 1970s.[11] This 'war' was in essence a struggle for influence between South Africa and the global anti-apartheid movement. The US and British governments adopted a pose of 'neutrality' in this conflict. This was considered justified by a conjunction of different factors: the all-encompassing Cold War; the scale of investments held by British and American companies in the Republic; the unwillingness of Britain and America to intervene in the domestic politics of an independent state; and the unstated but significant racially-based antipathy towards both the exiled liberation movements and the African, 'coloured' and Asian populations of the Republic. The central battleground in the struggle for representation was the Western media, which was regularly condemned by South Africa for supposedly focusing on negative news, and criticised by some members of the anti-apartheid movement for being 'soft on apartheid'.[12] This book attempts to assess this dual critique and in the process provide a guide to the contradictions, fractures and nuances inherent in the international media's treatment of South Africa.

The state of race relations within Great Britain and the United States of America undoubtedly influenced the coverage of South Africa. The United States of America, while remaining the scene of continuing racial tension, had just emerged from the civil rights struggle of the 1960s. The surface presentation of anti-racism, as exemplified by the 'melting pot' trope, was the accepted political consensus of the 1970s. American reporters who covered South Africa during this period had often cut their journalistic teeth reporting the civil rights movement. It is not surprising, therefore, that many American journalists and politicians viewed South Africa through the lens of their own country's unique racial experience.[13] Although British politicians and journalists normally discussed South Africa in a colonial or African context, the undercurrents of British racial tension during the 1960s and 1970s also influenced the development of the media treatment in the UK. In their study of race issues in four British newspapers between 1963 and 1970, Paul Hartman and Charles Husband observed that 'the press has reflected pressures that on the one hand have sought to exclude coloureds from British society and on the other have aimed to reduce discrimination against them'.[14] Ambiguities of this sort dominated the British media during this period and recurred with unerring regularity in the coverage of South Africa.[15]

Television broadcast news, which had achieved its ascendancy in the United States during the 1960s, began to dominate the dissemination of news in Britain during the 1970s. Partly as a response to this shift in media power, newspapers underwent a period of flux, during which they attempted to develop a distinctive new role as providers of complementary news. While broadcasters established a relatively new form of foreign news gathering (the use of 'firemen' or 'parachutists'), the newspapers began to cut back on their foreign staff.[16] South Africa was an exceptional case during this period as the number of correspondents and 'stringers' increased rapidly following the Angolan war, in contrast to many other areas of the world.[17]

In the years following the Tet Offensive in Vietnam (1968), the American media were popularly perceived as being capable of exercising extraordinary power. This power was tested in the conflict between the Nixon administration and the *New York Times* over the publication of the Pentagon Papers and reached its apotheosis during the *Washington Post*'s exposé of the Watergate scandal.[18] By 1977, Tom Bethell could comment without irony: 'we clearly do now have something very close to a new system of government, in which editors holding the equivalent of oversight Cabinet meetings have left the pamphleteers with portable presses ... very far behind'.[19] The British media of this period demonstrated less overt power due to the continuing exercise of restrictive libel laws, the Official Secrets Act and the government's application of D-Notices. However, the print and broadcast media were also subject to the exhortations of the growing networks of right- and left-wing political agencies during the 1970s. From the right, these voices emerged in the form of interventionist lobby groups, public relations companies and publishing outlets. From the left, a number of pressure groups and sociologists accused the media of being incapable of representing the news either fairly or accurately.[20] It was into this controversial field that the South African Department of Information launched its programme of manipulating the media. It utilised the left-wing refrain of unfair treatment by the media, while simultaneously employing elements of the pragmatic interventionism of the burgeoning New Right lobbyists.

During this period, the foreign news coverage of the print and broadcast media was generally subservient to the perceived national interest of its country of origin and the Cold War and its ramifications were treated as a genuine war. Newspapers and television programmes were able to suggest that British or American foreign policy was misguided, foolish or doomed, but they did not express support for the 'enemy', which in the main was communism. This made the coverage of South Africa particularly problematic. The British and US governments consistently condemned apartheid but they rarely backed their statements with actions. In effect, they practised a system of 'structural hypocrisy'.[21] The African National Congress (ANC) and the South African Communist Party (SACP) were perceived as being allied to the Soviet Union and were thus associated with the 'enemy'. This confusion created a large area of representational opportunity for correspondents or columnists writing about South Africa but it also, paradoxically, increased the need for official guidance. Barbara Rogers explains how the guidance system operated in Britain:

> diplomatic and foreign correspondents of all the major news media attend daily press conferences on foreign affairs at the Foreign and Commonwealth Office (FCO); the same applies to most London-based correspondents of news agencies and major foreign media. Although access to these press conferences is fairly easy, it is a privilege which could be withdrawn if the correspondent published something which seriously embarrassed the government. The press conferences themselves help to shape news reporting on international affairs, providing background information on current news topics which correspondents can use for instant analysis ... There is, in addition, a system of regular briefings for correspondents from the major British media, which are a much more powerful instrument for influencing the news. Access to these briefings is seen quite explicitly as conditional on good behaviour, and there have been cases of major newspapers being excluded from them for a while, as retribution for undesirable news coverage or comment. The briefings are perhaps the major source of news and background information on foreign affairs for the British media, and therefore help to shape the coverage by the newspapers, radio, television, overseas broadcasting and the news agencies. The process is, if anything, becoming even more influential as the number of foreign correspondents each organisation can afford dwindles. A cosy relationship of mutual convenience has been built up behind the scenes in Whitehall, in which direct orders about how to present the news are often unnecessary; a hint may be all that is required.[22]

James Thomson recalls that the relationship between the press and the US government overseas was both mutually supportive and mutually productive: 'in foreign postings for both officials and journalists, mutual learning is the name of the game. The best of the Foreign Service officers and the best of the overseas press corps are fundamentally in the same business. Everyone from ambassador and bureau chief on down is in the business of information gathering, analysis and transmission ... Inevitably, they seek out and use each other.'[23] Governmental influence appears to have permeated the production of news by the media on a number of different levels. However, it should also be recognised that debates within the news media and the fractures and nuances within the coverage, while reflecting tensions and discrepancies in government policies, could, on occasion, lead to shifts within these policies. This degree of influence was directly related to the press's perceived ability to represent and reflect public opinion. As Leon Sigal has observed, 'Especially important among the imponderables in the official's calculus is the state of public opinion ... because of the difficulty of ascertaining public opinion on any given issue, officials rely on the opinions of commentators and editorial writers for a "quick reading of the public mind". As a consequence, the press ... *is* public opinion in the eyes of officials'.[24]

The final influence which demands mention is South Africa's domestic English-language press. During the 1970s, newspapers such as the *Rand Daily Mail* were perceived by the South African government as being little short of an unelected opposition. However, South African government propaganda also relied upon the existence of a 'free' press and judiciary as evidence that the country was 'democratic'.[25] The South African English-language media performed a critical function during the apartheid years but it was under almost constant threat from a government which was intent on using the existence of the South African press for propaganda purposes while attempting to control it.[26] The manifold influence of the domestic English-language media was crucial to the construction of the international media's treatment of the Republic. The struggle for the representation of South Africa can therefore be seen as a multi-faceted process in which many voices contributed to, and contested, the final text.

The claim that newspapers compose the 'first draft of history' is an obvious exaggeration. It is, perhaps, more accurate to say that the media contribute a complex web of clues towards an early interpretation of events. These clues reflect the structure and condition of their cultural production. The images and texts produced by the news organisations are thus best described as *refracted* representations of reality.[27] While all texts are, to a certain extent, refracted representations, the significance of media texts is that readers and viewers assume that they are attempts at representing reality. As Maria explained in Mark Pedelty's *War Stories*, 'Many [journalists] speak of finding *the truth*, or presenting *the reality* ... but there are many realities and there are many truths'.[28] The issue of ideology has dominated academic studies of the media during the last 25 years.[29] For the purposes of this thesis, Herbert Gans's assessment of the form of ideology functioning in the media is particularly useful because it recognises the existence of fluid or shifting representations:

> If the news includes values, it also contains ideology. That ideology, however, is an aggregate of only partially thought-out values which is neither entirely consistent nor well integrated; and since it changes somewhat over time, it is also flexible on some issues. I shall call this aggregate of values and the reality judgements associated with it paraideology, partly to distinguish it from the deliberate, integrated, and more doctrinaire set of values usually defined as ideology, but it is ideology nevertheless.[30]

It is possible to detect Gans's paraideology in the consensus system which dominates the work of the international media. Observers as varied as Walter Lippmann and Noam Chomsky have discussed the media's tendency towards 'manufacturing consent' and this is clearly one of the unstated central tasks of journalism.[31] Herman and Chomsky are correct to assert that the media is subject to a series of filters which 'fix the premises of discourse and interpretation and [define] what is newsworthy in the first place'.[32] However, the suggestion that these filters amount to a 'propaganda system' implies a determinism which bears similarity to Althusser's theory of Ideological State Apparatuses.[33] A less rigid analysis might explain the media's manufacture of consent as an example rather of the Gramscian concept of hegemony.[34] Todd Gitlin's observation that 'journalists' values are anchored in routines that are at once *steady* enough to sustain hegemonic principles and *flexible* enough to absorb many new facts; and [that] these routines are bounded by perceptions of the audience's common sense and are finally accountable to the world views of top managers and owners' reflects very neatly the fusion of contradiction and coalescence which appears to be such a central part of the construction of news.[35] Mark Pedelty, in his anthropological study of correspondents in El Salvador, emphasises the importance of the reporters' working practices (or routines) in anchoring and controlling 'complex issues':

> Reporters are usually in a tertiary relationship to the news events they
> cover. Since they are rarely at the scene of breaking events ... they must
> collect and evaluate interpretations thereof. Given their emphasis upon
> elite sources, who themselves are usually hearing about events second-
> and third-hand, reporters are often evaluating others' interpretations
> of others' interpretations, and so on. The journalist must comb through
> complex layers of interpretation and representation, hoping to derive
> a more concretized sense of the original event. Pseudo-events are a great
> aid in this interpretive process ... Like legal trials, pseudo-events reduce
> complex realities into two-dimensional form, producing manageable
> outlines of complex issues. Journalists complete the process among
> themselves in intra-press negotiations, reducing 'the story' to its most
> significant, or at least its most marketable, elements.[36]

The process of news-gathering as practised by individual journalists
was, as Pedelty discovered, both complicated and chaotic. It appears
to be subject on multiple levels to both manipulation and the random
factor. Daniel Hallin noted, in his book on the coverage of the Vietnam
war, that 'The ideology of the Cold War was ideally suited to the
reduction of this complexity: it related every crisis to a single, familiar
axis of conflict.'[37] However, in the case of South Africa, Cold War
ideology was only really significant from 1974 and was partly negated
by the fact that race relations in the Republic conflicted with the
consensual representation of race relations in Britain and the United
States. This tension (or partial negation) established a small degree of
flexibility within the media's consensus. Recognising this flexibility, or
potential for shift, is central to any understanding of how the media,
and the forces which attempted to influence the media, operated.
International news is, in effect, the site of an ideological struggle for
(and of) representation. In this struggle, the power of capital possesses
a distinct advantage. However, as Hallin has suggested, there is the
consistent potential for conflict and chaos at the heart of the system:

> Corporate control of the mass media does not guarantee that the
> media's cultural products will consistently serve the interests of the
> capitalist system as a whole, any more than corporate control of energy
> guarantees against an energy crisis ... If the anarchy of production
> leaves the capitalist system vulnerable to economic crisis, why should
> the anarchy of ideological 'production' not leave it similarly vulnerable
> to cultural crisis?[38]

The coverage of foreign news, especially the foreign news of a
country whose political system is regularly criticised by the national

governments of the international media, exaggerates the potential for what Edward Said has called 'eccentric, unexpectedly original, even aberrant' moments.[39] In order to examine both the original and the orthodox in the construction of foreign news, it is essential to determine who comprises the international media. Unfortunately, the sociological and anthropological traditions of media analysis have consistently underplayed the role of the individual journalist. As David Morrison and Howard Tumber have commented:

> insufficient attention has been paid to how the journalist as an individual exercises his own judgement in negotiating his role, and more than that, the critical politicizing of research in the area of mass communications has meant that the journalist as news gatherer has been pushed out of sight. He no longer fits, or rather researchers cannot find a place for him, in the grand indictment of the news as the reproduction of the dominant ideology.[40]

This depersonalising of the media has led to a profound dichotomy between the bulk of mass communications research and the institutional histories of newspapers or memoirs of editors and journalists. It is almost always a case of 'never the twain shall meet'. Travelling between the two, one is struck by the extraordinary degree of tension that has built up between the two approaches during the last 20 years.[41] This tension is particularly disappointing because, as Morrison and Tumber discovered in their research for *Journalists at War*, many reporters are willing to discuss the issues arising from the problems of news-gathering. Research of this sort reveals a fascinating oral tradition of myth, anecdote and observation. Even more critically, the failure to examine the role of individuals within news organisations has permitted a shroud of invisibility to surround the work of vast numbers of journalists, a shroud which has allowed individuals to progress in their careers without justified examination or criticism.[42] Research into the backgrounds and identities of journalists often reveals useful insights into why the coverage emerges in the form that it does. Thus, in an article for the *New Statesman*, Chris Mullin reported that:

> Few readers of the *Daily Telegraph* will, for example, have realised that the paper's Salisbury stringer – Brian Henry – is the same as the *Daily Mail*'s Peter Norman who is the same person as the *Guardian*'s Henry Miller. And that all these people are in real life a Rhodesian journalist called Ian Mills who, as it happens, is also the *BBC* correspondent.[43]

There is a growing academic literature on war correspondents that does address the issues of journalistic identity.[44] Unfortunately, studies of foreign correspondents in regions that are not technically at war are still rare.[45]

The lack of study of the journalist as an individual contributor to the news-gathering process leads on to a lack of analysis of the significant role of the internal media discourse. On one level, this internal discourse relates to the question of who the journalist believes that s/he is writing for. Robert Darnton remembers of his days working for the *New York Times* that 'We never wrote for the "image persons" conjured up by social science. We wrote for one another.'[46] If the primary 'public' for a journalist's work is his/her contemporaries, the secondary public is often the (official) sources themselves. Darnton asserts that 'The reporting of news runs in closed circuits: it is written for and about the same people, and it sometimes is written in a private code.'[47] Penetrating such codes should be one of the central tasks of media analysis.

In 1972, Timothy Crouse recorded the conservatism which dominated the media: 'Journalism is probably the slowest-moving, most tradition-bound profession in America. It refuses to budge until it is shoved into the future by some irresistible external force.'[48] This is partly due to the symbiosis which often develops between reporters and their sources.[49] However, while symbiotic relationships do emerge, so do severe antagonisms. Evidence of these antagonisms rarely appears in a blatant form in the media, but the clues are there. The only effective method for unearthing long-standing tensions in the media is to tap into the oral history of the journalists in question.

Another facet of the internal media discourse which is particularly significant to historians is the system of precedents which appears to presage shifts in representation. It is a matter of record that exposés are rarely anything of the sort. They are often prefigured by a long history of references, indicators and pointers. For the journalist, these precedents provide a useful support in the 'selling of the story'. While the precedents for a shift in representation can be overwhelming, on other occasions they can be virtually non-existent and this in itself can be instructive. During 1978, Trevor Brown investigated the coverage given to Steve Biko before his death in September 1977. He found that the 'internationally known' South African leader had barely received any press coverage during the preceding years. Brown engaged in telephone interviews and correspondence with journalists on various newspapers and was informed by Jim Hoagland (*Washington Post*) that 'A reader of the [*New York*] *Times* and the *Post* over the years ... would have known of Biko.'[50] The only evidence to support Hoagland's assertion was three articles in the American media.[51] Brown did not examine the similar sparsity of reference to Biko in anti-apartheid publications.

To understand the media's employment of standardised and stereo-typed representations, the reader needs to engage in active inter-pretation. The media are, in effect, a store of historically loaded representations. Shifts and tensions within these widely accepted representational assumptions are crucial clues to the condition of the hegemonic culture. In one form or another, they are always present.[52] Walter Lippmann described the system of stereotypes as constituting:

> an ordered, more or less consistent picture of the world, to which our habits, our tastes, our capacities, our comforts and our hopes have adjusted themselves. They may not be a complete picture of the world, but they are a picture of a possible world to which we are adapted. In that world people and things have their well-known places, and do certain expected things. We feel at home there. We fit in ... There we find the charm of the familiar, the normal, the dependable; its grooves and shapes are where we are accustomed to find them. And though we have abandoned much that might have tempted us before we creased ourselves into that mould, once we are firmly in, it fits as snugly as an old shoe.[53]

Robert Darnton recalled that journalists 'simply drew on the traditional repertory of genres. It was like making cookies from an antique cookie cutter. Big stories develop in special patterns and have an archaic flavor, as if they were a metamorphoses of *Ur*-stories that have been lost in the depths of time.'[54] In effect, the 'news' is subject to the influence of long-standing cultural determinants. These determinants define what is 'news', what the 'story' should be and how it should be told. The inheritance of these story-telling tropes, determinants or techniques, and their employment in conjunction with the composition of news creates the neat match or 'fit' described by Lippmann. Interestingly, Darnton employed a similar metaphor to describe the same process:

> It is the neatness of the fit that produces the sense of satisfaction, like the comfort that follows the struggle to force one's foot into a tight boot. The trick will not work if the writer deviates too far from the conceptual repertory that he shares with his public and from the techniques of tapping it that he has learned from his predecessors.[55]

Lippmann suggested that, without reform (or in periods of great social tension), the system of stereotypes could culminate in the creation of absolute representations:

> a system of all evil, and of another which is the system of all good ... Real space, real time, real numbers, real connections, real weights are lost. The perspective and the background and the dimensions of action are clipped and frozen in the stereotype.[56]

Fifty-two years after the publication of Lippmann's *Public Opinion*, Alexander Cockburn addressed the issues of foreign correspondence in an ostensibly humorous article for the journalism review, *More*. Discussing the work of the veteran roving *New York Times* correspondent, C.L. Sulzberger, Cockburn observed:

> What has C.L. Sulzberger got to do with the practice of foreign reporting, people ask. 'Why, he's an embarrassment at the [*New York*] *Times*,' a *NYT* staffer told me. Far from it. It seems to me that C.L. is the summation, the platonic ideal of what foreign reporting is all about. It's true that we do not find him courageously observing Cambodian soldiers on the outskirts of Pnom-Penh, but this is incidental. C.L. has divined the central mystery of his craft, which is to fire volley after volley of cliché into the densely packed prejudices of his readers. There are no surprises in his work ... *He never deviates into paradox*. His work is a constant affirmation of received beliefs.[57]

Bearing in mind Darnton's assessment that 'foreign correspondents ... bring more to events they cover than they take away', media analysis should be particularly concerned with the cultural context and history of news production.[58] In addition, it is essential to recognise that the stereotypes and standardised representations described by Lippmann, Darnton and Cockburn are subject to rare but significant adjustments. These reformations can, perhaps, be described as 'representational paradigm shifts' because their evolution bears some resemblance to a softer version of Thomas Kuhn's revolutionary scientific paradigms:

> novelty emerges only with difficulty, manifested by resistance, against a background provided by expectation. Initially, only the anticipated and usual are experienced even under circumstances where anomaly is later to be observed. Further acquaintance, however, does result in awareness of something wrong or does relate the effect to something that has gone wrong before. That awareness of anomaly opens a period in which conceptual categories are adjusted until the initially anomalous has become the anticipated.[59]

Lippmann suggested that 'any disturbance of the stereotypes seems like an attack upon the foundations of the universe'.[60] Indeed, the innate conservatism of the media does resist change, especially change which threatens or contradicts the traditional image repertoire. The reasons behind a shift in representation are varied and can be related directly to the power of the original source. In the case of foreign news, shifts are usually due to the intensity and drama of the events being reported. On extremely rare occasions, however, they can be influenced by the work of individual journalists. In summary, the media does not reflect reality. It provides refracted representations which are a product of cultural consensus, paraideology and a degree of chaos. The chaos in the system can either be the result of the individuality of the journalists themselves, who are not automatons, or the potential randomness of the news, which is only partly predictable. The refracted representations produced by the media serve, on one level, as an internal media discourse and on another level, as a system of stereotyped and standardised paradigms. These representational paradigms are subject to occasional adjustment or shift. Above all, the media is rarely neutral or objective.

This is not a study of what the international media should have been, but what it was. As an historian I do not feel that it is my task to inform my historical subject how s/he should have acted.[61] I am concerned to examine how and why the media representations of South Africa during the 1970s emerged in the forms that they did. Among the issues which this book attempts to address are: the sources of influence and manipulation in the media; the media's construction of news stories; the role, significance and occasional adjustments in the media's traditional image repertoire; and the fractures, nuances and 'blips' (the chaotic element) which randomly affected its system of representation. I have done this by studying the textual coverage of South Africa during the 1970s in both the British and American print and broadcast media and interviewing as many of the people responsible for reporting the news from South Africa as was possible.[62] The central purpose of these oral interviews was an attempt to get 'behind the news' in order to understand, in the language of journalism, 'the who, what, when, where and why' of foreign correspondence in South Africa. Examining the news-gathering structures of the various media organisations was an essential consideration before any analysis of foreign correspondence in South Africa could be attempted. Finally, the results of the fusion of the textual analysis and supporting interviews were tested against the existing history and political science texts on the events of the period in three case-studies.

There are few models for a study of this type. The majority of academic examinations of the international media's coverage of foreign affairs concentrate on periods of time that are too short for constructive historical analysis, and focus on too small a selection of media to be representative of the whole. Comparative studies of the coverage of British and American news-gathering of any one country are virtually non-existent. The most useful models were Daniel Hallin and Todd Gitlin's work on the US media's coverage of the Vietnam war and the Peace Movement, respectively. These two studies offer many useful clues towards a workable methodology, most notably in their fusion of textual analysis and supporting interviews with journalists.[63] Although there is a growing literature on the domestic South African media, no single book has, as yet, focused upon the international media's representation of South Africa.[64] Trevor Brown's essay on the US press coverage of Biko remains the only academic example, discussing the 1970s, of textual research followed up by investigative interviews.[65]

Although failing to provide a model analysis, a useful source on the media were the media themselves. Journalistic critiques of the media were relatively rare in the British press of the 1970s.[66] In the United States, however, the growth of schools of journalism and the increasingly high profile of investigative reporting contributed to a significant body of pragmatic and penetrative media criticism. Magazines as varied as *Harper's*, the *Nation* and *Esquire* carried regular examinations of the media. These were complemented by the observations of *Columbia Journalism Review*, *More* and *Nieman Reports*. Even *Time* and *Newsweek* carried regular columns on the press. While there has been an abundance of books by journalists on the media during the 1970s, very few commentators have attempted to offer a viable method of media analysis.[67] The final chapter of Martin Walker's *Powers of the Press* stands as a rare exception.[68] In this, Walker discussed the histories of 12 of the world's most famous newspapers. He then proceeded to test their reputations by considering their respective reporting of Iran during the 1970s. The system that he used merged a simple form of content analysis (collating the number of articles on Iran per year, and their subject) with a recognition of the relative importance of differing writers and reports. Walker's conclusions manage to be critical, realistic and convincing, a conjunction rarely achieved in academic media analysis.

This study does not employ statistical content analysis for the simple reason that I am not convinced that it is particularly useful. The fundamental problem with content analysis is that it normally treats its limited sample in isolation. The wider context in which the news is constructed, the Cold War for instance, is normally forgotten.

Perhaps, most significantly, content analysis fails to provide any system for judging the relative impact of separate reports or articles. Yet, on admittedly rare occasions, an individual article can launch or accelerate a 'moral panic' and thereby influence a flood of coverage by other news media. Articles of this sort are obviously worth more than countless mundane news agency reports. As Morrison and Tumber have suggested, content analysis 'cannot go beyond its own methodology to explain how the picture was arrived at ... To understand the creation of news as distinct from social relationships as demonstrated by the news, it is essential to get to grips with people as operatives within a system rather than operators of a system.'[69]

In order to address the question, how are media representations constructed and, in part, as compensation for the lack of an analytical system, I have allowed the case-studies in this book to expand beyond the usual minimal sample in orthodox media analysis. The range of the media examined in this study was also, in part, an acknowledgement of Carol Weiss's research into the diverse media readership habits of American 'leaders' and Henry Grunwald's assertion that ' "the media" are a great many large and small, often contradictory if not warring, newspapers, magazines, broadcasters, columnists, editorial writers, reporters, publishers – together providing a mass of reportage and opinion that defies any single bias'.[70] Although small circulation publications and stringer journalists are featured throughout this book, the core sources, predictably, proved to be the elite media of Britain and the United States. This was because the elite press during the 1970s still tended to designate more space for foreign news and comment than either the television or the tabloid press.

The reasoning behind this book's extensive trawl of media sources was also an attempt to address Morrison and Tumber's observation that 'There is no absence of material on foreign correspondents, but studies are rare ... the very few academic studies which do exist fail in the clarification of basic questions because it is unclear who is being referred to by the title "foreign correspondent" '.[71] During the process of interviewing, I discovered that many of the most informed and informative journalists had worked on the periphery of the media. A study which had limited the size of the media under analysis would have missed the true scale of the internal media discourse, a discourse that at times served as a running commentary on itself. The research for this book suggests that the 'foreign correspondent' was only the most visible player in the construction of foreign correspondence. In the case of the newspapers for example, news about South Africa was also constructed by the editorial writers, columnists, cartoonists, photographers, sub-editors, foreign editors, stringers, visiting correspondents and, most significantly, South African (black and white) reporters. Examining the diversity of the media also reveals a number of profound differences as well as similarities in the representation of news. As Daniel Hallin explains of the American media:

> Because of their different audiences ... and because of television's special need for drama, TV and the prestige press perform very different political functions. The prestige press provides information to a politically interested audience; it therefore deals with *issues*. Television provides not just 'headlines', as television people often say, nor just entertainment, but ideological guidance and reassurance for the mass public. It therefore deals not so much with issues as symbols that represent the basic values of the established political culture. This difference is certainly not absolute. Newspapers too can play the role of moralist ... And television has always been torn between a desire to belong to the inner circle of serious journalism and its other identity as storyteller-moralist.[72]

A recognition of the different traditions and differing working methods of the newspapers, news-magazines, news agencies and broadcast media is an important addition to knowledge of the identities of the journalists. These structural differences are multiplied in an examination of the British and American media. Chapter 2 provides a relatively prosaic guide to the structures of the international media which takes into account such factors as the density of South African coverage in the respective newspapers; the opening of bureaus in the Republic; visits by columnists and members of the editorial staff; and the publication of surveys and special reports on South Africa. It is complemented by Appendix A, which provides brief biographies of the main correspondents and stringers. Detail of this sort establishes a bedrock on which the later analysis of the three case-studies can take place.

Since studies of the media have established conclusively that journalists are dependent upon, and often manipulated by, their sources, it is particularly surprising that little academic attention has been given to the pressure groups whose primary purpose is to influence media representations. Robert Darnton recalled:

> Press spokesmen and public relations men are often former reporters, who adopt a tone of 'we are all in this together' and try to seem frank or even irreverent in their off-the-record comments. In this way they can influence the 'angle' or the 'slant' of a story – the way it is handled and the general impression it creates.[73]

Karen Rothmyer's report on the role of public relations companies in the United States during the Biafran war concluded by warning that 'the Government or the news media rely too heavily on such firms rather than their own investigation ... The farther away geographically the story occurs, the more likely it is that special-interest groups will be successful in influencing its telling'.[74] The case of South Africa during the 1970s demonstrates many of the elements Rothmyer reported in the coverage of the Biafran war. In New York, Washington DC, and to a certain extent, London, a maze of public relations companies, lobbyists and secret organisations campaigned and manipulated on South Africa's behalf. These were opposed by the global network of anti-apartheid groups. Chapter 3 examines the propaganda programme put into action from 1972 by South Africa's Department of Information. Chapter 4 discusses the attempts by the British and American anti-apartheid movements to influence the international media's representation of the Republic.

The three case-studies in Chapters 5, 6 and 7 are based upon a fusion of oral interviews and textual analysis. The interviews, in particular, proved to be a very rich source. I did not offer interviewees the option to remain anonymous, although I did accept a small amount of material given 'off the record'.[75] The interviews (which lasted, on average, one hour) were concerned with questions arising from my textual analysis, the structures of news-gathering, the relationship between the correspondent/stringer in South Africa and the editorial staff of the publication, and the journalistic internal discourse. On many occasions, responses to questions unearthed observations or details that would have been impossible to recognise if I had relied solely on a reading of the newspapers. A significant amount of information gathered during the oral research for this book proved unsuitable for use. Most of this information consisted of amusing anecdotes, unsubstantiated stories and allegations about other journalists. However, determining the veracity of stories, 'chasing leads' and negotiating the traditional representations that often dominate the reporter's anecdote provided me with both an education in investigative journalism, and a number of useful insights into the journalists' impressions of the 'reality' of news production.[76]

There were also problems relating to the textual analysis. The primary stage of the textual research was a matter of studying the cuttings files on South Africa at the Royal Institute of International Affairs (RIIA).[77] The RIIA collection was then compared with the existing indexes of the newspapers.[78] Finally, with certain unindexed newspapers and magazines that were not available at the RIIA, I was forced literally to comb through each edition of the publication. This research was then complemented by a similar system in South Africa and the United States of America. Gaining access to broadcast media proved more difficult. My extensive survey of the print media provided a list of all the television programmes on South Africa that had attracted the attention of the press. Actually viewing these programmes and news reports was nearly impossible.[79] From the British Broadcasting Corporation (BBC) and Independent Television News (ITN) it is possible to gain access to the 'day lists' for news programmes from the 1970s.[80] The BBC Written Archive at Caversham possesses transcripts for most BBC documentaries screened on the subject of South Africa in the 1970s. Other transcripts were obtained from the regional broadcasters.[81] The only other method for getting access to broadcast material was by appealing to the producers or directors of the television programmes. This proved successful in some instances. Once again, similar methods were employed in the US and South Africa.[82] Without actually viewing or listening to the majority of the broadcast media coverage of South Africa, I might have under-played the significance of the medium in this study. I have consistently tried to be aware of this danger.

The three case-studies in this book examine exceptional moments in the international media's coverage of South Africa during the 1970s. They should be read in the context of the struggle for representation between South Africa's Department of Information and the global anti-apartheid movement, described in Chapters 3 and 4. Chapter 5 considers the *Guardian*'s wage starvation exposé (March 1973) and the resulting debate in the British media. Chapter 6 examines the international media's coverage of the South African invasion of Angola (1975–76) and Chapter 7 analyses the shifts in representation which followed the Soweto uprising (1976). I chose the three case-studies because each one established precedents for the coverage of the 1980s: the economic sanctions issue; South African military intervention; and violent unrest in South Africa. In addition, each chapter demonstrated a different facet of the international media: the investigative exposé backed by a newspaper campaign (Chapter 5); war correspondence (Chapter 6); and dependence upon South African journalism (Chapter 7).[83] Chapter 8 attempts to draw together the various strands of the analysis by considering the influence which South African journalism exerted over the coverage of the country; the transformations in the society of the foreign correspondents and stringers during the decade; and the results and implications of the South African government's attempts to manipulate the media. The final chapter considers the similarities and differences in the British and American interpretation of apartheid and poses the question: in view of the differences in the

British and American traditions of journalism and their interpretations of the significance of the South African 'story', why, over the long term, were their representations so similar?

Academic analysis of media coverage often neglects the historical context of news production. Contemporary historical studies often utilise media sources with little examination or criticism. This book is an attempt to combine a critical analysis of the international media's coverage of South Africa with a history of the 1970s. The case-studies, which are by nature experimental, offer guides to the histories of a number of notable South African stories, while tracking a series of shifting representations and noting the competing voices of South Africa's Department of Information and the anti-apartheid movements. Greg Dening has suggested that:

> History is all the ways we encode the past in symbol form to make a present. It is in this sense very vernacular. It is an everyday, every moment act. Making History is our constant cultural exercise. We express the past and by that make our social relations and our social structures ... We create change, we establish the status quo in our History making.[84]

The international media's news production might not be a valid 'first draft of history' but it is an example of 'history making'. The print and broadcast media are not scientific, they do not produce news to any single pattern. Edward Said has observed that 'We do not ... live at the mercy of a centralised propaganda apparatus, even though a great deal of what is actually propaganda is churned out by the media'.[85] Through a study of the media, the organisations whose central function was to influence the media, and the news which the media created, this book attempts to analyse and explain the contradictions which dominated the representations of South Africa during the 1970s.

NOTES

1. Edward Behr, *'Anyone Here Been Raped and Speaks English?': A Foreign Correspondent's Life Behind the Lines* (Sevenoaks, New English Library, 1982), pp. x–xi.
2. Robert Darnton, *The Kiss of Lamourette: Reflections in Cultural History* (London, Faber & Faber, 1990), p. 60, originally published as 'Writing News and Telling Stories', *Daedalus*, Vol. 104, No. 2 (Spring 1975), pp. 175–94.
3. Dan O'Meara, *Forty Lost Years: The Apartheid State and the Politics of the National Party, 1948–1994* (Randburg, Ravan Press, 1996), p. 170.
4. The best recent history of South African politics during the 1970s is O'Meara, op. cit. See also Tom Lodge, *Black Politics in South Africa since 1945* (London, Longman, 1983).

5. In some respects, following the events of 1974, the global anti-apartheid movements also adopted a domino theory for southern Africa. This was in recognition of the fact that the global institutions, South Africa and the Western governments were more open to influence on the lesser (and, some would have said, more urgent) subjects of Rhodesia and Namibia than on South Africa.

6. See for instance the US Ambassador to the United Nations, Andrew Young's off-hand remark that South Africa was an illegitimate regime (Graham Hovey, 'Young Sets Off Furor by Agreeing South Africa Rule is "Illegitimate"', *New York Times*, 16 April 1977); and Vice-President Walter Mondale's ambiguous statement in favour of 'full political participation' within South Africa (Roy Lewis, 'Vorster–Mondale Talks End on a Note of Disagreement and Mutual Incomprehension', *The Times*, 21 May 1977).

7. On US–South African relations see Rene Lemarchand (ed.), *American Policy in Southern Africa: The Stakes and the Stance* (Washington DC, University Press of America, 1978); William Minter, *King Solomon's Mines Revisited: Western Interests and the Burdened History of Southern Africa* (New York, Basic Books, 1986); Christopher Coker, *The United States and South Africa, 1968–1985: Constructive Engagement and Its Critics* (Durham, NC, Duke University Press, 1986); James Barber and John Barratt, *South Africa's Foreign Policy: The Search for Status and Security 1945–1988* (Cambridge, Cambridge University Press, 1990); Zaki Laidi, *The Super-Powers and Africa: The Constraints of a Rivalry, 1960–1990* (Chicago, University of Chicago Press, 1990); Deon Geldenhuys, *The Diplomacy of Isolation: South African Foreign Policy Making* (Johannesburg, Macmillan, 1984); Cyrus Vance, *Hard Choices: Critical Years in America's Foreign Policy* (New York, Simon & Schuster, 1983); Donald B. Easum, 'United States Policy toward South Africa', *Issue*, Vol. 5, No. 3 (Fall 1975), pp. 66–72. For an insight into the South African Department of Information's perception of the relations, see Daan Prinsloo, *United States Foreign Policy and the Republic of South Africa* (Pretoria, Foreign Affairs Association, 1978). Jack Robinson, 'Pretoria's Texas Oil Baron', *To The Point*, 21 June 1974, p. 44, was a profile of John G. Hurd, the US Ambassador to South Africa, 1970–75.

8. Beyond the general academic texts discussing South Africa's foreign relations (above), there are few studies of Britain's relations with South Africa during the 1970s. An exception is Geoff Berridge, *Economic Power in Anglo-South African Diplomacy: Simonstown, Sharpeville and After* (London, Macmillan, 1981). The memoirs of senior British politicians of the period skirt over the subject. A lone exception is David Owen, *Time to Declare* (London, Michael Joseph, 1991). See also David Scott, *Ambassador in Black and White: Thirty Years of Changing Africa* (London, Weidenfeld & Nicolson, 1981). During 1977, Scott stated in a speech to the Cape Town Press Club: 'We [Britain] now find ourselves with very little ammunition left to defend ourselves against intense international criticism that we are leaning over backwards to defend South African internal policies ... I have spoken frankly, but I hope you will accept that I have spoken as a friend.' (p. 195). Following his term as Ambassador to South Africa, 1976–79, Scott was appointed Vice-President of the United Kingdom–South Africa Trade Association (UKSATA), 1980–85. In this appointment, he was following Sir Arthur Snelling, who had served as Ambassador to South Africa from 1970–72 and was Vice-President of UKSATA from 1974 to 1980. Snelling regularly contributed pro-South African articles to the newspapers during the 1970s, see, for example, Sir Arthur Snelling, 'The Wages of Africans', *Financial Times*, 30 March 1973; 'Viewpoint: Labour and Apartheid', *Financial Times*, 19 April 1974; 'Developing the Bantustans', *Financial Times*, 15 January 1975. See also Patrick Wall, *Prelude to Détente: An In-depth Report on South Africa* (London, Stacey International,

1975). Wall was a Conservative MP. See 'Obituary: Major Sir Patrick Wall', *Daily Telegraph*, 19 May 1998.

9. Vance, op. cit., pp. 261–2; Owen, op. cit., p. 284.

10. The compliant stage of this process reached its climax during the Angolan war at the end of 1975. The South Africans, who claimed that they had been encouraged by the United States to invade Angola, felt that they were abandoned by the Western powers. (See Chapter 6).

11. Military metaphors recur with regularity within statements originating from the Department of Information. See, for example, Keith Abendroth, 'Rhoodie Ready to Bruise a Few Toes for South Africa', *Rand Daily Mail*, 24 October 1972: 'The fight would continue for more money to improve the service. "After all we cannot expect to use an air rifle against tanks," [Rhoodie] said.'

12. In the context of this book, I am using the term 'Western media' as being interchangeable with 'international media'. The importance of the term, 'international', is that many of the news agencies, newspapers, news-magazines and broadcast media studied in this book were genuinely international, in that they were republished or available in many countries, not the least South Africa. My central sources have been the English and American media. Of course, a study which also included an analysis of other country's media would be more accurate. It would also have been impossible in the time available. The reasons for focusing on the English and American media were two-fold: first, most foreign correspondents in South Africa from 1972 to 1979 were British or American; secondly, the South African government and media were most intensely concerned about the representation of their country in the English and US media.

13. The US media had experienced a representational shift on the subject of racism during the 1950s and 1960s. By the 1970s, the consensual media position was one of anti-racism. However, this had not as yet led to a situation where the number of African-American journalists working for the elite media reflected their percentage of the population. See for example Richard A. Pride and Daniel H. Clarke, 'Race Relations in Television News: a Content Analysis of the Networks', *Journalism Quarterly*, Vol. 50 (Summer 1973), pp. 319–28; Churchill Roberts, 'The Presentation of Blacks in Television Network Newscasts', *Journalism Quarterly*, Vol. 52 (Spring 1975), pp. 50–55.

14. Paul Hartman and Charles Husband, *Racism and the Mass Media* (London, Davis-Poynter, 1974), p. 144. See also Andrew Stephen, 'Uganda Asians and the Press', *New Statesman*, 8 September 1972, p. 310, which concludes: 'All of which illustrates the mixed-up, schizophrenic attitude of the British media on race issues.' During the 1970s, the number of Afro-Caribbean and Asian journalists working for the national British newspapers was, as now, pitifully small.

15. See Stuart Hall, 'The Whites of their Eyes: Racist Ideologies and the Media', in Manuel Alvarado and John O. Thompson (eds), *The Media Reader* (London, BFI Publishing, 1990); Centre for Contemporary Cultural Studies, *The Empire Strikes Back: Race and Racism in 70s Britain* (London, Routledge, 1982).

16. 'Firemen' or 'parachutists' are journalists who arrive to report an event and then leave. The use of this type of reporter is normal practice for broadcasting companies because the cost of keeping television bureaus in a large number of countries is prohibitive. Newspaper 'firemen' can be divided into two categories: staff and editorial writers, who are normally little more than visitors; and the reporter, covering countries which practice strict policies of censorship or limit the issue of visas, who knows that he or she will be unlikely to be allowed to return to the country again, and is therefore more critical than might have been the case if access to the story had been willingly provided. See Mort Rosenblum, *Coups and Earthquakes: Reporting the World for America* (New York, Harper

Colophon Books, 1981), pp. 10–11.

17. 'Stringers' are non-staff correspondents working for news publications. Sometimes they receive a financial retainer, sometimes they work on a freelance basis. For details on the increasing number of reporters in South Africa following the Angolan war, see Chapter 2.

18. For the story behind the publication of the Pentagon Papers, see Sanford J. Ungar, *The Papers and the Papers: An Account of the Legal and Political Battle over the Pentagon Papers* (New York, Columbia University Press, 1989). On the coverage of Watergate, see Carl Bernstein and Bob Woodward, *All The President's Men* (London, Quartet Books, 1974); James McCartney, 'The Washington "Post" and Watergate: How Two Davids Slew Goliath', *Columbia Journalism Review*, July/August 1973, pp. 8–22; Nat Hentoff, 'Lingering questions' and Laurence I. Barrett, 'The dark side of competition', in 'Woodward, Bernstein and "All The President's Men"', *Columbia Journalism Review*, July/August 1974, pp. 10–15; Philip Nobile, 'How The New York Times became Second Banana', *Esquire*, May 1975, pp. 85–99.

19. Tom Bethell, 'The Myth of an Adversary Press', *Harper's*, January 1977, p. 39. See also Kevin Phillips, 'Busting the Media Trusts', *Harper's*, July 1977, p. 23, in which Phillips discusses '"the media" as the decade's most notable economic, cultural, and political phenomenon'.

20. An example of right-wing pressure on the media was the organisation Accuracy In Media [AIM] which was launched in the mid-1970s, based in Washington DC, and published regular *Accuracy In Media Reports*. An example of left-wing pressure was the criticism of the media that came through 'media studies'. See, for example, Glasgow University Media Group, *Bad News* (London, Routledge & Kegan Paul, 1976); *More Bad News* (London, Routledge & Kegan Paul, 1980); and Greg Philo, John Hewitt, Peter Beharrell and Howard Davis, *Really Bad News* (London, Writers and Readers Publishing Co-operative Society, 1982). On the international stage, UNESCO conferences often provided regular criticism of the international media's coverage of developing countries. This was accompanied by the instigation of censorship in many of these countries, for example, India during the Emergency of 1975. See also Martin Woollacott, 'Where No News is Bad News', *Guardian*, 27 August 1975; Mort Rosenblum, 'Reporting from the Third World', *Foreign Affairs*, Vol. 55, No. 4 (July 1977), pp. 815–35.

21. For an explanation of the causes of the American version of this structural hypocrisy, see Donald B. Easum, 'United States Policy toward South Africa', *Issue*, Vol. 5, No. 3 (Fall 1975), pp. 66: 'Interests determine policies. Policies appear confused or ambiguous, or evoke controversy, when the interests they are designed to serve are themselves in conflict. A policy that promotes one particular interest may threaten the condition of some other interest. This interrelationship of interests and policies is of unusual significance in the case of US policies toward South Africa.'; Easum had served as Assistant Secretary of State for African Affairs between 1974–75. Easum's explanation could apply equally effectively to British policy toward the Republic.

22. Barbara Rogers, *The Image reflected by Mass Media: Manipulations. The Nuclear Axis: a Case Study in the Field of Investigative Reporting* (New York, UNESCO, 1980), p. 9. Rogers had worked for the British Foreign Office for 16 months, following university. (Interview with Barbara Rogers, 5 December 1995.)

23. James C. Thomson Jr, 'Government and Press: Good News about a Bad Marriage', *New York Times* magazine, 25 November 1973, p. 53. Thomson worked for the State Department and the White House for seven years during the 1960s. He later became the administrator of the Nieman Fellowship at Harvard University.

24. Leon V. Sigal, *Reporters and Officials: The Organization and Politics of News-making* (Massachusetts, D.C. Heath, 1973), p. 135.
25. Elaine Potter, *The Press as Opposition: The Political Role of South African Newspapers* (London, Chatto & Windrush, 1975), pp. 208–9.
26. For details of the restrictions imposed by the South African state on its domestic media, see Frene Ginwala, *The Press in South Africa*, United Nations Unit on Apartheid, Notes and Documents No. 24/72 (November 1972); Alex Hepple, *Press Under Apartheid* (London, International Defence and Aid Fund, 1974). For further information on the compromised nature of the South African press, see Chapter 8.
27. Martin Walker, *The Powers of the Press: The World's Great Newspapers* (London, Quartet Books, 1982), p. 390, sums up the international print media's coverage of Iran in the 1970s as functioning like a 'distorting mirror'. Todd Gitlin, *The Whole World is Watching: Mass Media in the Making and Unmaking of the New Left* (Berkeley, University of California Press, 1980), p. 77, describes the shifts in the *New York Times*'s representation of the New Left as 'correspond[ing] to something real in society: not accurately, as a mirror image corresponds to a reflected object, but as a distortion of something actual'.
28. Mark Pedelty, *War Stories: The Culture of Foreign Correspondents* (New York, Routledge, 1995), p. 227.
29. See Stuart Hall, 'Culture, the Media and the "Ideological Effect"', in James Curran, Michael Gurevitch and Janet Woollacott (eds), *Mass Communication and Society* (London, Edward Arnold, 1977), pp. 315–48; Stuart Hall, 'The Rediscovery of "Ideology": Return of the Repressed in Media Studies', in Michael Gurevitch, Tony Bennett, James Curran and Janet Woollacott (eds), *Culture, Society and the Media* (London, Routledge, 1982), pp. 56–90; Ruth Tomaselli, Keyan Tomaselli and Johan Muller, 'A Conceptual Framework for Media Analysis', in Tomaselli, Tomaselli and Muller (eds), *Studies on the South African Media: The Press in South Africa* (London, James Currey, 1987), pp. 5–21; Gitlin, op. cit., pp. 249–82; See also Louis Althusser, 'Ideology and Ideological State Apparatuses', in *Essays on Ideology* (London, Verso, 1984), originally published in French, 1970.
30. Herbert J. Gans, *Deciding What's News: A Study of CBS Evening News, NBC Nightly News, Newsweek and Time* (New York, Pantheon Books, 1979), p. 68.
31. Walter Lippmann, *Public Opinion* (New York, The Macmillan Company, 1947), p. 248, originally published in 1922; Edward S. Herman and Noam Chomsky, *Manufacturing Consent: The Political Economy of the Mass Media* (New York, Pantheon Books, 1988); See also Henry Grunwald, 'Don't Love the Press, but Understand it', *Time*, 8 July 1974, pp. 74–75. Grunwald commented following the Watergate scandal, 'the press will have to help rebuild an American consensus'.
32. Herman and Chomsky, op. cit., p. 2.
33. Althusser, op. cit., suggested that the media were one of the ideological systems utilised by the state, in the 'private domain', to control, sustain and police capitalist society.
34. Antonio Gramsci, *Selections from Prison Notebooks*, ed. and trans. Q. Hoare and G. Nowell Smith, (London, Lawrence & Wishart, 1971). See also Dagmar Engels and Shula Marks (eds), *Contesting Colonial Hegemony: State and Society in Africa and India* (London, British Academic Press, 1994).
35. Gitlin, op. cit., pp. 272–73.
36. Pedelty, op. cit., p. 125.
37. Daniel C. Hallin, *The 'Uncensored War': The Media and Vietnam* (New York, Oxford University Press, 1986), p. 50.

38. Daniel C. Hallin, 'The American News Media: A Critical Theory Perspective', in John Forester (ed.), *Critical Theory and Public Life* (Cambridge, MA, MIT Press, 1985), p. 137.
39. Edward Said, *Covering Islam: How the Media and the Experts Determine How We See the Rest of the World* (New York, Pantheon Books, 1981), p. 48.
40. David E. Morrison and Howard Tumber, *Journalists at War: The Dynamics of News Reporting during the Falklands Conflict* (London, Sage, 1988), p. x.
41. See, for instance, David Remnick, 'Dept. of Disputation: Scoop', *New Yorker*, 29 January 1996: 'What most press critics ignore is that much of the reason for what actually appears in newspapers and on television screens has to do with the people who produce the words and images – with the wild range of talent among reporters and editors, with their folkways and habits …'; See also Howard H. Davis, 'Media research: whose agenda?', in John Eldridge (ed.), Glasgow University Media Group, *Getting the Message: News, Truth and Power* (London, Routledge, 1993), p. 46: 'It is well known that media studies have had a poor reputation in the practitioners' world, and that serious attempts to put research on a better footing in relation to broadcasters, for instance … have met with little success.' While arranging and conducting interviews with journalists for this book, I found that in some cases all I needed to say was that I was an historian not a media student, for them to agree to talk with me.
42. There is no comprehensive index or guide to journalists working in the international media in either Britain or the United States. In order to research the backgrounds of the correspondents who had covered South Africa, I had to interview them. In order to find out more about their reputations, I had to ask their contemporaries.
43. Chris Mullin, 'Rhodesia and the British Press', *New Statesman*, 25 February 1977, p. 247.
44. For example, Morrison and Tumber, op. cit.; Pedelty, op. cit.
45. One recent exception is Stephen Hess, *International News and Foreign Correspondents* (Washington DC, The Brookings Institution, 1996).
46. Darnton, op. cit., p. 62.
47. Ibid., p. 76.
48. Timothy Crouse, *The Boys on the Bus* (New York, Ballantine Books, 1973), p. 321.
49. For a detailed examination of journalists and their sources, see Gans, op. cit., pp. 116–45; Sigal, op. cit., p. 54; and Tom Wicker, 'The Greening of the Press', *Columbia Journalism Review*, May/June 1971, p. 7: '[The] biggest weakness [of the American press] is its reliance on and its acceptance of official sources.'
50. Cited by Trevor Brown, 'Did Anybody Know His Name? US Press Coverage of Biko', *Journalism Quarterly*, Vol. 57 (Spring 1980), p. 37.
51. Donald Woods, 'South Africa will Regret Banning its Black Leaders', *Christian Science Monitor*, 14 September 1976, originally published as 'Remember the Name Well', *Rand Daily Mail*, 27 August 1976; later republished as 'Make a Note of Steve Biko', *Washington Post*, 27 September 1976; See also John F. Burns, 'A Jailed Black Relays Warning to Kissinger', *New York Times*, 19 September 1976.
52. See Frank Johnson, 'What the Devil shall We Say about Blair?', *Daily Telegraph*, 8 March 1997: 'Sooner or later – usually sooner – an idea takes hold about a Prime Minister. Nearly everyone suddenly agrees with it, and it becomes almost impossible for the politician to rid himself or herself of it.' The 'idea' that Johnson considers is the representational stereotype.
53. Lippmann, op. cit., p. 95.
54. Darnton, op. cit., p. 86.
55. Ibid., pp. 87–88. See also Gitlin, op. cit., p. 267: 'stereotyping solves an enormous

number of practical problems for journalism'.

56. Lippmann, op. cit., p. 156.

57. Alexander Cockburn, 'How to Earn your Trench Coat', *More*, May 1974, p. 24. For details on C.L. Sulzberger's connections with the CIA, see Carl Bernstein, 'The CIA and the Media', *Rolling Stone*, No. 250 (20 October 1977), pp. 59–61. See also Robert D. McFadden, 'Obituary: C.L. Sulzberger, Columnist, Dies at 80', *New York Times*, 21 September 1993.

58. Darnton, op. cit., p. 92.

59. Thomas S. Kuhn, *The Structure of Scientific Revolutions* (Chicago, University of Chicago Press, 1970), p. 64. Although genuine revolutions in representation are rare, 'when paradigms change, the world itself changes with them. Led by a new paradigm, scientists adopt new instruments and look in new places. Even more important, during revolutions scientists see new and different things when looking with familiar instruments in places they have looked before.' (p. 111)

60. Lippmann, op. cit., p. 95.

61. Pedelty, op. cit., pp. 219–30, concludes with suggestions for methods to improve the media.

62. For the print and broadcast media sources examined within this thesis, see the Bibliography. The vast majority of journalists agreed to speak to me. However, it should be acknowledged that the interviews were often only made possible by a barrage of telephone calls, faxes and letters. A small number of journalists were untraceable or refused to speak with me – See Appendix A for details.

63. Hallin, op. cit.; Gitlin, op. cit. See also Elaine Windrich, *The Cold War Guerrilla: Jonas Savimbi, the US Media, and the Angolan War* (New York, Greenwood Press, 1992), which is an exceptional example of a study which recognises the significance of propaganda in the construction of news. Windrich, however, did not follow up her analysis with interviews with the journalists.

64. Richard Pollak, *Up Against Apartheid: The Role and the Plight of the Press in South Africa* (Carbondale and Edwardsville, Southern Illinois University Press, 1981), contains one chapter (pp. 78–90) which discusses the international media; William A. Hachten and C. Anthony Giffard, *The Press and Apartheid: The Role and Plight of the Press in South Africa* (London, Macmillan, 1984), contains a brief section (pp. 275–81) on foreign journalists. See also Sanford J. Ungar, 'South Africa in the American Media', in Alfred O. Hero Jr and John Barratt (eds), *The American People and South Africa: Publics, Elites, and Policymaking Processes* (Massachusetts, Lexington Books, 1981), pp. 25–46.

65. Trevor Brown, 'Did Anybody Know His Name? US Press Coverage of Biko', *Journalism Quarterly*, Vol. 57 (Spring 1980), pp. 31–44.

66. Exceptions included the *New Statesman*, *Time Out* and *Private Eye*.

67. For some of the most successful examples, see A.J. Liebling, *The Press* (New York, Ballantine Books, 1961); Crouse, op. cit.; Rosenblum, op. cit.; David Halberstam, *The Powers That Be* (New York, Alfred A. Knopf, 1979); Gay Talese, *The Kingdom and the Power* (London, Calder & Boyars, 1981); Behr, op. cit.; Philip Knightley, *The First Casualty. From the Crimea to the Falklands: The War Correspondent as Hero, Propagandist and Myth Maker* (London, Pan, 1989).

68. Walker, op. cit., pp. 342–93.

69. Morrison and Tumber, op. cit., p. x.

70. Carol H. Weiss, 'What America's Leaders Read', *Public Opinion Quarterly*, Vol. 38, No. 1 (Spring 1974), pp. 1–22; Grunwald, 'Don't Love The Press ...', *Time*, 8 July 1974, p. 75.

71. David E. Morrison and Howard Tumber, 'The Foreign Correspondent: Date-line London', *Media, Culture and Society*, Vol. 7, No. 4 (October 1985), pp. 445–46.

72. Hallin, op. cit., pp. 125–26. Although the situation in Britain was very different

because of the public-service ethos of the BBC, Hallin's basic distinction stands. The conservatism of television media is magnified in motion pictures. For examples regarding South Africa, see Kenneth M. Cameron, *Africa on Film: Beyond Black and White* (New York, Continuum, 1994).

73. Darnton, op. cit., p. 75.
74. Karen Rothmyer, 'What Really Happened in Biafra?', *Columbia Journalism Review*, Fall 1970, p. 47. See also Windrich, op. cit. In the UK, there were fewer public relations companies than in the United States.
75. Gans, op. cit., p. xiii: 'I told the people I studied I would not use names; ... anonymity is an old fieldwork tradition. Sociologists are more concerned with the roles people perform ... than with individual personalities'; Pedelty, op. cit., listed his interviewees by first name only; Hallin, op. cit., and Gitlin, op. cit., permitted some of their interviewees to remain anonymous. 'Off the record' means not for attribution.
76. During the 1994 elections in South Africa, for example, The *Independent*'s correspondent, John Carlin, permitted me to travel with him while he observed the voting. We also discussed the work of foreign correspondents in South Africa. Carlin provided me with a crucial entrée to the world of news gathering, as it is practised now.
77. During the 1970s, the RIIA still subscribed to an extensive selection of British and US newspapers.
78. Indexes exist for *New York Times, Washington Post, Los Angeles Times, Wall Street Journal, Christian Science Monitor, Chicago Tribune, San Francisco Chronicle, The Times, Sunday Times, Guardian, Daily* and *Sunday Telegraph* (1979 only), *The Economist, Spectator, New Statesman, US News and World Report, Nation, New Republic, National Review* and [Johannesburg] *Financial Mail*.
79. The vast majority of television broadcasts before 1980 were shot on film and have not been transferred to video-tape.
80. 'Day lists' provide information on the running orders of news programmes. In the case of ITN's archive, they also include the lengths of the news clips and the names of the reporters.
81. One exception was Thames Television which lost its franchise some years ago and now runs its library on a massively reduced budget. Films were only available on commercial terms.
82. The South African Broadcasting Corporation (SABC)'s archive of 1970s broadcast material is in an appalling state. Only a tiny sample of material remains viewable.
83. Other case-studies could, perhaps, have included the treatment of South Africa's attempts to circumvent the sports boycott (1972–74); the 'Independent homeland' policy and the 'independence' of the Transkei and Bophuthatswana (1976–77); the nuclear programme (1977–79); and the representation of Gatsha Buthelezi, throughout the 1970s.
84. Greg Dening, *History's Anthropology: The Death of William Gooch* (Lanham, University Press of America, 1988), p. 2.
85. Said, op. cit., p. 44.

2

Structures of International News

Mention South Africa, and most people immediately think of apartheid. But there's more to this country than its politics, as many businessmen are discovering. The rising price of gold has sent the economy soaring – with a 6% real growth rate projected for this year. And it has sent businessmen rushing to Johannesburg. American Express estimates that the influx of Americans has increased about 20% during the past four months. South Africa isn't the vacation capital of the world by a long shot. Shops close at 1 p.m. on Saturdays, and movies never open on Sundays. And don't expect the likes of *Last Tango in Paris*. You won't find *Penthouse* or *Playboy* on newsstands, either. In fact, don't bring in any reading material that's even slightly blue. Customs officials have an astonishing lack of humour and will probably confiscate your material and fine you as well. There are after-hour annoyances, too. You can buy drinks in your hotel, but you will have to bring your own liquor to some unlicensed nightclubs and restaurants outside hotels. And women are typically banned from drinking spots, except for hotel 'Ladies' Bars'. You'll also have to tolerate the 'white only' signs in restaurants, cinemas, and elsewhere. Nonetheless, you can have a pleasant stay.[1]

When somebody asked the other day what change I had seen in South Africa, I found myself giving the very subjective answer that life was much pleasanter now for the visiting British journalist. The former enmity had been replaced by at worst indifference, at best friendly interest. In the early sixties, in the aftermath of Macmillan's 'wind of change' speech, the resentment shown to reporters was sharp ... a great many white South Africans now suspect that the journalists may have been right all along and that separate development is not only unjust but unworkable. Hostility to the English journalist has also declined for a less welcome reason – the South Africans no longer give a damn what we think of them ... The collapse of England's power has meant, among other things, that the English journalist here has been replaced as a bogey figure by the American journalist.[2]

In Chapter 1, this book suggested that foreign news is barely ever solely the product of the foreign correspondent. The construction of foreign news can best be understood by an examination of the news-gathering structures which contributed to and coalesced into the news material which then appeared in the newspapers and on the television.[3] This chapter considers the external contribution of the British and American news organisations to the coverage of South Africa in the 1970s by examining the newspapers, the news-magazines, the news agencies and the broadcasting companies. The exploration of the news-gathering structures of the international media should be read together with the mass of biographical and other detail provided in Appendix A.[4]

A simple guide to the British elite newspapers of the 1970s would probably place the *Daily* and *Sunday Telegraph* on the right, *The Times*, *Sunday Times* and the *Financial Times* in the centre, and the *Guardian* and the *Observer* on the liberal-left. These political descriptions fail to take into account, however, the fact that newspapers tend to function as 'broad churches'. On occasions, the ostensibly liberal *Guardian* adopted a right-wing stance and, similarly, the supposedly conservative *Daily Telegraph* sometimes carried liberal comment.

During the 1970s, *The Times* was still an 'establishment' newspaper. It offered Britain's only example of a 'newspaper of record'. With 18 foreign correspondents distributed throughout the world, *The Times*'s global representation was greater than that of any other British newspaper. The paper's Cape Town bureau had been reopened in 1969. *The Times*'s position on South Africa reflected the divisions within the British establishment. These tensions were replicated within the editorial structure of the newspaper. The foreign news editor, Jerome Caminada, had been born in South Africa and retained some sympathy for white South Africa's leaders and their problems. Kenneth Mackenzie, the chief foreign sub-editor, was also South African-born, but was a more forthright critic of the apartheid regime. Michael Knipe (correspondent, 1972–75) recalls: 'I took the view that I had two South Africans in London and therefore it was a damn sight easier getting my stuff in the paper than it was for anybody else.'[5] *The Times*'s correspondents in South Africa were supported by two stringers and the editorials were written by Roy Lewis. South African-born Marcel Berlins, the newspaper's legal correspondent, commented upon the Republic following his regular visits.[6] Louis Heren, the deputy and foreign editor of *The Times*, visited South Africa during the spring of 1978 and interviewed John Vorster. In the opinion pages of the newspaper, Bernard Levin devoted regular space to condemnations of the apartheid system and Lord Chalfont contributed a number of

articles which were gently sympathetic to the South African government.[7] Between 1973 and 1975, *The Times* carried three surveys of
the Republic and in 1978, a special report on the Transkei.[8]

The *Daily* and *Sunday Telegraph* divided their news pages (under
the control of managing editor, Peter Eastwood) from the opinion and
editorial pages (controlled by the editor).[9] The *Telegraph* kept a staff
of 13 correspondents world-wide, supported by 90 stringers. The
coverage of South Africa, as was the case with most newspapers,
was twinned with that of Rhodesia. Bill Deedes (ex-Conservative MP
and editor of the *Daily Telegraph* from 1974) was one of the few
editors in Fleet Street to comment openly on the subject of South
Africa.[10] The *Telegraph* also carried regular background articles by ex-
correspondents such as Douglas Brown.[11] Journalists on the *Telegraph*
visited the Republic more often than reporters with other British
newspapers.[12] Although the newspaper employed few South Africans,
Peregrine Worsthorne, the *Sunday Telegraph*'s columnist, had visited
South Africa on a regular basis during the 1950s and 1960s and
retained a deep affection for the country.[13] 'Peter Simple', the *Daily
Telegraph*'s columnist, was also a South African sympathiser. Columns
by guest writers in support of South Africa were normally sub-titled
'personal view'.[14] Unlike in *The Times*, articles opposing these views
were rare. During the autumn of 1977, the *Daily Telegraph* carried a
five-part series entitled 'What is South Africa's Future?', wherein
South Africans were invited to debate the country's prospects. Of the
five contributors, only one was African: the Chief Minister of the
'homeland' of Lebowa.[15]

The *Guardian* possessed the smallest overseas representation of the
elite British daily newspapers: eight correspondents and 32 stringers.
Throughout the 1970s, the newspaper was consistently refused its
request to situate a correspondent in the Republic and it was therefore
forced to depend upon South African stringers.[16] James MacManus
was appointed Africa correspondent in 1974 but was not allowed to
enter South Africa until March 1977; thereafter he returned with regularity. Because of its financial and logistical limitations, the *Guardian*
was the most accessible of the British newspapers to freelance and
visiting journalists.[17] The paper also employed a group of young staff
writers: Martin Walker, Richard Gott, Jonathan Steele and Adam
Raphael, who were all keen South Africa-watchers. Walker had
worked for the South African magazine *News/check* during the 1960s.
Steele and Gott had visited the country in 1970 and 1971, respectively.
Raphael and Steele were both married to South Africans.[18] However,
as Richard Gott recalls, 'The *Guardian* was a very pluralist ship.'[19]
Examples of the newspaper's 'pluralism' could be seen in the editorials

and articles written by Geoffrey Taylor, which recommended recognition of the Transkei, and the fact that the *Guardian* was the first of the British newspapers to carry articles by writers associated with the ANC and SACP in 1975.[20] The Anti-Apartheid Movement considered the *Guardian* to be one of the more sympathetic of the elite British newspapers.[21]

The international coverage of the *Financial Times* under the foreign editorship of J.D.F. Jones underwent a period of dramatic expansion following his appointment in 1967 at the age of 27. David Kynaston, in his history of the *Financial Times*, comments: 'At a time when most papers were cutting down on their foreign staff, the *FT* was doing quite the reverse and getting the people in place to provide full coverage and analysis.'[22] In 1976, following Jones's departure from the foreign editor's post, the *Financial Times* possessed 16 correspondents and 83 stringers. Jones, whose first job after university had been on the *Pretoria News*, retained an interest in South Africa and, following a term as managing editor, returned to South Africa as the newspaper's correspondent in 1981. One of his innovations as foreign editor had been the establishment of a structure of regional specialists, based in London, who periodically travelled and reported from their region. The regional specialist for Africa throughout the 1970s was Bridget Bloom.[23] Jones and Bloom visited South Africa regularly before the *Financial Times*'s appointment of a staff correspondent to the region in 1976.[24] Within South Africa, the *Financial Times* utilised the opportunities made possible by the newspaper's 50 per cent holding in the [Johannesburg] *Financial Mail* to employ a number of the latter's reporters as specialist stringers.[25] The South African-born columnist, Joe Rogaly, only rarely devoted his 'Society Today' column to questions relating to South Africa; when he did, however, the resulting articles normally attracted attention.[26] Between 1972 and 1975, the *Financial Times* published three surveys on South Africa.[27] J.D.F. Jones recalls that 'There was great pressure on us both from the [South African] Embassy and from the advertisers in South Africa to steer clear of politics [in the surveys].'[28] Jones and the *Financial Times* were not prepared to accept any editorial interference and, as a result, during the second half of the 1970s, the newspaper did not publish any surveys on the Republic.[29]

The *Sunday Times* employed only five correspondents and no more than a dozen stringers. In addition to Benjamin Pogrund's reports, coverage of South Africa during the early 1970s usually consisted of feature articles by *Sunday Times* visiting journalists. After some difficulty in obtaining a work permit from the Department of Information, Eric Marsden was appointed correspondent in 1977. On the staff of the newspaper in London was South African-born Denis Herbstein, who worked as a stringer in the Republic during 1976, until his application for an extension to his work permit was refused. Herbstein was also a regular contributor of sympathetic material on the A-AM in Britain. Hugo Young, editorial writer of the *Sunday Times*, also visited South Africa in 1972. The *Observer* was not permitted by the South African government to place a correspondent in the country and therefore, like the *Guardian*, depended upon South African stringers.[30] The newspaper commented in an editorial during 1976: 'If the South Africans are so keen to let the world know they have nothing to hide in their country, why do they persistently refuse entry visas to our reporters.'[31] David Martin, the newspaper's Africa correspondent (from 1974), was also not allowed to enter the Republic. Peter Deeley was eventually granted a work permit in 1979. The *Observer*'s global representation was similar to that of the *Sunday Times*. Of all the British Sunday newspapers, the *Observer* carried the largest number of feature articles on South Africa.[32] In Colin Legum, the *Observer* possessed one of Fleet Street's longest-standing and most dominant Africa experts.[33]

The fundamental difference between the British and the American newspapers chosen for analysis in this study results from the absence of South African journalists in the United States. Additionally, while most British newspapers were reducing their foreign coverage during the 1970s, their American equivalents were beginning to expand their networks of foreign correspondents. There is a grain of truth in W.A.J. Payne's assertion that 'In contrast to Britain and France, where journalists have made a prestigious lifetime career of becoming authorities on Africa, an American journalist is expected to approach Africa as a short-term assignment in the safari tradition.'[34] By the 1970s, however, the era of the British 'old Africa hand' had almost passed.[35] British journalists arriving in South Africa from the mid-1970s were often on a similar career assignment to their American counterparts. At the same time, American journalists were becoming increasingly knowledgeable about the countries that they were covering. The American newspapers discussed here can be tentatively divided politically as follows: the *Wall Street Journal* and the *Chicago Tribune* on the right; the *New York Times*, the *Washington Post*, the *Los Angeles Times* and the *Christian Science Monitor* in the centre; there were no major US newspapers on the liberal-left.[36]

The *New York Times* is often described as the United States of America's only 'newspaper of record'. The paper's foreign staff was the largest in the world: 32 correspondents, reporting from 23 bureaus, with the support of 25 stringers. Excluded from South Africa since the expulsion of Joe Lelyveld in 1966, the *New York Times* maintained correspondents in both Nairobi and Lagos. Before the newspaper was permitted to reopen its Johannesburg bureau, the Republic was covered annually by Charles Mohr (Nairobi correspondent, 1970–75). Editorials and background articles were written in New York by Graham Hovey.[37] C.L. Sulzberger, the newspaper's senior foreign correspondent visited South Africa during December 1975. Amongst the other *New York Times* columnists, the most regular commentator was Anthony Lewis. In addition to his two visits to the Republic in 1975 and 1979, Lewis turned his twice-weekly 'Abroad At Home – At Home Abroad' column to the subject of South Africa on more than 20 occasions.[38] Tom Wicker began to address the subject of South Africa during the Angolan war. It was at this time that issues relating to southern Africa entered the American political mainstream. Three years later, Wicker visited South Africa for a few weeks and filed his thrice-weekly 'In The Nation' column from the country.[39] During 1976, the *New York Times* was finally permitted to reopen its Johannesburg bureau. Intensive coverage of South Africa followed. One year later, Seymour Topping (managing editor) visited southern Africa and interviewed John Vorster.[40] In November 1977, the *New York Times* carried a powerful editorial which challenged South Africa's long-standing accusation that the world's media practised 'double standards' in its coverage:

> In our letters columns today, Johan Adler, the Deputy Consul General of South Africa asserts that his troubled country is 'a microcosm of the world' ... In fact, South Africa is not a microcosm of the world. Indeed, it is unique: the only state where an entire segment of the population – in this case, the nonwhite majority – is altogether denied participation in national politics solely because of race ... Ever since the horrors of Hitler's Germany became known during World War II, there has been almost universal agreement that deprivation and suppression based upon ascribed membership in a racial, religious, or ethnic group are morally unacceptable. South Africa is unique in its explicit attempt to build an entire society upon such racial suppression. It is therefore clearly deserving of censure.[41]

The *Washington Post* did not employ any foreign correspondents until the 1950s. Yet by the 1970s, the newspaper had 11 correspondents, supported by 23 stringers. South African coverage throughout the 1970s was handled by stringers with regular support from David Ottaway, the *Washington Post*'s Africa correspondent.[42] The newspaper's previous Africa correspondent, Jim Hoagland (1969–71) had won a Pulitzer prize in 1971 for his coverage of South Africa. Hoagland returned to the Republic for another visit in 1976.[43] Peter Osnos, the foreign editor, visited South Africa in 1978 in order to interview John Vorster. The *Washington Post*'s editor, Benjamin Bradlee, visited the country in 1979 with his wife, the paper's style editor, Sally Quinn.[44] With the notable exception of Jack Anderson, the *Washington Post*'s columnists did not assign much space to the subject of South Africa in the early 1970s. However, during the first 18 months of the Carter administration, Stephen Rosenfeld, Rowland Evans, Robert Novak and William Raspberry visited the Republic.[45] South Africa had clearly become a major policy story in Washington DC. The *Washington Post*'s editorials on South Africa were written by Stephen Rosenfeld and Karl Meyer.[46]

The *Los Angeles Times* was also involved in a programme of foreign expansion. In 1962, the paper had possessed only one overseas bureau, but by 1978 it had 18. In 1974, Tom Lambert had opened the *Los Angeles Times* bureau in South Africa, but he retired just before the Soweto uprising. Georgie Anne Geyer of the newspaper's foreign staff visited for a few days towards the end of June 1976. Veteran correspondent Jack Foisie arrived two months later and remained in the country until his retirement in 1984. In Los Angeles, editorials on South Africa were written by Louis Fleming, who had paid a visit to the country in 1974. However, *Los Angeles Times* correspondents received little assistance from either stringers or visiting staff writers.[47] Unlike other American newspapers which favoured a limited term for correspondents, the *Los Angeles Times* operated a system which encouraged both continuity and (a degree of) freedom. Jack Foisie later commented that 'Bob Gibson [the foreign editor] was not a great communicator with his staffers. I once chided him in a telephone conversation across ten thousand miles for not providing me with more "guidance". He replied sombrely, "You're getting paid to make judgements. When we think you're off base, we'll let you know."'[48] Although the *Los Angeles Times* did not possess any regular columnists of the calibre of those who wrote for the *New York Times* or the *Washington Post*, conservative opinion was expressed in William F. Buckley Jr's (the editor of the *National Review*) syndicated column and the paper also carried two articles by Barbara Hutmacher.[49]

The *Wall Street Journal* operated a system of foreign news gathering which was described by *Time* magazine in 1980 as 'lumbering after news instead of sprinting'. However, *Time* also acknowledged that 'The *Journal*'s editorial page is possibly the most influential conservative voice in the US.'[50] With only five overseas bureaus, coverage of Africa was organised from London before the appointment of an

Africa correspondent, Richard Leger, in 1977. There was often no more than one visit a year to the Republic by members of the *Wall Street Journal* staff. News from South Africa (which was rare) was normally left in the hands of South African stringers.[51] George Melloan, deputy editor of the paper's editorial page, was the only senior member of the *Journal*'s staff to visit the Republic during the 1970s. The *Wall Street Journal* carried one 'survey' on South Africa which appears to have been designed solely to offset the threat of sanctions.[52]

The *Chicago Tribune* did not possess a resident correspondent in South Africa during the 1970s. Beyond the rare visits of *Tribune* staff reporters, coverage depended primarily upon the news agencies.[53] The African-American columnist, Vernon Jarrett, only addressed the question of South Africa following the visits of South Africans to Chicago.[54] However, Patrick Buchanan's syndicated column offered a consistently conservative tone on the subject. Indeed, on a number of occasions, Buchanan served as the most sympathetic columnist the Republic had in the major US newspapers. His belief that 'the most virulent strain of racism in the world today is not anti-black, anti-yellow, or anti-red; it is anti-white' would have been shared by Eschel Rhoodie.[55] The *Chicago Tribune* did not devote a large number of reports and columns to the subject of South Africa but editorials on the subject appeared as often as those of the other elite American newspapers.

The *Christian Science Monitor* had the smallest circulation of the elite American newspapers discussed here but the newspaper was read by Christian Scientists within South Africa who regularly corresponded with the editorial staff in Boston.[56] The *Monitor* possessed eight foreign correspondents and 40 stringers world-wide. Throughout the 1970s, the Africa correspondent was responsible for the coverage of the entire region south of the Sahara.[57] John Hughes, the newspaper's editor, had reported from Africa between 1955 and 1961. Hughes and the *Christian Science Monitor*'s foreign editor, Geoffrey Godsell, were not born in the United States, being Welsh and English, respectively. Godsell visited South Africa in the summer of 1977 during which period June Goodwin introduced him to Steve Biko.[58] Godsell later contributed a six-part analysis of the Republic to the paper.[59] In keeping with many of the columnists on other newspapers, Joseph C. Harsch, the *Monitor*'s veteran columnist, did not address the subject of South Africa before Western involvement became a significant factor in the Angolan war.

A simple guide to the British news-magazines would tentatively place *The Economist* and the *Spectator* on the right and the *New*

Statesman on the liberal-left. Of these magazines, only *The Economist* offered a comprehensive coverage of South Africa during the 1970s. The unsigned reports were normally written by the South African journalist, Allister Sparks. Articles in other sections of the magazine were composed by Graham Hatton (business) and Benjamin Pogrund, amongst others. Reports in *The Economist* were edited but not rewritten.[60] The coverage was controlled by an Africa editor in London, operating to a similar news system as the *Financial Times*. John Grimond served in this post during the first half of the 1970s, during which time he visited the Republic on a regular basis.[61] *The Economist* carried one survey of South Africa between 1972 and 1979: a study of gold and its influence on the country.[62] Only the final pages of the survey addressed the internal politics of the Republic. The magazine also published a confidential 'Foreign Report', which, for a period during the 1970s, was edited by Robert Moss.[63]

The *New Statesman*'s opposition to the apartheid regime was normally pronounced. Stanley Uys provided regular background articles from South Africa (between 1972 and 1976) and was succeeded by Donald Woods (1976) and Roger Omond (1977). A large number of other writers commented on the Republic from London.[64] Christopher Hitchens exerted a continuous anti-apartheid influence through the editorials and the Crucifer diary, and, following his appointment as foreign editor, through articles written as a visitor to the country.[65] The *Spectator* carried fewer reports from South Africa than the *New Statesman*. During the first half of the 1970s, the *Spectator*'s regular commentator was Roy Macnab, who was also the London director of the South Africa Foundation.[66] During the second half of the decade, reports from South Africa were often supplied by Richard West.[67] *The Times*'s correspondent in the Republic, Nicholas Ashford, filed for the *Spectator* during 1979 while *The Times* was on strike. Other British publications which carried occasional commentaries on South Africa included the satirical magazine, *Private Eye*, the London listings magazine, *Time Out*, and *New Society*.

The seven American news-magazines discussed in the next few pages can be differentiated politically as follows: *US News and World Report*, *Business Week* and *National Review* on the right; *Time*, *Newsweek* and the *New Republic* in the centre; and the *Nation* on the liberal-left. The only American magazines to retain stringers in South Africa throughout the 1970s were *Time* and *Newsweek*.[68] *Time* had been excluded from the country since the expulsion of Lee Griggs in 1961 and depended during the early 1970s on the reports of Peter Hawthorne. Following the Soweto uprising, Lee Griggs was allowed to return for a brief visit.[69] In 1977, *Time* was permitted to reopen its

Johannesburg bureau under the stewardship of William McWhirter. Peter Hawthorne was retained as a stringer. In the build-up to re-opening the bureau, John Elson (a *Time* senior editor) had visited the Republic to interview John Vorster, and Henry Grunwald, editor of the magazine, had completed a two-week tour of the country. Grunwald's ensuing analysis rejected a 'one man – one vote' solution but did acknowledge that 'Comparisons should be made not with the rest of Africa, but with what the blacks' lot *could be* in South Africa ... As for the double standard, South Africa almost demands to be judged according to higher criteria by the very assets it proclaims.'[70]

Newsweek did not open a South Africa bureau during the 1970s, retaining its Nairobi base as the centre for the magazine's coverage of sub-Saharan Africa. Andrew Jaffe (Africa correspondent) was consistently refused a visa to enter South Africa. Peter Younghusband operated as *Newsweek*'s stringer in the Republic, receiving support from senior editors, Arnaud de Borchgrave and Andrew Nagorski (general editor of *Newsweek International*) during 1976.[71] Discussing *Time* and *Newsweek*, Mort Rosenblum has observed that 'the role of the desk [in New York or Washington DC] is so important that when *Newsweek* began giving by-lines it listed the writers in New York first and then followed with the correspondents who actually wrote the story ... the finished product often bears no resemblance in wording or style to what the correspondents originally wrote, although ideally the facts stay the same'.[72]

US News and World Report's coverage of South Africa was minimal in comparison to that offered by *Time* and *Newsweek*. The normal method of operation was an annual visit to the Republic by a staff reporter from the London bureau. An Africa correspondent was appointed in 1978. *Business Week* barely mentioned South Africa during 1972 and 1973, although coverage increased following the collapse of the Portuguese empire.[73] During April 1977, George Palmer, the ex-editor of the [Johannesburg] *Financial Mail* joined *Business Week* as the senior editor in charge of international business coverage. A correspondent, Jonathan Kapstein, was situated in South Africa during 1978. *Business Week* carried one 'special report' on the Republic during the decade.[74] The *Nation* was the first of the news-magazines to carry regular commentaries from an American stringer living in South Africa. Andrew Silk's reports for the magazine from 1976–77 demonstrated a degree of understanding, sensitivity and innovation that had not been present in previous reporters' articles on South Africa. The *Nation*, like its British equivalent, the *New Statesman*, provided regular space to those commentators who were opposed to apartheid.

Although the *New Republic* was less concerned with South African issues than the *Nation*, the magazine spoke for (and to) the American east-coast establishment. This was demonstrated on one level by the occasional commentaries on South Africa provided by James Thomson, curator of the Nieman Foundation for Journalism at Harvard University.[75] Following the Soweto uprising, the *New Republic* began to publish regular articles by Benjamin Pogrund. From 1979, the magazine carried articles by James North (Dan Swanson), an American stringer of the calibre of Andrew Silk.[76] The *National Review* adopted an extremely conservative position on South Africa in line with its role as the voice of the New Right. Publisher, William A. Rusher, was a loyal supporter of the Republic and the editor, William F. Buckley Jr, visited South Africa in 1974.[77] South Africa was only rarely the subject of feature articles in the *National Review* as the magazine did not employ a stringer or correspondent in the country. Coverage was normally limited to editorials, William Buckley's 'On the Right' columns, and the occasional report of a visitor to South Africa. In 1979, for instance, F.R. Buckley visited Soweto:

> Soweto is a settlement where blacks are segregated: a 'slum' it is not, failing the definition by as wide a margin as Watts. I've seen worse living conditions in St. Louis. In material circumstances it cannot be compared with the wretchedness of the shantytowns that ring Caracas, Bogota, Rio de Janeiro, or Santiago. On the basis of three hours of rubbernecking, plus the statistics – and with reasoned regard for the political, economic, and historical contexts – Soweto cannot be held up as representing any policy of *material* mistreatment of blacks, nor any racially motivated indifference to their well-being. To the contrary, and despite staggering obstacles, Soweto represents a continuing (since 1948) if sporadic effort by the white government to provide, *within the constraints of apartheid*, decent habitation for black miners and quarriers, with an inadequate, at times perplexed and ideologically loggerheaded – yet persistent – policy of improvements.[78]

In 1980, Sanford Ungar noted in his analysis of the American media's coverage of South Africa that '[the] magazines that tend to serve the American intelligentsia and the influential minority interested in foreign affairs – the *Atlantic Monthly*, *Harpers*, the *New Yorker*, *Commentary*, and the like – often feature articles about South Africa, both reportorial and philosophical'.[79] However, this is only an accurate assessment if one ignores the period between 1972 and 1976, when there had been no articles of any description on the apartheid regime in the four magazines. The *New Yorker* carried two major articles on South Africa during 1979, both of which were written by the veteran writer, E.J. Kahn Jr. The two essays discussed American investment in South Africa and life in South West Africa/Namibia.[80] Only *Esquire*, the radical monthly, *Ramparts*, the *Progressive* and the African-American publication, *Encore American and Worldwide News*, carried major articles on South Africa before the Soweto uprising.[81] In the period following the Soweto uprising, publications as varied as the *New York Review of Books*, *Commonweal*, *Fortune*, *Forbes*, *Rolling Stone* and the journalism review, *More*, devoted space to studies of South Africa.[82]

The three major international news agencies, Reuters, Associated Press (AP) and United Press International (UPI) differed significantly in their respective operations in South Africa. Reuters had a long-standing relationship with the South African Press Association (SAPA) with whom it exchanged foreign news for domestic South African reports. AP exchanged material with South African Associated News-papers (SAAN) and UPI exchanged reports with the Argus Group. AP and UPI also carried photographs, Reuters did not. AP did not have a broadcast media wing but UPI (United Press International Television News – UPITN) and Reuters (Visnews) did. All three agencies retained bureaus in South Africa throughout the 1970s, although it should be acknowledged that Reuters possessed a distinct advantage in the region. This advantage was a legacy of South Africa's colonial past. The same was true throughout Africa: 'By the early 1970s, Reuters had approximately 22 staff correspondents in Africa against Anglo-France Presse's (AFP) 24. The American agencies each had approximately half a dozen staff correspondents.'[83]

During the early 1970s, South Africa was a relative backwater for the news agencies, as indeed it was for the newspapers. Reuters concentrated on reporting the remunerative Johannesburg stock exchange for which it maintained the largest bureau of the agencies. Larry Heinzerling (AP bureau chief, 1974–78), oversaw a major expansion of the AP staff during his period in the Republic. By the end of the decade, AP had six correspondents and stringers in South Africa. UPI was forced by circumstances to work on a much smaller budget than Reuters or AP, and only employed one correspondent in the Republic until 1976. Recognising the historical advantage which Reuters possessed in the region, AP and UPI concentrated on feature articles and analysis. Surprisingly, none of the news agencies employed any African journalists during the 1970s, which perhaps explains why news agency 'scoops' were rare. One of the most dramatic reports filed by the news agencies, the visit by journalists to Robben Island in April 1977, was only an exceptional story because the international newspapers were excluded from the trip.[84]

Oliver Boyd-Barrett has noted that 'One of the most important features of the ... leading world agencies in their role as international news wholesalers is their fundamentally *national* character.'[85] Both AP and UPI remained dominant throughout the 1970s in the US market, whereas Reuters continued to possess a distinct advantage in the British market. Within South Africa, all three agencies hired at least half of their reporters locally. Reuters had a very large number of South African employees, while AP retained key posts for American journalists. UPI employed a significant number of British or South African staff writers. During the 1970s, in keeping with a number of the newspapers, there was a general trend amongst the news agencies to establish headquarters for continental coverage in Johannesburg. According to the AP foreign editor, Nate Polowetzky, the journalists' 'access and capacity to function is greater in South Africa than in any other country on the continent'.[86] Two 'radical' news 'feature' agencies were established in 1967 and 1973, respectively: Gemini (in London) and Africa News (in Durham, North Carolina).[87] Although few of the major newspapers credited articles to Gemini or Africa News, their influence grew over the decade.

In 1976, Aaron Segal noted that 'If US magazines and newspapers do not have enough reporters on the ground to begin to cover Africa, then radio and TV have yet to land. Neither has ever had a single full-time correspondent in Africa since World War II.'[88] This situation was transformed by the Angolan war, the Soweto uprising and the intensifying liberation struggle in Rhodesia/Zimbabwe. By 1978, the British Broadcasting Corporation (BBC), Independent Television News (ITN), Columbia Broadcasting System (CBS), National Broadcasting Company (NBC) and American Broadcasting Company (ABC) had all established television bureaus in South Africa. Before 1977, it had been normal practice for British and American broadcasters either to buy footage from UPITN, Visnews, or freelance reporters, or to send a 'fireman' into the Republic.[89] Television images and reports, therefore, lacked the continuity and fluency that might have been expected if resident correspondents had been situated in the country. One of the key factors in the establishment of international television bureaus was the launch of the South African Broadcasting Corporation (SABC)'s television service in 1976 which both provided footage to the international broadcasters and increased the number of South Africans who were trained to work in television production.

The rush to open bureaus in South Africa was, however, a shock to many of the journalists concerned. John Simpson later recalled: 'I'd taken the job of BBC radio correspondent in South Africa, having been told that there was no question of a television bureau being set up

there. Then, a few months later, out came John Humphrys – as television correspondent.'[90] Michael Nicholson (ITN), who had covered
the country for many years as a fireman, was the first correspondent
to establish a bureau. Humphrys followed soon afterwards. For the
British broadcasters, South and southern Africa proved to be a lucra-
tive asset, which would pay back, in part, British dependence upon the
American broadcasters in other areas of the globe. Although NBC and
ABC opened their own bureaus in the Republic during 1977, they
continued to exchange material with the BBC and ITN, respectively.
CBS had no such relationship with the British broadcasters and,
indeed, was the last to establish a base in South Africa.[91] While
Nicholson and Humphrys remained in Africa throughout the rest of
the 1970s, the turnover of US bureau chiefs was rapid. The first ABC
correspondent, Rex Ellis, was dismissed within a few months of arriving in South Africa 'when it was felt he failed to aggressively pursue
the story of Stephen Biko'.[92] Other American correspondents relied
heavily on locally recruited South African or Rhodesian cameramen,
technicians and producers.[93] During the two years following the
establishment of SABC television, a significant number of the newly-
trained SABC staff departed for jobs with the international broadcasters.

Although regular news reports from television correspondents
based in South Africa were a new development during the late 1970s,
British and American broadcasters had always possessed other means
of covering the country. Perhaps the most important of these was the
utilisation of documentary films, 'specials' or television series on the
subject. British television consistently discussed political developments in South Africa more regularly and at greater depth than the
Americans. The weekly BBC programme, 'Panorama', for instance,
carried reports or interviews from South Africa on more than half-a-
dozen occasions between 1973 and 1978.[94] On independent television
in Britain, Thames Television's 'This Week', Granada Television's
'World in Action' and London Weekend Television (LWT)'s 'Weekend
World' became increasingly concerned with issues relating to South
Africa in the period between 1976 and 1978. 'This Week', under the
influence of David Elstein and Jonathan Dimbleby, adopted a notably
anti-apartheid stance.[95] During the same period, South African politicians and the apartheid issue became a regular source of debate on
CBS's 'Face the Nation', ABC's 'Issues and Answers' and NBC's 'Meet
the Press'.[96]

Four programmes or series broadcast on British television during
the 1970s require additional comment.

On 12 December 1974, the BBC's 'Man Alive' screened an edited version of the independently-made film, 'Last Grave at Dimbaza', which provided a harrowing portrait of African poverty and infant mortality in the Eastern Cape. However, the BBC appeared to have succumbed to the entreaties of the South African Department of Information in that it also screened a propaganda film contributed by Vlok Delport, Director of Information at the South African Embassy in London. The pair of films was broadcast, in conjunction with a studio debate which pitted Albert Dhlomo (an ex-Robben Island prisoner), the film's director and a missionary who had recently visited South Africa, against Delport, L.E.S. de Villiers (the Deputy-Secretary for Information) and an African supporter of the South African government's policy of grand apartheid. Charles Curran, the Director-General of the BBC, later defended the programme by asserting that 'we shall go on ... with these unique balancing acts. And we shall do so, as we did on this occasion, without any pressure compelling us other than our own wish to be as fair as we can, even in the most emotive controversies'.[97] When 'Last Grave at Dimbaza' was screened on American public television ten months later, there was no accompanying South African propaganda film.[98]

Eighteen months later, the BBC screened a series of four programmes on 'The Philpott File' which addressed the issue of the introduction of television in South Africa. Unfortunately, these fundamentally lightweight programmes were broadcast during the Soweto uprising, in the context of which Philpott's faith in the liberalising effect of television must have appeared quite strange.[99] In complete contrast to the work of Trevor Philpott, the series of films, 'The South African Experience', made by Antony Thomas for Anglia Television (ATV) and screened during November and December 1977, was, in the words of Sadie Forman (*Anti-Apartheid News*), 'an historic document. Those watching were able to know, sometimes loud, sometimes muted but always clear, what is happening in South Africa right now and the definitive part played by Britain in shoring up apartheid.'[100] The three films, functioning as a triptych, examined the story of Sandra Laing, an Afrikaner child who was reclassified as 'coloured', the events of the Soweto uprising, and the international beneficiaries of the apartheid system, through an examination of the wages and conditions at Tate & Lyle, British Leyland and Sirdar (a clothes manufacturer).

Thomas, who started his film-making career working for the South African government during the early 1960s, but whose political beliefs had since changed, recalls that, although the Department insisted on providing him with 'minders' during the preparation of the documentary film, these were suddenly withdrawn in the days before filming commenced.[101] 'The South African Experience' had a profound impact on British viewers and Thomas was awarded the British Academy of Film and Television Arts Award for the best factual television series of 1977. Stanley Uys commented in the *Rand Daily Mail*: 'After this film ["The Search for Sandra Laing"], the South African Department of Information and all its associated publicists and propagandists, might as well fold their tents and steal away.'[102] However, it was the third film in the series, 'Working for Britain', which attracted the most political attention within Britain. Tate & Lyle claimed that the film 'contain[ed] grossly distorted statements which combine to give a totally unrepresentative picture'.[103] While Tate & Lyle managed to delay the showing of the film by one week, it failed to silence Thomas and ATV. The one-hour television debate after the showing of the film provided a platform for a genuine anti-apartheid voice, in the person of Abdul Minty. The failure of Chris van der Walt (the Director of Information at the South African Embassy) and Louis Luyt to provide an effective defence for South Africa had significant repercussions within the Department of Information.[104]

The films made by Antony Thomas were eventually screened in 30 countries, including the United States. *SA Digest* reported Eschel Rhoodie as commenting that 'Through [Thomas's] actions he ha[s] slammed the door tight in the face of other foreign TV film producers.'[105] Thomas recalls that ATV was 'very frightened by the experience'.[106] 'The South African Experience' represented the end of a period in which relatively radical documentaries on South Africa appeared on British commercial television. Within a few months, David Harrison arrived in the Republic to make a four-part series on the history of the Afrikaners for the BBC. He later explained that although 'we got a lot of stick over Antony Thomas' it was possible to make a series in South Africa because the Department of Information wanted the Afrikaners' story to be told: 'The argument that we had been getting ... was "You guys – all you talk about is the irritations of petty apartheid. You don't know anything about the history – you don't understand what we're trying to do – you never tell people about the grand design" ... so I said "okay, lets do it".'[107]

'The White Tribe of Africa' proved to be both retrogressive and confusing. Screened during January 1979, at the height of the Information scandal, the series might have revealed to the viewer Afrikaner culture in crisis. Instead, it offered a representation of the Afrikaner which had barely changed over the previous 20 years. In this respect, Harrison and the BBC were not alone. American documentaries also concentrated on the mysterious power of the mythologised 'white tribe'. The radical American film-maker, Peter Davis's work, 'The

White Laager', while attempting to emphasise the anti-apartheid position also 'documents the white power version of South Africa. No Black person speaks in the film, and scenes of Blacks are seen as if from white eyes.'[108] Among the most dramatic documentaries made by the network American broadcasters on the subject of South Africa during the 1970s was 'NBC Reports: Africa's Defiant White Tribe'. However, even this ostensibly intelligent treatment, which referred directly to the economic base of apartheid and discussed South Africa's nuclear programme, concentrated its focus on the Afrikaner. As the *Washington Post* television reviewer observed, 'Most of the interviews are with whites, who control the country. It's a fundamental way to look at an explosive situation.'[109]

While the failings of the American television broadcasters might be explained by the relative lack of knowledge in the US media about South Africa, no such excuse was available for the BBC. In his comprehensive study on the reporting of South Africa by the BBC between 1948 and 1961, Howard Smith has suggested that 'the frame of reference had been set immutably after Sharpeville' and that, since that time, the BBC 'could not be "neutral, unbiased or impartial"' on the subject of apartheid.[110] While this may be true at a formal level, in practice, the BBC's television coverage of South Africa during the 1970s demonstrated a significant degree of tolerance for the apartheid state.

Radio coverage of the Republic was particularly dominated by the BBC during the 1970s. In 1972, the BBC was the only radio broadcaster to have a resident correspondent in the country.[111] The BBC continued to differentiate between television reporters and radio staff, although on occasions journalists would be expected to utilise either medium. Turnover of correspondents was relatively rapid during the 1970s, with the average term of residency being 18 months. Within South Africa, BBC radio employed Peter Hawthorne as a stringer; in London, the most regularly called upon commentators were Bridget Bloom and Stanley Uys.[112] BBC Radio 4 covered events in South Africa in greater detail than the television broadcasters, with major news stories being reported on the 'Today' programme, the 'World at One', the 'PM' show and 'The World Tonight'. 'From Our Own Correspondent', the weekly foreign news programme, also featured many South African reports during the late 1970s. BBC domestic radio was, however, on occasions open to pro-South African opinion, and demonstrated much the same acquiescence and concern for 'balance' as BBC television.[113]

BBC World Service Radio provided the most comprehensive coverage of South African news on any British or American radio station.

World Service Radio, in addition to breaking a number of significant stories, was the first and only section of the international media to employ an African stringer in the Republic.[114] 'Focus on Africa', under the editorship of Israel Wamala, featured reports by BBC correspondents and background material by freelance reporters, stringers and print journalists such as David Martin. Following the Soweto uprising and the establishment of American television bureaus in the Republic, CBS Radio and ABC Radio began to broadcast reports to the United States.[115] By the end of the 1970s, National Public Radio, which was, in effect, a US version of the BBC, possessed a stringer in South Africa and programmes such as 'Morning Edition' and 'All Things Considered' regularly debated the apartheid issue.[116] With 'Africa News' and the *Christian Science Monitor*'s extensions into the production of radio news, the subject of South Africa became available to an increasingly large radio audience in the United States.

Information of the sort contained in this chapter, while prosaic on one level, is also central to any study of the media which wishes to address the issues raised in Chapter 1. The, often very brief, visits to South Africa by the senior members of the editorial staff of the news organisations were important because they demonstrated the perceived significance of the South African 'story'. At its core, this chapter has been an attempt to describe the complicated, and at times inchoate, discourse between the correspondents in South Africa and the editorial staff (and commentators) in Britain and North America. This discourse is examined further in the case-studies (Chapters 5, 6 and 7). Penetrating the media discourse and thereby influencing the development of the media's representations, was the central task of South Africa's Department of Information and the anti-apartheid movements. Their attempts to achieve this aim are examined in the next two chapters. The successes and failures of the news organisations in their coverage of South Africa and, perhaps most critically, the social and political forces which impinged upon the work of the correspondents and stringers will be examined in the conclusion to this book (Chapters 8 and 9).

NOTES

1. 'Personal Business: Booming South Africa Lures Businessmen', *Business Week*, 11 May 1974, p. 131.
2. Richard West, 'Toothless Bulldogs', *Spectator*, 5 March 1977, pp. 7–8.
3. For two studies of the US media's coverage of South Africa during the periods at either end of this book, see John Seiler, 'The Formulation of US Policy toward Southern Africa, 1957–1976: The Failure of Good Intentions', unpublished

PhD dissertation, University of Connecticut, 1976, pp. 5–42 (on the period 1957–71); and Sanford J. Ungar, 'South Africa in the American Media', in Alfred O. Hero Jr and John Barratt (eds), *The American People and South Africa: Publics, Elites, and Policymaking Processes* (Massachusetts, Lexington Books, 1981), pp. 25–46 (on the period 1979–80). There are no studies of the British media's coverage of South Africa during the 1970s.

4. See Appendix A for brief biographies of the correspondents and stringers in South Africa. For further information on the newspapers analysed in this study see Oliver Boyd-Barrett, 'The Collection of Foreign News in the National Press: Organisation and Resources', in Oliver Boyd-Barrett, Colin Seymour-Ure and Professor Jeremy Tunstall, *Studies on the Press: Royal Commission on the Press Working Paper Number 3* (London, HMSO, 1977); Michael Emery and Edwin Emery, *The Press and America: An Interpretive History of the Mass Media* (New Jersey, Prentice Hall, 1988); John C. Merrill and Harold A. Fisher, *The World's Great Dailies: Profiles of Fifty Newspapers* (New York, Hastings House, 1980); Dennis Griffiths (ed.), *The Encyclopedia of the British Press, 1422–1992* (London, 1992). See also the many histories of the newspapers and news organisations: Gay Talese, *The Kingdom and the Power* (London, Calder & Boyars, 1971); Harrison E. Salisbury, *Without Fear or Favor: The New York Times and its Times* (New York, Times Books, 1980); Ben Bradlee, *A Good Life: Newspapering and Other Adventures* (New York, Simon & Schuster, 1995); David Halberstam, *The Powers That Be* (New York, Alfred A. Knopf, 1979); Lloyd Wendt, *The Wall Street Journal: The Story of Dow Jones and the Nation's Business Newspaper* (Chicago, Rand McNally, 1982); Lloyd Wendt, *Chicago Tribune: The Rise of a Great American Newspaper* (Chicago, Rand McNally, 1979); Charles L. Robertson, *The International Herald Tribune: The First Hundred Years* (New York, Columbia University Press, 1987); Merle Miller, 'Why the Editor of Newsweek is not the Editor of Time, and Vice Versa, *Esquire*, June 1973, pp. 169–231; Howard Zinn, 'Rosebuds: Always Several Political Steps Ahead', *More*, December 1975, p. 3; Robert Sherrill, 'The New Regime at The New Republic', *Columbia Journalism Review*, March/April 1976, pp. 23–29; 'All the President's Magazines', *Time*, 15 December 1980, pp. 50–51; Andrew Kopkind, 'MacNeil/Lehrer's Class Act', *Columbia Journalism Review*, September/October 1979, pp. 31–38; John Grigg, *The History of The Times, Volume VI: The Thomson Years, 1966-1981* (London, Times Books, 1993); Alastair Hetherington, *Guardian Years* (London, Chatto & Windus, 1981); Geoffrey Taylor, *Changing Faces: A History of The Guardian, 1956-88* (London, Fourth Estate, 1993); Duff Hart-Davis, *The House that the Berrys Built: Inside The Telegraph, 1928-1986* (London, Hodder & Stoughton, 1990); David Kynaston, *The Financial Times: A Centenary History* (London, Viking Penguin, 1988); Harold Evans, *Good Times, Bad Times* (London, Weidenfeld & Nicolson, 1983); Frank Giles, *Sundry Times* (London, John Murray, 1986); Richard Cockett, *David Astor and The Observer* (London, Andre Deutsch, 1991); Ruth Dudley Edwards, *The Pursuit of Reason: The Economist, 1843-1993* (London, Hamish Hamilton, 1993); Donald Read, *The Power of News: The History of* Reuters, *1849-1989* (Oxford, Oxford University Press, 1994); Hugo Young, 'Rupert Murdoch and The Sunday Times: A Lamp Goes Out', *Political Quarterly*, Vol. 55, No. 4 (1984), pp. 382–90.

5. Interview with Michael Knipe, 12 April 1995.

6. As legal correspondent, Berlins reported the Biko inquest during November 1977 for *The Times*.

7. Levin was the most vociferous of the British columnists. He wrote 24 columns between 1972 and 1979 on the subject of apartheid. 'South Africa was very

important to me in the same way as the Soviet Union ... was important, because I care about basic human rights and freedoms.' (Letter from Bernard Levin, 10 July 1996). Levin was banned from visiting South Africa. Lord Chalfont, an ex-Labour politician, began writing regular columns on South Africa, following the Angolan war. He recalls that he saw himself as a 'centrist' on South African issues, during the 1970s. (Interview with Lord Chalfont, 12 March 1996.) Chalfont visited the Republic in 1977 in order to interview John Vorster for the BBC.

8. 'Business and Trade Centres of the World 8: Johannesburg', *The Times*, 12 June 1973; 'Export Corridors of the World: South Africa', *The Times*, 16 May 1974; 'Investment Centres of the World: Johannesburg', *The Times*, 26 August 1975; 'A Special Report: Transkei', *The Times*, 16 October 1978.

9. For a discussion of the divisions within the *Daily Telegraph*, see Hart-Davis, op. cit., pp. 236–39.

10. See, for example, William Deedes, 'Why Vorster has Written Us Off', *Daily Telegraph*, 8 December 1976.

11. Douglas Brown was the *Daily Telegraph*'s correspondent in South Africa during the 1950s. He later wrote a book about the country: Douglas Brown, *Against The World: A Study of White South African Attitudes* (London, Collins, 1966).

12. Ian Waller, political correspondent of the *Sunday Telegraph*, visited South Africa in 1973 and 1976; Graham Turner (*Sunday Telegraph*) visited in 1976; David Adamson, diplomatic editor of the *Daily Telegraph*, visited in 1976 and 1977; George Evans (*Sunday Telegraph*) interviewed Prime Minister P.W. Botha during March 1979; and Peter Taylor (*Sunday Telegraph*) visited in 1979.

13. Interview with Sir Peregrine Worsthorne, 15 January 1996. Worsthorne visited South Africa in 1977.

14. See, for example, Robin Page, 'Why South Africa Needs Us', *Daily Telegraph*, 29 May 1979.

15. Basil Hersov, Nic Rhoodie, Derrick de Villiers, Dr F. van Zyl Slabbert and Dr Cedric Phatudi, 'What is South Africa's Future? I–V', *Daily Telegraph*, 31 August–6 September 1977. Hersov was the President of the South Africa Foundation. Nic Rhoodie was the brother of the South African Secretary for Information.

16. The *Guardian*'s stringers in South Africa were Stanley Uys (until 1976) and Patrick Laurence (thereafter). The newspaper attempted to position Jonathan Steele as the correspondent in South Africa in 1974 but Steele was rejected by the Department of Information. (Interview with Ian Wright, 26 October 1994.)

17. Freelancers and stringers utilised by the *Guardian* included Roman Eisenstein, Richard Wagner, William Raynor (1972–73), Denis Herbstein (1976), John Kane-Berman and Steve Friedman (1979).

18. Interviews with Adam Raphael, 30 September 1994; Jonathan Steele, 15 November 1994; Martin Walker, 9 April 1996; and Richard Gott, 14 May 1996. See Jonathan Steele, 'The Other South Africa', *Guardian* 2–5 March 1970 and Richard Gott, 'Farther to the Right in South Africa', *Guardian*, 23 December 1971.

19. Interview with Richard Gott, 14 May 1996.

20. Geoffrey Taylor had been the *Guardian*'s foreign editor from 1960–69, northern editor from 1969–72 and assistant editor from 1973. See 'Independence for the Transkei' and 'The Transkei State of Mind', *Guardian*, 20 April and 28 May 1976; and his final statement on South Africa, a four-part series: 'Afrikanerdom Adrift in a Sea of Change', *Guardian*, 15–18 November 1976. For information on the *Guardian*'s publication of articles by ANC–SACP associated journalists, see Chapter 4.

21. Anti-Apartheid Movement, *Annual Report on Activities and Developments* (London, A-AM, 1977), p. 22.
22. Kynaston, op. cit., p. 376.
23. On Bridget Bloom, see Appendix A.
24. Following the appointment of Quentin Peel as the *Financial Times* correspondent in 1977, visits by Bloom decreased. Ian Davidson, foreign editor, visited South Africa in 1978.
25. At one point during the mid-1970s, [Johannesburg] *Financial Mail* journalists John Stewart (Cape Town), Stewart Carlyle (Durban), Richard Rolfe (mining) and John Kane-Berman (labour), were all stringing for the *Financial Times*. Although the *Financial Times* sold its holding in the [Johannesburg] *Financial Mail* in the mid-1970s, the connection persisted. Bernard Simon (*Financial Mail*) became the *Financial Times*'s chief stringer during the late 1970s.
26. See, for example, Joe Rogaly, 'Lombard: Mr Vorster is a Poor Risk', *Financial Times*, 17 September 1976; 'The West Cannot Win in Southern Africa', *Financial Times*, 2 November 1977.
27. *Financial Times*, 17 July 1972; 22 January 1974; 25 February 1975.
28. Interview with J.D.F. Jones, 3 November 1995.
29. Ibid. The *Financial Times* did not carry Club of Ten advertisements. See Chapter 3.
30. The *Observer*'s stringer in South Africa was Stanley Uys. Uys was succeeded by Hennie Serfontein. The *Observer* also published the Observer Foreign News Service (OFNS) which was syndicated world-wide. OFNS carried articles by a wide range of stringers and freelancers: Colin Smith, Richard Wagner (1972–73), John Borrell (1975–76), Donald Woods and Roger Omond (1976–77).
31. Editorial, 'Pretoria Propaganda', *Observer*, 19 December 1976.
32. Neal Ascherson, 'The Life-blood of Apartheid', *Observer*, 20 April 1975, republished in the American 'radical' publication, *Ramparts*, July 1975, pp. 11–13; Lord Goodman, 'A World of Tragic Disillusion' and 'Can the World Save South Africa?', *Observer*, 18 and 25 September 1977. Lord Goodman's parents had been born in South Africa; Anthony Sampson, 'The General's White Lies', 'The Spymaster and the Playboy' and 'The Long Reach of the Arms Men', *Observer*, 22 January–4 February 1979; Conor Cruise O'Brien, 'Metamorphoses of Apartheid' and 'The Guilt of Afrikanerdom', *Observer*, 22 and 29 July 1979. Cruise O'Brien was editor-in-chief of the *Observer*.
33. On Colin Legum, see Appendix A.
34. W.A.J. Payne, 'Through a Glass Darkly: The Media and Africa', in Helen Kitchen (ed.), *Africa: From Mystery to Maze* (Lexington, MA, Lexington Books, 1976), p. 219.
35. For an amusing, if romanticised, account of the 'old Africa hand', see Chris Munnion, *Banana Sunday: Datelines From Africa* (Rivonia, William Waterman, 1993).
36. The six major American newspapers analysed in this study were voted the best six US newspapers in an American survey in 1983. Among the 610 people surveyed were newspaper publishers, editors and journalism professors. ('Best in the USA', *Editor and Publisher*, 11 June 1983). On the basis that the elite US newspapers tended to exert a significant influence over the other areas of the American media, I decided that those newspapers which were judged 'best' in the above poll probably represented a good place to start my analysis.
37. Graham Hovey visited South Africa in 1975. See also Leonard Silk, 'Interest and Ideology', *New York Times*, 9 October 1973. Leonard Silk was a member of the *New York Times*'s editorial board during the early 1970s. He visited South Africa in 1973.

38. Exceptional articles by Anthony Lewis included: 'South Africa: The End is Inevitable but not Predictable', *New York Times* magazine, 21 September 1975, pp. 13–91; 'State of Violence', *New York Times*, 5 December 1977: 'We Learned the Cost of National Racism Once Before, and Said: Never Again'; 'State of Violence: II', *New York Times*, 8 December 1977: 'The logic of events is moving, and should move, toward American economic withdrawal.'

39. Exceptional articles by Tom Wicker included: 'Investing in Apartheid', *New York Times*, 6 December 1977; 'Should American Business Pull Out of South Africa?', *New York Times* magazine, 5 June 1979, pp. 31–75.

40. See Seymour Topping, 'Excerpts from Interview with Prime Minister Vorster on South African policy', *New York Times*, 17 September 1977; Seymour Topping, 'How Long can Africa's Whites Hold Out?', *New York Times* magazine, 13 November 1977, pp. 37–114.

41. Editorial, 'South Africa and the Double Standard', *New York Times*, 14 November 1977.

42. The *Washington Post*'s stringers in South Africa were Peter Younghusband (1972–74), Robin Wright (1974–77) and Caryle Murphy (1977–81). Murphy was eventually upgraded to the status of correspondent.

43. Jim Hoagland, 'Black Power vs. White Power: South Africa', *Washington Post*, 9–16 January 1977. Hoagland was permitted to enter South Africa for a six-week period on condition that he covered the 'independence' of the Transkei. (Interview with Jim Hoagland, 10 April 1996.)

44. Benjamin C. Bradlee, 'Images of Africa', *Washington Post*, 4 March 1979; Sally Quinn, 'The Afrikaner's Burden', 'Tea and Fury in Soweto', 'Questions of Color, Burdens of Proof' and 'An Alliance Going Sour', *Washington Post*, 4–7 March 1979.

45. Evans and Novak, June 1977; Stephen Rosenfeld, October 1977; the African-American columnist William Raspberry visited South Africa in April 1978.

46. Meyer also wrote editorials for the *New York Times*, from 1976.

47. During 1978 and 1979, David Lamb (Nairobi correspondent) and Alvin Shuster (managing editor) made short visits to South Africa.

48. Jack Foisie, 'A New Broom or an Old Hand?', *Nieman Reports*, Winter 1985, p. 16.

49. Barbara Hutmacher, 'A South African Editor Stands His Ground', *Los Angeles Times*, 10 February 1976; 'South Africa's Bottled-up Freedom', *Los Angeles Times*, 29 November 1977. Hutmacher was an American citizen, who had worked on the [East London] *Daily Dispatch* in the mid-1970s. See also Barbara Hutmacher, *In Black and White: Voices of Apartheid* (London, Junction Books, 1980).

50. 'A Leading Economic Indicator', *Time*, 7 July 1980, pp. 44–45.

51. The *Wall Street Journal*'s stringers were Neil Behrman (1972–76) and Stephen Mulholland (1977–84).

52. *Wall Street Journal*, 10 November 1978.

53. Visitors included James Yuenger and Clarence Page, 'Wheel of Hatred Turns, S. African Town Explodes' and 'Crisis in Black and White', *Chicago Tribune*, 20 and 27–30 June 1976. Clarence Page was an African-American, Yuenger and Page were accompanied by African-American photographer, Ernie Cox Jr. Clayton Kirkpatrick, 'Economic Pressure for Change Builds in South Africa'; 'More S. Africa Whites Muster Opposition to Apartheid'; 'South African Moderate Blacks' Goal: a Free and Fair Life'; 'The World has a Big Stake in a Peaceful South Africa', *Chicago Tribune*, 5, 7, 9 and 12 December 1976. Kirkpatrick was the editor of the *Chicago Tribune*. Ray Moseley, 'South Africa: At the Crossroads' and 'Industry Wants Halt to S. African Bias' and 'US

Companies Erasing Apartheid in S. African Plants', *Chicago Tribune*, 4–6 and 25–6 November 1979. Moseley was a renowned foreign correspondent.

54. See, for example, the following articles written by Jarrett after meeting Donald Woods: Vernon Jarrett, 'Racial War Closer in South Africa' and 'Some Good Advice from South Africa', *Chicago Tribune*, 21 May and 4 June 1978.

55. Patrick J. Buchanan, 'Young Slanders Black Patriots', *Chicago Tribune*, 27 March 1977. See also Patrick J. Buchanan, 'Who is Carter to Cast First Stone?', *Chicago Tribune*, 27 October 1977: 'And where does Carter come off lecturing South Africa on race relations? If memory serves, up until several months ago, Carter worshipped at a segregated Southern Baptist Church. Indeed, when an itinerant black preacher showed up to pray with Jimmy and the white folks, half the congregation wanted to interrupt "Nearer My God To Thee" to go up side his head.'

56. Interview with June Goodwin, 5 April 1996.

57. The *Christian Science Monitor* operated a strict limit on the length of terms for correspondents: Frederic Hunter (1969–73); Henry S. Hayward (1973–76); June Goodwin (1976–78); Gary Thatcher (1978–). The newspaper preferred its correspondents to be practising Christian Scientists although this was not obligatory. Unlike the *Los Angeles Times*, the *Monitor* also employed stringers within South Africa.

58. Interview with June Goodwin, 5 April 1996.

59. Geoffrey Godsell, 'Crisis in South Africa', *Christian Science Monitor*, 8–16 September 1977.

60. Interview with John Grimond, 29 January 1996.

61. Between 1974 and 1976, a number of freelance articles by John Grimond on southern Africa were published in the *New York Times*.

62. M.S. Mendelsohn, 'Kruger's Golden Rand: A Survey of Gold and South Africa', *The Economist*, 22 March 1975.

63. See Edwards, op. cit., pp. 900–1. On Moss, see Chapter 6.

64. Most notably, Suzanne Cronje (1972–74).

65. See Christopher Hitchens, 'Aspects of Southern Africa', *New Statesman*, 27 October 1978, pp. 534–35; 'Namibia: The Birth of A Nation', *New Statesman*, 3 November 1978, pp. 572–76. Another visitor to South Africa who filed a series of reports was Steven Lukes, 'Apartheid: Visible and Invisible', 'White Politics: the Limits of Change' and 'Black Politics: the Dangers of Disunity', *New Statesman*, 19 October–2 November 1979, pp. 586–87, 628–29, 676–77.

66. For information on the South Africa Foundation, see Chapter 3.

67. Richard West, who had previously written for the *New Statesman* and continued to write for *Private Eye,* financed his visits to South Africa by writing travel articles for holiday companies (interview with Richard West, 28 November 1995).

68. As a rule the vast majority of articles on South Africa in *Time* were only carried in the international edition. The domestic edition of the magazine only carried articles on foreign affairs when the subject matter directly related to the United States. All references to *Time* and *Newsweek* in this book refer to the international editions.

69. Lee Griggs was allowed to return to South Africa in order to cover the independence of the Transkei.

70. Henry Grunwald, 'Arguing with South Africa', *Time*, 27 June 1977, p. 19.

71. See Arnaud de Borchgrave, 'We Can Trump Russia', *Newsweek*, 17 May 1976, pp. 22–23; 'The Way the BOSS Sees it', *Newsweek*, 25 October 1976, pp. 19–20; Andrew Nagorski, 'A Matter of Color', *Newsweek*, 3 January 1977, pp. 18–20.

72. Mort Rosenblum, *Coups and Earthquakes: Reporting the World for America* (New York, Harper Colophon, 1981), p. 131.
73. See opening quotation, note 1.
74. 'Special Report: Doing Business with a Blacker Africa', *Business Week*, 14 February 1977, pp. 64–70.
75. Thomson visited South Africa during 1975 and proceeded to devote half of the *Nieman Reports*, Autumn/Winter 1975 edition to a close examination of South Africa, which included contributions from Benjamin Pogrund, John Corr (*Philadelphia Enquirer*), Gatsha Buthelezi and Percy Qoboza. In the editorial for the magazine ('Why South Africa?'), Thomson observed: 'This year's South African Nieman – Percy Qoboza ... is again a black, for the first time in a decade' (p. 61). During 1977 and 1978, and in conjunction with the persecution of African journalists and black consciousness groups in South Africa, *Nieman Reports* became one of the most vocal forces for liberal 'anti-apartheid' in the US establishment. For the campaign regarding Qoboza, see James C. Thomson Jr, 'African Nemesis?', *Nieman Reports*, Summer/Autumn 1977, pp. 2 and 31; 'The Percy Qoboza Case', *Nieman Reports*, Winter/Spring 1978, pp. 34–37; 'The Percy Qoboza Case: Continued', *Nieman Reports*, Summer 1978, pp. 46–49.
76. See James North, *Freedom Rising* (New York, New American Library, 1986).
77. See William A. Rusher, Letter to the editor, *New York Times* magazine, 16 November 1975, p. 105. During his visit in 1974, Buckley interviewed John Vorster for his network television show, 'Firing Line'.
78. F.R. Buckley, 'Soweto Visited: Another Country', *National Review*, 13 April 1979, p. 482. Compare Buckley's impressions of Soweto with Christopher Hitchens, 'Aspects of Southern Africa', *New Statesman*, 27 October 1978, p. 534: 'I expected to find that Soweto was pretty awful ... Wrong, of course. It is far worse than one has heard it is.'
79. Ungar in Hero and Barratt (eds), op. cit., pp. 28–29.
80. E.J. Kahn Jr, 'Annals of International Trade: a Very Emotive Subject', *New Yorker*, 14 May 1979, pp. 117–53; 'A Reporter at Large: Who Cares? ... We Do!', *New Yorker*, 25 June 1979, pp. 60–88.
81. Ian Robertson and Phillip Whitten, 'Sexual Politics in South Africa', the *Progressive*, September 1972, pp. 42–45; Tad Szulc, 'Why are We in Johannesburg?', *Esquire*, October 1974, pp. 48–91; Robert A. Manning, Tony Hodges and Paula Giddings, 'The South African Connection, Parts 1 and 2', *Encore American and Worldwide News*, 22 March and 5 April 1976, pp. 18–23 and 22–31.
82. Conor Cruise O'Brien, 'South Africa: an Ominous Lull', *New York Review of Books*, 27 September 1978, pp. 28–30; Peter Walshe, Alan Paton, William B. Gould and Thomas J. Downey, 'On the Brink in South Africa', *Commonweal*, 10 November 1978, pp. 713–22; Herman Nickel, 'The Case for Doing Business in South Africa', *Fortune*, 19 June 1978, pp. 60–74; John Train, 'South Africa: US, Don't Go Home', *Forbes*, 27 November 1978, pp. 33–35; Jan Morris, 'States in Siege, Part 1: South Africa', *Rolling Stone*, 2 June 1977, pp. 47–53; Patrick Laurence, Martin Schneider, Obed Kunene and Daniel Schechter, 'Banned in South Africa', *More*, December 1977, pp. 12–33. See also George W. Ball, 'Asking for Trouble in South Africa' and Benjamin Pogrund, 'The Anatomy of White Power', *Atlantic Monthly*, October 1977, pp. 43–60; Dan Jacobson, 'Among the South Africans', *Commentary*, March 1978, pp. 32–48.
83. Oliver Boyd-Barrett, *The International News Agencies* (London, Constable, 1980), p. 178.
84. Reuters, 'An Outsider's Look at a Special South African Jail', *New York Times*, 27 April 1977.

85. Boyd-Barrett, in Boyd-Barrett, Seymour-Ure and Tunstall, op. cit., p. 35.

86. Cited by Ungar in Hero and Barratt (eds), op. cit., p. 37.

87. See Richard Bourne, *News on a Knife-edge: Gemini Journalism and a Global Agenda* (London, John Libbey, 1995) and 'Our Turn: a Seventh Year for Africa News', Africa News, 20 July 1979, pp. 5–7.

88. Aaron Segal, 'Africa and the United States Media', *Issue*, Vol. 6, No. 2/3 (Summer/Fall 1976), p. 49.

89. UPITN was owned by UPI and ITN (25 per cent each) and Paramount Pictures (50 per cent, 1971–74); John McGoff (50 per cent, 1974–79), see Chapter 3. Visnews was controlled by Reuters and the BBC. Within the American market, ABC, NBC and CBS held shares in Visnews. For an introduction to the complexity of this system of image-production, see W. Stephen Gilbert and Patricia Williams, 'The News Bazaar', *Time Out*, No. 304, 9 January 1976.

90. John Humphrys and John Simpson, 'How We Met', *Independent on Sunday* magazine, 10 December 1995, p. 91.

91. 'Televising Africa for America', *Africa*, No. 87 (November 1978), pp. 96–97, reported that CBS opened its first African bureau in Nairobi during January 1977, under the stewardship of an African-American correspondent, Randy Daniels. Although Daniels did report from South Africa, visas to enter the Republic continued to prove difficult to obtain. During February 1977, Walter Cronkite, the CBS 'anchorman', visited South Africa and complained about the fact that 'We are not permitted to have a resident correspondent here – our requests for visas are largely denied. But we have a correspondent in the Soviet Union.' ('No Ban on Visas for CBS', *SA Digest*, 25 February 1977, p. 25. *SA Digest* was a Department of Information publication.) CBS opened a bureau in South Africa during 1978 with a white American correspondent.

92. Ellen Graham, 'Serious Competitor: ABC News Improves but Ratings Still Lag, under Arledge Regime', *Wall Street Journal*, 26 April 1978.

93. Interview with Heather Allen, 16 April 1996.

94. Subjects covered by 'Panorama' included the police shooting of miners in the Transvaal (September 1973); the Angolan war (January 1976); the Soweto uprising (June 1976); Kissinger's diplomacy (September 1976); an interview with John Vorster (February 1977); an interview with Roelof Botha (November 1977); and the breaking of the arms embargo against South Africa (November 1978). In 1974, 'Panorama' broadcast an interview with John Vorster which had originally appeared on William Buckley's 'Firing Line' in the US.

95. Clancy Sigal, 'Balance', *Spectator*, 26 November 1977, p. 32: 'Comparing current television coverage of news with the older newsreels, Dimbleby demolishes the concept of the objective reporter. "The obsession with balance" he insists, "distorts truth ... My fear is that when our successors look back on the coverage of events in South Africa ... by the British media today they will look back with the same kind of dismay that now we look back on the way the cinema covered the events in the 'thirties in Germany".'

96. John Vorster appeared on both 'Face the Nation' and 'Issues and Answers' in 1976 and 1977. Vorster was also interviewed on public television's 'The MacNeil-Lehrer Report', which regularly covered the South African story. (Ungar in Hero and Barratt (eds), op. cit., p. 38.)

97. Charles Curran, Letter to the editor, *Sunday Times*, 22 December 1974.

98. C. Gerald Fraser, '"Dimbaza", Film Smuggled out of South Africa, Won Aid of Church and Labor' and John J. O'Connor, 'TV: On Oppression in South Africa', *New York Times*, 27 October 1975. The WNET TV screening was followed by a debate between Anthony Lewis (*New York Times*) and the South African Ambassador to the US and UN, Roelof Botha.

99. 'The Philpott File: SA Faces Television', BBC 2, 8–29 July 1976. For an example of the tone of the programmes, see Trevor Philpott, 'The End of an Innocent Age?', *Listener*, 8 July 1976, pp. 2–4. See also Department of Information, *Report for the Period 1 January 1976 to 31 December 1976* (Pretoria, Government Printer, 1977), p. 6, which published a letter from Trevor Philpott to Eschel Rhoodie: 'We hope that we'll show that there is a good deal of entertainment and laughter in South Africa instead of the usual solemn and ominous view of the country which is so often the only one that is presented by the foreign media.' Philpott died in 1998 (Antony Jay and Alan Whicker, 'Obituaries: Trevor Philpott', *Independent*, 1 August 1998).

100. Sadie Forman, 'Working for Britain – Apartheid-style', *Anti-Apartheid News*, January/February 1978, p. 11.

101. Interview with Antony Thomas, 26 July 1996.

102. Stanley Uys, 'SA's Image Badly Slurred', *Rand Daily Mail*, 3 December 1977.

103. 'An Announcement by Tate & Lyle Limited', advertisement, *Daily Express*, 14 December 1977.

104. Luyt's television performance and the fact that 'Dr Rhoodie did not have much good to say about it' led, eventually, to Luyt and the Department of Information parting company. Within a few weeks, the first exposés of the Information scandal emerged in the South African press. (Mervyn Rees and Chris Day, *Muldergate: The Story of the Info Scandal* (Johannesburg, Macmillan, 1980), p. 118, citing Louis Luyt's evidence to the Mostert Commission.) See also Mervyn Rees, interview with Eschel Rhoodie, 1979, transcript, p. 382.

105. 'Door Closed', *SA Digest*, 9 December 1977, p. 9.

106. Interview with Antony Thomas, 26 July 1996.

107. Interview with David Harrison, 8 December 1995. See also David Harrison, 'In Search of the White Tribe', *Listener*, 1 February 1979, pp. 181–82, which recounts the problems faced during the filming of the series. These problems included Eschel Rhoodie's demands for a right of response. The second part of 'The White Tribe of Africa', which examined the Broederbond, was awarded the Royal Television Society Supreme Award for Best Documentary of the Year, 1979.

108. Kimberley Safford, 'Peter Davis' Film View of South Africa: An American review', *Critical Arts*, Vol. 1, No. 2 (June 1980), p. 96. Davis's second film study of South Africa, 'Generations of Resistance' (1980), viewed the society from the African perspective. 'The White Laager' (1977) was made in conjunction with the United Nations and screened on public television in the US.

109. Hollie I. West, 'Africa's Defiant White Tribe', *Washington Post*, 27 July 1977. For information on the making of the film, see Richard Pollak, *Up Against Apartheid: The Role and Plight of the Press in South Africa* (Carbondale and Edwardsville, Southern Illinois University Press, 1981), pp. 88–89.

110. Howard Smith, 'Apartheid, Sharpeville and "Impartiality": the Reporting of South Africa on BBC Television 1948–1961', *Historical Journal of Film, Radio and Television*, Vol. 13, No. 3 (1993), p. 291, citing Sir Hugh Greene, *The Conscience of the Programme Director* (London, BBC, 1965).

111. Voice of America covered events in South Africa from a neighbouring country.

112. For Hawthorne's list of strings, see Appendix A. Uys and Bloom also regularly appeared on BBC television and ITN.

113. For rumours regarding the attitude of senior editors at the BBC towards South Africa and the South African government, see 'Media News', *Private Eye*, No. 390, 26 November 1976, p. 3 and 'Street of Shame', *Private Eye*, No. 401, 29 April 1977, pp. 4–5. See also Editorial, 'No News', *Daily Telegraph*, 16 September 1976: 'Mr Desmond Taylor, the head of BBC news and current

affairs, lamented on Tuesday that South Africa was the freest country in Africa from which to report news.' This was at a time when the South African police were arresting African journalists and detaining them without trial.

114. Nat Serache, an African reporter on the *Rand Daily Mail*, was recruited as a stringer by the BBC World Service in 1975. See Chapter 8.

115. ABC possessed four separate radio networks, supplying 1,400 radio stations in the United States. CBS and NBC each owned one radio network. (Rosenblum, op. cit., p. 146.)

116. Ungar in Hero and Barratt (eds), op. cit., p. 38.

3

Information and/or Propaganda

[Eschel Rhoodie] was probably the most brilliant propagandist of the
century – I think he was better than Goebbels.[1]

I specifically said to [John Vorster]: 'I want you to approve, not an
information asset, but a propaganda war in which no rules or
regulations count. If it is necessary for me to bribe someone, then I
would bribe him or her. If it is necessary for me to purchase, for
example, a sable mink coat for an editor's wife then I should be in
a position to do so. If it is necessary for me to send somebody on a
holiday to the Hawaiian Islands with his mistress for a month, then I
should be able to do so.'[2]

The South African government's relationship with the international
media had been riven with difficulty since 1948. Indeed, in the immediate aftermath of the Sharpeville massacre (1960), the relationship
was tortuous. National Party (NP) politicians were well aware of the
power of the press, having been subject to anti-Afrikaner coverage in
the British media since the nineteenth century, and having utilised the
Afrikaans-language media throughout the long journey from nascent
nationalism to the election victory of 1948.[3] It would therefore be
completely inaccurate to suggest that NP politicians were 'anti-press'.[4]
They were, in fact, ardent supporters of the press, so long as it was
under their control and served their requirements. In 1950, the South
African government established a Press Commission of Inquiry with a
brief to investigate the domestic and the international press in South
Africa. The full findings of the Commission were finally published in
1964 and stretched to nearly 8,000 pages. The Commission employed
a system for judging the 'quality' of the coverage in the foreign media
which divided the reports into four categories: 'good', 'faulty', 'bad'
and 'very bad'. 'Very bad reporting' was described as 'either blindly
partisan or unscrupulously tendentious, the selection is so tendentious,
prejudiced and/or unscrupulous as to distort the South African political
and racial scene and the comment is so blindly partisan and/or

unscrupulous as to be generally unjustifiable'.[5] The reports of the full-
time correspondents in South Africa, between 1950 and 1955, were
evaluated as being 'good, 3.62; faulty, 1.02; bad, 14.70; and very bad,
80.66 per cent'.[6]

Between 1948 and 1972, the Information service of South Africa
was reorganised on a regular basis, most significantly in 1961 when
the Department of Information was founded.[7] However, it had long
been felt by a number of the Department's civil servants that it had
consistently failed to defend the country from international criticism.[8]
In 1968, for example, John Howland Beaumont, the editor of *South
African Panorama* (a Department of Information publication) resigned
and informed the press that 'Much of what was published by the
department to promote the official South African viewpoint abroad
… was misdirected and used the wrong tone, so that it often did South
Africa's image overseas more harm than good.'[9] This chapter examines
the activities of the Department of Information and South Africa's
other propaganda agencies during the 1970s by considering the
following: the Department of Information, during 1972–76, when
there was a concerted attempt to put a programme of media manipulation into action; the Information scandal ('Muldergate') which led
to the resignation of both the Minister and the Secretary for Information; the secret projects engineered by the Department in connection
with the international media; and the complementary roles played by
the South Africa Foundation, the private-sector propaganda agency,
and BOSS, South Africa's intelligence agency.

In 1968, Dr Connie Mulder was appointed Minister of Information.
Three years later, he undertook an extensive overseas tour with the
Secretary for Information, Gerald Barrie, in order to examine the
'propaganda offensive' facing South Africa. Mulder later informed
Deon Geldenhuys that 'The essence of their findings was that the
international propaganda offensive against South Africa was well
organised, highly sophisticated and generously funded … In a report
submitted to the prime minister it was recommended that South Africa
… should immediately and actively get involved in the propaganda
war and employ the same methods as its opponents.' Mulder instigated
the first secret projects upon his return from the tour. Heinz Behrens,
a German public relations specialist, was hired to feed articles into
the European media, and *To The Point* magazine was launched with
the support of government funds through extensive subscriptions.[10]
Meanwhile, Mulder encouraged the elevation of Gerald Barrie to the
post of Auditor-General and began the search for a Secretary and
Deputy-Secretary for Information capable of putting the new propaganda programme into action.[11] The civil servants who were chosen

were Eschel Rhoodie and L.E.S. ('Les') de Villiers.[12] Both Rhoodie and de Villiers had been affected by their experience of overseas anti-South African vitriol: 'As a press and information officer in the United States just after the Sharpeville shootings in 1960, I was spat upon by American students ... I therefore knew what it was to be humiliated for being a South African.'[13] Rhoodie's appointment was ratified in August 1972 against the wishes of the Public Service Commission.[14]

Rhoodie suggests in his memoir that his book, *The Paper Curtain*, had been central to Mulder's decision.[15] According to Rhoodie, the 'Paper Curtain' which afflicted South Africa differed 'from the Russian "Iron Curtain", East Germany's infamous "Wall" and Red China's "Bamboo Curtain" in that it is being drawn *not* by the people held responsible for all the "evil deeds" of apartheid but by the very people who claim that they wish to introduce reason into South Africa'.[16] Rhoodie's book also launched a number of criticisms of the international media which the Department of Information promoted throughout the 1970s. The most common of these were the concepts of 'double standards' and 'journalistic racism'. By double standards, Rhoodie meant that South Africa was being judged in isolation and not by the standards of other countries, while by journalistic racism he meant that 'the very same people who advocate this philosophy [the establishment of a non-racist South Africa] set an example of racialism (anti-White racialism) by ignoring crimes of Black against White and Black against Black'.[17]

A number of years later, Rhoodie recalled that his inspiration for *The Paper Curtain* had been an ex-CIA employee, whom he had met in the United States in the early 1960s. 'Mr Brown', or 'Brownie' as Rhoodie titled this mysterious figure, believed that 'The only way to influence the media was to own it, or to own some of the senior people in it.'[18] This analysis inspired Rhoodie's preoccupation with 'elite' politicians and newspaper executives. The suggestion that in order to influence the media one needed to own all or part of it later contributed to his downfall; ownership did not and could not mean *absolute* control. *The Paper Curtain* was an orthodox work of propaganda in that it lacked the degree of objectivity which would have made balanced analytical judgement possible. However, for all its contradictions, Rhoodie's book *was* a cunning polemic which managed to utilise the Afrikaner distrust of an uncontrolled media, while suggesting that resistance to the imagined misrepresentations was possible if the will, the funding and the ideas could be found. Rhoodie had, in effect, promoted himself as the only South African media analyst capable of taking on the task. Years later, he admitted to Mervyn Rees that the real reason for the Department of Information's involvement in covert propaganda activity was the unwillingness of private sector groups to do the job for South Africa: 'I heard so many times Afrikaans business leaders ... expressing their feelings of patriotism, but they never put their money where their mouths were.'[19]

During his first year as Secretary of Information, Rhoodie attempted to mobilise support in the South African government for the necessary funding required to transform the function of the Department of Information from what was in his opinion 'the official policy during the period 1955 to 1970 ... [which] was not to do anything' to something more substantial and proactive.[20] At the Perskor annual dinner in September 1972, Rhoodie attempted to convince leading Afrikaner politicians of the importance of launching a propaganda offensive which was prepared to employ 'whatever means necessary':

> There are certain factors, certain political realities, certain thrusts in foreign criticism of South Africa that we must take note of, side-step, blunt, meet head-on, try to avoid or to neutralise in order to promote a better image of South Africa ... It is difficult for us ... to counter [these factors, currents, and events] because our efforts will always be criticised as that of paid apologists for the government. But they are factors that can be countered by organising and making extensive use of existing goodwill among individuals, companies and organisations and, where they are non-existent, we should look to creating our own. Such non-governmental voices, independent, or ostensibly independent, whether South African or foreign, are very often more effective, are listened to and are considered more seriously than our own.[21]

One month later, Rhoodie discussed his plans for the Department with the *Rand Daily Mail*. In a peculiar interview littered with military metaphors ('in the front line trenches in the international battle for recognition and understanding') Rhoodie revealed that 'there would also be a change in the emphasis of publicity methods and he foresaw a time when 50 to 60 per cent of the department's methods would be "hidden", not in the sense of secrecy or subversion, but on an indirect basis. Events would be exploited to South Africa's advantage, even if they did not directly affect the country.'[22] An immediate innovation within the Department of Information was the promotion of Les de Villiers and Deneys Rhoodie to the position of joint-Deputy-Secretary. In addition, the Department's institutional structure was expanded from four divisions to eight. The Division for Planning and Special Projects which was, in effect, responsible for secret projects was headed by Les de Villiers.

New secret projects included two advertising front-organisations, the Committee for Fairness in Sport and the Club of Ten; a massive increase (30,000) in overseas subscriptions for *To The Point*; and the employment of two journalists, Bernard Lejeune and Karl Breyer.[23] Lejeune, a Frenchman, would later facilitate links between South Africa and Francophone African states. Breyer, a German photographer, used Department of Information funds (R26,000 per annum) to establish a photo-news agency which supplied material to a large number of European publications. Both Lejeune and Breyer had previously had their work published by *To The Point* and, according to Rhoodie and de Villiers, both journalists offered their services to the Department without being approached.[24] In addition, Rhoodie commissioned Richard Manville Inc., a New York public-relations firm, to engage in a market analysis at a cost of R280,000. The report, which eventually covered 14 countries and stretched to 17 volumes, proved very disconcerting for the Department of Information:

> Apartheid, it was confirmed, was the one word that popped into people's minds most frequently when questioned about South Africa. In most countries, the word and the general concept of what it signified made South Africa the most unpopular nation barring one – Idi Amin's Uganda. We rated well below Red China ... and Russia.[25]

The survey had an immediate impact upon members of the South African government who were privy to the data. Rhoodie later acknowledged that it 'contributed enormously to Vorster's eventual decision to launch the first in a series of two five-year propaganda campaigns. If South Africa's image was not much better than Uganda's, then previous methods, diplomatic and otherwise, had obviously failed.'[26]

On 3 December 1973, the Department of Information finally received the blessing of the Prime Minister. In a circular letter, which had actually been written by the Rhoodie brothers and de Villiers, Vorster informed Cabinet Ministers that 'In the light of increasing political and propaganda attacks against the Republic ... it has become necessary ... to adapt the functions of the Department of Information accordingly ... In the execution of his objectives it is left to the Minister of Information to decide what methods, medium and actions, whether public or secret, will be the most effective or necessary.'[27] Rhoodie's sense of power can be detected in the Department of Information's annual report for 1973: '[The Department's] instruction is to reach, convince and influence opinion-formers and decision-takers across the whole spectrum of public life in all countries that are of importance to us ... In order to give effect to this, no medium, channel or tactics will be overlooked.'[28]

During January 1974, Mulder and de Villiers visited the United States of America. During this tour, Mulder had a secret 40-minute meeting with Vice-President Gerald Ford. This meeting was arranged by the American publisher, John McGoff. Other meetings were held with Ronald Reagan, then Governor of California, and a number of Congressmen and Senators. In addition, Mulder and de Villiers visited the editorial board of the *New York Times*, where it was later claimed an agreement had been reached regarding the reopening of the newspaper's bureau in Johannesburg.[29] Soon after their return to South Africa, Mulder and de Villiers assembled in Cape Town with Eschel Rhoodie, Deneys Rhoodie, Nico Diederichs (the Minister of Finance), and John Vorster to discuss Rhoodie's proposal of a 'five-year-plan' for 1974–79.[30] Previous projects had cost R800,000 during 1973 and had been funded through BOSS. Rhoodie now estimated that his Department would need R15–25 million per annum in order to finance the expanded propaganda war. The 'five-year-plan' was approved and it was decided that funding would be supplied through P.W. Botha's secret Defence Special Account, which did not have to be declared to Parliament.[31] As Les de Villiers later explained, 'South Africa, like the United States, Russia and Germany before them ... had to buy, bribe or bluff its way into the hearts and minds of the world. We needed newspapers of world renown to speak up for us and if we could not get any to do so independently we should secretly buy our own.'[32]

The years 1974 and 1975 were relatively successful for the Department of Information. John Seiler acknowledged for example the 'immediate challenge to Swedish television reporters to prove their story of a "massacre" in the Caprivi strip. The resultant press investigation left both foreign and South African journalists satisfied that no massacre had taken place.'[33] In the field of secret or unorthodox diplomacy, on which Mulder, Rhoodie and van den Bergh (the head of BOSS) worked in unison, the détente with Black Africa attracted favourable international press coverage.[34] The visitor's programme which was developed in opposition to the existing 'liberal tour' was judged by Rhoodie 'to be the most important element of almost everything we did'.[35] The Department's annual report (1974) noted that events at the United Nations had also turned to South Africa's favour:

> Ironically the exclusion of our delegation from the deliberations of the General Assembly, seen by South Africa's enemies and hostile critics as a severe blow to our international prestige, in fact had the opposite effect among most news media, opinion-formers and decision-takers in

those countries whose opinions we value. The fact that the attack on South Africa was immediately followed up by an attack on Israel reverberated to the advantage of South Africa.[36]

With the new funds available from the Defence Special Account, Rhoodie and Mulder also began to involve themselves in grander schemes. The most dramatic of these was the attempt in 1974 to purchase the *Washington Star*. This project was conceived by Les de Villiers and the American publisher John McGoff. Rhoodie was particularly supportive because the concept managed to merge both the 'Brownie dictum' of controlling the press through ownership and the importance of establishing a discourse with the opinion-formers in the United States.[37] In September 1974, R8 million was placed in a Swiss bank account in order to finance McGoff's bid for the newspaper. This first major attempt by the Department to become secret international newspaper proprietors resulted in disaster.[38] An opposing bid for the *Washington Star* was accepted and McGoff purchased the *Sacramento Union* instead. Rhoodie claimed that McGoff informed the Department of Information that he had bought the *Sacramento Union* with the interest on the original R8 million. During 1976 it became clear that McGoff had actually used the original capital sum. The Department of Information had, in effect, been swindled and had little effective recourse.[39]

Failure to learn from their mistakes was Rhoodie and Mulder's most glaring error. In 1975, they attempted to neutralise a section of the South African domestic press by buying the SAAN publishing group. When this bid failed, the Department of Information decided that they would secretly launch their own English-language newspaper, the *Citizen*. This project would also be fronted by the Afrikaner businessman, Louis Luyt, who had led the bid for SAAN. During the 20 months which had followed the meeting in Vorster's office on 6 February 1974, the Department of Information had expanded their operations to include a bewildering array of different areas of influence. Les de Villiers recalled that by 1975 the Department was beginning to lose control of its 'investments':

> By then we had tens of spooks and more than a hundred secret projects under the direction of three of us – Deneys Rhoodie at his own insistence was also allowed by his brother Eschel to dabble in the dirty tricks division. I frequently found that payments had been made and orders given to spooks and front organisations without my knowledge; and I would register my disapproval. But time and again I would be reminded that only the three of us had to run the whole department –

both open and secret – and that day-to-day consultation was impossible. So the secrets slipped and the spooks ventured far from their cupboards and front organisations turned transparent.[40]

Eschel Rhoodie later admitted, in a rather quaint phrase, that 'I took too much on my fork.'[41] However, at this stage the chaos was containable, if expensive. As 1976 progressed a series of representational crises (in particular, South Africa's military withdrawal from Angola and the Soweto uprising) afflicted South Africa; in the wake of these crises, the Department of Information discovered that it was impossible to control its extraordinary level of operations *and* provide an effective voice for the beleaguered South African government. For Rhoodie, however, the failure of foreign governments and the international media to recognise the independence of the Transkei, and more particularly the duplicity of the South African state in its dealings with the 'independent' state, represented a crushing humiliation. In his memoirs, he discussed the hypocrisy of separate development: 'Separate [development] has no hope of success ... if, after independence, as happened with the Transkei, the inhabitants of that State are still treated like any other black person when they entered white South Africa. *This is the Achilles Heel of National Party policy.* It is the point where my belief in the honest objectives of separate development foundered on the rocks of reality.'[42]

During July 1976, Rhoodie, Mulder and van den Bergh assembled at the Montreal Olympics and developed a 'blueprint for change' which would be employed following the expected retirement or death of John Vorster. The core of this blueprint involved:

> the establishment of a thinktank comprising key civil servants, leaders of commerce and industry, scientists, technologists, political scientists, military strategists, representatives of the country's intelligence and law enforcement services. The thinktank would be responsible for all the country's forward planning on major political, socio-economic and capital works programmes. This thinktank, or supreme council, would make recommendations to the Cabinet – but the Cabinet would not be allowed to make decisions on its own, without the supreme council first discussing the issues.[43]

The plan involved Mulder's election as Prime Minister; van den Bergh's appointment as Chairman of the Supreme Council; and Rhoodie's appointment as 'the co-ordinating director of the thinktank'.[44] Twelve years later, Rhoodie described the plan as having symbolised 'the wish that there could be a dictatorship, which we qualified as "benevolent" or "verlig", to enforce separate development on an imaginative scale'.[45] However, the idea of benevolent dictatorship did not appeal to everybody within the Department and this eventually led to the leaks which assisted the investigations by the domestic South African press which began in earnest in 1977.[46]

Les de Villiers recalls in his memoirs that 'The speculation started almost from the day Mulder first served notice in Parliament in 1973 that he and his revamped and rejuvenated Department of Information had embarked on an unorthodox psychological war against its enemies abroad ... one question kept cropping up: Where do they get the massive amounts of money to feed this hidden war?'[47] During 1976, Gerald Barrie launched an investigation into irregularities in the Department of Information.[48] On 25 November 1976, Rhoodie 'issued instructions "on the advice of both Prime Minister Vorster and General van den Bergh" that we destroy all "unnecessary documentation"'.[49] Whether it was the threat posed by Barrie's investigation or a development related to the Montreal blueprint, the Department's annual report for 1976, submitted in May 1977, proved to be an extraordinary document. In the report, Rhoodie listed the problems that had faced South Africa during the year but, in contrast to previous reports, he cited a number of the media representations with very little criticism. For example, 'The Prime Minister was described ... as a man unable to control the direction of events and unable or unwilling to effect those changes in South Africa, which it was claimed, were necessary to prevent a race war.'[50] Rhoodie's prognosis for the year ahead was astonishing. In effect, he suggested that apartheid, in its current form, was unsaleable and required reform:

> All in all it will be a difficult year for the Department of Information and for its officials in South Africa and abroad. The Department has taken all precautions and has considered all possible strategies and actions. However, with the non-acceptance of the Transkei and in the wake of Angola, Rhodesia and the urban Black riots, foreign opinion at least will not easily be moved except by imaginative large scale moves in South Africa in the implementation of government policy to move away from racial discrimination and to structure a plurality of democracies for the country.[51]

Rhoodie later recalled that 'Vorster was furious at the report ... Any criticism of the Prime Minister by an official, even obliquely, was not only unheard of but also was considered bad form, disloyal, and, naturally, fatal to [the writer's] career.'[52] The events of 1977 only magnified Rhoodie and Mulder's problems. While Barrie's investigation began to unearth evidence of corruption within the Department, intermittent unrest continued to be a feature of life in South Africa's townships. During July 1977, Les de Villiers informed Rhoodie that he had decided to leave the civil service in order to accept a position as vice-chairman with the Department of Information's public relations firm, Sydney S. Baron and Company, in New York. Few knowledgeable observers were in any doubt that de Villiers was 'leaving a sinking ship'. De Villiers records in his memoirs that 'It was clear early in 1978 that the whole edifice of lies on which we had tried to launch South Africa back into the world was in imminent danger of being demolished by the Press.'[53]

By the autumn of 1977, the difficulties faced by the Department of Information were becoming insurmountable. Rhoodie recalled that they 'had a very strong suspicion that there was a mole right in our midst. We did not know who it was and we did not know how much was being leaked, or why it was being leaked to journalists from the SAAN group.'[54] In addition, Vorster constantly failed to arrange a requested meeting between Gerald Barrie and the Department of Information. Rhoodie began to believe that he was being abandoned.[55] His only remaining hope was that Vorster might resign and Mulder be elected to the premiership. During the same period, the Department of Information, which was now almost totally preoccupied with attempting to stop secret operations spiralling out of control, was called upon to explain the death of Steve Biko in police custody (September 1977), the banning of black consciousness groups and the closure of the *World* (October 1977). In this task, Rhoodie and others were found wanting. As the Secretary for Information commented in the Department's annual report for 1977:

> When the General Assembly of the United Nations proclaimed on December 14 last that 1978 was going to be the International Anti-Apartheid Year, it brought to a climax the worst period of anti-South African publicity and hostility in the country's history ... Reporting on the Biko case was extremely negative and widespread. It received the most in-depth coverage of any South African news story since the first heart transplant and was extremely damaging.[56]

In February 1978, the Auditor-General delivered his report to the Parliamentary Select Committee on Public Accounts, in which he criticised two unnamed officials of the Department of Information for misuse of public funds.[57] On 2 April, the [Johannesburg] *Sunday Express* published a story which detailed a state-financed vacation in the Seychelles which Rhoodie and others had taken in January 1977.[58]

In a desperate response to the pressure of the domestic newspapers, Rhoodie issued a statement on 5 May: 'I wish to state that the Department of Information has, for years, been asked by the government to undertake sensitive and even highly secret operations as counter-action to the propaganda war being waged against South Africa.'[59] Five days later, Mulder denied in the South African Parliament that the government was secretly financing the *Citizen*.[60] This would later lead to his resignation from the government and, eventually, the National Party. At this stage, however, the victims of the press exposé were the Rhoodie brothers who were forced into early retirement at the end of June 1978. The Department of Information was immediately subsumed within the Department of Foreign Affairs.

Three months later, the scandal re-emerged following the resignation of John Vorster and the election of P.W. Botha to the post of Prime Minister.[61] The revelation that the Department of Information had funded the publication of the *Citizen* was rapidly followed by Judge Anton Mostert's contribution to P.W. Botha's 'clean administration'; he released a 400-page report on exchange control contraventions which directly implicated leading South African politicians.[62] General van den Bergh accepted retirement, Eschel Rhoodie fled the country and the Botha administration established a Commission of Inquiry to investigate the 'alleged irregularities'.[63] The first report of the Commission was published in December 1978, by which point it was clear that the South African English-language press had uncovered an extraordinary tale of manipulation and corruption. Elements of the story continued to trickle out for the next three months and were complemented by two extensions to the Commission of Inquiry.[64] Anthony Lewis described the sense of expectation at the beginning of March 1979: 'Imagine Watergate at a point just before the cover-up of the cover-up began to come apart ... Three men involved in the affair have been fired or forced to resign. For the moment, the lid is on the story. But the three men are beginning to sound angry and if they talk ...'[65]

Mulder and van den Bergh remained silent, but Eschel Rhoodie, having been discovered in Latin America by Mervyn Rees, agreed to be interviewed.[66] Although Rhoodie provided a vast amount of evidence related to Information activity, many observers felt that the full story had not as yet been exposed.[67] The Information scandal finally ground to a halt in June 1979, following the resignation of John Vorster as President. The major effect in the international media of Rhoodie and Mulder's programme of media manipulation was a transformation in the representation of South Africa's Afrikaner leaders. As Stanley Uys (writing from London) explained:

I have often come across uncompromising critics of apartheid who have nonetheless remarked: 'But at least your country's leaders have clean hands.' This is the familiar view: that the men who were applying South Africa's reprehensible policies were not reprehensible themselves, except in a strictly political sense. Somehow, they had acquired an image of incorruptibility and austerity. They were mistaken and misguided, but they were not corrupt and venal. That was the image, and it was bolstered by the strongly religious flavour of National Party politics ... The Department of Information has ended all this.[68]

Amongst the earliest propaganda devices utilised by the Department of Information were the advertising front-organisations, the Club of Ten and the Committee for Fairness in Sport (CFS). Between April 1973 and June 1978, the South African state financed 32 advertisements by these organisations in the major newspapers of Europe and North America.[69] The CFS was headed by Gert Wolmarans, a former South African sports writer, and Louis Luyt.[70] The CFS was primarily concerned with protesting against the sporting isolation of South Africa. The Club of Ten's original administrator was Gerald Sparrow, author and one-time judge in the International Court in Bangkok. Sparrow had met Rhoodie during 1972 while visiting the Republic as a tourist. The targets of the Club of Ten advertisements, during Sparrow's stewardship, included the *Guardian*'s wage starvation campaign, the World Council of Churches and the United Nations. Sparrow later recalled that 'all the newspapers (with one exception, the London-published *Church Times*) accepted the advertisements with alacrity and competed with one another to offer the best space, coverage and terms for these profitable displays'.[71]

During 1974, the Department of Information agreed to sponsor a privately circulated quarterly entitled *Phoenix*, which was to be edited by Sparrow. The quarterly was intended to be 'devoted to the exposure of the politically motivated double standards ploy'. However, according to Sparrow, 'The first three issues ... met with the qualified approval of Dr Rhoodie but the last issue was not acceptable to the department ... I replied that in England it was not possible to have the policy of a paper dictated from outside.'[72] Following this contretemps, the Department of Information terminated its relationship with the judge. The Club of Ten re-emerged in February 1976 with a new administrator, Donald Boddie.[73] Rhoodie claimed that Boddie was not informed about the origins of the Club's finances.[74] The advertisements continued to criticise the usual bugbears, while adding new subjects for condemnation, such as the communist threat to southern Africa and the Western world's 'double standard' in not recognising the Transkei.[75] Following the resignation of Les de Villiers (who had originally been responsible for the writing of the advertisements) the concept of the Club of Ten became confused. The remaining ten advertisements continued to reiterate the theme of double standards but seemed to lose the ability to focus on a media error or a genuinely contradictory point. This, after all, had been the achievement of the original advertisements. The Club of Ten disappeared following the resignation of Eschel Rhoodie. *Elseviers* magazine later reported that the entire campaign had cost in excess of $1,000,000.[76]

To The Point was founded in January 1972 by a Dutch publisher, Hubert Jussen. The Department of Information did not technically own the magazine but it did make publication possible through extensive subscription. During the first two years of its existence, *To The Point* was published as a bi-weekly, thereafter appearing on a weekly basis. Before his appointment to the position of Secretary for Information, Eschel Rhoodie had been employed by the magazine as an assistant editor. Although conservative, *To The Point* did not serve solely as a propaganda tool for the Department of Information. The vast majority of its news columns and articles were relatively orthodox. The editorials, however, read as if they came straight from Rhoodie's pen.[77] Following the appointment of Dr John Poorter (ex-Department of Information director in London) as editor in 1973, the magazine began to carry an 'editor's memo' in addition to the editorials. This structural device suggests that Poorter needed to have his own editorial space; the editor's memo rarely echoed the same ideological message as the editorials. To a certain extent therefore, the editorials serve as a useful guide to the internal debates of the Department of Information.[78] Between April 1974 and October 1977, an international edition of *To The Point* was published from Antwerp.[79] Before 1976, the magazine played a complementary role to the South African government's détente with Africa. Following the Angolan war, coverage shifted towards the new concerns arising from the penetration of the Cold War into Africa. The Transkei's nominal independence was celebrated by a 16-page supplementary survey of the region.[80]

To The Point and *To The Point International* (*TTPI*) epitomised many of the paradoxes which dominated the Department of Information's secret projects. On one level, the magazines were no more than a feeble imitation of *Time* or *Newsweek*. However, they were able to publicise Rhoodie's ideas relating to double standards and journalistic racism, and did have a marginal impact.[81] In addition, the staff of *To The Point* wrote and designed the four financial and economic advertising supplements which appeared in *Business Week* between 1974 and 1977. These annual supplements, which in total amounted to more than 100 pages, were financed by the Department of Information's (secret) purchasing of advertising space.[82] Ultimately however, *To The Point* replicated the problems of control that the Department of Information had experienced in other spheres of its activities. This was most clearly demonstrated by the collapse of the magazine's international edition in the autumn of 1977. Following a protest by the European staff regarding the publication of material filed in Johannesburg, Hubert Jussen ordered a mass dismissal.[83] A press release by the staff of *TTPI* declared: 'All but one of the journalists ... have chosen to leave after being ordered to accept South African propaganda.'[84] The international edition was duly transformed into a précis of the domestic publication. Following the Information scandal, *To The Point* staggered on with the open sponsorship of the South African government until December 1980.

In 1975, John McGoff purchased a controlling 50 per cent share of United Press International Television News (UPITN) from Paramount Films. The money was provided by the Department of Information. As Karen Rothmyer has noted, 'With more than 100 clients in eighty countries, UPITN is, after Visnews, the second largest newsfilm producer and distributor in the world, and in many third world countries it may be the only source of foreign news. In the US it is relied on for foreign spot coverage in remote areas; its major American client is ABC, which sold its foreign news customer list to UPITN in 1976.'[85] With McGoff's associate, Clarence 'Dusty' Rhodes, appointed to the position of President and Chief Executive of UPITN in London, Rhoodie felt that the Department could now exploit the 'virtually unlimited access to all of the international outlets [available to] this television news distributing agency'.[86] Rhoodie later claimed that UPITN distributed programmes covering the independence of both the Transkei and Bophuthatswana, although the Department's greatest coup was staging an interview with John Vorster, for which Rhoodie had written both the questions and the answers.[87]

Although some of the material distributed by UPITN probably served the propaganda needs of the Department, Rhoodie recognised that the programmes could not be totally one-sided: 'Now and then David Oosthuizen was asked to produce a critical short for UPI[TN], critical of the South African Government, to protect Rhodes and the project.'[88] In effect, manipulating UPITN had proved as problematic as the other media interventions. After the Erasmus Commission revealed the financial basis of McGoff's stake in UPITN, Hugh Whitcomb, the editorial manager of ITN, stated that McGoff 'was never in a position to dictate editorial policy nor, as far as I know, did he ever try to do so'.[89] Karen Rothmyer investigated his other holdings and discovered that 'Former executives of various McGoff newspapers say that while they were occasionally ordered to run pro-South African articles and were supplied with magazines and other material extolling South Africa, they felt no concerted effort on McGoff's part to shape their editorial decisions.'[90]

In Great Britain, the Department of Information collaborated with two South African businessmen, David Abramson and Stuart Pegg, in its media-buying operation. During 1976, an attempt was made to raise the revenue needed to purchase the publishing group Morgan-Grampian. Rhoodie felt that 'Morgan-Grampian could be the very basis on which to build the *second five year programme*, due to go into operation in 1980.' He also felt that 'control of a major British publishing house, with contacts and outlets all over the world [would provide] a possible cover for the agents of General van den Bergh in countries where it would normally be difficult for Bureau agents to operate'.[91] Twenty-nine per cent of the shares in Morgan-Grampian were purchased but it proved impossible to raise the funds for a full take-over.[92] In 1977, Abramson and Pegg attempted to purchase the *Investors' Chronicle* with Department of Information funds. Stephen Mulholland, the *Wall Street Journal*'s stringer in Johannesburg, was pencilled in as the new editor.[93] IPC and the *Financial Times* decided not to sell the magazine after receiving warnings from the publishing group, Morgan-Grampian, regarding 'South African "funny money"'.[94] The Department of Information then proceeded to buy a 50 per cent share in the *Investors' Review* instead, but never managed to gain editorial control.

In addition to the surreptitious attempts to buy representation in the international media, the Department of Information possessed many other outlets for its opinions: these included the various book-publishing outlets either owned or sponsored by the Department; famous South African citizens, such as Gary Player and Christiaan Barnard; the visitors' tours; friendly (or pliable) American publishers; and the letters' columns and opinion pages of the newspapers.[95] In his evidence to the Erasmus Commission, Mulder observed that 'In Britain, you have to make an "understatement" while in America you have to storm a man head on.'[96] During his years as Secretary for Information, Eschel Rhoodie attempted to put Mulder's thesis into action. During April 1974, *Newsweek* carried an article by Peter Younghusband entitled 'The Afrikaner spirit'. Unfortunately, the article was brutally transformed by a sub-editor in the United States.[97] Rhoodie proceeded to engage in an extended correspondence with the editor of *Newsweek* which culminated in a ten-page letter detailing the errors in the original article and demanding Younghusband's dismissal. This was not forthcoming. As the *Financial Mail* later commented, 'surely the Secretary for Information has more urgent claims on his time than writing controversial letters like this?'[98]

Three years later, while Rhoodie was being investigated in South Africa, he became increasingly vociferous in his reaction to what he considered to be inaccurate reporting. In January 1977, for example, he objected to a series of articles by Jim Hoagland in the *Washington Post*.[99] When the *Washington Post* refused to publish Rhoodie's full response, the Department of Information bought advertising space in the newspaper to air its critique. Following the usual reiteration of the theory of journalistic racism, Rhoodie launched into an extended point-by-point refutation of the 'errors' in Hoagland's coverage. By the end of the advertisement, he was virtually hysterical: 'In conclusion. If Jim Hoagland wins a Pulitzer Prize for the misconceptions and ascertainable inaccuracies dished up as reliable in-depth report on South Africa, then *Pravda* also deserves one for its "accurate objective and dispassionate reporting on human rights and race relations in the USA". After all, neither Mr Hoagland nor the *Washington Post* holds a world copyright on intellectual dishonesty.'[100] An article which appeared in *National Geographic* in June 1977 received a similar response.[101]

During the Information scandal, Peter Younghusband wrote a summary of the career of the fallen Secretary in the *Capetonian* (a small-circulation magazine which Younghusband published). On the subject of Rhoodie's correspondences with the international media, he commented:

> as a psychological exercise they were a disaster, and reflected only that the Department of Information moved crudely and awkwardly in the sophisticated and cynical realms of the international press. It is possible that over the entire period of Dr Rhoodie's tenure of office, his aggressive and undiplomatic brow-beating of foreign editors, together with a heavy-handed policy of trying to 'manage' and pressure overseas newspapers and their correspondents by various means, caused more harm to South Africa abroad than the revelations confirmed in the Erasmus report ... The generally held view of the international press fraternity – from editorial executives to correspondents – was that Eschel Rhoodie was a man of considerable energy and ability, but was temperamentally unsuited to the job he held. He also lacked a grasp of the true principles of journalism and the functions of newspapers in democratic societies.[102]

Younghusband's commentary was obviously partly influenced by his own antipathy for Rhoodie because a number of journalists felt that, during the early 1970s, there was a relative improvement in the Department of Information's interaction with the international media.[103] Deon Geldenhuys has suggested that 'Information's often grandiose conception of international politics consisted of a strange compound of wishful thinking, naiveté and hard-headed *realpolitik*.'[104] Similarly, the Department's public relations operation can be summarised as demonstrating cunning and ignorance in almost equal measure. If cunning can be detected in the employment of frontmen or lobbyists, such as Sparrow and Donald deKieffer, who were married to people who were not white, ignorance, or perhaps, arrogance was consistently present in Rhoodie's endless attempts to draw attention to himself and the secret projects.[105] Mervyn Rees believes that 'with or without the press, he was his own worst enemy because he was going to shoot himself in the foot eventually: the lifestyle, the abuses – he attracted attention, he invited it'.[106]

Although the contradictions inherent in the Department of Information's interventions in the media were profound, and although they ended in exposure and scandal, some elements of the Rhoodie–Mulder programme were prescient. This can best be seen in South Africa's contribution to the establishment of the 'New Right' network which was emerging during this period in Britain and the United States. Karen Rothmyer wrote in 1981, with regard to Richard Mellon Scaife, that 'No longer, as in Spiro Agnew's day, are the media seen simply as the enemy; rather, they are regarded as an institution which, like any other, is capable of being influenced as well as intimidated.' Later in the same article, she observed how 'layers upon layers of seminars, studies, conferences, and interviews can do much to push along, if not create the issues which then become the national agenda of debate'.[107] In retrospect, it is clear that during the mid-1970s, Rhoodie had devised the rudimentary structure of a form of media manipulation that bears a striking resemblance to many of the practices which others later refined in the 1980s. It is also important to restate that the full panoply of Information activities has not yet been exposed. Les de Villiers suggests that 'There were a lot of people who never ... came to the surface, who did things for us and who were very successful.'[108]

The South Africa Foundation (SAF) was founded in December 1959 in direct response to the establishment of the Boycott Movement (the precursor to the Anti-Apartheid Movement). In the assessment of those opposed to apartheid, by the early 1970s, 'the Foundation [had] proved itself to be one of the most effective propaganda organizations in the Western world'.[109] The SAF did not attempt to defend apartheid, instead it concentrated upon keeping 'the Republic's international lines of communication open'.[110] During the 1970s it also began to develop a scholarly veneer in order to disguise its propagandistic purpose. This proved particularly effective in attracting foreign journalists, many of whom were willing to accept 'assistance' from a supposedly non-political source.[111] Under the presidency of Jan Marais (1974–77), the tone of the SAF annual reports became very close to that adopted by Rhoodie: 'There is no doubt that there is a strong politically based, well organised and liberally financed offensive against South Africa. This ... is the major sustaining factor in the campaign which has now been actively prosecuted for so many years.'[112] During 1973, Marais, in his role as chairman of the Trust Bank of South Africa, financed two advertisements which featured Lucas Mangope and Lucy Mvubelo opposing the application of economic sanctions against South Africa. The advertisements complemented those created by the Department of Information and were published in both British and American newspapers.[113]

The SAF retained offices and directors of operations in both London and Washington DC. Roy Macnab, an historian and poet, resigned from the South African foreign service in the 1960s and joined the SAF. In Britain, his work involved collaboration with the United Kingdom–South Africa Trade Association (UKSATA) and the provision of a subtle representation of South Africa's interests to both journalists and politicians.[114] Macnab also contributed occasional 'South African letters' to the *Spectator*, in which his byline described him as being, 'a South African author and former diplomat'.[115] Although Macnab's articles could hardly be described as propaganda, it is notable that he did not reveal to the readers that he was the London director of the SAF. He recalls that following the publication of the articles, 'there were official complaints to the President of the Foundation that I wasn't being patriotic enough'.[116] In the United States, John Chettle took a very active approach to his work. He recalls that, during the late 1970s, for example, 'We did some research into the extent to which the US media was concentrating on South Africa, as opposed to even the Soviet Union ... [We] gave it to Accuracy in Media and they made quite a bit of it.'[117] Beyond research, Chettle's other duties included: testifying on behalf of the SAF at the Africa Subcommittee of the Senate Committee on Foreign Relations; speaking on the subject of South Africa throughout North America; and keeping in regular contact with Donald deKieffer, the Department of Information's lobbyist.[118]

The similarities between the Department of Information and the SAF in this period were striking. In 1977, for instance, the SAF annual report noted that 'some subscribing members ... likened the situation to that of a salesman with a product to sell. The Foundation was the salesman and South Africa's image the product. If a product had characteristics which made it unsaleable in a given market, you had to change either the product or the market.'[119] No wonder then that Eschel Rhoodie is reputed to have described the SAF as an organisation 'which tries to do on a private basis what the Department of Information is doing on an official basis'.[120] Although many journalists availed themselves of the SAF's assistance, it is clear that a number of the correspondents in the Republic understood the true role of the Foundation. The [Johannesburg] *Financial Mail* reported in 1978 that 'At a press conference in Johannesburg this week, foreign pressmen peppered the Foundation's director-general, Peter Sorour, with questions about the organisation's stance on government policy. Obviously unsatisfied with Sorour's answers, one journalist openly commented: "It's a camouflage job." Said another: "You seem to be double-heading the Department of Information." '[121]

The complementary role that BOSS played in relation to the Department of Information during the 1970s remains a grey area. It is clear, however, that van den Bergh worked closely with Rhoodie and Mulder. This was not merely limited to the provision of secret funds, unorthodox diplomacy in Africa and the creation of the Montreal 'blueprint'. Gordon Winter has claimed that Chris van der Walt, the Director of Information in London during the late 1970s was actually a 'BOSS propagandist'.[122] Some years earlier, Adam Raphael made a similar accusation against Vlok Delport, van der Walt's predecessor.[123] It is also a matter of record that the Information scandal, and the ensuing resignations of Rhoodie, van den Bergh and Mulder, were rapidly followed by a number of defections from the South African intelligence agency.[124] Such defections had previously been rare, and led within a few months to the exposure of Craig Williamson.[125] Additionally, as Eschel Rhoodie admitted in his interview with Mervyn Rees, BOSS was the major supplier of information to the Department of Information:

> infiltration [into anti-apartheid groups] was done by the Bureau of State Security and they would provide us with information ... The Bureau ... produces a publication which is circulated only to the full Cabinet and I believe four or six people outside the Cabinet that included the Secretary for Foreign Affairs and myself ... [it] was a weekly and monthly and also a quarterly and annual summary ... a top secret summary of the state of the world in so far as it affects South Africa.[126]

South Africa, in conclusion, had two propaganda agencies (the Department of Information and the SAF) speaking on its behalf and an intelligence service which was directly concerned with the global representation of the Republic. Was ever a country better equipped to withstand the assault of an exiled opposition?

NOTES

1. Interview with Carl Noffke, 12 May 1995. Noffke was the Director of Information at the South African Embassy in Washington DC, from 1975.
2. Mervyn Rees and Chris Day, *Muldergate: The Story of the Info Scandal* (Johannesburg, Macmillan, 1980), p. 172, citing interview with Eschel Rhoodie.
3. On the role played by Afrikaans-language newspapers in the construction of Afrikaner nationalism, see Isabel Hofmeyr, 'Building a nation from words: Afrikaans Language, Literature and Ethnic Identity, 1902–1924', in Shula Marks and Stanley Trapido (eds), *The Politics of Race, Class and Nationalism in Twentieth Century South Africa* (London, Longman, 1987), pp. 95–123. Richard Pollak, *Up Against Apartheid: The Role and the Plight of the Press in South Africa* (Carbondale and Edwardsville, Southern Illinois University Press, 1981), p. 12, observed that 'A strong cross-pollination characterizes Afrikaner journalism and politics'. D.F. Malan was the editor of *Die Burger* before becoming Prime Minister; H.F. Verwoerd (Prime Minister, 1958–66) was the first editor of *Die Transvaler*. During the 1970s, many leading NP politicians served on the boards of the respective Afrikaner publishing companies, Perskor and Nasionale Pers.
4. Pollak, op. cit., p. 38.
5. *Second Portion of the Report of the Commission of Inquiry into the Press* (Pretoria, Government Printer, 1964), Appendix to Annexure XX, p. v.
6. Ibid., p. 1617.
7. See Deon Geldenhuys, *The Diplomacy of Isolation: South African Foreign Policy Making* (Johannesburg, Macmillan, 1984), pp. 16–17.
8. Eschel Rhoodie, *The Real Information Scandal* (Pretoria, Orbis SA, 1983), p. 82, described the Department of Information, before 1972, as being like a 'glorified post office'.
9. A.J. Wannenburgh, 'Ex-Information Editor Slates SA Publicity', [Johannesburg] *Sunday Times*, 15 September 1968.
10. Geldenhuys, op. cit., pp. 84–85.
11. Mulder believed Barrie to lack 'both the experience and the innovativeness [which he] sought in the Department's top official'. (Geldenhuys, op. cit., p. 85, citing interview with Connie Mulder.)
12. Eschel Rhoodie was born in 1932. He worked as a journalist during the mid-1950s for a South African Defence Force publication and *Die Vaderland*. In 1958 he joined the Information Service and between 1958 and 1972 served three terms in the United States of America, Australia/New Zealand and Holland. Rhoodie's doctoral dissertation compared the penal systems of the Commonwealth. This was rapidly followed by a trilogy of books: *South West: The Last Frontier in Africa* (Johannesburg, Voortrekkerpers, 1967); *The Third Africa* (Cape Town, Nasionale Bockhandel, 1968); *The Paper Curtain* (Johannesburg, Voortrekkerpers, 1969). During 1971, he was employed as Special Advisor to Connie Mulder. At the beginning of 1972, Rhoodie resigned from the Information Service in order to work as the assistant editor of *To The Point*. L.E.S. de Villiers was born in 1935. His full name was Lourens Erasmus Smit de Villiers and thus he was nicknamed 'Les'. De Villiers worked as a journalist with the

SABC and Nasionale Koerante (National Newspapers), and in public relations with an oil company during the 1950s. In 1960 he joined the Information Service and served two terms abroad in Canada and the United States of America, where he befriended an American publisher, John McGoff. An article by de Villiers on the representation of South Africa was published as 'A Scarecrow Image', *New York Times*, 3 August 1971. Neither Rhoodie nor de Villiers were members of the National Party or the Broederbond.

13. Rhoodie, *Real Information*, p. 79. See also Les de Villiers, *Secret Information* (Cape Town, Tatelberg, 1980), p. 26.
14. J.H.P. Serfontein, 'Verkramptes Upset over Rhoodie', [Johannesburg] *Sunday Times*, 3 September 1972.
15. Rhoodie, *Real Information*, p. 69.
16. Rhoodie, *Paper Curtain*, p. 81.
17. Ibid., p. 97. The Department also invoked a global metaphor in defence of the Republic: 'If we wanted to say something about the racial situation in South Africa, we should emphasise ... that this was a microcosmic of the world and just as there were no easy solutions to the problems of the world, there were no easy solutions to South Africa.' (Mervyn Rees, interview with Eschel Rhoodie, 1979, transcript, p. 402.)
18. Rees and Day, op. cit., p. 164.
19. Ibid., p. 204.
20. Rhoodie, *Real Information*, p. 42.
21. Ibid., p. 56.
22. Keith Abendroth, 'Rhoodie Ready to Bruise a Few Toes for South Africa', *Rand Daily Mail*, 24 October 1972.
23. On Breyer, see Rhoodie, *Real Information*, p. 61; on Lejeune, see de Villiers, op. cit., p. 50.
24. A third journalist who appears to have been financed by the Department of Information was Guy Lorraine. Lorraine's name appears on the Department's secret projects list as project G. 16 O, although there is no mention of him in the various memoirs relating to the subject (see Appendix B). Lorraine barely wrote any reports for the international media, except Guy Lorraine, 'Strike Trembles South Africa', *Christian Science Monitor*, 7 February 1973. None of the journalists who worked for the *Christian Science Monitor* during the 1970s has any memory of him.
25. De Villiers, op. cit., p. 108. See also Jack Anderson, 'The "Worst Leader" List', *Washington Post*, 16 March 1975, in which Vorster was placed eighth (after Idi Amin, Nguyen Van Thieu, Augusto Pinochet, Muammar Qaddafi, Lon Nol, Ferdinand Marcos and Kim Il Sung) by a poll of 30 foreign affairs experts.
26. Rhoodie, *Real Information*, pp. 60–61.
27. Ibid., p. 63.
28. Department of Information, *Report for the Period 1 January 1973 to 31 December 1973* (Pretoria, Government Printer, 1974), p. 6.
29. De Villiers, op. cit., pp. 65–66. Details regarding this meeting are problematic. A rumour emerged that the *New York Times* had agreed for the coverage by their correspondent, Charles Mohr's, to be evaluated over a specified period by the Department of Information. A *New York Times* journalist who was present at this meeting remembers nothing of the sort being agreed. (Interview with Jimmy Greenfield, 29 March 1996.) Les de Villiers suggests that the key to the meeting was winning Connie Mulder's support for the *New York Times* bureau to be reopened. (Interview with Les de Villiers, 18 April 1996.) At a second meeting between Mulder and the publisher and editors of the *New York Times* in the autumn of 1974, Mulder and Rhoodie agreed to allow the columnist and

editorial writer, Graham Hovey, to visit South Africa. (Letter from Graham Hovey, 18 October 1997.) See also 'Emissary Extraordinary', *Financial Mail*, 29 November 1974, p. 859; Peter Younghusband, 'How Eschel Rhoodie Fought the "Paper Curtain"', *Capetonian*, February 1979, p. 9.

30. Rhoodie, *Real Information*, pp. 82–84. See also de Villiers, op. cit., pp. 73–74.
31. Geldenhuys, op. cit., pp. 85–87.
32. De Villiers, op. cit., p. 110.
33. John Seiler, 'South African Perspectives and Responses to External Pressures', *The Journal of Modern African Studies*, Vol. 3 (1975), p. 460.
34. In September 1974, Vorster visited the Ivory Coast. This was followed by a visit to Liberia (February 1975) and the Victoria Falls Conference on Rhodesia (August 1975).
35. Rees, Rhoodie, transcript, p. 221. In 1973 for example, 82 foreign guests visited South Africa. Two of the four guests from Britain were journalists: Ian Waller, the political correspondent of the *Sunday Telegraph* and Jerome Caminada, the foreign news editor of *The Times* (*Southern African Information Service*, July–December 1973, p. 320 and January–June 1974, pp. 629–30). On the 'liberal tour', see Chapter 8.
36. Department of Information *Report for the Period 1 January 1974 to 31 December 1974* (Pretoria, Government Printer, 1975), p. 3. See Editorial, 'Pretoria, the PLO and the UN', *Washington Post*, 14 November 1974; Editorial, 'Self-destruct at the UN', *New York Times*, 15 November 1974.
37. See Carol H. Weiss, 'What America's Leaders Read', *The Public Opinion Quarterly*, Vol. 38, No. 1 (Spring 1974), p. 5, which revealed that 'After the three leading newspapers [the *Washington Post*, the *New York Times* and the *Wall Street Journal*], next in popularity is the *Washington Star*. Its readers are limited primarily to Washington-area residents for whom it functions apparently as a hometown newspaper.'
38. In 1973, the Department had attempted to purchase the independent *Natal Mercury*. See *Interim Report of the Commission of Inquiry into Alleged Irregularities in the Former Department of Information* (Pretoria, Government Printer, 1979), section f. 26–27, pp. 8–9; Rhoodie, *Real Information*, pp. 772–74.
39. Rhoodie, *Real Information*, pp. 382–91. See also Karen Rothmyer, 'The McGoff Grab', *Columbia Journalism Review*, November/December 1979, pp. 33–39.
40. De Villiers, op. cit., p. 50.
41. Rees and Day, op. cit., p. 186.
42. Rhoodie, *Real Information*, p. 881.
43. Rees and Day, op. cit., pp. 183–84.
44. Ibid., p. 184.
45. Eschel Rhoodie, 'PW: a Hero of His Own Crises', the [Johannesburg] *Star*, 25 September 1988.
46. During the leadership election in 1978, following the resignation of Vorster, Retief van Rooyen told Mervyn Rees, 'I knew I had to do something to stop [Mulder]. I had put my head through the door of potential dictatorship and what I saw there horrified the hell out of me.' (Rees and Day, op. cit., p. 72.)
47. De Villiers, op. cit., p. 151. Before 1977, investigations into South Africa's Department of Information by the international media were rare and normally associated with incidents or organisations in Britain. See Adam Raphael, 'How Vorster uses the Club of Ten', *Guardian*, 17 June 1974 and David Martin, 'Mystery Men Behind the Club of Ten', *Observer*, 23 June 1974, of which de Villiers later commented: 'in 1974, *Guardian* and its friends had tried to shake a Sparrow out of the Club of Ten tree-top. We had narrowly averted disaster'

(de Villiers, op. cit., p. 82). For other exceptional commentaries or exposés, see Adam Raphael, 'The Good News Machine', *Guardian*, 12 December 1974; Benjamin Pogrund, 'Battle for the Freedom of the Press', *Sunday Times*, 9 November 1975; Barbara Rogers, 'South Africa's Propaganda Machine', *Southern Africa*, Vol. 9, No. 7 (August 1976), pp. 5–9; David Martin and Rosanne Harvey, 'Apartheid's Millionaire Backers', *Observer*, 19 December 1976; Julian Burgess, Esau du Plessis, Roger Murray, Peter Fraenkel, Rosanne Harvey, John Laurence, Peter Ripken and Barbara Rogers, *The Great White Hoax: South Africa's International Propaganda Machine* (London, Africa Bureau, 1977). Rhoodie, *Real Information*, p. 232, records that Esau du Plessis, a coloured exile from South Africa and a member of the executive of the Dutch anti-apartheid movement 'succumbed to a tempting cash offer' and provided mailing lists and information regarding the Dutch and British Anti-Apartheid Movements to the Department.

48. *Report of the Commission of Inquiry into Alleged Irregularities in the Former Department of Information* (Pretoria, Government Printer, 1978), chapter 5.104, p. 27. Barrie later recalled that 'a chance conversation with Dr Deneys Rhoodie at Lisbon Airport in June 1974 gave rise to misgivings as to whether money was being spent by Information efficiently'. (Gerald Barrie, 'Rhoodie is Wrong', [Johannesburg] *Star*, 9 January 1984.)

49. De Villiers, op. cit., p. 152. See also *Report of the Commission of Inquiry*, chapter 5.117, p. 30.

50. Department of Information, *Report for the Period 1 January 1976 to 31 December 1976* (Pretoria, Government Printer, 1977), p. 3. See also Arnaud de Borchgrave, 'The Way the BOSS Sees It', *Newsweek*, 25 October 1976, pp. 19–20.

51. Department of Information, *Report 1976*, p. 10.

52. Rhoodie, *Real Information*, p. 80.

53. De Villiers, op. cit., p. 159. Les de Villiers left the Department of Information on 1 November 1977. See also Editorial, *South Africa Foundation News*, January 1978, p. 2: 'The recently retired No 2 of the Department of Information says that the Government's separate development policies are not saleable overseas.'

54. Rhoodie, *Real Information*, p. 420. See also Rees and Day, op. cit., p. 2; Hennie Serfontein, 'The Three Men Destroyed by Muldergate', *Observer*, 10 December 1978, in which he noted that in November 1977, 'One of the Nasionale Pers newspapers ... confronted Mr Vorster with the results of their investigation [into the Department of Information] ... Mr Vorster persuaded the [Afrikaans-language] newspapers not to publish saying that a large sum of money was at stake.'

55. Rhoodie, *Real Information*, p. 424.

56. Department of Information, *Report for the Period 1 January 1977 to 31 December 1977* (Pretoria, Government Printer, 1978), p. 3.

57. Rees and Day, op. cit., p. 18.

58. Kitt Katzin, 'Dr Rhoodie's Remarkable Jaunt', [Johannesburg] *Sunday Express*, 2 April 1978.

59. Eschel Rhoodie, Press statement, 5 May 1978.

60. 'Mulder Denial of Subsidy to Newspaper', *The Times*, 11 May 1978.

61. Botha won the leadership election against Mulder by 24 votes (out of 172). Vorster was elevated to the then ceremonial position of President.

62. Kitt Katzin, 'The Citizen: Secret Revealed', [Johannesburg] *Sunday Express*, 29 October 1978; The Botha government had attempted to stop Mostert from releasing his report. See also Mervyn Rees, 'It's All True!', *Rand Daily Mail*, 3 November 1978.

63. Following van den Bergh's retirement, BOSS was renamed the Department of National Security.

64. *Interim Report of the Commission of Inquiry into Alleged Irregularities in the Former Department of Information* (Pretoria, Government Printer, March 1979); *Supplementary Report of the Commission of Inquiry into Alleged Irregularities in the Former Department of Information* (Pretoria, Government Printer, June 1979).

65. Anthony Lewis (in Johannesburg), 'Three Loaded Guns', *New York Times*, 1 March 1979.

66. Extracts from Mervyn Rees's interviews with Eschel Rhoodie were published in the *Rand Daily Mail*, from 9 May 1979. See also David Dimbleby, interview with Eschel Rhoodie, 'Tonight Special', BBC 1, 21 March 1979.

67. Rex Gibson, 'The Information Scandal in Retrospect', in *South African Conference on the Survival of the Press and Education for Journalism, 4–6 October 1979* (Grahamstown, Department of Journalism, Rhodes University, 1979), p. 1, described the scandal as 'A conspiracy whose true extent has yet to be established'.

68. Stanley Uys, 'The Denting of a Nat Myth', *Rand Daily Mail*, 10 November 1978. See also 'Muldergate', 'Today', BBC Radio 4, 6 December 1978: 'the days of the politicians in South Africa running their country like a merchant bank are well and truly over.'

69. CFS advertisements: 'Who is Discriminating Now?', *New York Times*, 15 April 1973 and 'Fleet Street Blinkers', *The Times*, 16 April 1973; 'South African Sports News', *New York Times*, 22 December 1974; 'In South Africa more Black Golfers Play on the PGA Circuit than Anywhere Else in the World / In South Africa a Coloured Tennis Player was Chosen to Represent his Country at the Wimbledon Junior Championships 1975', *Guardian*, 20 October 1975; 'This is How we Discriminate in South Africa', *Washington Post*, 27 January 1977; 'Bias', *The Times*, 20 May 1977. Club of Ten advertisements: 'Does Britain have a conscience?', *The Times*, 28 July 1973; 'No Dealing with Diablos', *Guardian*, 28 August 1973; 'The Double Standard Game', *The Times*, 18 September 1973; 'Cowardice or Indifference?', *The Times*, 31 October 1973; 'Double Standards World Silence on this Massacre', *The Times*, 1 February 1974; 'An analysis of indignation', *Observer*, 9 June 1974; 'Now the Dust has Settled', *Guardian*, 31 August 1974; 'In God's Name Do Something: An Appeal to the World Council of Churches', *The Times*, 14 October 1974; 'The Free World Stands Today in Greater Danger than at any Time since the Darkest Days of World War II', *Daily Telegraph*, 6 February 1976; 'Can Britain Afford Double Think … Should a British Government Apply Double Standards?', *The Times*, 5 May 1976; 'Double Talk at World HQ', *The Times*, 16 December 1976; 'From the Guardian of December 6 1976', *Guardian*, 17 December 1976; '1976 A Year of Double Talk', *The Times*, 24 December 1976; 'A Challenge to Tom Jackson', *Guardian*, 8 February 1977; 'At 10pm on February 6, 1977, these Seven Jesuit Priests and Nuns were Murdered …', *The Times*, 23 February 1977; 'Moscow's Next Target in Africa', *Guardian*, 11 March 1977; 'Energy: the Peril Carter did not Reveal', *The Times*, 6 May 1977; 'The double standards game … and the rumour that mushroomed', *The Times*, 23 September 1977; 'The Double Standards Game: Why is the West Looking the Other Way?', *Washington Post*, 30 September 1977; 'The Double Standards of Mr Carter and the EEC', *The Times*, 7 October 1977; 'Double Standards on Capitol Hill?', *Washington Post*, 18 November 1977; 'The Double Standards Game (continued): The Strange Silence of Dr Owen', *The Times*, 1 December 1977; 'The Great Credibility Gap', *New York Times*, 23 December 1977; 'The Cuban Threat to Peace', *The Times*,

7 March 1978; 'The Great Majority Rule Hoax', *Washington Post*, 28 March 1978; 'Kolwezi ... the Double Standards of the British Press', *The Times*, 9 June 1978; 'The Stabilizing Influence of the Cubans in Africa!', *New York Times*, 14 June 1978.

70. In 1978, Rhoodie parted company with Luyt, and Gary Player was appointed as chairman of the CFS.

71. Gerald Sparrow, 'The Information File. Sparrow's Story Part II: How the Club of Ten Began', *Rand Daily Mail,* 27 June 1978. Club of Ten advertisements did not appear in the *Financial Times, Los Angeles Times, Wall Street Journal, Chicago Tribune* and *Christian Science Monitor*. Rhoodie later recalled that the advertisements had an immediate effect: 'There were letters coming in from all over the world, not by the tens or hundreds but literally by the thousands and there were cheques, small amounts [and] large amounts being sent in.' (Rees, Rhoodie, transcript, p. 264.)

72. Gerald Sparrow, 'The Information File. Sparrow's Story Part III: The Club and I Part Company', *Rand Daily Mail*, 28 June 1978.

73. Boddie had worked for the *Natal Mercury* in his youth, and had been the editor of the [London] *Evening News* from 1972 to 1974.

74. Dr Ferry A. Hoogendijk, 'Muldergate: The Eschel Rhoodie Story', *Elseviers*, 28 July–18 August 1979, news agency translation.

75. A notable advertisement during this period was 'Moscow's Next Target in Africa' (March 1977), reproduced, apparently without permission, from Robert Moss's series in the *Sunday Telegraph* (see Chapter 6). For this and other examples of Club of Ten and CFS advertising, see illustrations.

76. Hoogendijk, 'Muldergate', *Elseviers*.

77. This can be detected both in the writing style and the subject matter of many of the editorials. Poorter claims that Rhoodie did not exercise any influence over the magazine or the editorials. (Interview with Dr John Poorter, 26 May 1995; Letter from John Poorter, 20 November 1997.) Les de Villiers suggests that Rhoodie was involved in the editorial writing. (Interview with Les de Villiers, 18 April 1996.) See also de Villiers, op. cit., p. 133, which recalls that Louis Luyt felt that his problems with the Department of Information 'started with Rhoodie's persistent calls to the *Citizen* staff, feeding them government scoops directly and coaching them on editorials'.

78. See, for example, Editorial, 'No Time for Discord', *To The Point*, 11 July 1975, p. 17 and Editorial, 'Not our Controversy', *To The Point*, 25 July 1975, p. 21, which addressed the conflict between the Departments of Foreign Affairs and Information. *Rapport* (an Afrikaans newspaper) suggested that Rhoodie was responsible for the first editorial. The newspaper was fined at the Press Council for making this suggestion. (Geldenhuys, op. cit., pp. 111–12.)

79. *To The Point International* was only available on subscription, unlike the domestic edition. In 1975, Gordon van der Merwe (ex-SAPA correspondent in London and managing editor of *To The Point*), was appointed editor of the international edition. From this period, *To The Point International* carried different editorials to those in the domestic edition. These did not appear to have been written by Rhoodie.

80. 'Independence: A Special Survey of the Transkei', *To The Point*, 8 October 1976.

81. The only print interviews with John Vorster during the Soweto uprising were published by *To The Point*. See Gordon van der Merwe, 'Vorster: "Long-term Interests of S.A. are At Stake"', *To The Point*, 2 July 1976, pp. 7–8; Dr John Poorter, 'Situation is "Serious, But Not Critical", Prime Minister Vorster tells TTP', *To The Point*, 13 August 1976, p. 8. The magazine's commentaries also gained occasional reference in the international media, see 'Mirror of Opinion:

South Africa's "Bad Press"', *Christian Science Monitor*, 13 June 1977.

82. Hoogendijk, 'Muldergate', *Elseviers*. See 'Grow with South Africa', *Business Week*, 2 November 1974, pp. 41–72; 'Dynamic South Africa', *Business Week*, 10 November 1975, pp. 11–44; 'Doing Business with South Africa', *Business Week*, 22 November 1976, pp. 15–48; 'Invest in South Africa', *Business Week*, 21 November 1977, pp. 23–42.

83. Hubert G. Jussen, 'Publisher's Memo: A Matter of Principle', *To The Point International*, 12 September 1977, p. 5.

84. Press statement by former *TTPI* staff. (*Rand Daily Mail* archive, University of the Witwatersrand.) See also David Dale, 'Up to a Point ...', *New Statesman*, 23 September 1977, p. 390.

85. Karen Rothmyer, 'The McGoff Grab', *Columbia Journalism Review*, November/ December 1979, p. 37.

86. Rhoodie, *Real Information*, p. 391.

87. Ibid., pp. 392–94.

88. Ibid., p. 395.

89. 'Publisher Cited in South African Inquiry is Bought out by Partner in Film Agency', *Wall Street Journal*, 15 June 1979.

90. Karen Rothmyer, 'The South African Lobby', *Nation*, 19 April 1980, p. 456.

91. Rhoodie, *Real Information*, pp. 217–18. It is possible that some of the journalists covering Africa for *To The Point* served a similar function.

92. This was probably an early sign of Rhoodie's star beginning to wane in Pretoria. For Rhoodie's analysis see ibid., pp. 220–21. Ironically, the South African government made a profit of £1.2 million on the sale of the Morgan Grampian shares.

93. Rees, Rhoodie, transcript, p. 209 and 415. Mulholland claims that he has never heard of this plan. (Interview with Stephen Mulholland, 30 September 1996.) However, it is also claimed that Mulholland was a close friend of Abramson and Pegg. (Interview with Martin Welz, 4 October 1996.) In addition to his *Wall Street Journal* string, Mulholland also worked for the [Johannesburg] *Sunday Times*.

94. Rees and Day, op. cit., p. 127.

95. Pro-South African books were published through Valiant Publications or the South African Freedom Foundation (Rhoodie, *Real Information*, p. 264). On Player and Barnard, see Rhoodie, *Real Information*, pp. 181–90. See also Christiaan Barnard, 'And "A Good Deal that is Positive"', *New York Times*, 21 October 1977; Two exceptional American friends of the Department were Beurt SerVaas and C.W. Borkland. During the decade, SerVaas published a large number of articles which argued in favour of South Africa in his monthly publication, the *Saturday Evening Post*. With his wife, Cory (the editor of the magazine), he visited the Republic regularly during the mid-1970s and was a member of the Jussen syndicate which 'purchased' the *Citizen* from Louis Luyt in 1978. Borkland's publication, *Government Executive* carried a massive (30-page) six-part series of articles in 1978 on South Africa, based primarily upon Department of Information propaganda.

96. 'The Erasmus Evidence: A Hard-sell Strategy Born on Foreign Soil', *Rand Daily Mail*, 15 May 1980. James Srodes recalls that there was an 'invasion' of South Africans into Washington DC in the mid-1970s. He described the general tone at Embassy parties in the following terms: 'Hey look, we're nice people – have some more champagne.' (Interview with James Srodes, 11 April 1996.) Articles by Mulder in the US press included 'South Africa's Objectives,' *New York Times*, 14 May 1974; 'An Overture from a Pretoria Official', *Los Angeles Times*, 12 June 1975; 'US Policy on South Africa: "Anti-white Racism"', *New York Times*, 23 May 1978.

97. Peter Younghusband, 'The Afrikaner spirit', *Newsweek*, 29 April 1974; Young-husband recalls that Rhoodie suspected that the sub-editor was an African-American. (Interview with Peter Younghusband, 15 May 1995.)

98. 'Emissary Extraordinary', *Financial Mail*, 29 November 1974. The full Rhoodie correspondence was not published by *Newsweek*.

99. Jim Hoagland, 'Black Power vs. White Power: South Africa', *Washington Post*, 9–16 January 1977.

100. Dr Eschel Rhoodie, 'The Washington Post and its Reporting on South Africa: A Case of Intellectual Dishonesty?', advertisement, *Washington Post*, 24 April 1977. The *International Herald Tribune* which also carried the Hoagland reports, had published Rhoodie's critique as, Eschel Rhoodie, 'A South African Official Replies to Articles on his Own Country', 18 April 1977. See also Jim Hoagland, Letter to the editor, *International Herald Tribune*, 20 April 1977: 'Even a professional propagandist for the South African government could not have composed the collection of cheap shots, bare-faced lies and ad hominem attacks the Herald Tribune published under the name of Eschel Rhoodie ... I can only conclude that a trouble-maker intent on satirizing or discrediting Mr Rhoodie has obtained the Secretary's letterhead stationery and perpetrated a hoax on your readers.'

101. William S. Ellis, 'South Africa's Lonely Ordeal', *National Geographic*, June 1977, pp. 780–819; 'What National Geographic did Not Say ...', advertise-ment, *Washington Post*, 6 June 1977: 'These are some of the facts that National Geographic did not publish. The facts were made available to them but someone convinced the editors that facts are no longer sacred.'

102. Peter Younghusband, 'How Eschel Rhoodie Fought the "Paper Curtain"', *The Capetonian*, Vol. 1, No. 3 (February 1979), pp. 8–11.

103. Before leaving South Africa, Mike Keats, the UPI bureau chief, commented that he had 'experienced a definite feeling of more understanding from people in services like the Department of Information'. ('Freest in Africa', *South African Digest*, 15 February 1974, p. 3.)

104. Geldenhuys, op. cit., p. 119.

105. Sparrow was married to a Thai, deKieffer to a Japanese-Hawaiian. From 1976, the Department employed an African-American public relations representative in the United States. Andrew Hatcher had been an associate press secretary to President Kennedy in the early 1960s. ('South African Propaganda in the US Increases', *Southern Africa*, Vol. 9, No. 8 (September 1976), pp. 14–15.)

106. Interview with Mervyn Rees, 9 September 1996.

107. Karen Rothmyer, 'Citizen Scaife', *Columbia Journalism Review*, July/August 1981, pp. 45 and 48. Scaife purchased a 50 per cent share in the *Sacramento Union* in 1977.

108. Interview with Les de Villiers, 18 April 1996.

109. Ruth First, Jonathan Steele and Christabel Gurney, *The South African Connec-tion: Western Involvement in Apartheid* (London, Temple Smith, 1972), p. 222. See also Barry Cohen, 'Inside the "Club of Ten"', *New African*, May 1978, p. 54, which quotes Barbara Rogers as commenting: 'As an ostensibly independent organisation, the Foundation is accepted where representatives of the South African Government would not be.'

110. Geldenhuys, op. cit., p. 175.

111. Journalists who were either guests of, or who were assisted by, the SAF, included William Raspberry, Louis Heren, Lord Chalfont, Walter Cronkite, Henry Grunwald, Graham Turner, Israel Wamala, William Buckley, William Rusher, John Davenport (contributing editor of *Fortune*), John Ellison (foreign editor of the *Daily Express*), David Taylor ('Money Programme', BBC) and Ray Vicker

(London correspondent of the *Wall Street Journal*).

112. 'Presidential Address', South Africa Foundation, *Annual Report, 1972* (Johannesburg, SAF, 1973), p. 1. See also 'Presidential Address', South Africa Foundation, *Annual Report, 1974* (Johannesburg, SAF, 1975), p. 19: 'If the world news-media really want to embark on something worthwhile, here is a campaign they can launch – Comparative moralities and freedoms among nations.'

113. 'Economic Sanctions Make Me Shudder' and 'Don't Isolate Us', (advertisements), *The Times*, 20 and 25 September 1973; Jennifer Davis, 'Special: Black Sell-outs Sell Apartheid', *Southern Africa*, Vol. 6, No. 8 (October 1973), pp. 8–10. See also Burgess *et al.*, op. cit., pp. 25–26.

114. South Africa Foundation, *Annual Report, 1976/77* (Johannesburg, SAF, 1977), p. 28.

115. Roy Macnab, 'As Vorster Abandons Smith ...', the *Spectator*, 18 January 1975, p. 59.

116. Interview with Roy Macnab, 26 October 1996.

117. Interview with John Chettle, 23 May 1996. See 'Press Perverts Rights Picture', *Accuracy In Media Report*, Vol. 8, No. 3 (February 1979).

118. Interviews with John Chettle, 23 May 1996 and Donald deKieffer, 12 April 1996.

119. South Africa Foundation, *Annual Report, 1977/78* (Johannesburg, SAF, 1978), p. 1.

120. Burgess *et al.*, op. cit., p. 24, citing Eschel Rhoodie.

121. 'Shaky Foundation', [Johannesburg] *Financial Mail*, 17 March 1978, p. 817.

122. Gordon Winter, *Inside BOSS: South Africa's Secret Police* (Middlesex, Penguin, 1981), p. 469.

123. Adam Raphael, 'Club of 10's BOSS', *Guardian*, 25 June 1974: 'Delport ... is the head of operations for BOSS in the United Kingdom, according to informed diplomatic sources.'

124. The defectors included Gordon Winter, Alexander Lambert, Arthur McGiven and Ivan Himmelhoch. On Winter, see 'Interview with Gordon Winter', 'News', London Weekend Television, 29 June 1979; Winter, op. cit. On Lambert, see 'Portrait of a Defector', *New African*, December 1979, pp. 40–41. On McGiven, see Arthur McGiven, 'Inside BOSS's "Super Spook" HQ', 'The British "Targets" of BOSS' and 'How Army Bugged BOSS Spies', *Observer*, 30 December 1979–13 January 1980. On Himmelhoch, see Martin Bailey, 'BOSS at Work in Britain' and 'Foreign Policy Duality', *New Statesman*, 15–22 August 1980, pp. 8–9 and 12.

125. Hugh Lewin, Walter Schwarz and David Beresford, 'Pretoria's Agent was Responsible for Channelling Secret Funds to Anti-apartheid Workers', *Guardian*, 23 January 1980; Andrew Stephen, 'Scenes in the Life of a Super-spy', *Sunday Times* magazine, 8 February 1981, pp. 20–30.

126. Rees, Rhoodie, transcript, p. 197.

4

The Anti-Apartheid Movements

One of the weaknesses of the anti-apartheid movement in Britain and in the United States has been that whites have played most of the leadership roles. In most cases, the criticism that white American or English liberals are working out guilt complexes about their country's own situations by becoming deeply involved in fighting the battle for South Africa's blacks may be an overstatement. But it contains enough appearance of truth ... to damage their credibility on the issue.[1]

The Anti-Apartheid Movement is more than a pressure group: it is Britain's conscience on southern Africa.[2]

In Chapter 3, I examined the rise and fall of the South African Department of Information. In this chapter, I consider the activities of the anti-apartheid groups in Britain and the United States. Previous assessments of anti-apartheid campaigns have differed in their conclusions. David Wiley, for example, suggested, in 1979, that 'the movements in the Western nations have been fraught with divisiveness, sectarianism, and an inability of the protagonists to cooperate in common strategies of change. Frequently, the movements have more leaders than constituents and their interpretations of events in Africa frequently reflected more their own ideologies than the realities of the African needs and movements'.[3] In contrast, Hugo Young commented of the Stop The Seventy Tour (STST) that 'It is hard to think of a single large political campaign which has had anything like so immediate an impact.'[4] In an attempt to explain these contrasting assessments, this chapter considers the organisations which opposed apartheid South Africa; their attempts to influence the media representation of the Republic; the coverage of, and the tensions within, the anti-apartheid movements; the historical precedent established by the Clapham Sect and the origins of the Free Nelson Mandela campaign.[5]

The two major organisations spearheading the anti-apartheid pressure groups in Britain and the United States were the Anti-Apartheid Movement (A-AM) and the American Committee on Africa (ACOA), respectively.[6] As George Houser, the Executive Director of the ACOA, later recalled, 'South Africa provided the spark' which led to the foundation of the ACOA in 1953.[7] During the 1960s, the ACOA published a magazine, *Africa Today*, which was relaunched in 1966 as a quarterly publication under the aegis of the University of Denver. By the 1970s, the organisation was primarily preoccupied with issues relating to southern Africa. As with the A-AM in Britain, the major campaigns of the 1970s were disinvestment, the sports boycott, the enforcement of the arms embargo, defence and aid activities, lobbying in Washington and at the United Nations, and South Africa's illegal occupation of South West Africa/Namibia.

Anti-apartheid protest in Britain was originally voiced in the early 1950s by Reverend Michael Scott (the Africa Bureau) and Canon John Collins (Christian Action, and later Defence and Aid). As George Shepherd has noted, 'Both the Africa Bureau and Christian Action have roots back into the Anti-Slavery Society, which was founded in 1906 and in turn emerged out of earlier antislavery groups.'[8] In 1959, the Boycott Movement was established in response to the call by Albert Luthuli, the ANC President, for sanctions against South Africa.[9] The Boycott Movement tapped into the same tradition as the other organisations while also utilising the talents of a number of Indian South African exiles who were resident in London.[10] Following the Sharpeville massacre (1960), the Boycott Movement was renamed the A-AM. The early 1960s was a relatively successful period for the A-AM: South Africa was forced to leave the Commonwealth in 1961 and the Labour government, elected in 1964, introduced an arms embargo against the Republic.[11] The issue of economic sanctions, however, remained unresolved. From 1965, the A-AM published a monthly newspaper, *Anti-Apartheid News*. Assistance was provided in this venture by a number of journalists, most notably, Anne Darnborough, Bruce Page and Gus Macdonald.[12]

Although the A-AM and the ACOA were the two major organisations opposing apartheid South Africa, there were a number of other groups which campaigned with equal vociferousness. On the radical end of the American spectrum, the South African Committee (SAC) emerged 'out of a widespread student concern for research on imperialism and racial problems'.[13] The SAC published a monthly magazine, *Southern Africa*, and members of the organisation founded Africa News.[14] Jennifer Davis, a South African exile who worked for the ACOA and the SAC, recalls that '*Southern Africa* magazine was where we had freedom ... there we really did work it as a collective ... the politics was more interesting, we pushed a little further left'.[15] In Britain, the work of the A-AM was complemented by the

International Defence and Aid Fund (IDAF). IDAF had originated from the British Defence and Aid Fund, an organisation established by Canon Collins in the mid-1950s to provide funds for those arrested and imprisoned during the Treason Trial in South Africa. By the 1970s, IDAF was also concerned with educational issues, information gathering, the promotion of links with sympathetic European groups and an extensive publishing programme. Other organisations involved in campaigns against South Africa included the African-American Institute (A-AI) in the United States, which published the magazine, *Africa Report*.[16] Jennifer Davis comments, recalling the A-AI's lack of enthusiasm for mobilising for sanctions, that 'We regarded them as almost the other side.'[17] In Britain, the Africa Bureau, established by Reverend Michael Scott and supported by David Astor and Colin Legum, campaigned with the purpose, among others, of opposing 'racial tyrannies in Africa ... [and promoting] the achievement of nondiscriminatory majority rule in Africa'.[18]

The networks of organisations opposed to South Africa worked in conjunction (and sometimes in conflict) with a multitude of non-governmental organisations of which, perhaps, the most important were the churches. The decisions, in 1970, by the World Council of Churches (WCC) in favour of disinvestment, and, in 1971 and 1973, to give humanitarian aid to the liberation movements, the ANC and the Pan-Africanist Congress (PAC), were particularly significant.[19] However, despite the support of the WCC, profound divisions existed in the opposition to apartheid. In the main, these divisions were concerned with the issue of support for the ANC and the PAC and, by extension, support for the armed struggle.[20] Kader and Louise Asmal, who were Vice-Chairman and Honorary Administrative Secretary of the Irish A-AM, respectively, believed that the A-AMs were 'partners of the liberation movements in joint campaigns to change public opinion and alter the policy of governments'.[21] In contrast, Amnesty International (AI) refused to endorse the adoption of the armed struggle.[22] In effect:

> two different anti-apartheid strategies [emerged]: one in the direction of domestic reforms with minimal external pressure and the other in favour of disengagement and support for liberation. The former stems from the gradualist, reformist ideas institutionally expressed through the AAI ... and the Africa Bureau ... while the latter reflects the abolitionist pressures of the AAM, the ACOA, SAC, and particularly the American black activists.[23]

In the 1970s, the collapse of the Portuguese empire, the intensification of military action in Rhodesia/Zimbabwe and the Soweto uprising all transformed the terms of the debate regarding the armed struggle. By the mid-decade, it was clear that the moral questions associated with support or opposition to violent action were peripheral. Southern Africa was in turmoil. This brought with it fresh problems for the anti-apartheid movements and, most dramatically, the introduction of the Cold War into the sub-continent. While there were many similarities between the campaigns of the ACOA and the A-AM, there were also fundamental differences between Britain and the United States as operating sites for pressure groups. In the United States, for instance, African-American politicians became, during the 1970s, crucial to the anti-apartheid campaign. The appointment of Congressman Charles C. Diggs Jr to the posts of Chairman of the Subcommittee on Africa of the Committee on Foreign Affairs (1969) and the first Congressional Black Caucus (1971) was an important element in this process. Diggs was a supreme publicist of the liberation cause in South Africa. His 'Action Manifesto' of 1972, for example, was not afraid to address the thorny issue of violence: 'Our government, at present, decries violence as a means of liberation, without condemning the violence which the South African government uses to enforce the subjugation of the majority of the people. The United States must recognise that any means are legitimate so long as the recalcitrance of the South African government continues.'[24]

The annual hearings of the Subcommittee on Africa into US investment in Southern Africa (1971–73) unleashed a flood of information which complemented the A-AM disinvestment campaign and later proved useful to protest organisations as the disinvestment campaign spread through the American university campuses in the late 1970s. The marshalling of African-American protest by Diggs and others influenced a shift towards a more pronounced anti-apartheid position in George McGovern's Presidential campaign pledges of 1972.[25] The importance of this shift among Democratic Party candidates was demonstrated by the priorities of the Jimmy Carter Presidential campaign in 1976.[26] During the same year, the Black Leadership Conference on Southern Africa brought together more than 120 black organisations to draw up an African-American manifesto on southern Africa which, amongst a welter of other proposals, endorsed the armed struggle. In July 1977, TransAfrica was established as a lobbying organisation for Africa and the Caribbean.[27]

In contrast, in Great Britain, the failures of the Labour governments (1964–66 and 1966–70) to fulfil their policy commitments regarding southern Africa contributed to a sense of resignation when a Labour government was elected in 1974.[28] As Guy Arnold, the director of the Africa Bureau, commented, 'Traditionally there has always been far more sympathy with Black African causes among the ranks of the Labour Party than amongst the Tories. Sympathy is one thing, however, and action when in power is something quite different.'[29] Although Joan Lestor, a Vice-President of the A-AM, was appointed to the position of junior minister (with responsibility for Africa) in the 1974 Labour government, Labour policies towards South Africa rarely stretched beyond 'gestures'. The most significant of these was the announcement of Britain's withdrawal from the Simonstown naval base in 1974. However, as the debates in the newspapers made clear, this decision could be justified on economic, geopolitical or strategic grounds, thereby rendering the concession to the A-AM little more than a 'sop'.[30] There were no Afro-Caribbean or Asian Labour Members of Parliament (MPs) during the 1970s. This was not unique to the Labour Party. The A-AM had a similar problem as it acknowledged: 'The AAM is still faced with the difficult task of mobilising in the black community in Britain. Some developments have taken place but there is much more to be done in this area.'[31]

The second major difference between anti-apartheid activities in Britain and the United States related to the number of South Africans in the respective countries, and the popular (or assumed) knowledge of the Republic. The large number of exiled (or South African-born) journalists working in the British media during the 1970s was discussed in Chapter 2. A similar number of South Africans could be found within the British organisations opposed to apartheid. Figures such as Ruth First, Ronald Segal, Abdul Minty and Ethel de Keyser were among the dominant voices in the campaign in Britain during the early 1970s.[32] Except for Jennifer Davis, Dennis Brutus and Dumisani Kumalo, there were few exiled or émigré South Africans within the American anti-apartheid movements. This difference in South African involvement was reflected in the different forms of the debate in the two countries. Popular knowledge (and perceptions) of South Africa in Britain, while contributing to its relatively high level of public exposure in the media, also meant that the work of the A-AM in Britain was regularly challenged by well-informed opponents. To a significant extent in the United States, the ACOA and the SAC were campaigning within a less informed or opinionated milieu.[33]

The third major difference between the operations of the anti-apartheid movements related to the political cultures of the respective countries. In Britain, the A-AM was able to organise a national campaign, due in part to the relative smallness and homogeneity of the country. The expansion of A-AM offices across Britain during the 1960s and 1970s laid the ground for the genuine mass movement which emerged during the 1980s. In the United States, the traditional core of anti-apartheid activity had been the east coast. This remained true during the 1970s, although the ACOA opened a new office in Chicago (under the stewardship of Prexy Nesbitt) and there were pockets of activity in California.[34] Although the movement spread throughout the universities of North America during the late 1970s, anti-apartheid never became an issue of national concern in the US.[35]

The final difference between Britain and the United States related to the continuing tensions within the anti-apartheid organisations. In Britain, the central division related to the willingness or otherwise of 'liberals' to work with Africans and 'communists'. This tension was at its most extreme amongst the South African exiles and émigrés and was rooted in long-standing strategic arguments about the liberation struggle which dated back to the 1940s and 1950s.[36] In the United States, communists played a less significant role in the anti-apartheid movement. There, tensions tended to be dominated by the issue of race.[37] However, while there were structural racial distinctions between the anti-apartheid groups in the US, Jennifer Davis recalls that, in the broad American student movement, 'in a sense, people were dealing with South Africa because they couldn't deal with American racism and so this was like a displacement'.[38]

The major area of A-AM and ACOA activity during the 1970s was the United Nations. Newell Stultz has recorded that between 1963 and 1970, 14 resolutions were passed by the General Assembly of the UN condemning apartheid. Between 1970 and 1976, this figure increased to 60: 'Before 1970 all votes on South African issues in the General Assembly were to some degree split-votes, that is, non-unanimous. But from 1970 to 1976 there were six resolutions ... where either the voting was unanimous or there was no recorded vote at all; that is, the motion was, as the record reads, "passed without objection".'[39] The increase in the passage of resolutions condemning South Africa was complemented by a series of conferences held by the UN on the subject of apartheid.[40] In 1972, the General Assembly accepted the principle of armed struggle in much the same language as Charles Diggs's 'Action Manifesto'.[41] A year later, the General Assembly declared 'that the South African regime has no right to represent the people of South Africa and that the liberation movements recognised by the Organization of African Unity are the authentic representatives of the overwhelming majority of the South African people'.[42] In 1974, the General Assembly took the critical decision to suspend South Africa from the United Nations.[43] While this resolution represented a vital stage in the isolation of South Africa, it also led to increased sympathy for the Republic in the columns of a number of Western newspapers.[44]

On 1 January 1976, the UN established the Centre against Apartheid at the United Nations Secretariat. Following the World Conference for Action against Apartheid held in Lagos during August 1977, the tone of UN resolutions hardened, as the use of the phrase 'racist regime' in a Security Council resolution dated October 1977 indicates.[45] Four days later, the General Assembly passed the most significant resolution of the decade pertaining to South Africa, enforcing a mandatory arms embargo against the Republic. As Secretary-General, Kurt Waldheim, stated in the Security Council: 'We have today clearly witnessed a historic occasion. The adoption of this resolution marks the first time in the 32-year history of the Organisation that action has been taken under Chapter VII of the Charter against a Member State.'[46] The declaration that the period between 21 March 1978 and 20 March 1979 would be proclaimed International Anti-Apartheid Year brought to a close a period in which the anti-apartheid movements had made great advances on the international stage. These advances, however, were greatly assisted by escalating repression and resistance inside the Republic. As George Houser recalls, 'It was always in response to events in South Africa that it was possible to do things outside.'[47]

The A-AM and the ACOA were as different in their relations with the media as they were in their national contexts. The A-AM started the 1970s with a relatively high profile following its role in the sports campaigns of 1969 and 1970. Its success in conjunction with the ad hoc group, Stop the Seventy Tour, in causing the abandonment of South Africa's cricket tour of England (1970), had given the A-AM a much needed publicity boost. The direct action employed during the protests, however, also led most of the British media to demonise the campaign. As Peter Hain later noted, 'One of our failures, and one of the opposition's few successes, was that the public distinction between militant non-violence and violence became very blurred.'[48] While the campaign to enforce a sports boycott attracted a new generation of younger activists to the A-AM, the media's treatment of the post-1968 generation exacted a degree of damage from the A-AM's carefully cultivated respectable image.[49]

Within months of its success in halting the cricket tour, the A-AM relaunched the sanctions campaign with a new focus on the withdrawal of British capital from the Republic. This fresh agenda was directly linked to the burgeoning campaign against Barclays Bank, which was gathering support throughout the universities of Britain. During 1972, Ruth First, Jonathan Steele and Christabel Gurney wrote *The South African Connection*, which would become the crucial anti-apartheid text of the period.[50] However, as the wages paid by British companies entered the mainstream of media discourse, the A-AM, among the first instigators of the debate, was increasingly isolated by the development of the story.[51] The years 1974 and 1975 were very discouraging for the A-AM and the liberation organisations. The forays of the South African Department of Information into the world of international diplomacy and the changed conditions in southern Africa following the fall of the Portuguese empire took the organisation by surprise: 'Events since the end of 1974 have been well-publicised and the western press has made a special point of casting Vorster as Africa's Peace-Maker. Never before have we seen such a major and concerted offensive to cast South Africa in a favourable light. The Pretoria regime has taken every opportunity to exploit what it considers to be a more favourable climate of opinion.'[52]

In the United States, the ACOA experienced a similar degree of isolation, which Houser later described as 'the cooling enthusiasm toward Africa of the seventies ... [making] itself felt'.[53] One area in which both the British and American anti-apartheid organisations could publicise their cause and, occasionally, influence the external coverage of South Africa was through the medium of publishing. During the 1970s, the production of anti-apartheid magazines and pamphlets escalated. The circulation of the A-AM's monthly newspaper, *Anti-Apartheid News*, remained at 7,000 throughout the decade, approximately half of which were supplied to members of the Movement. *Anti-Apartheid News* was a slightly haphazard publication, providing news, commentary, exposés, extracts from anti-apartheid books, statements by the A-AM and the ANC, details on campaigns, and, from the mid-1970s, critiques of the British media's treatment of South Africa. It was not a predictable newspaper, being, in effect, pragmatic and earnest in equal measure. Among the many journalists who contributed during the decade were Jonathan Steele, Antonio de Figueiredo, Paul Foot, Christopher Hitchens and Rupert Pennant-Rea.[54]

Anti-Apartheid News was extraordinarily dependent upon the goodwill and talent of its volunteer contributors. An example of this dependence can be seen in the design quality of the newspaper's front page which suddenly deteriorated during the mid-1970s following the departure of a team of young advertisement designers led by Malcolm Gluck, who had originally been encouraged to assist the A-AM by Ethel de Keyser.[55] The only comparable magazine in the United States was the SAC's monthly publication, *Southern Africa*. The SAC was a less populist organisation than the A-AM and this could be detected in the style of the organisation's magazine. *Southern Africa* offered extensive analysis and a comprehensive survey of the coverage of

South Africa in the global media, but rarely replicated *Anti-Apartheid News*' sense of a campaigning publication.

The ACOA did not publish a newspaper or magazine of its own during the 1970s, concentrating instead upon the production of pamphlets and briefing papers.[56] The IDAF produced the six-monthly *Southern African Information Service*, a survey of all references to South Africa in governmental publications and the media, until 1974. During 1975, the IDAF launched *Focus on Political Repression in Southern Africa*, a news bulletin which concentrated on reports of human rights abuses in the Republic. Throughout the decade, the ANC continued to publish *Sechaba* and the SACP issued the quarterly periodical, the *African Communist*. Neither publication was particularly effective at promoting the cause of the ANC–SACP to the uncommitted reader, which, perhaps, was not their purpose. During the mid-1970s, *Sechaba* was relaunched for a few years as a quarterly publication.[57] The *African Communist* remained rigidly ideological throughout the decade, offering a Marxist analysis of events which gave little priority to the provision of information on the international struggle against apartheid.[58] There appears to have been little cooperation between the British and American anti-apartheid publications.

In addition to the pamphlets published by the A-AM and the ACOA, the IDAF engaged in a concerted publishing exercise which addressed many areas of South African life. Exceptional examples which bore the IDAF imprint included Hilda Bernstein's study of the Biko inquest, Barbara Rogers's examination of the 'Bantustans', and a survey of the activities of BOSS.[59] The Africa Bureau also published pamphlets and in 1976 financed *The Great White Hoax*, which proved to be the first comprehensive study of the secret operations of South Africa's Department of Information.[60] Taken in its entirety, the published efforts of the underfunded anti-apartheid movements of Britain and the United States provided an abundance of information and posed a significant threat to the propagandists of South Africa.[61] No wonder then that Eschel Rhoodie informed Mervyn Rees: 'As far as Britain was concerned we were mostly concerned … with countering the operations of the Anti-Apartheid Movement.'[62] Despite the concerns of the Department of Information, relations between the anti-apartheid movements and the media in Britain and the United States were always problematic. The A-AM normally assessed this relationship in terms of the manner in which the media had reported the activities of the organisation. At times during the 1970s, the A-AM's tone could verge on the patronising:

The bulk of [the] reporting [on the 'détente' initiative] has tended to give a highly misleading impression of the situation and the Movement has endeavoured to correct this and to convey the true perspectives of the situation, through contact with individual reporters, through letters and numerous press statements. ... Of the national daily and weekly newspapers covering Southern African issues in depth, special mention must be made of the *Morning Star*, which also unfailingly reported AAM activities, *The Guardian*, *Tribune* and *West Indian World*. *The Sunday Times*, *The Observer* and *The Times* have also covered the issue though to a lesser extent. The Movement's connection with individual journalists in the press is maintained but a greater effort is needed in this field to ensure that the realities of the Southern African situation are reflected with greater accuracy.[63]

Placing articles by A-AM (or ANC) representatives in the British media was extremely difficult. The only newspaper which regularly found space for anti-apartheid comment was the communist daily, the *Morning Star*.[64] During 1975, the 'women's page' of the *Guardian* carried an article on the ANC–SACP member, Hilda Bernstein.[65] Following the Soweto uprising, the *Guardian* began to commission articles on South Africa from Bernstein.[66] In 1978, an article on the conditions on Robben Island was republished in both the *Los Angeles Times* and the *Washington Post*.[67] The key to the international media's acceptance of Hilda Bernstein's work was only partly an increased interest in the validity of the ANC position, however. The more significant factor was that Bernstein was a balanced and creative journalist.[68]

In America, penetration of the media by supporters of the anti-apartheid cause was equally tortuous. Francis Kornegay, a representative of the Washington Task Force on African Affairs, commented in 1973 that 'One of the woefully neglected areas by Southern Africa groups and other organizations with interest in building an informed public on African issues has been, we feel, mass communications.'[69] As with the A-AM, American organisations could not afford to employ a staff member whose sole task was to engage in public relations. George Houser describes the normal method of media relations for both British and US anti-apartheid organisations when he recalls that 'We all had a finger in the pie.'[70] However, the British organisations did possess the advantage of operating in a country where the media was interested in South Africa. One cannot read George Shepherd's comments on the A-AM's relations with the press without detecting a touch of envy: 'press visibility has extended the influence of AAM into levels of British society not yet touched by counterpart groups in the United States'.[71] The ACOA (which was based in New York) retained

useful contacts with journalists on the *New York Times* but found its
most productive relationship to be with the African-American media.[72]

Neither the British nor the American anti-apartheid movement felt
that it was fairly treated by its national media. The A-AM's assertion
that 'The correspondence columns of *The Times* constantly ignore
letters from the AAM and its supporters', was repeated by the ACOA
in relation to the *New York Times*.[73] The events of June 1976 caused
some concern within the organisations over the relative invisibility of
the ANC.[74] Following Mike Terry's appointment to the position of
Executive Secretary of the A-AM in 1976, the approach to media
relations was re-examined. Terry recalls that, although 'It took me
quite some time to get on top of [media relations]', the eventual
analysis was that the newspapers perceived the ANC as isolated and
disconnected from events in South Africa. The new media programme
was designed:

> to try and shift the agenda about how news itself was reported from
> South Africa. Secondly, to try and ensure that the media heard the voice
> of the liberation movement ... thirdly, to try and get coverage of our
> own events ... Our task, above all, was to try and persuade people that
> [apartheid] was an evil system that they had to act against and that the
> fundamentals hadn't changed.[75]

There is no doubt that the A-AM's relationship with the British media
was contradictory. In 1977, for example, the A-AM annual report
confirmed that 'For the first time in many years press coverage on
political prisoners and detainees was fairly wide. Feature articles
appeared in both *The Times* and the *Observer*; deaths in detention
were covered by the daily press on many occasions and the TV documentary on deaths in detention, *The Lawbreakers*, was screened.'[76]
Within days, however, in the aftermath of Steve Biko's death, *Anti-
Apartheid News* commented: 'If the press had spoken out earlier
against the torture and murder by the South African authorities, Steve
Biko and the others who have died at the hands of the South African
security police might be alive today.'[77] Ethel de Keyser believes that
the contradictions in the A-AM relationship with the media originated
in the problem of 'negotiating for peace and conducting a war'.[78]

In 1975, the Secretary-General of the ANC, Alfred Nzo, stated in a
Secretariat report that the 'imperialist news-media were prepared to
sink to the lowest depths in an effort to confuse world public opinion
... into accepting the success of the "detente" manouvre'.[79] Following
the Angolan war, *Anti-Apartheid News* began to carry commentaries
upon the media.[80] In 1977, the A-AM suggested in its annual report

that 'the role of *Anti-Apartheid News* has become more important ... in counteracting the biased reporting of the national media'.[81] Although it had always been a particularly unlikely ambition, the failure to meet one of the three targets of the post-1976 media policy – influencing the coverage within South Africa – led, eventually, to an almost blanket condemnation of the British media's correspondents in southern Africa.[82] The BBC's coverage became, during the late 1970s, a constant (and quite possibly, justifiable) bone of contention. *Anti-Apartheid News* launched a campaign at the beginning of 1977 which urged readers: 'When you see or hear biased reporting of events in Southern Africa on television or radio, COMPLAIN!'[83] The insert contained the telephone numbers of various broadcast media with the BBC at the top of the list. Within 12 months the BBC broadcast a documentary film which 'highlight[ed] Britain's role in bolstering Apartheid and tells you how you can help support the A-A struggle'.[84]

One of the stated functions of the A-AM's media relations was to encourage the press and television to report on the organisation and its campaigns. Beyond the BBC documentary in 1978, there is little evidence that the Movement was particularly successful in this task.[85] As Abdul Minty recalls, 'There wasn't continuous publicity [because] there weren't continuous events.'[86] During the first half of the decade there appeared, to the media, to be no likelihood of any major social unrest in the Republic. Between 1976 and 1980, the Cold War dominated any discussion of the subject, and the end of white rule in Rhodesia/Zimbabwe was considered by most correspondents to be the essential story.[87] The A-AM, therefore, had to attempt to influence a media which between 1972 and 1975 denied that a resistance movement existed, because there was little evidence of ANC activity within the Republic. During the second half of the decade, the A-AM had to defend itself against the accusation that it was little more than a communist front-organisation.[88]

Les de Villiers claimed in 1975 that 'South Africa's foes have no problem in cornering the best part of any discussion programme on TV or obtaining reams of column inches in leading liberal journals for their vitriolic message'.[89] In reality, the A-AM, as an organisation, received very little direct coverage. While the campaigns were reported by the media, the A-AM was rarely credited for its role in promoting information about South Africa, or its international and governmental lobbying. An article by Hugh Hebert in 1974, on the occasion of the A-AM's 15th anniversary, cast the organisation as 'chipping away' at the edifice of apartheid.[90] Three years later, Jack Foisie (*Los Angeles Times*) visited the A-AM. The ensuing article was notably confused. It opened as follows: 'At the top of a wobbly staircase in a decaying house in West London is the headquarters of the Anti-Apartheid Movement. By the standards usually used to measure the strength of pressure groups, the movement appears to be as feeble as the house.'[91] Predictably, friendlier articles on the A-AM were published in *Africa* magazine and the ANC journal, *Sechaba*.[92] There was barely any coverage of the ANC in the British or American media except in the *Morning Star*.[93] Ethel de Keyser was being generous when she recalled that 'The ANC at that stage was barely visible above the parapets.'[94]

In Foisie's article on the A-AM, he recorded that Peter Hain was 'the most publicized of the anti-apartheid crusaders'.[95] In fact, Hain's high public profile created a degree of tension within the A-AM. This stretched back to the days of the joint A-AM–STST campaign. In *Don't Play with Apartheid*, Hain stated: 'My particular role was to act as public spokesman for STST and to coordinate activities. The fact is that the communications industry needs individuals to explain a movement and "public personalities" are simply the children of this need.'[96] Ethel de Keyser felt that '[Hain] was an excellent public face but that the role played by the A-AM should have been recognised. What people in the A-AM resented was the lack of such recognition in his book.'[97] The tension over Peter Hain was an example of the A-AM's unwillingness to tolerate high-profile, semi-independent, spokespeople. This unwillingness was particularly apparent when the spokesperson was perceived by members of the A-AM as an 'interloper'. The problem with Hain was not his politics, it was his media status.[98] De Keyser recalls that 'Anti-Apartheid was unaccustomed to being a member of anything, other groups were members of Anti-Apartheid. This was an attitude generated, I think in the very early days of the A-AM.'[99] The failure to surmount (or at least, disguise) these tensions was one factor which contributed to the A-AM's reputation as a domineering and opportunistic organisation.[100]

Similar tensions emerged when Donald Woods arrived in Britain in 1978. Woods, having been the editor of the [East London] *Daily Dispatch*, understood the media and was eager to tell his story. During the first three months of his exile, Woods travelled extensively in Britain and the United States, speaking on the subject of South Africa. His personal campaign attracted extraordinary media attention.[101] Sally Quinn reported in the *Washington Post*:

> I am aware there's a 'comment' quality about me now ... so I must say what I've got to say quickly ... There is a very strong likelihood that if I try to sustain this too long my colleagues will start looking for a new angle. There are different ways to head this off, and Donald Woods, a

close friend of the late black leader, Steve Biko, has chosen an unusual one. Woods is on a media blitz in America speaking to groups ranging from campus seminars to business organizations, to President Jimmy Carter ... 'This trip,' he says, 'is political. It is sponsored by the African American Institute to spread the word. To try and seriously bugger around people like Mr Van Rooyen and the South African embassy; a task to which we must all strive.'[102]

Woods' appearance as the first private citizen to address the UN Security Council and his call for the withdrawal of American business from South Africa complemented the burgeoning sanctions debate in the United States.[103] However, in Britain, he was not particularly welcomed by the A-AM.[104] This was strange because, upon his arrival from South Africa, Woods had visited Oliver Tambo, the President of the ANC, and offered his services to the liberation movement. Woods recalls that Tambo informed him that 'You can do us far more good as a non-ANC person – You can go to America; the UN Security Council have asked you to speak there ... it is so much more powerful for you to say "Let us have economic sanctions," if you are not saying it as a member of the ANC.'[105] Ronald Segal's review of Woods' book, *Biko*, sheds more light on the tensions which accompanied Woods' arrival. Segal's review opened with a comprehensive condemnation of the Black Consciousness Movement (BCM): 'Its ideology was a rag-bag of protest thought ... Its economic dispensation [was] based on a more or less romanticised historical communalism ... It reflected and fed only a mood.' Although Segal acknowledged Woods' contribution and conversion to the cause of economic sanctions, he also asserted that '[Woods] is likely to be disappointed. For he makes his call ultimately to the conscience and good sense of the West ... All this only serves to remind black South Africa once again that it must find its release in revolution.'[106] Donald Woods, in effect, was perceived by some members of the A-AM not only as a high-profile white South African interloper, but also as an apologist for the recently-martyred leader of the increasingly criticised BCM.[107]

Similar tensions dominated the A-AM's relationships with journalists who were sympathetic to the anti-apartheid cause but determined to follow a path of their own in the struggle. Barbara Rogers was, perhaps, the most active anti-apartheid journalist during the 1970s.[108] Her interest in South African propaganda and Britain's foreign investment in the country began when she was appointed to the South West Africa/Namibia desk at the Foreign Office in 1969. She left the Foreign Office during 1970 and visited the Republic in 1971. During the years that followed, Rogers worked as an assistant (and speech-writer) for Congressman Diggs in the United States and wrote a large number of books, pamphlets and articles on a wide variety of subjects relating to South Africa. She recalls that 'The main problem trying to write about southern Africa, especially in Britain, was the deadening effect of the Anti-Apartheid Movement if you were not part of it, or if you wanted to express a different opinion from their line.'[109]

Len Clarke emigrated to South Africa from Australia in 1954. In 1966, he moved to Britain whereupon he wrote *The Seeds of Disaster*, under the pseudonym, John Laurence.[110] Throughout the 1970s, Clarke worked in advertising, while writing occasional articles for the *Guardian* and other publications.[111] He also wrote a vast number of letters to the newspapers on the subject of South Africa. His letter-writing represented a small-scale example of what Edward Herman and Noam Chomsky have called 'flak'.[112] Clarke was a tireless campaigner and should have been a model member of the A-AM, yet his relationship with the organisation was not without its problems: 'When you've got a massively organised propaganda system, the best thing to do – and I tried to get the A-AM to understand this but they largely ignored it – is to stress the fact that what you are hearing from the white side in South Africa is propaganda ... Therefore study what they are saying ... instead the A-AM was usually concentrating on anti-propaganda, or their own sort of propaganda.'[113] The failure to cooperate fully with committed anti-apartheid campaigners of the calibre of Rogers and Clarke was a major weakness of the A-AM. The ACOA and the SAC do not appear to have had such a difficult relationship with individual writers or journalists or to have suffered from the power struggles which were a consistent feature of exile politics in London. Jennifer Davis believes that this was because the organisations in the US were not as centralised as the A-AM: 'if you're not trying to control everything, then every [contribution] is synergy'.[114] It is, however, important to acknowledge that the American anti-apartheid campaigners were less directly concerned than the ANC and the SACP in Britain with a particular outcome to the South African 'revolution'.

Having discussed the failings of the anti-apartheid movements at some length, it is only fair to conclude with the recognition that the organisations were faced with almost insurmountable obstacles during the 1970s: lack of funding; a liberation struggle which for long periods of time was barely visible within South Africa; a general public and media which espoused anti-racism while harbouring negative representations of Africa; governments that practised 'structural hypocrisy'; and the natural wastage of campaigners who volunteered their support, money and effort for a campaign which never seemed to end. As Christopher Hitchens recalls of the A-AM in the mid-1970s, 'it was going through the motions ... you had that feeling of breaking rocks and treading water'.[115] In addition, a distinct sense of resentment against the media had built up amongst long-term campaigners and the representatives of the liberation movements. Reg September, for example, justifies the stern, authoritarian tone of his correspondence with the press by explaining that 'For years we knocked on those doors ... Maybe I was affected by [that]. I think we always recognised the power of the press, but ... we were always on the receiving end ... we didn't have the infrastructure of a state.'[116]

The similarities between the A-AM and the anti-slave trade campaign, engineered by the Clapham Sect during the late eighteenth and early nineteenth centuries, are startling: the length of the campaigns; the employment of boycotts; the education, and later support, of the British public; the opposition of entrenched British capital; the involvement of campaigners with local knowledge (South Africans and white 'West Indians'); and the association of the campaigns with a foreign ideology. Ernest Marshall Howse noted, in his study of the Clapham Sect, the debilitating effect that 'The cloud of republicanism' had on the campaign following the French Revolution of 1789.[117] The Cold War caused similar problems for the A-AM–ANC during the 1970s. While there were, of course, many differences between the campaign to abolish the slave trade and the struggle to defeat apartheid, it is telling that the responses of the capitalist interests were so similar: exaggerated claims of the effects of abolition/withdrawal on the British economy; a slow and grudging acceptance of a policy of gradualism; and the assertion that life for the African was better than that described by the campaigners.[118] In many ways both in its tactics and the opposition which it faced, the A-AM was a natural descendant of the Clapham Sect.

Although the 1970s was a particularly difficult decade for the A-AM, the organisation finally found a campaigning device which would eventually create a powerful resonance in Britain and the United States. The idea for a 60th birthday celebration for the imprisoned ANC leader, Nelson Mandela, originated from E.S. Reddy's discovery of the date of Mandela's birthday. He contacted Mike Terry with the suggestion that a celebration of Mandela's birthday might be an effective way to draw attention to the plight of political prisoners in South Africa.[119] *Anti-Apartheid News* and *Sechaba* duly carried tributes to the imprisoned leader.[120] There was little media coverage of the first Mandela campaign, but the A-AM annual report recounted the immediate success of the idea:

Special cards were distributed in Britain and internationally, and the South African press estimated that thousands were sent to Robben Island. The AAM also produced a blown-up card which was signed by many prominent figures in Britain, including several Cabinet members, David Steel, Leader of the Liberal party, and trade union leaders. On 18 July a delegation consisting of former AAM president Barbara Castle MP, Bob Hughes MP, AAM chairman, and Joan Lestor MP, AAM vice president, were refused permission to deliver the card at South Africa House. In Parliament the Prime Minister [James Callaghan] sent greetings to Nelson Mandela on behalf of the government.[121]

The 'Free Nelson Mandela' campaign, which in effect represented a personalisation of the liberation struggle, had begun.[122] Mike Terry recalls that the idea had received the full backing of the ANC, while also noting that 'from some people's point of view, [it was] an opportunity to increase the focus on Mandela and the ANC'.[123] It was clear, towards the end of the 1970s, that the A-AM was beginning to break out of the 'stranglehold' that had kept the organisation in either a demonised or an isolated position throughout the decade. It would still, however, be a number of years before the emergence of the United Democratic Front (UDF) in South Africa, and the ensuing development of a more productive relationship between ANC supporters and the foreign correspondents within the country.[124]

NOTES

1. Jim Hoagland, *South Africa: Civilizations in Conflict* (London, George Allen & Unwin, 1972), p. 358.
2. Suzanne Cronje, 'Africa's British Allies', *Africa*, No. 29 (January 1974), p. 66.
3. David Wiley, 'Anti-Apartheid Movements versus Government Policy in US and UK' (a review of George W. Shepherd Jr, *Anti-Apartheid: Transnational Conflict and Western Policy in the Liberation of South Africa* (Connecticut, Greenwood Press, 1977)), *Africa Today*, Vol. 26, No. 1 (1979), p. 63. In the early 1970s, David Wiley was a spokesman for the Madison Area Committee on Southern Africa.
4. Hugo Young, 'Introduction', in Derek Humphry, *The Cricket Conspiracy* (London, National Council for Civil Liberties, 1975), p. 7.
5. There are, as yet, no independent, academic studies of the anti-apartheid movements, either in Britain or in the United States, during the 1970s. Shepherd, op. cit., is a useful account, but Shepherd was the (part-time) Executive Director of the American Committee on Africa (ACOA) from 1953–55. For information on the ACOA during the 1960s, see John Seiler, 'The Formulation of US Policy toward Southern Africa, 1957–1976: The Failure of Good Intentions', unpublished PhD thesis, University of Connecticut, 1976, pp. 108–20.
6. Most of the various British and American anti-apartheid archives were either in transit or in the process of being catalogued while the research for this book was being prepared.

7. George M. Houser, 'Meeting Africa's Challenge: The Story of the American Committee on Africa', *Issue*, Vol. 6, No. 2/3 (Summer/Fall 1976), p. 16.

8. Shepherd, op. cit., p. 33.

9. Abdul S. Minty, 'The Anti-Apartheid Movement and Racism in Southern Africa', in Peter Willetts (ed.), *Pressure Groups in the Global System: The Transnational Relations of Issue-Orientated Non-Governmental Organizations* (London, Frances Pinter, 1982), p. 28.

10. Indian South Africans such as Vella Pillay played a major role in the A-AM until 1994. Many of the Indian members of the A-AM were also members of the Indian National Congress (INC) and the South African Communist Party (SACP).

11. Austin Mitchell, 'Pipe Dreaming', *New Statesman*, 14 February 1997, p. 16, citing Marcia Williams: '[Upon entering Number 10], the first thing he [Wilson] did was to put out an order that the Foreign Office and the Defence Department must be told that no arms be sold to South Africa.' See Oliver Wright, Confidential memo to P.W. Carey, Board of Trade, 17 October 1964 (PRO: PREM 13/092): 'the prime minister has directed that all shipments of arms to South Africa should cease forthwith'.

12. A friendly relationship was developed, in particular, between the A-AM and the *Sunday Times*, for whom Bruce Page worked. In the 1970s, Denis Herbstein became the major contact for the A-AM at the *Sunday Times*. (Interviews with Bruce Page, 17 May 1996; Denis Herbstein, 7 February 1996.)

13. Shepherd, op. cit., p. 42.

14. 'Organizational Initiatives: Liberation in Southern Africa', *Issue*, Vol. 3, No. 4 (Winter 1973), p. 52: '*Southern Africa* ... is the only magazine in the United States that covers every month news concerning liberation struggles in Southern Africa, news of what is going on in South Africa, interpretations and news about what is going on in the rest of the world in relation to Southern Africa.'

15. Interview with Jennifer Davis, 8 November 1996.

16. Shepherd, op. cit., p. 33: '[The A-AI], founded in 1953 in Washington DC ... had from its inception a semiofficial character, as it derived much of its funding from United States government sources.' See also Dan Schechter, Michael Ansara and David Kolodney, 'The CIA as an Equal Opportunity Employer', *Ramparts*, June 1969, pp. 25–33.

17. Interview with Jennifer Davis, 8 November 1996.

18. Shepherd, op. cit., p. 35, citing 'AIMS', Africa Bureau, mimeographed, London, 1952. See also Richard Cockett, *David Astor and The Observer* (London, André Deutsch, 1991), pp. 182–86. Mary Benson, a South African émigré, was a key figure within the Africa Bureau.

19. The church organisations did not interact with the media, preferring to demonstrate their support for the anti-apartheid cause through the usual A-AM and ACOA channels.

20. The technical brief of the A-AM was to oppose apartheid. The A-AM therefore purported to speak for both the ANC and the PAC, although in practice it was always closer to the ANC than the PAC. The ACOA adopted a similar position. (See George M. Houser, Letter to the editor, *Christian Science Monitor*, 15 February 1977.)

21. Kader and Louise Asmal, *Anti-Apartheid Movements in Western Europe*, United Nations Unit on Apartheid, No. 4/74 (March 1974), p. 6.

22. Interview with Abdul Minty, 4 October 1996. Minty was the Honorary Secretary of the A-AM. AI did not publish a report on human rights in South Africa in the 1970s until *Political Imprisonment in South Africa: An Amnesty International Report* (London, Amnesty International Publications, 1978).

23. Shepherd, op. cit., pp. 43–44.
24. Charles C. Diggs, Jr, 'Action Manifesto', *Issue*, Vol. 2, No. 1 (Spring 1972), p. 52. The other major campaigner against apartheid in the US legislature was Dick Clark, senior Democratic Senator from Iowa.
25. C. Gerald Fraser, 'Nixon Denounced on Africa policy', *New York Times*, 5 November 1972.
26. For Jimmy Carter's pre-election concerns regarding South Africa see 'Playboy Interview: Jimmy Carter', *Playboy*, Vol. 23, No. 11 (November 1976), p. 70: 'It might be that now I should drop my campaign for President and start a crusade for black-majority rule in South Africa or Rhodesia'.
27. William Minter, *King Solomon's Mines Revisited: Western Interests and the Burdened History of Southern Africa* (New York, Basic Books, 1986), p. 280.
28. For the A-AM's impressions of the Labour government (1964–66), see Anne Darnborough, *Labour's Record on Southern Africa: An Examination of Attitudes before October 1964 and Action since* (London, Anti-Apartheid Movement, 1967).
29. Guy Arnold, 'Britain and Southern Africa', *Africa*, No. 36 (August 1974), p. 69.
30. See, for example, Henry Stanhope, 'Britain Simply Does Not need Simonstown', *The Times*, 4 June 1974; Colin Legum and Andrew Wilson, 'The Simonstown Trap', *Observer*, 10 November 1974; Lord Chalfont, 'Simonstown: What is All the Arguing About?', *The Times*, 11 November 1974. The Simonstown Agreement was formally terminated in June 1975.
31. Anti-Apartheid Movement, *Annual Report of Activities and Developments: October 1977–September 1978* (London, A-AM, 1978), p. 24.
32. Other South Africans in key positions within the British anti-apartheid movements included Phyllis Altman, Hugh Lewin, Allen Brooks and John Sprack. The biographical details of a number of people involved in the anti-apartheid movements and the ANC can be found in Thomas Karis and Gwendolen M. Carter, *From Protest to Challenge: A Documentary History of African Politics in South Africa, 1882–1964*, Gail M. Gerhart and Thomas Karis, *Volume 4: Political Profiles, 1882–1964* (Stanford, Hoover Institution Press, 1977); Frene Ginwala, *The Press in South Africa*, United Nations Unit on Apartheid, No. 24/72 (November 1972), pp. 30–32. See also Shula Marks, 'Ruth First: A Tribute', *Journal of Southern African Studies*, Vol. 10, No. 1 (October 1983), pp. 123–28.
33. Although the debate in the United States was less intense than that in Britain, the director of the South Africa Foundation in Washington DC felt that 'The most effective critics of South Africa are exceedingly well informed about conditions in [South Africa] ... it is no longer correct to assume that their hostility arises from scant understanding.' (M.R. Christie, 'Foreign Report: Washington', *South Africa International*, Vol. 4, No. 3 (January 1974), p. 181.)
34. The Washington office of the ACOA was reopened in 1972 as an independent Washington Office on Africa, sponsored by the ACOA and the Methodist, Presbyterian, United Church of Christ and Episcopalian churches.
35. On the spread of the anti-apartheid issue through the American universities, see Edward B. Fiske, 'South Africa is New Social Issue for College Activists', *New York Times*, 15 March 1978; Editorial, 'Heading for the Exit in South Africa', *New York Times*, 2 April 1978; Barry Mitzman, 'US Students vs. Apartheid: The Divestiture Demonstrations', *Nation*, 13 May 1978, pp. 563–67.
36. See David Everatt, 'The Politics of Non-racialism: White Opposition to Apartheid, 1945–1960', unpublished DPhil thesis, Oxford University, 1990, p. 275: 'The disputes which followed the rise of the ANC – over the place of class struggle, the efficacy of parliamentary action, and others – were fought

out over the form that racial co-operation should take, and the place of whites in "the struggle against apartheid".'

37. See, for example, the debate on the subject by two *Washington Post* columnists: William Raspberry, 'Israel and South Africa: Toward US Tension', *Washington Post*, 21 April 1976 and Stephen S. Rosenfeld, 'Blacks and Jews: Tension over Diplomacy', *Washington Post*, 23 April 1976.

38. Interview with Jennifer Davis, 8 November 1996.

39. Newell M. Stultz, 'The Apartheid issue at the General Assembly: Stalemate or Gathering Storm', *African Affairs*, Vol. 86, No. 342 (1987), pp. 37–38.

40. Before 1972, there had been two conferences or international seminars on the subject of apartheid. Between 1972 and 1979, the United Nations organised 13 (seven conferences, five seminars and a symposium). The most significant of these were the International Conference of Experts for the Support of Victims of Colonialism and Apartheid in Southern Africa, Oslo, 9–14 April 1973, and the World Conference for Action against Apartheid, Lagos, 22–26 August 1977. See also the extensive publishing programme of the United Nations Unit on Apartheid.

41. The General Assembly referred to the legitimacy of struggle 'by any available means'. (Scott Thomas, *The Diplomacy of Liberation: The Foreign Relations of the African National Congress since 1960* (London, Tauris, 1996), p. 117, citing RES. 2923 E [XXVII] 1972.)

42. 'General Assembly resolution: Policies of apartheid of the Government of South Africa – Situation in South Africa resulting from the policies of apartheid', A/RES/3151 G (XXVIII), 14 December 1973, *The United Nations and Apartheid, 1948–1994* (New York, Department of Public Information, United Nations, 1994), p. 328.

43. 'Ruling by the President of the General Assembly, Mr Abdelaziz Bouteflika (Algeria), concerning the credentials of the delegation of South Africa', A/PV.2281, 12 November 1974, ibid., p. 333.

44. See Chapter 3.

45. 'Security Council resolution: The question of South Africa', S/RES/417 (1977), 31 October 1977, *The United Nations and Apartheid*, p. 347.

46. 'Statement by Secretary-General Kurt Waldheim in the Security Council after the adoption of resolution 418 (1977) concerning a mandatory arms embargo against South Africa', S/PV.2046, 4 November 1977, ibid., p. 348. The mandatory arms embargo against South Africa was the successful resolution to a campaign in which the A-AM and the ACOA had been engaged for 15 years. (Interview with Abdul Minty, 4 October 1996.)

47. Interview with George Houser, 17 April 1996.

48. Peter Hain, *Don't Play with Apartheid: The Background to the Stop the Seventy Tour Campaign* (London, Allen & Unwin, 1971), p. 200.

49. The A-AM's respectability as an organisation was a crucial component in its attempts to win support for its cause amongst politicians and members of the British establishment. (Interviews with Ethel de Keyser, 9 November 1995; Christabel Gurney, 6 August 1996.)

50. Ruth First, Jonathan Steele and Christabel Gurney, *The South African Connection: Western Involvement in Apartheid* (London, Temple Smith, 1972). Steele recalls that the impetus for the book came from Ruth First. (Interview with Jonathan Steele, 15 November 1994.)

51. See Chapter 5.

52. Anti-Apartheid Movement, *Annual Report on Activities and Development, October 1974–September 1975* (London, A-AM, 1975), p. 3. See also Dan O'Meara, *Forty Lost Years: The Apartheid State and the Politics of the National*

Party, 1948–1994 (Randburg, Ravan Press, 1994), p. 192: 'So successful was the détente initiative that a senior ANC functionary later told me that by mid-1975 his organisation had begun to fear that it might be excluded from every African state south of the Sahara.'

53. George M. Houser, 'Meeting Africa's Challenge: The Story of the American Committee on Africa', *Issue*, Vol. 6, No. 2/3 (Summer/Fall 1976), p. 22.

54. Rupert Pennant-Rea later became the Deputy-Governor of the Bank of England. The contents and direction of *Anti-Apartheid News* was overseen by an editorial board which included ANC–SACP members, Brian Bunting and Ruth First. Bunting was the Tass correspondent in London.

55. Gluck and his friends had previously designed the famous A-AM poster for the 1970 sports boycott campaign, which featured a white policeman beating an African and bore the legend, 'If you could see their national sport, you might be less keen on their cricket.' An example of the poor front-page designs which followed Gluck's departure would be *Anti-Apartheid News*, July–August 1976, p.1, which failed to feature a photograph of the Soweto uprising. Gurney recalls: 'I think we were so concerned with getting the message right that we didn't realise that what you needed was a picture – we were very keen on getting the words right.' (Interview with Christabel Gurney, 6 August 1996.)

56. See, for example, Sean Gervasi, *Continuing Escalation in the Angola Crisis*, The Africa Fund, New York, 1975. See also David Martin, 'American Warships are "Off Angola"', *Observer*, 11 January 1976.

57. The editor of *Sechaba* and the ANC's Director of Publicity, M.P. Naicker died in 1977. He was succeeded by Francis Meli, an SACP member.

58. *African Communist* also featured a number of articles offering a historical perspective on the struggle and particularly venomous book reviews. Due to its quarterly periodical status (as with *Sechaba* during the mid-1970s), it suffered from an inability to respond quickly, in print, to events within South Africa.

59. Hilda Bernstein, *No. 46 – Steve Biko* (London, International Defence and Aid Fund for Southern Africa, 1978); Barbara Rogers, *Divide and Rule: South Africa's Bantustans* (London, International Defence and Aid Fund for Southern Africa, 1976); *BOSS: The First Five Years* (London, International Defence and Aid Fund for Southern Africa, 1975).

60. Julian Burgess, Esau du Plessis, Roger Murray, Peter Fraenkel, Rosanne Harvey, John Laurence, Peter Ripken and Barbara Rogers, *The Great White Hoax: South Africa's International Propaganda Machine* (London, Africa Bureau, 1977).

61. IDAF and the ACOA published occasional fund-raising advertisements in the British and American newspapers. See, for example, IDAF, 'Remember Soweto', advertisement, *The Times*, 16 June 1977.

62. Mervyn Rees, interview with Eschel Rhoodie, 1979, transcript, p. 188. For an example of South African 'dirty tricks' against the A-AM, see Martin Walker, 'Anti-Apartheid Finds Forgeries', *Guardian*, 14 March 1977; and Robin Lustig, 'Riddle of a "Dirty Tricks" petition', *Observer*, 25 March 1979.

63. A-AM, *Annual Report*, 1975, p. 22.

64. The A-AM also sustained a productive relationship with *Africa* magazine, which carried articles by Ruth First, Frene Ginwala and Ethel de Keyser during the early 1970s. See also Editorial, 'Nuclear Conspiracy: West Germany and South Africa', *Africa*, October 1975, p. 7, which published an appeal by the ANC regarding South Africa's nuclear programme.

65. Suzanne Lowry, 'Miscellany', *Guardian*, 29 August 1975.

66. See Hilda Bernstein, 'Back to Black', *Guardian*, 4 October 1976; 'Did he fall or was he pushed?', *Guardian*, 22 February 1977; 'The Woman South Africa Locks Up in the Place Without a Name', *Guardian*, 5 July 1977. See also

M.P. Naicker, 'Demolishing the Bridge-building Myth', *The Times*, 8 September 1976.

67. Hilda Bernstein, 'Inside Apartheid's Gulag Archipelago', *Los Angeles Times*, 29 January 1978, republished as 'The Relentless Racism in S. African Prison', *Washington Post*, 5 February 1978. The article had originally been published as 'Two South Africans from the Island', *In These Times*, 18–24 January 1978, pp. 9–10. *In These Times* was a radical American weekly.

68. Bernstein suggests that it is possible that her reputation as a published author and public speaker made her views more acceptable to the media. (Interview with Hilda Bernstein, 15 July 1996.)

69. 'Organisational Initiatives: Liberation in Southern Africa', *Issue*, Vol. 3, No. 4 (Winter 1973), p. 44.

70. Interview with George Houser, 17 April 1996. See also Suzanne Cronje, 'Interview Abdul Minty', *Africa*, No. 29 (January 1974), p. 69: 'We do not have a research department, not even a research officer. We don't have the resources to employ full-time personnel to sift publications, but we have individuals in Britain and elsewhere who send us material; and sometimes the press comes to us for comment, as a result of which we get to know what is happening.' Jennifer Davis recalls that 'We always knew [that media relations] were important. We just didn't do much.' (Interview with Jennifer Davis, 8 November 1996.)

71. Shepherd, op. cit., p. 39.

72. Interview with George Houser, 17 April 1996. See also Daniel Schechter, 'Media Myopia', *More*, December 1977, p. 31. A noted achievement for the ACOA was the publication of George M. Houser, 'Communism and the War in Angola', *New York Times*, 14 December 1975. SAC members and founders of Africa News, Reed Kramer and Tami Hultman had a degree of success in placing anti-apartheid articles in the US publications. See, for example, Tami Hultman and Reed Kramer, 'Investing in South Africa is investing in Apartheid', *Los Angeles Times*, 9 April 1978.

73. Anti-Apartheid Movement, *Annual Report of Activities and Developments, October 1975–September 1976* (London, A-AM, 1976), p. 23. See also 'South Africa Courts US through "Back Door" Contacts and Intensive Propaganda', *Southern Africa*, Vol. 7, No. 7 (July–August 1974): 'the [*New York*] *Times* did not publish letters received from Africa Fund researcher Jennifer Davis and lawyer Joel Carlson'. The Africa Fund was a subsidiary organisation of the ACOA. The *Guardian* regularly carried correspondence from the A-AM and the ANC.

74. Ethel de Keyser recalls a logistics meeting called by the ANC during the late 1970s which was attended by five people including Frene Ginwala and herself: 'We sat down to work out how we could tell the people of this country [Britain] about the ANC because people didn't know [anything about the organisation].' (Interview with Ethel de Keyser, 9 November 1995.) The ANC and the A-AM concern regarding the media profile of the ANC was directly related to the Soweto uprising and the belated coverage of the Black Consciousness Movement (BCM). During the period June–September 1976 barely any journalists or media organisations bothered to ask the ANC to comment on the unrest in South Africa.

75. Interview with Mike Terry, 14 December 1995.

76. Anti-Apartheid Movement, *Annual Report on Activities and Developments, October 1976–September 1977* (London, A-AM, 1977), p. 12.

77. 'Steve Biko: AAM Demands International Enquiry', *Anti-Apartheid News*, October 1977, p. 1. *Anti-Apartheid News* had not carried any significant reports on the Black Consciousness leader during the year before his death.

78. Interview with Ethel de Keyser, 9 November 1995. The 'negotiations' were with the international media, the 'war' was the struggle against apartheid South Africa.

79. Alfred Nzo, 'The ANC fights back: abridged and edited version of the Secretariat Report submitted to the Special Extra-ordinary Meeting of the National Executive Committee of the African National Congress', *Sechaba*, Vol. 9, No. 5 (May 1975), p. 16. See also B.J., 'Propagandists for Apartheid' (a review of Burgess *et al.*, op. cit.), *African Communist*, No. 71 (Fourth Quarter 1977), p. 109: 'Far too many communists ... underestimate the extent and significance of the lie machines which our opponents operate everywhere ... If this booklet does nothing else than make people aware of the danger of being brainwashed by the media of the bourgeoisie in all countries it will have served a useful purpose.'

80. Christabel Gurney, 'British Press Leaps to Defence of Rhodesian Racism' and J.S. Marsh, 'What the Papers Said on Angola', *Anti-Apartheid News*, April 1976, pp. 6 and 11.

81. A-AM, *Annual Report*, 1977, p. 21.

82. See, for example, 'Smith's Press Puppets', *Anti-Apartheid News*, December 1977, p. 5. Beneath a photograph of a number of journalists 'being entertained at Rhodesian Breweries', *Anti-Apartheid News* commented: 'Foreign journalists in Rhodesia share the life style of the white minority.' For a more balanced form of media analysis, see Karen Rothmyer, 'US Press: Telling It Like It Isn't', *Southern Africa*, Vol. 11, No. 10 (December 1978), p. 5.

83. *Anti-Apartheid News*, January–February 1977, p. 12.

84. BBC Written Archives Centre at Caversham. 'Open Door: South Africa – The Rifle, the Saracen and the Gallows', BBC 2, 20 and 25 February 1978. The programme was introduced by Neil Kinnock. Copies were not available for viewing.

85. Abdul Minty and George Houser occasionally appeared on television as representatives of the A-AM and the ACOA, respectively. These television appearances were normally in opposition to South African propagandists.

86. Interview with Abdul Minty, 4 October 1996. See also Ethel de Keyser's comment: 'What we did wasn't an issue every day.' (Interview with Ethel de Keyser, 9 November 1995.)

87. '[Rhodesia] was the prime pump of news from [Africa] for the *Guardian* and every other newspaper for that decade.' (Interview with James MacManus, 16 October 1995.)

88. Mike Terry was a member of the Communist Party of Great Britain (CPGB). Ethel de Keyser, Executive Secretary of the A-AM until 1974, had not been a member of the SACP. See the friendly relationship between the A-AM–ANC and the *Morning Star*. See also Editorial, 'Making Way for Marx', *To The Point*, 26 September 1975, p. 22: 'Britain's Anti-Apartheid Movement has fallen on hard times compared with two or three years ago. Its present influence is a shadow of what it was during Peter Hain's "Stop the 70 Tour" campaign ... In recent months hard-line Marxists, having infiltrated the AAM, have been winning the power struggle. Whereas the movement originally stood mainly for multiracial sport at all levels, now ... the demand is for destruction of the entire SA political system.' Friends of the A-AM also believed that communists were playing too significant a role: 'As often happens to movements that go into remission or decline ... they get taken over by rather dreary second-rate, fellow travellers of the Communist Party.' (Interview with Christopher Hitchens, 15 April 1996.)

89. Les de Villiers, *South Africa: A Skunk Among Nations* (London, International Books, 1975), p. 103.

90. Hugh Hebert, 'Boer War Veterans', *Guardian*, 29 June 1974. See also 'Freedom Lock', *Time Out*, No. 226, 28 June 1974, p. 8.

91. Jack Foisie, 'Apartheid Foes Attack on Many Fronts', *Los Angeles Times*, 12 July 1977. The A-AM office was in Charlotte Street, W1, not in West London. Some months after Foisie visited the A-AM, the *Wall Street Journal* published a profile of the ACOA: Derek Reveron, 'Pamphlet Power: Small Group of Activists Puts Pressure on Big Firms to Get Out of South Africa', *Wall Street Journal*, 23 February 1978. The article reported that 'most of the faces around ACOA headquarters are white'; described the offices as 'unkempt'; and quoted Houser as saying, 'You fight for a lot of things you don't expect to happen.'

92. Suzanne Cronje, 'Africa's British Allies' and 'Interview: Abdul Minty', *Africa*, No. 29 (January 1974), pp. 66–71; 'No Collaboration with Apartheid', *Sechaba*, Vol. 8, No. 3 (March 1974), pp. 14–18; 'AA: 20 Years of Struggle', *Sechaba*, September 1979, pp. 17–18.

93. Exceptions included Suzanne Cronje, 'South Africa Speaks', *Africa*, No. 27 (November 1973), pp. 32–39, this was an interview with Reg September, the ANC's representative in Britain; Martin Walker, 'ANC Alarmed by Pretoria detente', *Guardian*, 27 March 1975; Colin Legum, 'African Nationalist Movement in Crisis', *Observer*, 28 December 1975; Linda Melvern, 'Free Arms for Blacks – "We Just Ask"', *Evening Standard*, 29 July 1977. The first significant article on the ANC in an American newspaper was Gregory Jaynes, 'Blacks in Exile Carry On War Against South Africa', *New York Times*, 20 June 1980. See also 'CBS Reports: The Battle of South Africa', CBS, 1 September 1978. In his review of the film, Jim Hoagland commented: 'No African guerrilla organization – described on the program with the systematically loaded label of "liberation organization" – has ever received the exposure in America that the African National Congress gets from this edition of *CBS Reports*.' (Jim Hoagland, 'Battle of South Africa', *Washington Post*, 1 September 1978.)

94. Interview with Ethel de Keyser, 9 November 1995.

95. Jack Foisie, 'Apartheid Foes Attack on Many Fronts', *Los Angeles Times*, 12 July 1977.

96. Hain, op. cit., p. 202.

97. Interview with Ethel de Keyser, 9 November 1995.

98. Hain continued to be a high-profile opponent of the South African government and a member of the A-AM. He was regularly called upon by the media to comment upon the sports boycott. In 1973, he stated: 'I accept the arguments advanced by Ruth First and her co-authors in *The South Africa Connection* that the only way to fight apartheid is to disengage completely.' ('Interview: Peter Hain', *Africa*, No. 19 (March 1973), p. 45.) Hain was national chair of the Young Liberals, 1971–73. He was subject to a letter bomb attack in 1973 and two prosecutions. In both cases he was found to be substantially innocent: the first (a private prosecution, financed from South Africa), in 1972, related to conspiracy over the STST campaign although Hain was found guilty of the minor charge of sitting down on a tennis court; the second was concerned with a petty bank robbery in Putney. See Jackie Leishman, 'Hain: the Inadmissible Evidence', *Guardian*, 22 August 1972; Humphry, op. cit., Peter Hain, *A Putney Plot?* (Nottingham, Spokesman, 1986).

99. Interview with Ethel de Keyser, 9 November 1995.

100. Many journalists felt that the A-AM were too judgmental of journalists who were merely doing their jobs: 'There was a feeling and it was very powerful in the A-AM that if you did any kind of analysis of the National Party [which recognised that reform was slowly occurring] – you were going soft. So this was a major discouragement.' (Interview with Stanley Uys, 24 March 1995.)

Raphael felt that the A-AM attempted to co-opt him following the publication of the wage starvation stories, see Chapter 5. (Interview with Adam Raphael, 30 September 1994.)

101. See Donald Woods, 'Cry My Beloved Country', *Observer*, 1 January 1978; Marcel Berlins, 'Fugitive Editor Fears Civil War', *The Times*, 7 January 1978; Donald Woods, 'No Easy Walk to Freedom', *Observer*, 8 January 1978; Alexander MacLeod, 'Donald Woods: champion of the blacks', *Listener*, 12 January 1978, p. 49, adapted from 'Profile: Donald Woods', BBC Radio 4, January 1978; William McWhirter, 'Critic in Exile', *Time*, 16 January 1978, p. 31; Peter Younghusband, 'The Great Escape', *Newsweek*, 16 January 1978, p. 16; The two *Observer* articles were syndicated in the *New York Times*, 8 January 1978, *Washington Post*, 8–9 January 1978 and *Chicago Tribune*, 15 January 1978; See also Donald Woods, 'To an Exiled South African Editor, Apartheid is a "Collective Tyrant"', *Los Angeles Times*, 5 March 1978; Paula Giddings, 'Exile with a Mission', *Encore American and Worldwide News*, 20 March 1978, pp. 16–21; Donald Woods, 'South Africa's Face to the World', *Foreign Affairs*, Vol. 56, No. 3 (April 1978), pp. 521–28; 'Biko's Friend', *New Yorker*, 29 May 1978, pp. 21–23. Woods was named Editor of the Year in the Granada Television 'What the Papers Say' awards.

102. Sally Quinn, 'After Escaping South Africa, Donald Woods Hits Back', *Washington Post*, 6 February 1978. The reference to Retief van Rooyen refers to an argument which Woods had with van Rooyen at an impromptu press conference, following Woods' visit to the Senate Subcommittee on African Affairs. Van Rooyen, who was the police's barrister in the Biko inquest, was 'visiting' Washington at the time.

103. The text of Woods' speech to the UN was published as Donald Woods, 'Mobilizing Effective Moral Force Against Apartheid', *Objective: Justice*, Vol. 9, No. 4 (Winter 1977/78), pp. 14–19.

104. *Anti-Apartheid News*, for example, only carried one article on Woods's escape from South Africa and ensuing 'media blitz'. '"Ostracise SA" – Banned Editor', *Anti-Apartheid News*, March 1978, p. 10.

105. Interview with Donald Woods, 19 June 1995.

106. Ronald Segal, 'Beyond Grieving' (a review of Donald Woods, *Biko* (London, 1978)), *Guardian*, 13 April 1978. Segal was a long-standing ANC member, a close friend of Oliver Tambo and the editor of the Penguin Africa Library. Aida Parker, 'Secret US War Against SA: Part Six', *Citizen*, 20 June 1977, described him as 'the most dangerous propagandist against South Africa'.

107. Toussaint, 'Fallen among Liberals', *African Communist*, No. 78 (Third Quarter 1979), pp. 18–30, took the criticism of the BCM and the denigration of Donald Woods a stage further. The article concluded of Steve Biko, 'that the path he was following led to a dead end' (p. 30). Woods's book on Biko is also condemned as a source: 'It contains much second hand account of things Biko is said to have said in the presence of Woods. For these there is only Woods's recollections … such recollections may well be faulty due to the lapse of time, or even be unconsciously distorted by the selective memory of the writer' (p. 19). Woods's reputation took another blow when he was condemned by the Writers Association of South Africa (WASA) for exploiting the memory of Steve Biko. (Patrick Laurence, 'Blacks Criticise Exiled Editor', *Guardian*, 4 July 1978.)

108. Barbara Rogers' work on South Africa included 'South Africa's Propaganda Machine', *New Statesman*, 15 January 1971, pp. 69–70; *South Africa's Stake in Britain* (London, Africa Bureau, 1971); *White Wealth and Black Poverty: American Investments in Southern Africa* (Connecticut, Greenwood Press, 1976); *Divide and Rule*; Burgess *et al.*, op. cit.; with Zdenek Cervenka, *The*

Nuclear Axis: Secret Collaboration between West Germany and South Africa (London, Julian Friedman Books, 1978); *The Image Reflected by Mass Media: Manipulations. The Nuclear Axis: A Case Study in the Field of Investigative Reporting* (New York, UNESCO, 1980). See also her articles in *Sechaba*, *Africa Today*, *Anti-Apartheid News*, *Southern Africa* and *Africa Report*.

109. Interview with Barbara Rogers, 15 December 1995.

110. John Laurence, *The Seeds of Disaster* (London, Victor Gollancz, 1968). Barbara Rogers recalls that this book contributed to her interest in South African propaganda. (Interview with Barbara Rogers, 5 December 1995.) Laurence had become interested in South Africa's external propaganda 'when I was Copy Chief of SA's largest ad agency, and we were appointed by the SA Dept. of Information to write four large ads for the UK press. The briefing by a Department official began with "Your task will be to create material which will help our friends in the British Conservative Party to oust the Wilson Labour Government".' (Letter from Len Clarke, 21 May 1997.)

111. Clarke's work on South Africa in the 1970s, published under the name John Laurence, includes *Countering South Africa's Misleading Racial Propaganda*, United Nations Unit on Apartheid, 18 March 1972; 'Censorship by Skin Colour', *Index on Censorship*, Vol. 6, No. 2 (March/April 1977), pp. 40–43; Burgess *et al.*, op. cit.; *Race, Propaganda and South Africa* (London, Victor Gollancz, 1979). See also the articles in *Gemini*, the *Guardian* and *Anti-Apartheid News*.

112. Edward S. Herman and Noam Chomsky, *Manufacturing Consent: The Political Economy of the Mass Media* (New York, Pantheon Books, 1988), pp. 26–28: '"Flak" refers to negative responses to a media statement or program.' During the 1970s, Clarke wrote to nearly every British national newspaper and magazine. He was able to read all the reports on South Africa, because the advertising agency at which he worked subscribed to every newspaper. Clarke recalls that only a tiny percentage of all the letters that he sent to the media were ever published. During the second half of the 1970s, he became particularly concerned with the BBC: 'the BBC, to my mind, has been the main pro-South African propaganda organ in this country, particularly because of [the supposition that] the BBC is totally impartial'. (Interviews with Len Clarke, 22 June and 7 July 1995.)

113. Interview with Len Clarke, 22 June 1995. See A-AM, *Annual Report*, 1976, p. 22: 'As the struggle intensifies, *Anti-Apartheid News* is becoming more important as the main propaganda weapon through which the Movement can put forward its distinctive view on the situation.'

114. Interview with Jennifer Davis, 8 November 1996.

115. Interview with Christopher Hitchens, 15 April 1996.

116. Interview with Reg September, 17 May 1995.

117. Ernest Marshall Howse, *Saints in Politics: The 'Clapham Sect' and the Growth of Freedom* (London, Allen & Unwin, 1953), p. 45.

118. Ibid., p. 33; 'Lord Penrhyn ... assured the Commons that the tales of the Middle Passage were begotten in fanaticism and nurtured in falsehood, and that the captive slave looked upon the voyage from Africa as "the happiest period of his life".'

119. Interview with Mike Terry, 14 December 1995.

120. 'Release Nelson Mandela!' and Sadie Forman, 'Another Day in the Life of Nelson Mandela', *Anti-Apartheid News*, July/Aug, 1978, pp. 1 and 6; Editorial, 'Mandela – 60 Years Old', 'Nelson Mandela and our Revolution' and 'Life on Robben Island', *Sechaba*, Vol. 12 (Third Quarter 1978), pp. 1–18.

121. A-AM, *Annual Report*, 1978, p. 8. The birthday celebration was held on 18 July

1978. See also Nicholas Ashford, 'Prayers Said for Robben Island Prisoner No. 466/64', *The Times*, 18 July 1978; John F. Burns, 'Key Black Leader Turns 60 on South African Prison Isle', *New York Times*, 19 July 1978; *Observance of Mr Nelson R. Mandela's Sixtieth Birthday*, United Nations Centre against Apartheid, Notes and Documents No. 23/78, August 1978.

122. The Mandela campaign re-emerged in South Africa, two years later, in a campaign organised by Percy Qoboza through the pages of the African newspaper, *Sunday Post*. See Eric Marsden, 'Free Mandela Movement Grows', *Sunday Times*, 13 April 1980; John F. Burns, 'South African Seeking Freedom for "the Black Pimpernel"', *New York Times*, 21 May 1980.

123. Interview with Mike Terry, 14 December 1995.

124. 'The UDF ... made a conscious decision to use the commercial press, the white press and to woo individual journalists.' (Interview with Patrick Laurence, 12 May 1995.) The ANC, in exile, continued to experience difficulties with the media for a number of years. Denis Herbstein comments: 'It took a long time for them to get their act together.' (Interview with Denis Herbstein, 9 March 1995.) See also Joseph Lelyveld, *Move Your Shadow: South Africa, Black and White* (London, Michael Joseph, 1985), pp. 336–37.

5

'Starvation Wages', 1973–74

Starvation wages in South Africa – the most effective Guardian investigation in my time.[1]

the one story that I remain genuinely proud of having written.[2]

Towards the end of 1972 and throughout 1973, African workers went on strike in South Africa. Most historians now accept that the Durban strikes, as they became popularly known, were the first major example of a revived African industrial resistance which had been crushed, but not destroyed, during the repression of the early 1960s.[3] The international media failed to acknowledge the extraordinary significance of the African workers' agency, devoting little more coverage to the subject than had been awarded to the (white) student unrest that had occurred during 1972. However, as the ANC journal, *Sechaba*, acknowledged, 'in Britain, the strike wave triggered off a great deal of soul-searching about the morality of British investment in South Africa … it took the direct challenge of the workers themselves to the cheap labour system to jolt liberal consciences into realising the scandalous exploitation of the Black workers in South Africa, and to force foreign capital on to the defensive'.[4]

The payment of poverty wages to African workers in South Africa was of course not exceptional, having been common practice throughout the twentieth century. This chapter will demonstrate that the *Guardian*'s campaign on the subject of wage poverty *was* extraordinary in its handling, development and retreat from the implications of the original exposé. The contradictions which emerged in the *Guardian*'s campaign reflected the difficulties which news organisations experience when they challenge the liberal consensus. This chapter considers the exposure of Adam Raphael's reports and the coverage which ensued; Raphael's sources and the precedents for, and contexts of, the story; the consequences and critiques of the campaign; and, finally, the ambiguous tone of the treatment and the passive representations of Africans which came to dominate the story.

On 12 March 1973, the *Guardian* led with a story entitled 'British Firms Pay Africans Starvation Rate'. The report was a summary of Adam Raphael's research undertaken during a three-month working vacation in South Africa. There had been previous stories broaching this subject in the British newspapers but none was delivered in such a sensationalist style, or with the full backing of the newspaper concerned. Raphael's front-page story opened:

> The majority of British companies in South Africa are paying substantial numbers of their African workers below officially recognised subsistence levels. An investigation of 100 British companies found only three – Shell, ICI and Unilever – who were paying all employees above the minimum for an African family to avoid malnutrition. Some prominent British companies earning large profits in South Africa are paying between a third and a half of this minimum subsistence standard. 'If your income is below the poverty datum line (£10–£11 a week for a family of five) your health must suffer. In a real sense this is starvation,' said the research officer for Johannesburg's Non-European Affairs Department. This comment proved to be no exaggeration. On two wattle farms owned by Slater Walker SA, I saw several children suffering from open sores, distended stomachs and weakened limbs.[5]

The report listed ten other British companies (Associated Portland Cement, Tate & Lyle, Metal Box, Courtaulds, General Electric, Reed, Rowntree Macintosh, Chloride Electrical, Associated British Foods and British Leyland) whose subsidiaries were paying wages below the poverty datum line. Raphael's article was accompanied by two photographs which he had taken at the Boscombe estate wattle farm owned by Slater Walker.[6] A supporting article explained the methodological determination of the poverty datum line and noted that American companies had a more progressive policy with regard to African working conditions. The article also punctured the argument that South African wages were fixed under apartheid law by citing a British government Department of Trade advice document which stated that 'The impression that this legislation effectively prevents employers from improving the wages or conditions of service of non-white employees is mistaken: employers retain a good deal of flexibility in these areas.'[7] The *Guardian*'s editorial opened a debate on the 'scandal of African labour' by posing the question: 'What are we going to do about South Africa?'[8]

The other newspapers responded quickly. *The Times* acknowledged that 'The *Guardian* is to be congratulated for bringing into prominence the fact that well-known firms whose head offices or holding

companies are in London are among the worst employers in South
Africa ... it will not do. How can it be stopped? The slave trade was
stopped.'[9] The *Financial Times* suggested that 'The best policy would
be to find the right mix between higher pay, better living and working
conditions, and greater efficiency.'[10] In contrast, the *Daily Telegraph*
carried a news report which implied collusion between Raphael and
the Anti-Apartheid Movement (A-AM): 'Most British companies are
sensitive to charges of exploitation of the African worker levelled at
them by anti-apartheid groups.'[11] As the week proceeded, the
Guardian persisted with coverage of the repercussions of the original
story. These included calls for a debate and questions to the Prime
Minister by Labour MPs in the House of Commons; responses by
the directors of companies accused in the report; A-AM student campaigns designed to force universities to disinvest; demands for an
inquiry by the British Council of Churches; a critical statement by Reg
September, chief representative of the ANC in London; and an article
by John Laurence on African infant mortality in South Africa.[12] In
addition, the newspaper ran two further editorials which attempted,
rather unsuccessfully, to grope their way towards a resolution of the
question, 'What is to be done?'[13]

The other newspapers covered the scandal less intensely although
there was a flurry of letters to *The Times* on the subject, including a
defensive correspondence from the Chairman of Tate & Lyle followed
by further evidence from Adam Raphael.[14] On Sunday 18 March, the
Observer contributed an editorial: 'The keen public response stirred
by the Guardian's disclosures about starvation wages paid by many
British firms in South Africa shows how strongly the British conscience
feels about this country's involvement in the harshly discriminatory
practices of apartheid.'[15] Colin Legum, in London, recognised the
importance of South Africa's economic dependence on foreign investment but criticised the supposed impracticality of the disinvestment
lobby: 'Then there is the call for full and complete disengagement,
which is usually put forward vehemently. But how is this to be
achieved, and if it were achieved, what would be the consequences?
... Would not such a development, in effect, throw away the West's
'economic lever'? To these crucial questions no sensible answers have
been provided.'[16] Three months later, Suzanne Cronje explained:

> Colin Legum ... is the chief activist behind ... the 'Study Project on
> External Investment in South Africa and South West Africa (Namibia)'
> ... The dubious nature of such work becomes clear when it emerges
> that it proceeds in close co-operation with those circles most anxious
> to maintain the status quo in the land of apartheid – the Foreign Office,

the Confederation of British Industry, Barclays Bank, Rio Tinto Zinc, and similar concerns.[17]

Benjamin Pogrund, writing from South Africa, commented in the *Sunday Times*: 'it has all been reported ad nauseam and no one, either in South Africa or Britain, can possibly claim to have been ignorant of what was happening – particularly the large number of British businessmen busy making money there … The 500 or so British companies have had … enormous capacity either to initiate progress or to maintain and bolster the status quo. They have constantly chosen the latter path.'[18] The *Sunday Telegraph* reported that 'The South African Government … is delighted with the way in which the "hypocrisy" of the British, so ready to criticise apartheid, has been exposed.'[19] The *Sunday Mirror* carried an editorial which reflected the contradictions of the emerging debate:

> The *Guardian* newspaper last week uncovered an unknown scandal that ought to be on the conscience of every caring person in Britain … Already the idiot lobby is demanding that all British firms should be compelled to pull out of South Africa. That wouldn't help anybody … The correct solution is for each company publicly and openly to raise African earnings at least to subsistence level as a first step – This won't bankrupt anyone! … The vast pressure of public opinion will insist that every other company that has failed to maintain proper standards follows these examples … Just as the *Sunday Times* came so brilliantly and successfully to the rescue of the thalidomide children, life will be better for some of the poorest souls in the world – thanks to the *Guardian* and its reporter, Adam Raphael.[20]

On 19 March, the *Daily Telegraph* published an editorial on the subject. Following an assessment of the possibility of strike activity leading to violent disorder, the editorial explained that 'there can be no principle yet of equal pay for equal work between white and black in the complicated South African labour field, but the movement must be to relate wages much more closely to subsistence'.[21] The media gaze of the daily and Sunday newspapers began to wane after the first week as the campaign became almost solely associated with the *Guardian*. None of the news-magazines viewed the scandal as worthy of cover-story status. *The Economist*, in its business section, cited a number of the warnings that the story was going to break. While contributing little new information, the magazine stated that 'The storm that has broken over the heads of British companies … is largely deserved.'[22] *New Society* praised 'the *Guardian*'s fine reporting on African wages – a tribute to the virtues of a near sensationalist approach in a quality paper'.[23] The *New Statesman* published a three-page analysis which criticised the simplicity of newspaper campaigns with regard to wages but offered little tangible alternative.[24] The *Spectator* praised the 'tigerish tenacity [with which] the *Guardian* [had] followed up the story with more reports, interviews and a barrage of leaders'. Contextualising the wage reports in the aftermath of the Durban strikes, the article concluded with a powerful indictment: 'a first lesson to be learned by the British may be that one cannot touch pitch without being defiled. It is no longer a secret that British investment buttresses the South African way of life'.[25]

At the beginning of the second week, the *Guardian* turned its campaign towards support for the Labour Party's demands for an investigation by a Parliamentary Select Committee. Adam Raphael reported the exposé-related events and responses in Britain while Stanley Uys provided the supporting news from South Africa. In an editorial, the newspaper warned that 'The issue cannot again be allowed to drift into oblivion after a brief outcry, as some companies hope it will.'[26] This editorial was accompanied by another supporting article by Adam Raphael which attempted to clear up any misunderstanding in potentially libellous statements which had been published by the newspaper during the preceding period.[27] By the third week of the campaign, the *Guardian*'s coverage was beginning to grow weary; reportable effects were decreasing and the government was only slowly moving towards an acceptance of the viability of a Select Committee. The paper seemed to imply as much in an editorial on 28 March: 'Enough has surely been said already to show that the facts need to be established.'[28]

On 3 April, the *Guardian*, perhaps in the knowledge that the government was about to give way on the investigation, ran the longest editorial to date; the text occupied the complete editorial space for the day, two-fifths of a page. The editorial announced that the newspaper would soon publish a revised version of Adam Raphael's questionnaire for British businesses in South Africa to assist shareholders in the questioning of the boards of the relevant companies.[29] Detailing the brutality of the apartheid state, the editorial commented on the recent South African Special Branch interrogations of a number of the students and staff of the University of Natal who had helped Raphael during his research. Having noted the World Council of Churches decision to disinvest in South Africa, the newspaper came to a different conclusion:

> The right course is to work on a number of fronts simultaneously – persuading employers to pay Africans a living wage, breaking down job

reservation, fighting the pass laws, discouraging any new white immigration to South Africa, looking hard at any proposals for further investment there, providing education and training for Africans, and maintaining the international ostracism of the South African government. The will of white South Africans to preserve apartheid may eventually be broken.[30]

On the facing page, the newspaper carried a full page of proposed improvements which could be introduced by British companies in South Africa. In effect, the *Guardian* was stating that it favoured 'involvement' rather than 'withdrawal', so long as certain conditions were met. In the 'Society Today' column in the *Financial Times*, Joe Rogaly assessed the issues surrounding the question of starvation wages. While stating that it was essential that the pressure was kept up on British businessmen, he defended the campaign against critics on both sides:

> Those who argue that economic forces will in the long run erode the barriers of apartheid may be sincere: the equally sincere reply is that after three-quarters of a century of increasingly rapid economic development in South Africa the barriers that keep Africans voteless, without security of tenure, forced to carry 'passes' and subject to the brutal attentions of the police whenever any of them step out of line, are still there. It is on this ground that some of those who favour revolution are horrified that any company might treat its black workers better, lest the fervour that is imagined to exist should die down. In my view paying Africans enough to live on will not make much difference to the timing of any revolt, either way: what it will do is make the lives of a number of individuals just that much more tolerable.[31]

Rogaly concluded by assessing that the starvation wages scandal had occurred because of 'a curious conglomeration of circumstances: the publication of excellent reports about a long-standing injustice, coming at a (possibly brief) moment when at least the major British companies are conscious of a need to be seen acting decently'. The *Guardian*'s campaign reached its immediate conclusion on 9 April with the announcement of an inquiry by the Trade and Industry Sub-Committee of the House of Commons' Select Committee on Expenditure. On the same day, Slater Walker, the company most prominently named in Adam Raphael's original report, announced that it had doubled the wage rate of the lowest-paid African workers at its subsidiary company in South Africa.[32] During the four weeks between the publication of the original story and the decision to launch the

parliamentary inquiry, the *Guardian* had published ten related editorials, an extraordinary number when one compares this to the single
editorial which had discussed the Durban strikes.[33] The *New York
Times*'s correspondent was quite accurate when he reported that 'it
makes the fuss about American involvement in South Africa seem mild
indeed'.[34]

Adam Raphael had started work at the *Guardian* in 1966. Between
1968 and 1972 he worked as its Washington correspondent, during
which period he married Caroline Ellis, the daughter of a former
editor of the *Rand Daily Mail*. In his memoir of the 'starvation wages'
story he explains why he seized upon the idea of looking at British
companies in South Africa:

> Partly because I had married a South African, I was a keen observer
> during my years in Washington as the pressure increased on big
> American companies like Polaroid and IBM to justify their continued
> operations in the Republic. A Congressional Committee led by a black
> Congressman, Charles Diggs, began holding a series of hearings on
> Capitol Hill into the wages and conditions of African workers employed
> by American firms ... This spotlight of publicity ... achieved results.
> Under the pressure of public opinion leading American firms began to
> change their employment practices in South Africa.[35]

The second major influence on Raphael was *The South African
Connection* by Ruth First, Jonathan Steele and Christabel Gurney.[36]
The text's central thesis, that the apartheid state was unreformable and
that disinvestment was therefore the only tenable strategy, was ignored
by Raphael. He concentrated on the chapters which dealt with the
dishonesty and hypocrisy of British companies, recognising that this
information could transcend the investment/disinvestment debate.
With three months holiday due, Raphael decided to visit South Africa
with his wife and child, ostensibly to meet his in-laws. He comments:
'It was my first trip to South Africa and, heavily influenced by my
American experience, I thought I should spend at least some of my
time looking at the employment practices of British companies ...'[37]
Upon arriving in the Republic, Raphael paid a visit to South Africa's
newly-appointed Secretary for Information, Eschel Rhoodie, who
'said something in passing which led me to suspect that I was on the
right track: "There are a number of British companies in this country
with prominent reputations in the world who are paying their workers
less than they should."'[38] Although it is not clear what Rhoodie was
attempting to achieve by making such a suggestion, there is little doubt
that, as the *African Communist* observed, 'some Nationalists were

gloating that it was Durban, the English city, which was hardest hit by the strikes, thus demonstrating that the English, who were always blaming the Government for African poverty, were amongst the worst employers of Black labour'.[39]

Between 22 December 1972 and 25 February 1973, Raphael filed 14 stories for the *Guardian* on a variety of subjects, while researching the wages and conditions of African workers in British companies. Through the mediations of South African journalists, Stanley Uys, Donald Woods and Tony Heard, Raphael was introduced to African trade unionists, academic researchers and student activists.[40] Uys remembers: 'He was sitting down the corridor from me [in the *Cape Times* offices] and you could see that [the story] was gathering its own momentum, the more he inquired, the more he dug around … he'd really struck a very rich seam.'[41] After a visit to the South African Institute of Race Relations, Raphael decided that the best method for judging the behaviour of British companies was by using the poverty datum line (a theoretical minimum wage for a family to survive without malnutrition) as a yardstick. Concentrating on a handful of companies with the worst reputations, he obtained information on the wages being paid through direct contact with the African workers, 'standing outside factory gates to get [their] pay slips'.[42] He also drafted a questionnaire on wages and conditions which was sent to 100 British companies and followed up with telephone calls. Answers were obtained from one-third. Upon his return to England, Raphael felt excited with the material he had gathered:

> I'd never worked on a story for three months, I'd done a lot of work by the time I came back … The foreign editor [Ian Wright] … expressed boredom with the story and eventually said 'well, it might make a leader page article'. I did create a bit of a row – I mentioned to the editor that there was a news story there as well. It was going to go on the back page of the (Monday) Guardian and just by fluke, sheer fluke, the story that was meant to lead the paper was the French election results and for some reason they didn't come through and my story was promoted to the front page.[43]

However, it should also be acknowledged that Adam Raphael had an exceptional gift for 'placing copy', as Ian Wright recalls: 'He had a brilliant ability to aim a story at a particular part of the paper and get it there – which all of us envied.'[44] Raphael also possessed another skill, that of choosing his target carefully. The decision to focus the original story on the wattle farm owned by Slater Walker SA was almost certain to garner a level of coverage not normally associated with an economic story.[45] The precedents for Raphael's exposé were legion, it was his execution and delivery which were original.[46] In August 1970, for example, Neil Wates, the director of a large construction firm, had attracted media coverage for his decision, following a visit to South Africa, that he was not prepared to invest in the country even though his company would undoubtedly have made huge profits from the exploitation of cheap labour.[47] A few months after Wates's statement, Denis Herbstein, a South African-born journalist was visiting the Republic when he received a telephone call from the foreign department of the *Sunday Times*: 'Pogrund had put up this idea [to investigate working practices in British companies] ... and they asked me to do it.'[48]

Herbstein's research had been intended to include 16 British companies and he managed to conduct interviews with ten. Herbstein's article was published on 18 April 1971. The Unilever director in Durban, T.B. Higgins, was quoted as commenting on Herbstein's inquiry: 'the article will be so controversial you should consider whether you would be loyal to British interests by publishing it'.[49] Notably, by the time of Raphael's investigation, Unilever, whose pay was amongst the lowest in Herbstein's survey, had improved its performance. Herbstein's report possessed many of the elements that would later lie at the core of the *Guardian*'s treatment: an equivalent measure to the poverty datum line; malnutrition ('A survey showed that 80% of the unskilled labour force ... suffered signs of malnutrition'); and insensitive quotations from managing directors ('In this country I couldn't care less about politics. We are here to make a profit'). The key differences between the two were in the areas of style and tone. Adam Raphael emphasised the negative in a style which was designed to make the story big news. Herbstein attempted constructive criticism, including an eight-point plan: 'If the British companies are serious about "bridge building", there are a number of girders and nuts and bolts they could use as a minimum programme which would not involve challenging the law yet would convince the black masses of their desire to help.' The most significant difference between the articles, however, lay in the backing provided by their respective newspapers. Denis Herbstein's article was 'buried' in the business section and, with no supporting editorial or front page 'splash', was destined to be forgotten. He explains why this happened:

Harry Evans [the editor of the *Sunday Times*] who was quite close to Pogrund had said this was a top priority story ... unfortunately that week Harry was away. Everybody who saw it said that this is a great piece, although in 1971, South Africa was still a bit off the map ... I don't know what happened in the engine room of the *Sunday Times*, I'd only been at the paper for two or three years and this was the first big story I did ... it went into business news and that, I was told, was the decision of the deputy editor, Frank Giles ... [who] was really a Foreign Office man, he was close to South Africa House ... he very diplomatically placed [the story] where it would have less effect.[50]

Although Herbstein's report did not lead to a widespread debate in the British media, those concerned with promoting South Africa's interests were well aware of its implications. Roy Macnab, the South Africa Foundation (SAF)'s London director, reported that 'both *The Times* and the *Sunday Times* have had men in South Africa to report on the race relations record of British business subsidiaries there and a strenuous effort was made to shame them before public opinion at home. British business, however, appears to be tough enough to take it.'[51] Following a visit to South Africa during May 1972, Jeremy Thorpe (the leader of the Liberal Party) gave a press conference in which he 'called on fellow MPs to buy shares in British companies operating in South Africa to improve conditions for African workers ... he said he was appalled by the "slave conditions" [in the Republic]'. Thorpe was also quoted as stating that 'Those who call for the withdrawal of British investment in South Africa will achieve nothing.'[52] Thorpe's employment of the slavery trope in conjunction with a moral vindication of further investment prefigured the eventual course of the Raphael–*Guardian* campaign.

Inspired by the need to develop the sanctions debate, Ruth First, Jonathan Steele and Christabel Gurney set about the task of compiling a text which would expose the degree to which Western (and, especially, British capital) financed and fortified the apartheid system. *The South African Connection* used as one of its sources, Denis Herbstein's unpublished notes for his article on British companies. Published in the autumn of 1972, the book served to expand the parameters of the economic argument and was widely reviewed. Douglas Brown (*Sunday Telegraph*) was critical: 'The authors, obsessed by racial politics, stand every socio-economic argument on its head. They ignore the universal experience that prosperity increases the power of a proletariat to the point that enables it to break out of any political straight-jacket.'[53] In contrast, Clifford Longley was impressed by the cogency of the book's argument: 'The case against many British businesses remains to be answered.' He continued: 'Is public opinion changing on the question of British investments in South Africa? Recent indications suggest that it may well be doing so.'[54]

During October 1972, the A-AM announced in its annual report that it intended to intensify its campaign against British companies investing in South Africa.[55] The penultimate precedent for the Raphael story was provided by the South African government, however: 'The Minister of the Interior, Dr C.P. Mulder, announced in October [1972] that he had had enough of foreign visitors' investigations of foreign companies' employment practices, and would in future refuse them entry to the country.'[56] This was the metaphorical 'red rag to a bull'. By the beginning of 1973, the British media were primed for the emergence of a major story on the scandal of African wages in South Africa. In effect, the groundwork had been laid and the media could not claim ignorance of working conditions in the Republic. As Bridget Bloom commented some months after the wage starvation scandal had become public knowledge, 'it was inevitable that sooner or later the spotlight would be turned in the British direction. The articles published in the *Guardian* ... were new in the manner they were presented rather than the facts they contained.'[57]

As with any media story, the contexts within which the story breaks, prospers or dies, often reveal as much as the story itself. The early 1970s was a period in which investigative journalism was particularly fashionable. In effect, newspapers were slightly more prepared to take a risk with a well-researched story than might have been the case in more conservative times. Successful investigations during this period included Seymour Hersh's My Lai massacre exposé, the *Sunday Times*'s Insight team's Thalidomide stories and the concurrent Watergate revelations. In 1973, the *Guardian* did not have a resident lawyer and, as Raphael points out, the copy was not read for libel:

> there was nothing cut out – the *Guardian* has a tradition that the writer has a high degree of control. Those pieces weren't read for libel and they weren't altered for libel either. It went in virtually unedited – I do not remember any correction at all. I had total control over it. For a start no-one else knew anything about the story – I had all the stuff in my notebooks ... There was such a row after as to whether I had the proof to say what I had actually said – all those questions should have been asked before. It shows ... how accidental newspapers are.[58]

The appearance of the *Guardian* story also related to the shifting British interests in Africa. Between 1971 and 1973, British exports to South Africa decreased by 12 per cent and, during 1972, exports to African Commonwealth countries (most notably, Nigeria) exceeded those to South Africa for the first time.[59] By 1973, the Conservative government, which had entered power in 1970 with a strong commitment to resume arms sales to South Africa, was in the process of adjusting its foreign policy to match the new economic realities. One week before the Raphael story appeared in the *Guardian*, Patrick Keatley had explained that 'The bitterness of a Radio Rhodesia commentator a few nights ago confirms that something significant is happening. British anxiety about oil supplies – Nigeria now provides 10 per cent of this country's needs – was, apparently more important than ancient ties of blood, he said. Kith and kin were going to be "thrown to the wolves".'[60] In addition, Britain's entry to the European Economic Community (EEC) on 1 January 1973 had transformed the terms of its trade with South Africa. The 45 per cent of South African exports to Britain which had previously been admitted duty free or at a reduced tariff would now incur the increased rates of the EEC's Common External Tariff. Although, there was a transitional period of two years of reduced EEC tariffs until 1 January 1975, the traditional relationship between Britain and South Africa had changed significantly. Douglas Evans observed 'As Britain buys 75 per cent of South Africa's canned fruit and ... imports more than the whole of the rest of the EEC, these are far from trifling issues.'[61]

An additional context of the wage starvation reports related to the question of the 'social responsibility' of capital. Originating from Ralph Nader's one-man campaigns in the United States, the issue of corporate responsibility (especially with regard to the environment) had entered the public consciousness. The concept of companies being answerable to their shareholders, and to a certain extent the media and the general public, was not extraordinary in 1973. Indeed, an organisation known as Counter-Information Services (CIS) had been publishing 'anti-reports' on major British companies since the previous summer.[62] The first of CIS's targets had been Rio-Tinto Zinc, the mining company with extensive interests in Namibia.[63] The second report issued by CIS targeted the General Electric Company. As the *Guardian* noted, 'In a 36-page booklet modelled on the company's own annual report, CIS accuses GEC of creating large-scale unemployment, under-paying its South African black workers, and of supplying equipment for the Vietnam war.'[64]

However, the most important context for the *Guardian*'s campaign was the ambiguous responses of the South African government, (white) population and media to both the Durban strikes and the wage revelations. Stanley Uys, reporting from the South African Parliament in Cape Town on 9 February, noted that 'Mr Vorster was in unusually sombre mood when he spoke about the strikes ... [he] said there was a lesson to be learned in them by everyone – the Government, Government-appointed wage boards, and employers.'[65] Five weeks later, Uys quoted a statement that the National Party MP, and later

Prime Minister, F.W. de Klerk, had given to the Afrikaans-language newspaper, *Rapport*: 'In so far as the present storm in the British press cleaves open the hypocrisy of these employers and helps to force them to pay fair wages to their black employees one is inclined to welcome the campaign in Britain.'[66]

In the aftermath of the Durban strikes, Ian Waller commented: 'The most remarkable feature of the Durban strike, which undoubtedly hastened a settlement, was the upsurge of support for the Africans from white South Africans, who suddenly realised how African workers were being exploited.'[67] Researching his story on starvation wages during this period provided Raphael with the insight to reflect the ambiguous concerns of white South Africa. Following the *Guardian*'s publication of Raphael's story, the *Rand Daily Mail* declared: 'When an overseas company accused of paying starvation wages to its African employees in South Africa says it didn't know, we find such a confession almost as disturbing as the initial accusation ... Mr Slater['s] ignorance of how his South African companies treat black workers is typical of many overseas enterprises operating here – particularly British enterprises.'[68] In retrospect, it is clear that the Durban strikes represented a significant juncture in the context of the British media's treatment of South Africa. However, it also displayed profound contradictions. As Stanley Uys explains:

> I don't think any of us really got a feel of the historical movement, looking back on it now. I think you saw the media at its best in the first couple of decades (the initial opposition to apartheid) ... and then a certain confusion set in, particularly when the blacks started flexing their muscles. I think also there was a certain ambivalence on the part of Rhoodie and others in the Department [of Information], they felt that firstly there was Raphael attacking the British employers – that in a sense what he was saying was that these were the worst of South African employers – in a way he was exonerating the Afrikaners. On the other hand they realised that this was a kind of Achilles heel ...[69]

The short-term effects and long-term consequences of the international media's treatment of the wage starvation story were varied. For Adam Raphael the story was a once-in-a-lifetime opportunity; he was feted on television and awarded the Granada Investigative Journalist of the Year and British Press Awards Journalist of the Year prizes for 1973.[70] For the *Guardian*, the story opened up a series of problems relating to litigation and advertising revenue. Alastair Hetherington recalled in his memoir that, following the publication of the wage starvation stories, 'there was undoubtedly a levelling off after a period of good growth in advertisement volume'.[71] Legal action and the threat of further litigation also served to enforce a level of moderation on the *Guardian*'s continuing treatment of the wages story.[72] Herein lies the explanation for the shift after the intensity of the first week's coverage towards the more restrained campaign for a Parliamentary Select Committee and the ensuing transformation of the story from exposé to domestic standard news (the reporting of a parliamentary inquiry).[73]

For the British businesses in South Africa which had been vilified by the media and were facing a degree of embarrassment in front of the parliamentary inquiry, the immediate response was a scramble to introduce marginal wage increases for African workers. Hetherington recalled in his memoir the case of Lord Stokes, the chairman of British Leyland: 'When he said that his company accepted "custom and practice" in South Africa, he was asked whether, if he had been in the cotton industry in the early nineteenth century, he would have accepted slavery as inevitable.'[74] However, by March 1974, W.E. Luke, the chairman of the United Kingdom–South Africa Trade Association (UKSATA) could claim an increase, on average, of over 50 per cent in the wages of African workers employed by British companies. He seized the opportunity to enjoy a sneer: 'Not fast enough for the *Guardian* but fast enough for most other people.'[75] It bears repetition to state that the increases in African wages were nevertheless minimal, raising wages only marginally above the poverty datum line.[76]

The effect on the Church of England General Synod was ambiguous and no conclusive decision was reached on the question of the sale of shares in British companies operating in South Africa. The British Trades Union Council (TUC)'s response to the scandal was to send a delegation (during October 1973) to investigate trade union conditions in the Republic. The TUC delegation published its report on the mission to South Africa on 15 December 1973. The report disappointed the A-AM by declaring a willingness to reconsider the TUC opposition to British investment in South Africa, if British businesses could show 'in a practical way that they were encouraging and recognising genuinely independent trade unions for African workers'.[77]

The report of the Trade and Industry Sub-Committee of the House of Commons' Select Committee on Expenditure, *Wages and conditions of African workers employed by British firms in South Africa*, was presented on 6 March 1974. Under the chairmanship of William Rodgers (Labour MP), the inquiry found that 63 of 141 British companies investigated had been paying wages below the poverty datum line. A small number of companies, whose names were not released, had refused to take part in the investigation. The report's main recommendations were: first, that a new code of practice should be established for British firms operating in South Africa; secondly, that British companies should create a timetable towards the payment of all African workers at the minimum effective level (50 per cent above the poverty datum line); and, finally, that the practice of lawful collective bargaining between companies and African employees should be established. The Sub-Committee referred directly to the media when it stated: 'The expectation that employment practices will be subject to public scrutiny would seem to be a potent force for progress.'[78]

The proposals issued by the British government amounted to a voluntary code of conduct for British companies. In this respect, the report resembled the code adopted by the EEC and the Sullivan principles announced in the United States of America in 1977. The significance of these principles or codes of conduct, in the opinion of William Minter, was that 'they fitted within parameters judged acceptable to the South African government, and diverted attention from the issue of apartheid's survival as a system to the narrower question of conditions within specific companies'.[79] Commentators described the report as 'a damp squib', 'the firework that didn't' and 'a mouse'.[80] This was partly due to the fact that the report was published in the interval between the British general election and the assembly of Parliament and therefore there was no debate on the subject, or questions to Ministers. Although the immediate impact of the Parliamentary Select Committee appeared to be relatively innocuous, it did, however, contribute to a tightening of focus on all things South African. As Malcolm Brown explained, 'If anything has been achieved in these early months of the campaign ... it is a change in the ground rules of the argument. It has been established that financial involvement in South Africa *is* a moral question.'[81]

The South African Department of Information's response to the Raphael–*Guardian* campaign demonstrated a number of ambiguities. During the immediate aftermath of the exposé, *To The Point* suggested that 'The present outcry for better wages is a clear defeat for the dis-investment lobby. The pendulum seems to be swinging towards the advocates of greater involvement. To this extent, we may approve it.'[82] A year later, following the publication of the report, a second editorial commented that 'We must overlook the subtle moralising tone which underlies reports like these, regarding them tolerantly as a remnant of the days of paternalism ... What, then, is the positive aspect of the report? It puts the British Labour Government firmly behind the idea of influencing the South African economic and political structure rather than isolating it.'[83] However, other voices within the Department of Information were preoccupied with negating and neutralising the campaign. Les de Villiers, for instance, claimed that 'It became abundantly clear, as this campaign developed, that wages were not the major concern. It was simply a way of getting at South Africa and embarrassing British business into either fighting "the system" or pulling out of the country.'[84] While detailing his perception of the 'over-the-top' coverage devoted to the subject, de Villiers criticised the fact that 'other areas where Britain had business interests and paid much lower wages remained almost hidden from public view'.[85] The suggestion that South Africa was not alone in playing host to exploitative foreign business had accompanied the Raphael story almost from the beginning.[86] Patrick Wall (Conservative MP) picked up the theme during a televised debate: 'why aren't we sending our teams to India [to] see what British firms are doing there? American firms are paying much less to their workers *I am told* in India, than they are in South Africa'[87] [my emphasis]. Two months later, the Club of Ten placed a half-page advertisement in *The Times* which reiterated the theme.[88]

There was also criticism of the *Guardian*'s campaign from another direction. Within days of the original appearance of the story, Nkomo Kairu stated in a letter to the editor: 'Why the white liberal patronage for Southern Africa now? By any chance a desire to mend, reform and sophisticate so white capitalism remains firmly on top considering the now threatening resurgence of black masses?'[89] Jonathan Steele, who was writing for the *Guardian* on the subject of Eastern Europe during the period of the newspaper's campaign, recalls :

> I felt that there was an element of show-business about this whole campaign ... First of all, we didn't look at the wider context of the South African economy ... The second thing that was unfortunate was that we tended to come out with the message that bad though British companies were, they were better than South African companies ... there was a sort of relativity that came into that ... and ipso facto, that we could lead the way in civilising the South African labour market ... The third thing, which was perhaps really the most important, was that it defused the disinvestment campaign.[90]

Nor was this statement made simply with the benefit of hindsight. In a letter to the *Guardian* in 1974, Steele noted that both the media campaign and the parliamentary inquiry had been side-tracked by the question of starvation wages ('which are not unique to South Africa'), and in the process failed to expose the central scandal of the growing gap between white and African wages.[91] While continuing to support the disengagement option in his letter, Steele diplomatically made no reference to his own experience of the *Guardian*'s unwillingness to discuss British economic withdrawal from South Africa: 'I did submit an article to the editor which was arguing the disinvestment case ... and it was turned down ... it was a political decision and it was explained as such.'[92] Reg September, the ANC's representative in London, offered a further criticism of the *Guardian*'s stance. Noting the newspaper's editorial comment that 'The answer seems to be that British investment in South Africa is an odious necessity both for Africans and for us', September described the *Guardian*'s faith in employers, to encourage and recognise African trade unions, as astounding and naive. Significantly, September also referred to the sub-text of the South African Department of Information's response to the coverage: 'South Africa is now very worried about the question of investments, judging by their international advertising and publicity campaigns'.[93]

The *Guardian* campaign was eventually forced to face the contradictions of its origins. By focusing on the brutal exploitation of the passive, 'starving', African, Raphael had invoked a representation which would strike a powerful chord with the readers of the British newspapers. In this respect it is not surprising that the story should be carried by the liberal *Guardian*. The passivity of Raphael's portrayal conjured up images of both the slave and the colonised subject. Although genuinely effective at rousing public opinion in Britain, this passive representation was fundamentally inaccurate. Without balancing the representation of the (passive) suffering of African workers in the context of *active* responses, such as the Durban strikes, which only a small amount of the coverage actually did, the end result was bound to be paternalistic, external, superior and separated. The passive nature of the representation also affected the journalists who followed Raphael. Few bothered to consult the African workers upon the question of wages, preferring to consult the managers of the British companies or subsidiaries.[94] Raphael himself cannot be held responsible for this as his original article did not refer to slavery, and he did consult Africans on the subject of their conditions of employment. Nevertheless, the lasting representational tone of the story was one of passivity. This dominant theme of passivity was exemplified by the fact that the Parliamentary Committee 'managed to avoid taking evidence from a single black South African ... after some pressing, the committee ... agreed to accept written evidence from the Anti-Apartheid Movement ... As for the African National Congress and the numerous South African exiles now living in London, the committee did not bother to consult them.'[95]

While the passive tone of the coverage was both somewhat offensive and misleading, passivity as a representational device did mobilise a reaction in the British press, amongst the British public and, finally, achieved a form of recognition in the parliamentary report. The most dramatic aspect of this passivity was the media's repeated use of slavery tropes. Even *Anti-Apartheid News* included the word 'slavery' in a sub-heading within the newspaper.[96] In her seminal account of British identity and popular consciousness in the eighteenth and early nine-teenth centuries, Linda Colley has noted the ambiguous impact of the anti-slavery campaign: the solidification of a sense of moral integrity which effectively negated the extension of the public debate. Colley's description of the parliamentary debates on the abolition of the slave trade as being 'as riddled with national pride and complacency as they are with genuine humanity' is strikingly similar to the ambiguity that dominated the entire British media's coverage of the wage starvation scandal.[97] The resilience of the slavery trope in the context of South Africa was not completely destroyed until the Soweto uprising and the well-publicised re-emergence of African agency.

Beneath the surface of the *Guardian*'s campaign, a struggle was being waged between those who were committed to the reform of South Africa and the business interests that suggested that increased investment would eventually transform the lot of the African worker and break down the apartheid ideology. The theory of reform through investment was developed by Michael O'Dowd, an official of the Anglo-American Corporation, and was often dubbed the 'Oppen-heimer thesis'. As Barbara Rogers has observed, the thesis 'played a useful role for investors in dividing and confusing the critics of financial support for South Africa'.[98] In addition, South African capital (and international capital invested in South Africa) had benefited from a period of extraordinary growth during the 1960s. This growth had been accompanied by favourable media reports which reflected O'Dowd's theory in slogans such as 'Richer is Lefter', and the assertion that 'South Africa's economic growth must continue to surge forward, bringing a rapid increase in the standard of living of all its peoples.'[99] In 1970, Frederick Johnstone, a radical political scientist, had demon-strated the many fallacies in the Oppenheimer thesis, most notably the miserable poverty which afflicted the vast majority of African workers. As he noted:

> All of the major white interest groups share responsibility for these conditions; they are not the product of apartheid policies alone. The employers, who in the prevailing thesis are pictured to be basically in conflict with white supremacy, in fact play an important role in

determining African wage rates. The very low wages of African workers, ... indicate what the response of employers to the rightlessness of African workers has tended to be. They have sought, and obtained, cheap labour.[100]

The contradictions inherent in the theory of reform through investment were brought into stark relief by the Durban strikes and the ensuing publicity devoted to African poverty. The *Guardian* campaign, therefore, served a dual function: on one level, the attention which was focused on British companies represented a warning of the potential for a public campaign in favour of disinvestment; on another level, the coverage defused the demand for a full-scale disinvestment campaign.[101] The response of both the British government and the opposition was to bury the subject in an inquiry. As Alan Watkins commented in the *New Statesman*, 'the inquiry is an exercise, at the lowest, in hypocrisy and, at the highest, in evading an issue. For the issue – and to say this is not to depreciate Mr Raphael or the *Guardian* – is surely not what wages firms pay in South Africa but whether they should be there at all.'[102] This ambiguity was reflected in the *Guardian*'s own decision to retain its company's pension fund investments in South Africa 'provided that the fund's influence is exerted to improve pay and conditions'.[103] This decision left the *Guardian* open to charges of hypocrisy. Indeed, *Private Eye* had commented within days of the original appearance of the Raphael story:

> The reek of humbug is strong over the Grays Inn Road offices of the *Grauniad* [Guardian], following the paper's pious crys of horror at the low wages paid to South African labourers by British firms ... Unfortunately for the *Grauniad*'s virgin-white conscience, the employees of the paper are not themselves free of the matter ... the *Grauniad*'s pension ... fund is run ... by Rothschilds the bankers and these wise and enterprising City men have seen fit to invest the *Grauniad*'s money where the pickings are richest, i.e. in South Africa ... nor can the *Grauniad* offer up the flimsy excuse that, like Jim Slater, they knew nothing about this. The issues was raised at an NUJ meeting over two years ago since when nothing has been done.[104]

In some ways the Raphael–*Guardian* campaign had marked an aberrant moment in the British media's treatment of South Africa. For a short period, the opportunity had been available to extend the reformist debate regarding South Africa into more radical areas. However, the Raphael story did have one long-term consequence: its example as a recurring reminder to international capital in South

Africa that there was now a partial measure for the duplicity of international capital. As William Rodgers had suggested in 1974, 'Public scrutiny and a live public conscience are the best means of ensuring that the recommendations of my Committee continue to produce results.'[105] Following the exposé in 1973, the wage starvation story continued to reappear at regular intervals in the British media.[106]

NOTES

1. Alastair Hetherington, *Guardian Years* (London, Chatto & Windus, 1981), p. 285.
2. Adam Raphael, *Grotesque Libels* (London, Corgi, 1993), p. 143.
3. A vital precedent to the Durban strikes was the strike by contract workers in Namibia (1971–72).
4. 'Black Workers' Mighty Movement', *Sechaba*, Vol. 7, No. 9 (September 1973), p. 18.
5. Adam Raphael, 'British Firms Pay Africans Starvation Rate', *Guardian*, 12 March 1973.
6. In addition to the photographs, Raphael also recorded a few minutes of 8mm film which was broadcast on 'First Report', ITN, 12 March 1973. Raphael's willingness to utilise different forms of media undoubtedly contributed to the impact of his exposé. He recalls that 'At one time I had glamorous ideas of being a picture journalist.' (Interview with Adam Raphael, 13 October 1995.) See also 'Lunchtime News', ITN and 'News at Ten', ITN, 12 March 1973.
7. Adam Raphael, 'The Company We Keep: Britain's Shame in Africa', *Guardian*, 12 March 1973.
8. Editorial, 'Scandal of African Labour', *Guardian*, 12 March 1973.
9. Editorial, 'Connivance in Wage Slavery', *The Times*, 13 March 1973.
10. Editorial, 'Economic Sense in South Africa', *Financial Times*, 13 March 1973.
11. John Miller, 'Pledge by British Firms in S Africa Over Black Wages', *Daily Telegraph*, 13 March 1973.
12. See Adam Raphael, 'Action After SA Pay Report', *Guardian*, 13 March 1973; Adam Raphael, 'Embarrassing Study on Africans' Wages', *Guardian*, 14 March 1973; Patrick Keatley and Christine Eade, 'Thorpe Wants MPs to Act as "Vigilantes" on S. Africa Firms', *Guardian*, 14 March 1973; Alec Hartley, 'Students Step Up Battle', *Guardian*, 14 March 1973; Reg September, Letter to the editor, *Guardian*, 14 March 1973; Ethel de Keyser, Letter to the editor, *Guardian*, 14 March 1973; Adam Raphael, 'Firm Promises Wage Rise for Africans', *Guardian*, 15 March 1973; Adam Raphael, 'More than 100 MPs Condemn British Pay in South Africa', *Guardian*, 16 March 1973; John Laurence, 'From the Cradle to the Grave', *Guardian*, 16 March 1973.
13. Editorial, 'The Case to be Answered', *Guardian*, 14 March 1973; Editorial, 'Above the Poverty Line', *Guardian*, 16 March 1973.
14. John O. Lyle, Letter to the editor, *The Times*, 15 March 1973; Adam Raphael, Letter to the editor, *The Times*, 16 March 1973.
15. Editorial, 'Starvation Wages', *Observer*, 18 March 1973.
16. Colin Legum, 'The Wages of Apartheid', *Observer*, 18 March 1973.
17. Suzanne Cronje, 'Black Wages', *Africa*, No. 22 (June 1973), p. 59. See also Reverend Michael Scott, 'Report on a Study Project on External Investment in South Africa and Namibia', *Objective: Justice*, Vol. 7, No. 4 (October–December

1975), pp. 31–3.

18. Benjamin Pogrund, 'No One Can Say: We Didn't Know about Black Workers', *Sunday Times*, 18 March 1973.
19. 'Behind the South African Workers' Row', *Sunday Telegraph*, 18 March 1973.
20. Editorial, 'The Unknown Scandal', *Sunday Mirror*, 18 March 1973.
21. Editorial, 'Wages in South Africa', *Daily Telegraph*, 19 March 1973.
22. 'They Should Have Known Someone Would Blow the Gaff', *The Economist*, 17 March 1973.
23. Editorial, 'Capital Illusion', *New Society*, 22 March 1973, pp. 631–32.
24. Adrian Guelke and Stanley Siebert, 'South Africa's Starving Work Force', *New Statesman*, 23 March 1973, pp. 407–9.
25. Peter Rodda, 'Et Tu, Britain', *Spectator*, 24 March 1973, pp. 362–63.
26. Editorial, 'A Select Committee Soon', *Guardian*, 19 March 1973.
27. Adam Raphael, 'A Chance Now to Look Beyond the Balance Sheet', *Guardian*, 19 March 1973.
28. Editorial, 'Time to Audit our Shame', *Guardian*, 28 March 1973.
29. 'Questions for Shareholders', *Guardian*, 13 April 1973.
30. Editorial, 'South Africa: Does British Money Bolster Apartheid?', *Guardian*, 3 April 1973; Editorial, 'Apartheid: The Long Battle', *Observer*, 8 April 1973, also favoured the 'multi-target approach'.
31. Joe Rogaly, 'The City's Duty to Black South Africa', *Financial Times*, 3 April 1973.
32. Adam Raphael, 'Slater Doubles the Lowest African Wages', *Guardian*, 9 April 1973.
33. Editorial, 'Why South Africa Prospers', *Guardian*, 9 February 1973.
34. 'South Africa Ties Troubling British', *New York Times*, 8 April 1973. See also John Allen May, 'British Firms Boost Pay of South African Blacks', *Christian Science Monitor*, 20 March 1973: '"The Guardian has done more for the Bantu people of South Africa in two days certainly in terms of income, than has been done in all the past ten years," my City of London informant declared.'
35. Raphael, *Grotesque*, pp. 143–44.
36. Interview with Adam Raphael, 30 September 1994. Ruth First, Jonathan Steele and Christabel Gurney, *The South African Connection: Western Involvement in Apartheid* (London, Temple Smith, 1972).
37. Raphael, *Grotesque*, p. 144.
38. Ibid., p. 145.
39. Editorial, 'The Frame Case', *African Communist*, No. 53 (Second Quarter 1973), p. 10.
40. Raphael's investigation used as its central source, the research into farm workers' wages gathered by the Wages Commission at the University of Natal, Pietermaritzburg (UNP), 1972. However, having checked the material with Mike Murphy (the chair of the commission and coordinator of the research during 1972), he was then guided around the Natal Midlands by Marc Dubois (the chairman in 1973). Dubois was at that time a lecturer in the UNP Geography Department. (Letter from Mike Murphy, 25 July 1995.)
41. Interview with Stanley Uys, 22 September 1994.
42. Raphael, *Grotesque*, p. 146.
43. Interview with Adam Raphael, 30 September 1994.
44. Interview with Ian Wright, 26 October 1994.
45. For information on Slater Walker, see Charles Raw, *A Financial Phenomenon: An investigation of the Rise and Fall of the Slater-Walker Empire* (New York, Harper & Row, 1977). As evidence that Raphael chose Slater Walker SA for its usefulness as a target rather than the fact that it was the worst of the British

employers, see B. Pogrund, 'African Workers Live in Squalor, Claim Students', *Sunday Times*, 25 March 1973. Describing the conditions on three wattle plantations owned by a subsidiary company of Courtaulds, Marc Dubois was quoted as saying, 'I think the conditions on this estate are far worse than on the estates owned by Natal Tanning & Extract Company [Slater-Walker SA].'

46. For the sake of brevity and because Raphael's reports failed to make any impact in the United States, this chapter only details the British precedents, although it should be borne in mind that the attention applied to US investments in South Africa had been one of Raphael's inspirations for the investigation. Precedents in the United States included Timothy H. Smith, *The American Corporation in South Africa: An Analysis* (New York, United Church of Christ, 1970); The Polaroid 'Experiment', advertisement, *New York Times*, 13 January 1971; *US Business Involvement in Southern Africa: Hearings before the Subcommittee on Africa of the Committee on Foreign Affairs*, parts 1 and 2 (Washington DC, US Government Printing Office, 1972); J.H. Chettle, 'US Corporations and South Africa', *South Africa International*, Vol. 2, No. 1 (July 1971), pp. 47–54; Michael Reisman, 'Polaroid Power: Taxing Business for Human Rights', *Foreign Policy*, No. 4 (Fall 1971), pp. 101–10; Charles C. Diggs Jr, 'Action Manifesto', *Issue*, Vol. 2, No. 1 (Spring 1972), pp. 52–60; John Blashill, 'The Proper Role of US Corporations in South Africa', *Fortune*, July 1972, pp. 48–91; Jim Hoagland, *South Africa: Civilisations in Conflict* (London, George Allen & Unwin, 1972), pp. 338–83; Frederic Hunter, 'Is Slavery Really Dead?', *Christian Science Monitor*, 27 June 1972; Wilfred Jenks (Director General, International Labour Office), 'Labour and Wages in South Africa', *Objective: Justice*, Vol. 4, No. 4 (October–December 1972), pp. 20–26.

47. Neil Wates' report to the board of Wates Construction was reprinted as a pamphlet: Neil Wates, *A Businessman Looks at Apartheid*, United Nations Unit on Apartheid, October 1970. Peter Hain recalls that Wates 'said that the Stop The Seventy Tour campaign had made him much more aware – so when he went out to South Africa, he started looking at it through [new eyes]'. (Interview with Peter Hain, 4 March 1996.)

48. Interview with Denis Herbstein, 17 November 1994. This is confirmed in a letter from Pogrund, who says: 'Yes, I remember passing this idea to Harry Evans. I can't recall how I got into this issue of what UK companies were paying but I knew it was important and it was too big and needed too much time and travelling for me to handle.' (Letter from Benjamin Pogrund, 25 May 1996.)

49. Denis Herbstein, 'South Africa: Do British Companies Set a Good Example or Just Collect the Profits?', *Sunday Times*, 18 April 1971 and all unattributed quotations from here. See also John Sackur, 'Casualties of the Economic Boom in South Africa', *The Times*, 26 April 1971. On Sackur's intelligence connections, see Harold Evans, *Good Times, Bad Times* (London, Weidenfeld & Nicolson, 1983), p. 73; Phillip Knightley, 'The Inside Story of Philby's Exposure', *British Journalism Review*, Vol. 9, No. 2 (1998), pp. 35–38.

50. Interview with Denis Herbstein, 17 November 1994. Hugo Young suggests that the reality might be less sinister and that the decision to place the story in the business section was probably due to Frank Giles's poor news judgement. (Interview with Hugo Young, 21 November 1995.)

51. Roy Macnab, 'Foreign Report', *South Africa International*, Vol. 2, No. 1 (July 1971), p. 65.

52. 'Thorpe Urges Pressure on Vorster with Shares', *Daily Telegraph*, 2 June 1972. For the ANC's response to Thorpe, see 'Dear Eartha Kitt: An Open Letter to Jeremy Thorpe and Eartha Kitt, With Friends Like These, Who Needs Enemies', *Sechaba*, Vol. 6, No. 9 (September 1972), pp. 2–3. For *Sechaba*'s contribution

to the precedents to the Raphael story, see Barbara Rogers, 'The Standard of Living of Africans in South Africa', parts 1 and 2, *Sechaba*, Vol. 6, Nos 7 and 8 (July and August 1972), pp. 22–24 and 21–24.

53. Douglas Brown, 'Economics and Apartheid', *Sunday Telegraph*, 24 September 1972.

54. Clifford Longley, 'Investment in South Africa: A Manual for the Opponents of Apartheid', *The Times*, 29 September 1972. Longley was the paper's religious affairs correspondent. See also Hugo Young, 'Any Other Business: The Black Facts about Britain's South African Connection', *Sunday Times*, 1 October 1972; Melvyn Westlake, 'Barclays on the Apartheid Hook', *The Times*, 22 November 1972; the *Guardian* carried a full page of excerpts from *The South African Connection* on 20 September 1972; See also Ruth First, *Foreign Investment in Apartheid South Africa*, United Nations Unit on Apartheid, No. 21/72 (October 1972); Two pages of extracts from *The South African Connection* were also carried in *Anti-Apartheid News*, November 1972, pp. 6–7. See also Ruth First, 'Foreign Investment in Apartheid South Africa', *Objective: Justice*, Vol. 5, No. 2 (April–June 1973), pp. 24–30.

55. Anti-Apartheid Movement, *Annual Report, September 1971–August 1972* (London, A-AM, 1972), pp. 11–12.

56. Muriel Horrell, Dudley Horner, John Kane-Berman and Robin Margo, *A Survey of Race Relations in South Africa, 1972* (Johannesburg, SAIRR, 1973), p. 119. The final precedent was William Raynor, 'Our Steel, S. African Stealth', *Guardian*, 19 December 1972. This full-page article contained a crucial statement from a board member of the British Steel Corporation (International): 'We must always be able to defend our behaviour as a business in the international context.' In addition, the article carried a photograph of an ironic advertisement placed by the Garment Workers Industrial Union of Natal: 'Wanted: Slaves At Starvation Wages'.

57. Bridget Bloom, 'Black Workers Blocked by the Law', *Financial Times*, 4 October 1973.

58. Interview with Adam Raphael, 30 September 1994.

59. Muriel Horrell and Dudley Horner, *A Survey of Race Relations in South Africa, 1973* (Johannesburg, SAIRR, 1974), p. 106; 'The Way the Cookie Crumbles', *The Economist*, 4 August 1973, p. 31.

60. Patrick Keatley, 'U-turns, No Signals', *Guardian*, 5 March 1973. See also Suzanne Cronje, 'Black African Backlash', *New Statesman*, 26 May 1972, pp. 695–96.

61. Douglas Evans, 'Many Happy Returns from South Africa', *The Times*, 15 March 1973.

62. Hugh Geach, one of the two founders of Counter-Information Services, had also been one of the instigators of the Stop the Seventy Tour campaign. Geach was involved in Young Liberal activity with Peter Hain.

63. Counter-Information Services, *The Rio-Tinto Zinc Corporation Limited Anti-Report* (London, CIS, 1972). See also 'The Anti-report on RTZ', *Financial Times*, 18 May 1972.

64. 'Radicals Hit Out at GEC', *Guardian*, 14 September 1972. Counter-Information Services, *The General Electric Company Limited Anti-Report* (London, CIS, 1972).

65. Stanley Uys, 'Whites Rethink after Durban', *Guardian*, 10 February 1973.

66. Stanley Uys, 'South African MP Hits Out at British Employers' "hypocrisy"', *Guardian*, 19 March 1973.

67. Ian Waller, 'S. Africans Learn Lesson of Durban, *Sunday Telegraph*, 11 February 1973.

68. Editorial, 'Their Business to Know', *Rand Daily Mail*, 15 March 1973.
69. Interview with Stanley Uys, 22 September 1994.
70. Raphael was 'banned' from re-entering South Africa in October 1973.
71. Hetherington, op. cit., p. 42.
72. For details on the legal action, both actual and threatened, against Adam Raphael and the *Guardian*, see Raphael, *Grotesque*, pp. 150–53, 158–63.
73. The *Guardian* did, however, continue to cover the story more intensely than any other newspaper. See Adam Raphael, 'All in Black and White', *Guardian*, 8 May 1973, on the plight of Ovambo workers in Namibia; David McKie, 'UK Firms "Still Paying Below Poverty Level"', *Guardian*, 13 June 1973, which carried extracts from Raphael's written evidence to the House of Commons Select Committee.
74. Hetherington, op. cit., p. 291.
75. Raphael, *Grotesque*, p. 155.
76. The 50 per cent increase in wages raised the rate to the 'minimum effective level'. This raised wages from a subsistence level (the poverty datum line) to the bare minimum acceptable for the purchase of food, heat, light and clothes. See Christian Concern for Southern Africa (CCSA), *British Companies in South Africa* (London, CCSA, 1974), pp. 5–9.
77. Muriel Horrell, Dudley Horner and Jane Hudson, *A Survey of Race Relations in South Africa, 1974* (Johannesburg, SAIRR, 1975), p. 318. For a trenchant critique of the TUC delegation's comments, see Suzanne Cronje, 'White-faced Trade Unionism', *New Statesman*, 2 November 1973, p. 642.
78. Adam Raphael summarised the report in 'Fair-play Code for British Firms in South Africa', *Guardian*, 7 March 1974. See also Joe Rogaly, 'Lombard: British Companies in South Africa', *Financial Times*, 19 August 1974: 'The public reminders keep on coming and they will continue to keep on coming.'
79. William Minter, *King Solomon's Mines Revisited: Western Interests and the Burdened History of Southern Africa* (New York, Basic Books, 1986), p. 288.
80. Benjamin Pogrund, 'How the Whites See It', *Sunday Times*, 10 March 1974; 'The Firework that Didn't', *The Economist*, 16 March 1974; Jonathan Steele, '"Pleasingly Moderate" Report Welcomed by White South Africans', *Anti-Apartheid News*, April 1974, p. 7.
81. Malcolm Brown, 'Apartheid: The Screw Turns', *The Times*, 15 March 1974.
82. Editorial, 'Black Wages', *To The Point*, 7 April 1973, p. 19.
83. Editorial, 'A Shift of Emphasis', *To The Point*, 17 May 1974, p. 19. Roy Macnab, of the SAF, was equally unconcerned: 'The fact that the *Guardian*, followed by the media generally, by its action – and its apparent success – has become willy-nilly an agent towards amelioration, must be a blow to them ... Political parties and the Press may argue *ad infinitum* the issues involved in contact with South Africa ... but in the City of London commercial considerations remain and, significantly, a South African share is still called by a name that is unmentionable in any other context.' (Roy Macnab, 'Foreign Report: London', *South Africa International*, Vol. 4, No. 1 (July 1973), pp. 58–59.) South African shares continued to be referred to as 'kaffir shares' during the 1970s.
84. Les de Villiers, *South Africa: A Skunk Among Nations* (London, International Books, 1975), p. 159.
85. Ibid., p. 161.
86. See, for example, David Blundy, 'Coloured Seamen Paid £4 a Week on British Ships', *Sunday Times*, 1 April 1973.
87. 'Money at Work: The South African Connection (Part 2)', BBC 2, 4 May 1973. Patrick Wall was a noted friend of South Africa. A few weeks later, the *Sunday Telegraph* instituted an examination which supported Wall's position. Staff

writers (including A.J. McIlroy), 'Close Up Investigation: Is the Black Boss Any Better than the White?' and 'Cures for Africa's Black Exploiters', *Sunday Telegraph*, 27 May–3 June 1973.

88. The Club of Ten, 'Does Britain have a Conscience?', *The Times*, advertisement, 28 July 1973. See illustrations. During August 1973, Gordon Winter visited Hong Kong (on the advice of General van den Bergh) to research a story on the wages paid by British companies to Chinese employees. Gordon Winter, *Inside BOSS: South Africa's Secret Police* (Middlesex, Penguin, 1981), pp. 421–26). See Gordon Winter, 'British Shame in Hong Kong', [Johannesburg] *Sunday Express*, 9 September 1973. The story was repeated by Richard Hughes, 'Children in Scandal of 36,000 Jobs', *Sunday Times*, 16 September 1973.

89. Nkome Kairu, Letter to the editor, *Guardian*, 24 March 1973.

90. Interview with Jonathan Steele, 15 November 1994.

91. Jonathan Steele, Letter to the editor, *Guardian*, 9 March 1974. See also Suzanne Cronje, 'Whitewashing Apartheid', *Africa*, No. 33 (May 1974), pp. 68–69.

92. Interview with Jonathan Steele, 15 November 1994.

93. Reg September, Letter to the editor, *Guardian*, 9 March 1974; Editorial, 'Our Employees in South Africa', *Guardian*, 4 March 1974. For previous ANC or A-AM statements on the issue of wage starvation, see Reg September, 'Withdraw Now, says ANC', *Anti-Apartheid News*, May 1973, p. 3; A-AM, 'Poverty Wages', *Sechaba*, Vol. 7, No. 6 (June 1973), pp. 21–22. See also Alan Brooks, 'Parliamentary Committee Defends British Capital', *Anti-Apartheid News*, April 1974, pp. 6–7.

94. An exception was David Taylor's report for 'Money at Work: The South Africa Connection', BBC 2, 27 April 1973. Having utilised the same guides as Raphael, Taylor visited a sugar plantation owned by Tate & Lyle. In response to Chief Buthelezi's comment that South Africa had a 'tradition of slavery', Taylor asserted 'the African worker is no longer a passive slave figure. The Durban strikes prove this.'

95. 'Open File', *Guardian*, 29 December 1973. See also Alan Brooks, 'Parliamentary Committee Defends British Capital', *Anti-Apartheid News*, April 1974, p. 7.

96. '"Respectable" Firms who Cash in on Slavery', *Anti-Apartheid News*, May 1973, p. 7. There was obviously a significant degree of confusion within the A-AM representation of the wage starvation subject: the cover of the same edition of *Anti-Apartheid News* displayed a portrait of 'active' striking workers, with the subtitle: 'When massive TV and newspaper exposure can't persuade greedy British bosses to pay African workers a living wage, don't they deserve what's coming to them?' Only the South African Communist Party journal, *African Communist*, managed to avoid all mention of slavery.

97. Linda Colley, *Britons: Forging the Nation, 1707–1837* (New Haven, CT, Yale University Press, 1992), p. 358. For example, Colin Legum, 'The Wages of Apartheid', *Observer*, 18 March 1973. 'Not since the early part of the nineteenth century, when the campaign for the abolition of slavery was led by an influential part of the Establishment, have British businessmen had to face such a moral challenge to their right to profit from black men's sufferings as they face now over their role in South Africa's economy.'

98. Barbara Rogers, *White Wealth and Black Poverty: American Investments in Southern Africa* (Westport, CT, Greenwood Press, 1976), p. 70.

99. Norman Macrae, 'The Green Bay Tree', survey, *The Economist*, 29 June 1968, pp. x and xlvi. See also Norman Macrae, 'Foreign Report: What Will Destroy Apartheid?', *Harper's Magazine*, March 1970, pp. 30–42. 'It is known that both Nixon and Kissinger read Norman Macrae's version of the O'Dowd thesis' (Rogers, op. cit., p. 159).

100. Frederick A. Johnstone, 'White Prosperity and White Supremacy in South Africa Today', *African Affairs*, Vol. 69, No. 275 (April 1970), pp. 135–36. Johnstone also observed that the real value of African wages had actually decreased during the period of exceptional South African economic growth (p. 135).

101. Voices favouring disinvestment were extremely rare in the mainstream British media. One notable exception was 'Money at Work: The South African Connection', BBC 2, 27 April 1973, which included an interview with David Hemson in which he stated that 'I do feel that the right line is to withdraw British capital because it's the only way in which we will really get change.' Hemson was 'banned' by the South African government on 1 February 1974.

102. Alan Watkins, 'Spotlight on Politics: South Africa and The Commons', *New Statesman*, 4 May 1973, p. 638.

103. *Guardian*, 16 May 1973. Out of 206 potential National Union of Journalists (NUJ) voters, 155 actually voted. Of these, 82 voted for the motion; 38 voted for disinvestment and 15 voted 'for keeping the investment solely to maximise the return'.

104. *Private Eye*, No. 294, 23 March 1973, p. 5. The term 'Grauniad' was a joke which referred to the regular printing errors in the *Guardian*. See also 'Gnome', *Private Eye*, No. 294, 23 March 1973, p. 5; *Private Eye*, No. 340, 10 January 1975, p. 4: 'Never Mind the Wages, Feel the Dividend.'

105. *British Companies in South Africa* (London, CCSA, 1974), foreword.

106. Joe Rogaly, 'Society Today: Questions British Firms Should Answer', *Financial Times*, 18 November 1975. Following a fresh survey by CCSA: Adam Raphael, 'Firms Ignore Black Pay Call' and 'Why the Law Must Act on this Neglect', *Guardian*, 26 April 1976; Denis Herbstein and David Blundy, 'Apartheid: The Workers Britain Betrayed', *Sunday Times*, 16 May 1976; Following an analysis of company information sent to the Department of Trade: Adam Raphael, 'Starvation Wages from Firms in South Africa' and Editorial, 'The Wages of Shame', *Observer*, 18 December 1977. During the same month, Anglia Television (ATV) broadcast a documentary film made by Antony Thomas which examined working conditions in British companies in South Africa: 'The South African Experience', ATV, 21 December 1977. Tate & Lyle Ltd objected to its representation in the documentary and attempted to have the programme withdrawn. It also placed an advertisement to protest: 'An Announcement by Tate & Lyle Limited', *Daily Express*, 14 December 1977.

6

The 'Little Mistake', 1975–76

A mixture of secrecy, propaganda, outright lies and obstruction from both sides has made coverage of the war a nightmare of frustration. None of the three factions has yet permitted reporters to accompany its troops along the shadowy battlefronts, nor witness any of their reported engagements ... only the accidents of the war – the capture of some of its participants – have indicated who is fighting it and where it is being fought.[1]

The world's knowledge of the war comes from reporters sitting in cities usually many miles from the fighting, assessing how much truth there is in the inflated claims being pressed on them and then sending their stories to editors who have to look at reports from all sides and attempt to see where the truth lies.[2]

The previous chapter examined Adam Raphael's wage starvation exposé and discussed the debate that ensued. Raphael's story originated from an individual's research, was confined to the British media and, despite its precedents, was a genuine aberration. In contrast, the coverage of the war in Angola represented no more than another chapter in the long history of war correspondence. South Africa's military intervention in a neighbouring country, although extraordinary in 1975, became a regular event during the 1980s. The original 'incursion' in Angola, however, remains the subject of speculation. Genuinely reliable sources are rare, while most official sources are still closed, but it is possible to construct a chronology (albeit, contested) from the media reports of the period, memoirs and academic studies.[3] The chronology that emerges from an amalgam of these sources suggests that the South African Defence Force (SADF) entered Angola as early as June 1975.[4] The paucity of references to Cuban involvement during the summer of 1975 reveals that the long-standing debate regarding who intervened first, the Cubans or the South Africans, was at best a distraction, and at worst a smokescreen.[5] This distraction had the effect of disguising (and indirectly justifying) the internationalisation of the Angolan war, thereby promoting the supposition that both the Cubans and the South Africans were functioning as proxy representatives of the Soviet Union and the United States, respectively.

In 1977, Robin Hallett wrote an article for *African Affairs* entitled 'The South African Intervention in Angola, 1975–76'. While acknowledging the 'official smoke screen [or] deliberately created miasma' which accompanied the war, he expressed his trust in 'having at his disposal a remarkably wide range of press reports, the work of enterprising and level-headed observers, drawing their material from a wide range of informants'.[6] However, Hallett did not consider it necessary to investigate the backgrounds or identities of these 'level-headed observers'. Robert Moss, for example, was far more than 'an Australian journalist based in London' who just happened to be 'an ardent supporter of Savimbi'.[7] Moss was suspected of having extensive intelligence contacts and his books, *Chile's Marxist Experiment* and *The Collapse of Democracy* had provided 'the rationale for extreme Right-wing government in Chile and Britain, respectively'.[8]

The media coverage of the South African invasion of Angola is examined in this chapter through a consideration of the problems of reporting from areas controlled by the Popular Movement for the Liberation of Angola (MPLA) and the National Union for the Total Liberation of Angola (UNITA); the exposure of the South African involvement; the shifts in the positions adopted by the commentators and editorial-writers; and the partiality of the coverage. The coverage of the Angolan war falls somewhere between what has been regarded as the 'open' access of the Vietnam war and the 'closed' nature of the Falklands and Gulf wars. In some respects, the manipulation of reporting in Angola represented the first stage in a process which would be developed further during the war in Afghanistan. The journalist in Angola undoubtedly faced many problems. Bridget Bloom, reporting from Luanda, commented on the eve of independence:

> communiqués are infrequent and hardly informative ... all information is strictly controlled ... Trying to find the source and particularly to examine the truth of the multitude of rumours is what journalists should be doing here just now, but the task is far from easy ... Just as important in terms of news gathering is that there is (for obvious reasons) no contact with the rival liberation movements ... and, less understandable, now that we all have our credentials reaffirmed very little with the MPLA itself – it was announced for example on Wednesday [5 November] that no one in Government would grant interviews until after independence [11 November].[9]

While the situation in Luanda was undoubtedly critical during the period of Bridget Bloom's visit, the MPLA does appear to have had a particularly antipathetic relationship with Western journalists. This was demonstrated by the number of journalists expelled from Luanda: a BBC 'Panorama' team was arrested and expelled at the beginning of November 1975; a CBS television crew was detained on 22 November; Reuters had no representative in Luanda from 16 November; and, during February 1976, A.J. McIlroy and an ITN film crew were ordered to leave the country.[10] Perhaps the most powerful example of the MPLA's poor relationship with the international media was the harassment which occurred during the night of 4 November 1975. Nicholas Ashford reported:

> I was awakened at 4.30 am, with a loud knocking on the door. When I opened it two Africans in civilian clothes burst into the room brandishing automatic pistols ... I was forced to get dressed at gun point while the soldiers conducted a cursory search of my room. I was then taken downstairs and made to wait in the hotel lobby for about three hours. Eventually, having inspected my press credentials, they allowed me to return to my room. Other journalists were not so fortunate. Some who were staying in a neighbouring hotel, including the correspondents of the *New York Times* and *Le Monde*, were taken away and kept in cells until about 10 am.[11]

As the critical period of November 1975 passed and the invading South African force became stalled, the MPLA developed a structure designed to aid the distribution of news.[12] Will Ellsworth-Jones, who covered Luanda for the *Sunday Times* between January and February 1976, explained how the media relations system functioned during this period: 'reporters were effectively divided into four categories for the purpose of getting anywhere near the front ... first [in] were the Cuban reporters ... next came the Eastern bloc ... third in line came the Western sympathisers ... last came the Western reporters who usually made it a minimum of two weeks after any town had been captured'.[13] However, journalists who had been in Luanda at the time of independence commented in their articles on how much less restrictive the reporting process had become.[14] In contrast to the MPLA, Jonas Savimbi seemed to thrive on publicity, as Chris Munnion explains:

> Savimbi had a natural flair for public relations. Hacks attempting to cover the situation in Angola were meeting great resistance from the government in Luanda which, if they approved a visa, would lay on a

strictly regimented 'programme'. The South Africans were similarly discouraging about visits to the northern border of Namibia and Angola.
The flamboyant and vain Savimbi found foreign correspondents only
too willing to visit him in the territory he controlled and, inevitably, to
put across his case and his views.[15]

Savimbi was, in reality, trapped within a public relations contradiction. He needed positive publicity in which he would be applauded
as an 'anti-communist' in order to appease his international backers,
but he could not afford his links with the South Africans (or the
Portuguese) to be made public.[16] Before December 1975, UNITA's
media relations team managed to control the representation of their
organisation and leader with some success. The claim that Savimbi was
the 'peace candidate' (he had entered the war after the National Front
for the Liberation of Angola (FNLA) and the MPLA) was promoted
alongside the assumption that UNITA would win a democratic
election (and, by extension, was therefore democratic).[17] Perhaps most
significantly, Savimbi's willingness to be interviewed helped to convince the journalists that he was 'a rather friendly character with not
too much in the way of pure doctrine to impede him in negotiations'.[18]
As Savimbi's relationship with the South Africans began to become
apparent, especially following the display of the South African
prisoners by the MPLA (13 December 1975), UNITA's propaganda
became confused. This confusion involved completely contradictory
statements.[19] To compound the problem, Jorge Sangumba (the foreign
affairs spokesman of UNITA) began to permit large numbers of
journalists to report from UNITA territory. While the majority of the
correspondents continued to be hypnotised by Savimbi's 'charm',
others began to discover a darker side to UNITA.[20] Henry Kamm, for
instance, noted that journalists and photographers were having their
camera films 'seized at gunpoint'.[21]

Although J.S. Marsh asserted that 'Prevented from filing the stories
they liked from Luanda, the press ... decamped to UNITA territory',
this failed to recognise that most reporters found it equally difficult
to perform their task in UNITA territory. Michael Kaufman quoted a
French photographer who had recently been in Huambo as saying:
'I've been waiting for two weeks to see action ... They promise and
they promise and meanwhile they take me for tourist junkets to nice
towns and cities where the people come out to cheer their leaders.'[22]
Sinister evidence also began to emerge that journalists who disobeyed
regulations were locked up and forgotten. During a visit to interview
three Cuban prisoners held by UNITA in Silva Porto, journalists
reported that 'Two white men who had not been seen before emerged

with the Cubans. They were barefoot, wearing ragged clothes and looking extremely dejected ... Journalists questioned them and they replied in French, that they also were journalists.'[23]

On the whole, the media's treatment of Jonas Savimbi was sympathetic. One example of this was the UPI report which commented that UNITA's 'public-relations efforts have either been totally incompetent or deliberately infiltrated by enemies. There have been a series of inexplicable and highly embarrassing incidents recently to fuel these fears.'[24] The UPI reporter did not suggest that Savimbi and his supporters had been engaging in attempts to manipulate the media. Following UNITA's defeat, very few journalists followed up the reports of the discovery of mass graves in the liberated territories.[25] By this point, the representation of Savimbi as an anti-communist guerrilla fighter had been well-established.[26] To summarise, while the war (and the South African involvement in it) was by no means a secret, it did possess a certain 'Alice in Wonderland' quality. Few, if any, journalists actually witnessed any fighting, and only a few seconds of film of the South Africans ever appeared.[27] This surreal quality was exaggerated by the journalists' dependence upon sources in Lusaka, Kinshasa and Pretoria and the fact that these sources were consistently manipulated by bogus statements issued by the CIA, amongst other intelligence agencies.[28] As journalists became aware of the degree of covert propaganda, all official statements became suspect. This eventually meant that any statements from the FNLA, UNITA or the MPLA were considered problematic until verified and, as has been noted, verification was often impossible.[29]

In his book, *The First Casualty*, Phillip Knightley maintains that the changes in news-gathering which journalists experienced in Rhodesia in the late 1970s originated in the theory that the correspondents in Vietnam had been responsible for the American defeat: 'Throughout the world governments took note ... [and] saw the danger of giving the media unfettered access to the war zone, and made contingency plans to control the flow of information if war should come. Suddenly, from Rhodesia to Afghanistan, correspondents found doors closed to them.'[30] Angola represented a very early stage in this process; this partly explains the 'Wonderland' quality of its war. The available evidence also suggests that the CIA used Angola as a testing ground to see whether the media could be manipulated during a civil war. Roger Morris, who had been Henry Kissinger's former African Affairs assistant in the US National Security Council, quoted a source as saying: 'I think Kissinger saw [Angola] as the place to find out if you could still have covert operations.'[31] It is also significant that the turnover of journalists in Angola was rapid. Only a handful of correspondents saw both sides of the conflict; the vast majority made one-off visits to either Luanda or Huambo.[32] Indeed, journalists who managed to stay in the same place for an extended period often filed for a number of different news organisations.[33] The fact that very few British or American journalists spoke Portuguese also benefited UNITA at the expense of the MPLA. Jane Bergerol believes that 'The British and American press ... are powerless to appreciate any situation where English is not a vehicle ... The MPLA did not speak good English and therefore were at a major disadvantage.'[34] As if to confirm the importance of the language issue, Max Hastings commented in one of his reports that 'we had dinner with two young UNITA officers, both educated ... both of whom spoke English well'.[35]

The first report in the international media on the subject of South African troops in Angola appeared in the *Diario de Noticias* (a Lisbon daily newspaper) on 11 August 1975.[36] *The Economist*'s response was to suggest that the South Africans might intend to annexe the Ruacana dam.[37] The *Financial Times* reported the MPLA's fears that South Africa might take advantage of the civil war to encourage a 'balkanisation' of the country: 'a "Katanga-type" solution'.[38] Nevertheless, during the months of September and October 1975, very few British or American journalists examined South African military activity in southern Angola; the handful who did comment noted that South Africa had not interfered with Mozambique's independence. In addition, as Antonio de Figueiredo reported from Lisbon, 'Conflicting reports of South African and mercenary activity in Angola meet with indifference here because everyone is too absorbed with Portugal's internal situation.'[39]

Leslie Gelb's investigative account of CIA activity in Portugal and Angola neglected to mention South Africa, although South African activity in Angola was actually intensifying during this period.[40] 'White mercenaries' were occasionally referred to in reports, but these were normally assumed to be Portuguese. The emphasis of articles continued to be influenced by 'well-informed sources' in Lusaka. An example was a report in *The Times* (24 October) in which it was suggested that between 1,400 and 1,700 Cubans were either in, or on their way to, Angola. Almost as a footnote, the newspaper recorded that 'A military spokesman for MPLA ... said in a radio broadcast that the "massive" South African force was moving towards the town of Sa da Bandeira, some 130 miles north of the border with Namibia.'[41] Disregarding this announcement, the international media continued to downplay MPLA claims (or 'accusations').[42] During early November, as the South African column drew closer to Luanda and the number of correspondents in the city increased due to Angola's impending independence, a handful of journalists began to unearth details which implied (even if they did not prove) direct South African involvement.[43]

Fred Bridgland's (Reuters) first visit to Angola had been on 21 September. He recounts in his uncritical biography of Jonas Savimbi that 'Very little attention was being paid to Angola. Rhodesia, the aftermath of Vietnam, Mrs Indira Gandhi's suspension of democracy in India, and the ever-simmering Middle East attracted international media attention ... when a UNITA representative in Lusaka offered a flight into the country, it sounded like an interesting diversion from Rhodesian nationalist politics.'[44] Bridgland, accompanied by Nicholas Ashford, lodged in the former Portuguese governor's residence in Silva Porto. On the next day, they interviewed Savimbi. Bridgland was impressed and remained in Angola until 7 October, when, disappointed by UNITA's refusal to take him to the military front, he returned to Lusaka. Three weeks later, following the reports of the military successes of the anti-MPLA forces, Bridgland returned to Angola 'to try to discover what had turned the tide in UNITA's favour'.[45] Arriving at Silva Porto on 1 November, he spotted two trucks towing brand new armoured cars and approached one of the drivers:

> I greeted him in Portuguese. When that brought no response I asked him in English what language he spoke. 'English' he replied – except that the gravelly accent was a product of southern Africa, not some genteel English county. I asked him where he came from and he replied grudgingly and gutturally: 'I am from Inger-land.' I sauntered to the second armoured car where another young white sat in the driving compartment ... when I asked him where he came from he said: 'I am a mercenary.' Good, but from which country? – 'I cannot say.' However, the accent, obviously developed at his mother's knee south of the Orange and Limpopo rivers, spoke for him.[46]

Four days later, Bridgland returned to Lusaka to file his report, which at this time made no mention of the South African 'mercenaries': 'two or three armoured cars whose white drivers declined to confess they were South African soldiers were insufficient evidence to back up a story for my international news agency of an invasion of another country by Pretorian hordes'.[47] Bridgland's companion on this flight was Robert Moss, who later provided an account of his visit for the *Spectator*. Moss's article referred to the 'allegations of South African and Western backing for the "rebel" movements', and claimed that the MPLA 'propagandists were shifting tack in an attempt to blame their reverses on the intervention of the South African and Portuguese "mercenaries"'.[48] Michael Nicholson (ITN) had also arrived at Silva Porto on 1 November. After two days of waiting in the governor's mansion, Nicholson decided to investigate for himself:

> I walked to UNITA's headquarters at the airfield and wandered from empty room to empty room until I heard voices. A door was open. I saw an official at his desk. I entered, and very quickly the door was held firm, blocking me, but I had already seen the leg: a long, tanned leg … It didn't mean, of course, that the South African military were there in any numbers but having sighted one of them, all we needed to do was to find his friends and we had something of a sensational story to send home.[49]

Nicholson returned to Lusaka on 9 November, sharing his flight with Fred Bridgland. The two journalists pooled their suspicions of the South African incursion and decided that they would work together in an attempt to unravel the riddle.[50] On 10 November, they returned to Angola with Andrew Jaffe (*Newsweek*), ostensibly to report UNITA's independence celebrations. The flight landed at Huambo and Jaffe was encouraged to leave the aeroplane.[51] The pilots, who had befriended Nicholson during the previous evening, allowed Bridgland and Nicholson to remain on board while the aeroplane detoured to the Caprivi Strip in Namibia for refuelling: 'The pilots said they would show us something which would interest us as journalists. The conditions were that we agreed not to report either the flight or anything we saw or ask too many questions.'[52] The sight from the aeroplane window convinced Nicholson and Bridgland that they were at the military staging post for South Africa's war in Angola. Many years later, Bridgland commented: 'It seemed slightly unreal: for some reason best known to themselves, for we never asked them, the pilots had guided us directly to the firmest evidence possible of South Africa's involvement in Angola.'[53] Returning to Huambo, the aeroplane picked up Jaffe, and Nicholson's camera crew, and continued to Benguela. During the drive from the airstrip to the town, their bus was stopped at a roadblock which was manned by 20 white soldiers: 'One … was unmistakably South African. There were no identification marks on his uniform … even the man's name – normally stencilled over the right-hand breast pocket – had been inked out … Nor were we looking at mercenaries, but neat, spruce, young men with clipped hair and pressed uniforms – conscripts, who made up the bulk of the South African army.'[54] While returning to the aeroplane, Nicholson's cameraman, Alan Downes, managed to record some film of the South African soldiers.[55] The journalists proceeded to Huambo in order to cover the independence celebrations. On 12 November, they returned to Lusaka.

In order to gather more supporting evidence for their scoop, Bridgland and Nicholson returned to Angola. They managed to find Savimbi in Lobito and, during a press conference, questioned him on the subject of South African involvement. Savimbi, however, continued to shroud his answers in ambiguity: 'I need people to fight with armoured cars that we cannot operate ourselves, maybe they are South African [or] Rhodesian, but there are more French ... The MPLA they had Russians with them. We had to address ourselves to people who could match them.'[56] Eventually, Savimbi lost patience with his questioners. Grabbing Jaffe's arm, he said: 'Here I am fighting Communism. Trying to stop the Russians from taking over Angola. And instead you hold me up to ridicule over the whites. You do this to your own Presidents too, don't you? What's the matter – don't you want to live in a democracy?'[57] Bridgland's and Nicholson's reports were filed simultaneously on 14 November in keeping with their agreement to release the news at the same time. Although both journalists had achieved the exposé of the Angolan war, somewhat surprisingly the immediate impact was not that great. One explanation can be found in the fact that Nicholson's film was not particularly convincing: the 'snatched' film was only 25 seconds long and the (two) white faces in long shot were only on the screen for 11 seconds. In addition, Nicholson's report began with a survey of the conquest of Lobito in which there was no mention of Cuban troops, although one Soviet-made weapon was held up to demonstrate 'how totally reliant the MPLA is on Russian supplies'.[58]

Tony Hodges, who had been at Benguela with Nicholson, Bridgland and Jaffe, filed his report for the *Observer*.[59] The story was not considered worthy of front-page treatment. Andrew Jaffe's commentary for *Newsweek* failed to state that South African soldiers were fighting inside Angola.[60] Bridgland records that when he submitted his copy on 14 November, Reuters 'were still nervous about stating categorically that South Africa had invaded Angola' so the news agency retained the 'white mercenary' safety clause.[61] The story received by the international subscribers opened as follows: 'Columns of armoured vehicles manned by whites are rolling across wide stretches of Angola through the defences of the MPLA, informed sources said, amid reports of a build-up of Russian, Cuban and Mozambican troops in the MPLA stronghold of Luanda. The major unanswered question remains the origin of the white soldiers.' Towards the end of his report, Bridgland quoted a Portuguese informant, working with UNITA, as stating that 'The South Africans are doing a good job. They are professionals.'[62] The overall effect of Bridgland's story was not clarity but confusion. Six days later, Reuters capitulated and ran a more assertive report: 'South African regular troops are fighting many hundreds of miles … inside Angola.'[63]

Following the publication of Bridgland's (unabridged) report in the *Washington Post*, John Stockwell, the CIA Chief of the Angola Task Force, commented in his memoirs: 'The propaganda and political war was lost in that stroke. There was nothing the Lusaka station could invent that would be as damaging to the other side as our alliance with the hated South Africans was to our cause.'[64] Yet although Stockwell, Bridgland and Nicholson, among others, believed that the 14 November scoop established a negative image of UNITA, the evidence tends to suggest something quite different. It was in fact the conjunction of Cuban reinforcements, and disinformation from the CIA stations in Kinshasa and Lusaka that transformed the war from a struggle between three African factions (and their backers) 'over an obscure piece of African real estate' into a chapter in the Cold War.[65] An example of this was the editorial in the *New York Times* published under the title, 'Angola Intervention': 'There was a time when the United States would have responded to such a massive and menacing intervention with its own show of force, but that is something that the American people would never countenance now.'[66] This diatribe against Soviet imperialism did not mention the South Africa engagement. To a certain extent, the escalation of the war shielded the South African state from global recrimination. While the majority of the observers of the Angolan war became distracted by the Cold War implications, only the vigilant few concentrated on the South African presence.[67]

Marsha Coleman's study of elite American newspapers' coverage of the Angolan war correctly asserts that 'the US press underreported the fact of South African intervention and when it did report this, failed to do so in the same negative and emotional terms in which it reported the Cuban involvement'.[68] However, Coleman's thesis neglected to acknowledge either the dominance of the Cold War paradigm or the relative transformation which the American media underwent in their treatment of Angola following the reporting of the South African invasion. This shifting position was directly related to:

> [the] unprecedented series of 'leaks' to the press by various members of Congress and other opponents of US intervention in government agencies … Over the next two months [from 7 November] there were so many leaks about American covert activities in Angola that, according to one knowledgeable source in State Department intelligence, only minor details escaped the attention of the public; 'all of the essential facts were published in the newspapers'.[69]

Does Britain have a conscience?

Britain is concerned about its business reputation abroad. Prompted by the press, Members of Parliament are investigating black wages paid by British Industry in South Africa. *It is encouraging to hear that the South African government also sees a need to improve black wages; and reassuring to know that our companies operating out there have never been inhibited by law in this respect.*

But does Britain really have a conscience or is it simply reacting to anti-South African pressures? *After all,* that country represents only 15% of our total investment abroad.

Let us insist that Members of Parliament also probe British wages in India, Black Africa, Ceylon and Hong Kong and all the other areas that make up 85% of our commitment abroad.

And while we are in the midst of this conscience crisis, how about wages at home *where charity is supposed to begin?* On May 9, The Times reported: "Most Asian seamen in the British Merchant Fleet are Indians, who now earn a basic £24.48 a month. There are also 1,600 Pakistanis, who earn a basic £14.69 a month and 1,000 Bangladeshi earning £16.73 a month. Minimum rates for British seamen are now £94.00 a month."

Does Britain really have a conscience?

Let us write to our MPs and insist that all wages be investigated at home and abroad before we answer that question.

SPONSORED BY:
THE CLUB OF TEN, 2 GREAT MARLBOROUGH STREET, LONDON W.1

1. Club of Ten, 'Does Britain Have a Conscience?', *The Times*, 28 July 1973. This advertisement was a direct reponse to the Adam Raphael/*Guardian* starvation wages exposé. See Chapter 5.

AN ANALYSIS
OF INDIGNATION

It is almost a year ago that a series of articles by Mr Adam Raphael on black wages in South Africa appeared in The Guardian. This series earned Mr Raphael a press award as news reporter of the year.

Our Parliamentarians took over where Mr Raphael signed off. A Government committee probed British operations in South Africa and provided these companies with "guidelines" on wage increases.

In the end it was claimed that Mr Raphael's series on South Africa led to a dramatic string of wage rises. Mr Harry Oppenheimer, Chairman of Anglo American, however, contended in London recently that changes were taking place in any event—without interference from Britain.

In his speech at Chatham House, Mr Oppenheimer hinted that the concern shown by Raphael for black employees of British firms in South Africa "is not felt in anything like the same degree in regard to British firms operating, say, in Hong Kong or India, or elsewhere in the African continent."

Mindful of the fact that Mr Raphael may want to earn another press award in this field, we have taken great care not to scoop him on the real in-depth story of labour conditions at British establishments in Hong Kong, Sri Lanka, Singapore and a host of black African countries, but these facts are beyond dispute:

We found that on sugar plantations in South Africa, workers earned something like five times the wages of the tea-leaf pickers in Sri Lanka—the island we used to know as Ceylon. In a Daily Mirror report on November 2, 1973, Dr S Vijeratnar described working conditions on tea plantations in Sri Lanka as follows: "It is worse than a prison camp. Their quarters aren't fit for animals, let alone human beings."

Consider our Crown Colony, Hong Kong, where a Chinese worker doing the same job as a European is normally paid only one-seventieth to one-hundredth of the European's wages. There are an estimated thirty thousand child labourers in Hong Kong where such exploitation is illegal.

A Telegraph report published in May 1973 showed that an unskilled black worker earns between £25.40 and £44 per month in South Africa, while in Kenya wages for the unskilled varied between £4 and £14.50 a month. A semi-skilled black worker in South Africa earns between £30.80 and £55.40 while in Uganda he is paid between £12 and £24.50; and a skilled black worker in South Africa earns between £37.50 and £92.40, while in Liberia he earns between £21 and £63 a month. Add to this brief comparison between the black worker's position in South Africa and the rest of the continent, free food, clothing and housing and medical advantages which he enjoys in South Africa.

Now let's carry on, Mr Raphael. Let's have a close look at Sri Lanka, Hong Kong, India and a host of other African countries. It must not be thought that you and The Guardian are being selectively indignant—of being more intent on South Africa-baiting than on improving the lot of the workers employed by British firms abroad.

THE CLUB OF TEN,
PO Box 4AA
LONDON W1.

2. Club of Ten, 'An Analysis of Indignation', *Observer*, 9 June 1974. As for illustration 1.

NOW THAT THE DUST HAS SETTLED...

The main aim of The Club of Ten, a private group of citizens, has always been to expose the hoaxing of the public by double standards in international affairs whereby everything that Communist governments do is applauded as progressive and nobly inspired in the interest of the people, whereas the motivation of countries that reject socialism or communism is denounced as sinister and oppressive.

Pursuing this line of argument, the Club of Ten, some months ago, inserted an advertisement in three national newspapers under the title AN ANALYSIS OF INDIGNATION. This criticised a series of articles by Mr Adam Raphael of THE GUARDIAN attacking the wages paid by British firms operating in South Africa. We extended an invitation to The Guardian to investigate similar wages paid in Hong Kong, Sri Lanka and Singapore and in the independent African countries under black rule. We pointed out that, unlike the Communist countries whose problem is to prevent their own citizens escaping to the West, in South Africa the concern is to control a flood of black labour from outside the country who wish to work in South Africa because of the higher wages paid there, the better living conditions, and the rule of law which prevails.

The Guardian did not accept the invitation. Instead it started a campaign of denigration against the Club of Ten, insisting that the Club of Ten was a " front " for the South African Government.

The Club of Ten promptly supplied the Foreign Office with the names of four of the chief contributors to the funds of the Club of Ten, all private individuals from three friendly countries. After investigating the activities of the Club of Ten, the authorities stated that there was " no evidence of irregularities or illegalities in the Club's activities." This was in accordance with a principle long established in Britain that both sides should have the right to be heard, a part of the basic democratic right of free speech.

Now the Club of Ten has invited the Press to meet a leading contributor to the Club of Ten who is in London on business and has handed over a cheque to the spokesman of the Club of Ten as a contribution to their forthcoming advertising campaign and the cost of publishing a quarterly magazine, The Phoenix, devoted to the exposure of the politically motivated double standards ploy.

Now that the dust has settled, we again invite The Guardian and its reporter to carry on the investigation into wages paid in the countries we have named. Otherwise we will have to conclude that The Guardian is more interested in South Africa baiting than in an impartial investigation of black wages and living standards.

**The Club of Ten,
PO Box 4AA
London W1.**

3. Club of Ten, 'Now that the Dust Has Settled …', *Guardian*, 31 August 1974. This advertisement followed a series of articles by Adam Raphael and others examining the Club of Ten and its sponsors. See Chapter 3.

4. Club of Ten, 'The Free World Stands Today in Greater Danger than at any time Since the Darkest Days of World War II ...', *The Times*, 6 February 1976. This advertisement addressed the Angolan War, Soviet 'expansionism' and the Organisation of African Unity. The bottom picture shows 'automatic weapons from behind the Iron Curtain carried by MPLA soldiers'. In fact, the weapons were Israeli Uzi sub-machine guns. See Chapter 6.

5. Club of Ten, 'Moscow's Next Target in Africa', *The Times*, 11 March 1977. This advertisement reproduces the final page of Robert Moss's four-part series on the Angolan War (originally published in the *Sunday Telegraph*, two-and-a-half weeks earlier). See Chapters 3 and 6.

6. Photograph by Sam Nzima, 1976.

7. Photograph by Sam Nzima, 1976.

8. Photograph by Peter Magubane, 1976.

While the impact of this process was slow and the US media were guilty of both 'simplistically portraying the Angolan conflict as "Communism" versus "anti-Communism"' and 'uncritically parroting the administration's distortions of events in Angola', the American media did manage to adjust their treatment as new information emerged.[70] The catalysts for this change included Oswald Johnston's and Seymour Hersh's investigative journalism which suggested that the United States had been the first to escalate the conflict by supplying secret funds to the FNLA; an increasing sense of the complexity of US involvement as demonstrated by David Anable's article for the *Christian Science Monitor* exposing Gulf Oil's relationship with the MPLA ('Ironically, … American elements are aiding and bankrolling opposite sides'); and the realisation that the United States was deeply involved in an alliance 'with the perpetrators of apartheid, the white rulers of the Republic of South Africa', and the potential diplomatic damage that this could cause to relationships with other African states, not least, Nigeria (at that time the United States' second major source of foreign oil).[71]

The spectre of Vietnam was consistently invoked by the American media alongside a vast number of other historical analogies: the Congo crisis, the Spanish civil war, the Biafran war and the Cuban Missile crisis.[72] Of comparable importance to the Vietnam analogy in influence during this period were the ongoing revelations of the Pike Committee into CIA activity.[73] Slowly, senior political commentators began to express doubts about US involvement in Angola. These included both Anthony Lewis and Walter Cronkite.[74] During this period of American introspection, the MPLA displayed four South African prisoners to the press in Luanda (13 December). Five days later, the US Senate, in a crucial vote (54 to 22), decided to impose a complete ban on further aid to UNITA and the FNLA. Almost immediately, the media treatment adjusted to reflect the new realities. This did not mean that the US media suddenly became sympathetic to the MPLA but it did become more balanced. Leslie Gelb, for example, reported on the fact that Pentagon officials were unhappy with the United States' growing identification with South Africa.[75] Condemning President Ford's denunciations of Cuba, an editorial in the *Washington Post* stated: 'we do not hear Mr Ford criticising Zaire or South Africa, which have soldiers in Angola backing the "American" side. For the Post's part, we oppose all foreign intervention in Angola. But Cuba can at least make the claim on solid racial grounds (as Fidel Castro just has) that the blood of Africa "runs abundantly through our veins".'[76]

A few journalists even permitted themselves the indulgence of imagination. Anthony Lewis, for instance, hypothesised: 'Suppose the United States had immediately objected when South African troops entered Angola in force last October. This country would now have a degree of credibility in Africa as a friendly, disinterested power.'[77] The *Wall Street Journal* also reflected the shift in US coverage. On 19 December, an editorial had tentatively suggested support for the Ford administration's plan to increase the funds for UNITA–FNLA.[78] Four days later, following the passage of the Tunney–Clark amendment, a staff writer commented: 'the outlook for American interests isn't particularly bright ... the US is backing the less competent, more poorly organized side. It is also the side with the weaker political credentials – 14 African nations have recognised the MPLA regime so far. "The MPLA have the brightest people, and most of Angola's management skills," concedes one US official.'[79] By early January, the American media had undergone a major shift in the consensus regarding US involvement in Angola. While this was undoubtedly due to the 'several key miscalculations' made by the US strategists, it is revealing that the *Washington Post* considered one of these miscalculations to be the underestimation of 'the degree to which the United States would be impaled publicly as "the collaborator" of racist South Africa when Pretoria's troops entered the conflict, even prior to Havana's'.[80] The factor which made this shift in the consensus in the United States' coverage particularly extraordinary was that President Ford continued to talk 'tough' on the Angolan question throughout the period.[81]

The British media did not moderate its stance in tandem with the Americans, as might have been expected. Indeed, a number of 'liberal' commentators sustained a position which can only be described as violently anti-communist. The *Guardian*, which had been running an editorially-based anti-MPLA campaign even before detailed knowledge of South African involvement emerged, barely adjusted its tone. This was peculiar because in general the work of the newspaper's correspondents and columnists was balanced. An editorial on 22 November led on the UNITA statement that 20 Russian soldiers had been captured, a statement which was later proved to have originated from the CIA disinformation unit in Lusaka.[82] By 16 December, editorial suggestions were beginning to resemble ideas emanating from South Africa: 'The UNITA leader, Dr Savimbi, sees in the conduct of South Africa a desire that Angola should be balkanised ... "Balkanisation" is the emotive word for "partition"; unless Angola is to be fought over by the Big Powers and their proxies, this is the only solution worth pursuing.'[83] On 6 January 1976, the *Guardian* carried a letter from an African reader offended by the editorial position:

> Your persistent opposition to a total MPLA victory ... and your equally
> persistent support for the other factions supported by South Africa and
> America (sorry – Kissinger, CIA and Ford) shocks me as an African,
> especially when your paper hitherto has enjoyed wide respect in Africa
> ... Your paper is backing obvious losers and the sooner you realise it
> and become objective about Angola the better ... It is South Africa which
> should be condemned and forced to withdraw.[84]

No such transformation was forthcoming: the very next day, an
editorial condemned Father Adrian Hastings, who had had the
effrontery to suggest, in a letter to *The Times*, that a swift MPLA
victory might not be a bad outcome.[85] The *Guardian* persisted
with this editorial position until Huambo had fallen to the MPLA
(9 February) and UNITA had announced its reversion to guerrilla
activity. During this period, Geoffrey Taylor wrote the editorials on
Africa for the newspaper. James MacManus later recalled that
'Geoffrey became the object of hostility by a group at the *Guardian*
who thought he was getting it all wrong.'[86] In December 1975, Taylor
had suggested that, if the conflict were to spread to the borders of
South Africa, 'That situation would present the West with the ultimate
in unpopular choices: whether to support the Soviet Union or South
Africa.'[87] In other words, the choice would have been between
institutionalised communism and institutionalised racism. Taylor's
editorials on Angola, during this period, demonstrate clearly which
position he would have adopted. At the *Observer*, there appears to
have been a similar degree of conflict. In December, David Martin
wrote a powerful condemnation of the allegations around the question
of the South African engagement:

> the propaganda continues. The MPLA is described as Marxist, which
> it is not. True, the movement includes some Marxists. But it prefers to
> call itself 'progressive', a word the Western press refrains from using,
> but one which indicates the varying ideological tendencies. South
> Africa's invasion, CIA funding and all other Western involvement is
> described as a response to the Soviet arms build-up. Again this is untrue.
> Russian arms began to arrive in May [1975] in clear response to the
> September 1974 plot to exclude Neto and the November 1974 FNLA
> military moves. And it must be added that Cuban troops training the
> MPLA's expanded army did not become involved in the fighting until
> early November south of the railhead at Benguela, when the South
> African column was already 800 kilometres inside Angola.[88]

However, this article which directly contradicted the editorial
position of the *Observer*, was published by the Observer Foreign News

Service (OFNS), not the British newspaper.[89] Martin recalls that while Legum was responsible for the composition of editorials on Africa and the stories which went in the newspaper, he could not exert any influence over the stories carried by the OFNS.[90] Within a few weeks, Legum had taken the opposing argument into the international arena with an article published in the *New Republic*. He continued to propagate the myth of Savimbi's support, charisma and all-round pliability, while condemning the isolationism displayed by American liberals in relation to Angola. Legum also suggested that liberal America's treatment of Henry Kissinger was unfair. He continued: 'I don't need reminding of the stupid errors made by Kissinger and Nixon in southern Africa – errors that some of us have tried (but mostly failed) to get liberals to pay serious attention to because of preoccupation with Vietnam.'[91]

The failure of the liberal newspapers in Britain to adjust their position following the news of the South African invasion facilitated a shift to the right by the *Daily* and *Sunday Telegraph*. However, this shift and its associated support for South Africa was partly disguised by a series of attacks on the weakness of the American (and British) response to the advance of communism. Peregrine Worsthorne declared that 'For the first time since the end of the war, the American will has been tested and found wanting. Nor has Britain helped in this dire moment of strain, despite the fact that Southern Africa is an area where the British role could have been highly influential. This failure, too, needs to be exposed with ruthless rigour.'[92] Two weeks later, a columnist on the *Daily Telegraph* addressed the issue of apartheid: 'Apartheid might be vicious in practice, it might be evil in fact, but, if the alternative to this system really is bloody chaos such as we have seen in other parts of Africa, do we in a relatively secure England, have the moral right to urge such a course?'[93] This conclusion had been made acceptable in the context of the (liberal) debate over communism versus racism. As if to demonstrate the anti-communist tone in the British press, on the day following the fall of Huambo, Max Hastings composed an 'obituary' for UNITA:

> In any internal power struggle in Africa the personal risks for those involved of execution or exile have always been high. So when entering such a struggle, everybody likes to be sure that their side has at least a remote chance of winning. The message of Angola is that it pays to be on the side of the Russians. They win. Whatever amiable mutterings the American Ambassador whispers into receptive ears, when it comes to the crunch he cannot deliver the cash, votes or guns from Washington to back them.[94]

The coverage of the Angolan war represents one of the lowest points in British journalism's treatment of African news. Only the *Financial Times* sustained a consistent level of balance in its coverage and, as we shall see, even this was problematic.

British correspondents were the most obviously partial during the Angolan war. Fred Bridgland's attachment to Jonas Savimbi is clear from the biography of the UNITA leader which he wrote in the mid-1980s.[95] Michael Nicholson confessed in his memoir that 'I wanted Savimbi to win, and was loath to make public a story [the SADF exposé] that could do him such damage.'[96] A.J. McIlroy, reporting from Luanda, covered the MPLA and its Cuban allies with antipathy. Commenting upon a Cuban officer, he descended into cliché: 'A Havana cigar clenched unlit in a mouth that flashed silver teeth when he smiled ...'[97] Following a visit to Cabinda, McIlroy filed a report which claimed that the MPLA was planning to nationalise the oilfields.[98] This was not only incorrect, it was also completely illogical: the future revenues from Gulf Oil were essential to the survival of the government in Luanda. McIlroy was duly expelled from Angola on 2 February 1976. Although the *Daily Telegraph* dedicated an editorial to the subject of McIlroy's expulsion, it was no surprise to his contemporaries, amongst whom his nickname was 'A.J. Make-it-up'.[99]

Bruce Loudon was the only correspondent in Angola officially to 'recognise' the UNITA–FNLA 'government'. For a few days in early December 1975 his byline read: 'Huambo, provisional capital, UNITA–FNLA Democratic Republic of Angola'.[100] Loudon's previous career explains his partiality. Until 1974, he had been the *Financial Times*'s and *Daily Telegraph*'s stringer in Lisbon. Following the Portuguese revolution, reports emerged in the Portuguese press that Loudon's relationship with the Caetano regime had developed far beyond the realm of normal journalistic practice. These reports had been inspired by copies of correspondence sent by Loudon, in 1973, to Portuguese government officials.[101] Upon the receipt of translations of the transcripts of the Portuguese articles, J.D.F. Jones, the foreign editor of the *Financial Times*, telephoned Loudon and summarily dismissed him with the admonition that he 'would never get a job with any respectable newspaper again, ever'.[102] The *Daily Telegraph*, however, retained Loudon's services. In 1976, *Time Out* gained access to the letters:

Upon his return to Lisbon [in 1973], Loudon started a correspondence with Dr Pedro Feytor Pinto, 'Director of Information' at the Portuguese dictatorship's Secretariat of State for Information and Tourism. 'Above all else,' Loudon wrote, 'I have the deep conviction that allegations such as those in connection with "massacres" in Mozambique gain rapid international acceptance because of the consistent failure of Portugal to launch effective counter campaigns.' Loudon believed, he wrote, that 'something must be done very urgently to combat this propaganda campaign, and to present the realities of the situation in Mozambique in a positive and effective manner.' What was needed, Loudon proposed, was 'a daily flow of information from Mozambique to a central point in Lisbon, from which it can be disseminated both to the international news media and to Portuguese representatives, as well as to other opinion formers.' ... Though he was only a 'humble foreigner', Loudon wrote, 'I stand ready to help in any way I can over the next few critical months.'[103]

One can only concur with *Time Out*'s conclusion: 'In view of his relationship with the former Portuguese dictatorship, it would seem that Loudon would be one of the least impartial men to send to cover the war in Angola.'[104] Partiality was also apparent amongst more liberal reporters. Jane Bergerol, the *Financial Times*'s stringer in Luanda, had her articles heavily edited in order to remove biased comment.[105] As Bridget Bloom remembers, 'It was impossible for the *Financial Times* – it was virtually propaganda for the MPLA ... it was not the sort of thing we could have published in the *Financial Times* without losing out completely on objectivity.'[106] The *Financial Times*'s sub-editors certainly performed their task with great skill; Bergerol's published reports appear to be amongst the most objective of the war.

While partiality was most obvious in the work of British journalists, the most disturbing element of the international media's coverage of the South African invasion of Angola was its emphasis. Throughout the period in question, the majority of the British and American correspondents and commentators accepted the version of events which blamed the South African incursion on Soviet–Cuban escalation. *The Times*, for example, commented as late as mid-January 1976 that 'The South Africans are the only military force that can check a determined Russian–Cuban–MPLA advance; yet South African intervention has been disastrous for the western position. It should have been discreet – it was almost as blatant as the Russian–Cuban, which it followed.'[107]

The US media, hampered by the strictures of objective journalism and the importance of sources, consistently underplayed the role of South Africa while focusing on the grander Cold War implications. Attempts to understand the planning behind the South African incursion were mainly confined to the British media, although these interpretations were normally influenced by the belief that the South African action was reactive rather than proactive.[108] To what extent this emphasis was exaggerated by confidential British and American government sources remains difficult to assess. As the American academic, Gerald Bender, acknowledged in the *Los Angeles Times*, however, 'The stream of government information on the number and type of Russian arms shipments to Angola has been so voluminous and detailed that one wondered if the supply sergeants of the ... MPLA were as knowledgeable about their Russian stocks as the average American newspaper reader.'[109]

Equally difficult to assess is the influence of the Western intelligence agencies in Angola, although this does seem to have been important. Far from working in unison, there appears to have been no small degree of tension between the British Secret Intelligence Services (SIS), the CIA, the French Service de Documentation Extérieure et Contre-Espionage (SDECE) and South Africa's BOSS. Stockwell later recalled that 'The South Africans and French accepted voluminous intelligence reports and detailed briefings from [the Pretoria and Paris] CIA stations but never reciprocated with much information about what they were doing in Angola.'[110] It would appear that one of the repercussions of the Pike Committee's investigation into the CIA was a partial breakdown in the relations between the international intelligence agencies. An article in *To The Point* explained the difficulties of the period: 'spies and their organisations are going through a tough time. Those that used to cooperate now mostly distrust each other.'[111]

The lack of cooperation can be seen in a number of strange incidents which occurred during this period in which intelligence and journalism were merged. Stockwell notes that the CIA arranged the expulsion from Kinshasa of 'one European reporter, whom we knew only as Germani'.[112] Hans Germani was actually an employee of *To The Point*, a long-standing front-organisation of South Africa's Department of Information. Equally strange was an article in the *Washington Post*'s series on spies, by the newspaper's London correspondent, Bernard Nossiter: 'An unknown number [of SIS officers] are posing as journalists. "Fleet Street relies on the secret vote to keep its operatives in the field these days," one authority insists. The secret vote is the figure publicly published for the SIS budget.'[113] Jonathan Bloch and Patrick Fitzgerald later commented: 'Most of the British intelligence officers who arrived in Angola had been spotted fairly quickly, although one or two posing as journalists had a certain amount of success.'[114]

The failure of the South African intervention in Angola had an immediate effect in the Republic. The tone of the Club of Ten advertisement, 'The Free World today stands in greater danger than at any time since the darkest days of World War II', which appeared in February 1976 suggested genuine desperation.[115] Eschel Rhoodie later commented that 'From a propaganda point of view the Angolan "mistykie" [little mistake] was, in fact, a God-send to our enemies. Diplomatically speaking it was an equal disaster.'[116] The 'little mistake' was disastrous for a number of additional reasons: it destroyed the pretence that South Africa's policy was one of non-intervention in foreign countries; and it contradicted the prior image of South Africa as the 'military strongman' of the continent. *West Africa* magazine declared: 'when the dust has cleared, it will be remembered in Africa only that the South Africans were worsted in their first encounter with an African army'.[117] Within South Africa, the failed intervention served as a form of inspiration for many in the African population, as Benjamin Pogrund noted in an article for the *Spectator*:

> all the factors which make for white dismay act in reverse in regard to the country's blacks. On the specific issue of Angola there would seem to be considerable support for the MPLA – if only because South Africa is opposing it. In more general terms, blacks feel that the succession of events in the sub-continent is on their side, that the tide of history is flowing in their favour. Black confidence is slowly mounting, and greater assertiveness and aggression are likely.[118]

Angola had also attracted the full attention of the international media. The war convinced many columnists and commentators that southern Africa would succeed Vietnam as the epicentre of the Cold War. A number of specialist war correspondents were duly dispatched to report from Rhodesia/Zimbabwe, South Africa, Angola and Mozambique. The central exposé of the Angolan War, the revelation that South African combat troops were in the country, had been the work of a news agency reporter (Bridgland) and a television broadcaster (Nicholson). Within two years, all the major broadcasting companies in Britain and the United States would open bureaus in Johannesburg. Despite the confusion and contradictions in the reports, the Angolan war had transformed the South African 'story'. During the next three years, South Africa would be subjected to a degree of coverage not hitherto experienced in its history.

NOTES

1. Tom Lambert, 'Angola War: Secrecy and Propaganda', *Los Angeles Times*, 16 January 1976.
2. Will Ellsworth-Jones, 'Messages from the Front', *Sunday Times*, 8 February 1976.
3. A number of the most important sources originally appeared in the media, these include: Gabriel Garcia Marquez's account of the Cuban engagement in Angola

which was published in the Mexican weekly publication, *Proceso*, January 1977 (*Washington Post*, 10–12 January 1977, republished extracts in translation; *New Left Review*, No. 101–102 (February–April 1977), pp. 123–37, published the full article in translation); Robert Moss, 'Castro's Secret War Exposed', *Sunday Telegraph*, 30 January–20 February 1977, contained extensive information gathered during a major investigation. See also Gerald Shaw, 'The *Cape Times* and the Angola War: August 1975–March 1976', unpublished summary of events; Ryszard Kapuscinski, *Another Day of Life* (London, Pan Books, 1987), originally published in Polish, 1976. Official sources include the South African Defence Force version of events which was released on 3 February 1977, in response to Moss's series ('The Angolan War', *South African Panorama*, March 1977, pp. 6–7); Willem Steenkamp, *South Africa's Border War 1966–1989* (Gibraltar, Ashanti Publishing, 1989), contains new information on the SADF; John Stockwell, *In Search of Enemies: A CIA Story* (New York, W.W. Norton, 1978), is an account by the CIA officer directly responsible for Angola. Stockwell resigned from the CIA in 1977. Academic sources include: Gerald Bender, 'Kissinger in Angola: Anatomy of Failure', in Rene Lemarchand (ed.), *American Policy in Southern Africa: The Stakes and the Stance* (Washington DC, University Press of America, 1978), pp. 65–143; Colin Legum and Tony Hodges, *After Angola: The War over Southern Africa* (London, Rex Collings, 1976); John A. Marcum, *The Angolan Revolution Volume II: Exile Politics and Guerrilla Warfare (1962–1976)* (Massachusetts, MIT Press, 1978); R.W. Johnson, *How Long will South Africa Survive?* (London, Macmillan, 1977), pp. 137–63; Graeme Norris Addison, 'Censorship of the Press in South Africa during the Angolan War: A Case Study of News Manipulation and Suppression', unpublished MA thesis, Rhodes University, 1980.

4. Marcum, op. cit., p. 268. Francis Campredon, Agence France Presse (AFP), 10 June 1975. See also Nathaniel Davis, 'The Angola Decision of 1975: A Personal Memoir', *Foreign Affairs*, Vol. 57, No. 1 (Fall 1978), p. 121. There appears to have been more than a small degree of confusion during the intervention in June, SADF soldiers attacked National Union for the Total Liberation of Angola (UNITA), MPLA and South West Africa People's Organisation (SWAPO) forces, before withdrawing to Namibia.

5. Although, Cuban advisors are reported to have been in Angola since early 1975, the majority of commentators accept that Cuban combat troops did not arrive in Angola until late September 1975. For recent research see Piero Gleijeses, 'Havana's Policy in Africa, 1959–76: New Evidence from Cuban Archives', *Cold War International History Project Bulletin*, No. 8/9 (1997), pp. 5–18; Odd Arne Westad, 'Moscow and the Angolan Crisis, 1974–1976: A New Pattern of Intervention', *Cold War International History Project Bulletin*, No. 8/9 (1997), pp. 21–32.

6. Robin Hallett, 'The South African Intervention in Angola, 1975–76', *African Affairs*, Vol. 77, No. 308 (July 1978), p. 347. Hallett's core sources were the accounts listed in footnote 3: Gabriel Garcia Marquez, Robert Moss and the official statement of the SADF. Hallet's primary 'observers' included Jane Bergerol (*Financial Times*), Bruce Loudon (*Daily Telegraph*) and Stanley Uys (*Guardian* and *Observer*). Secondary correspondents included Nicholas Ashford (*The Times*), James MacManus (*Guardian*), A.J. McIlroy (*Daily Telegraph*), Will Ellsworth-Jones (*Sunday Times*) and David Martin, Tony Hodges and Colin Legum (*Observer*).

7. Hallett, op. cit., p. 348.

8. R.W. Johnson, op. cit., p. 139. Robert Moss, *Chile's Marxist Experiment* (Newtown Abbot, David & Charles, 1973); *The Collapse of Democracy* (London,

Temple Smith, 1975). Moss was the editor of *The Economist*'s confidential 'Foreign Report', the spokesman for a right-wing pressure group, the National Association for Freedom (NAFF) and the author of Mrs Thatcher's 'Iron maiden' speech. See also Peter Chippindale and Martin Walker, 'Only the Views We Want You to Read', *Guardian*, 20–21 December 1976; Jane McLoughlin, 'This Disturbing Case of the Writer and the CIA', *Daily Mail*, 22 December 1976; 'The Spies who Went Out of the Fold', *Private Eye*, No. 393, 7 January 1977, pp. 17–18; Crispin Aubrey, 'NAFF And The Tory Connection', *Time Out*, No. 380, 8 July 1977, p. 5. Within a month of the *Sunday Telegraph*'s publication of Moss's 'history' of the Angolan war, the Club of Ten had placed an advertisement which reproduced the last page of the Moss series in *The Times*, *Guardian*, *New York Times* and *Washington Post*. See illustration.

9. Bridget Bloom, 'Independence at Gunpoint', *Financial Times*, 10 November 1975.
10. UPI, *Guardian*, 30 October 1975; Reuters, 'Angolans Release Two CBS Newsmen', *New York Times*, 12 December 1975; Reuters, 'Luanda Regime Ousts Reuters for Shooting-incident Report', *New York Times*, 16 November 1975. Nicholas Ashford, 'Luanda Launches Attack on Reuters', *The Times*, 28 January 1976; 'MPLA Expel Telegraph Reporter', *Daily Telegraph*, 3 February 1976. See also A.J. McIlroy, 'Angola Threatens Shipping Lanes', *Daily Telegraph*, 6 February 1976; 'ITN News Team Ordered Out of Angola', *Daily Telegraph*, 4 February 1976.
11. Nicholas Ashford, 'Police Swoop on Foreign Journalists in Angola', *The Times*, 5 November 1975. Bridget Bloom remembers that night as 'one of the scariest incidents in my whole life as a journalist'. (Interview with Bridget Bloom, 21 March 1995.)
12. J.S. Marsh, 'What the Papers Said on Angola', *Anti-Apartheid News*, April 1976, p. 11, later commented uncritically, 'Early on, MPLA recognised the dangers of … unsubstantiated reporting and issued warnings to newsmen about false reports and distortions, eventually taking control of the communications media to check the dispatches leaving Luanda.'
13. Will Ellsworth-Jones, 'Messages from the Front', *Sunday Times*, 8 February 1976.
14. Michael T. Kaufman, 'Luanda Confident', *New York Times*, 23 January 1976.
15. Chris Munnion, *Banana Sunday: Datelines from Africa* (Rivonia, William Waterman, 1993), p. 366.
16. UNITA's international backers included the US and Great Britain: Nicholas Ashford, 'Arms Race Among Rival Factions Turns the Angola Conflict into an International Issue', *The Times*, 25 September 1975; Leslie H. Gelb (Diplomatic correspondent), 'US Aides Tell of Covert European Help to Angolans', *New York Times*, 10 March 1976. For details on Savimbi's links with right-wing elements within the Portuguese colonial administration, see William Minter (ed.), *Operation Timber: Pages from the Savimbi Dossier* (New Jersey, Africa World Press, 1988).
17. For the first instance of this claim, see Charles Mohr, 'In Angola's Political Manoeuvering, a Moderate Gains Support', *New York Times*, 24 April 1975, wherein Mohr suggested that UNITA would win 45 per cent of the vote, the MPLA 30–35 per cent and the FNLA 20–25 per cent. His source for this appears to have been an earlier poll conducted by a domestic newspaper in Luanda. These figures are based on the assumption that Angolans would vote solely according to ethnic groups.
18. Will Ellsworth-Jones, 'What Marxism Means in Luanda', *Sunday Times*, 11 January 1976. Ellsworth-Jones had not been to UNITA territory and was

therefore summarising the opinions of the other correspondents, the contents of the cuttings files and information provided in background briefings.

19. See, for example, 'Unita Denies Aid from South Africa', *The Times*, 9 December 1975. Obfuscation was the normal method adopted by UNITA whereas the South Africans favoured domestic censorship and international denials. The international media were briefed by the South African government in Pretoria on 27 November and taken on a 48-hour visit to southern Angola on 2–4 December 1975. Journalists were encouraged to believe that South African support consisted mainly of 'advice and logistical support'. (Addison, op. cit., p. 216.)

20. Peter Younghusband, 'A Prophet Who Strikes Back', *Newsweek*, 19 May 1975, p. 15: '[Dr Savimbi possesses] an easy charm that attracts all who meet him'. See also Max Hastings, 'No Brakes on the Line to Luso', *Evening Standard*, 19 January 1976: '[Savimbi] is an advertising man's dream of an African guerrilla leader: beard, green beret, bangles and bracelets and pistol and black leather jacket – charm, charisma, sexuality and physical presence'. For the 'dark side' see Tom Lambert, 'Angola War: Secrecy and Propaganda', *Los Angeles Times*, 16 January 1976: 'In eight days in central Angola, this reporter spent most of the time as a courteously treated near-captive of UNITA.'

21. Henry Kamm, 'Southern Angola Found Under Uncertain Control', *New York Times*, 22 January 1976. On 21 January, Francois Campredon (AFP) reported seeing 'half a dozen soldiers in South African brown combat uniforms inspecting a rail bridge over the Cuanza River', he also recalled that 'UNITA had recently confiscated film shot by two American television teams of a convoy carrying white soldiers'. (Addison, op. cit., pp. 40–41.) See also Fred Bridgland, *Jonas Savimbi: A Key to Africa* (Edinburgh, Mainstream, 1986), p. 166.

22. J.S. Marsh, 'What the Papers Said on Angola', *Anti-Apartheid News*, April 1976, p. 11; Michael T. Kaufman, 'Sight and Sound of War Prove Elusive in Angola', *New York Times*, 31 December 1975.

23. Pooled dispatch, 'French Journalists Held in UNITA Prison', *The Times*, 8 January 1976. The majority of the newspapers carried this report but otherwise accepted Savimbi's explanation without further examination. Reports are only ever 'pooled' when the journalists are either incapable of transmitting the story through the usual channels, or as a form of collective protection against potential punishment. Eight days after this pooled dispatch, Max Hastings reported that 'Two French journalists are in jail for asking embarrassing questions about the South Africans.' (Max Hastings, 'War for Carcass of Angola', *Evening Standard*, 16 January 1976.)

24. UPI, 'The Quest for Facts in Angola', *New York Times*, 18 January 1976.

25. See AFP, 'MPLA Show "Mass Graves" Found in Angola', *The Times*, 16 February 1976; 'MPLA Consolidates Despite Massacres', *Africa News*, Vol. 6, No. 8 (23 February 1976), p. 2; Jane Bergerol, 'Civilians were Slaughtered in Angola Retreat', *Observer*, 29 February 1976.

26. Elaine Windrich, *The Cold War Guerrilla: Jonas Savimbi, the US Media and the Angolan War* (New York, Greenwood Press, 1992), suggests that the construction of 'Savimbi' took place during the late 1970s. In 1973, Leon Dash, 'The War in Angola', *Washington Post*, 23–26 December 1973, provided a crucial contribution to the early representation of Savimbi. Dash was an African-American journalist who had attended university with Jorge Sangumba. He was awarded a Pulitzer prize in 1974.

27. Addison, op. cit., p. 40, suggests that 'the war became a field for investigative journalism whose object was to expose those involved'.

28. Stockwell, op. cit., pp. 191–202.

29. 'One of the most bizarre aspects of the war in Angola is that hardly anyone has seen it … information on the fighting is limited to secondary sources'. (Kaufman, 'Sights and Sound of War Prove Elusive in Angola', *New York Times*, 31 December 1975).

30. Phillip Knightley, *The First Casualty. From the Crimea to the Falklands: The War Correspondent as Hero, Propagandist and Myth Maker* (London, Pan, 1989), p. 428.

31. Roger Morris, 'The Proxy War in Angola: Pathology of a Blunder', the *New Republic*, 31 January 1976, p. 21.

32. Only senior correspondents such as Michael Kaufman, Nicholas Ashford, Peter Younghusband and Chris Munnion saw both sides of the conflict. Ingeborg Lippman, an American photographer who worked as a stringer for the *New York Times* remained in UNITA territory for many weeks. She recalls that the vast majority of foreign correspondents barely stayed any longer than one night. Many correspondents only remained in Huambo for two or three hours, before returning to Lusaka. (Interview with Ingeborg Lippman, 14 August 1996.)

33. Jane Bergerol in Luanda filed copy for the *Financial Times*, the *Observer*, *The Economist* and BBC 'Africa Service'.

34. Interview with Jane Bergerol (Wilford), 22 May 1995. Exceptions included Bruce Loudon (*Daily Telegraph*) and Barry Hillenbrand (*Time*), both of whom were reporting from UNITA territory.

35. Max Hastings, 'No Brakes on the Line to Luso', *Evening Standard*, 19 January 1976.

36. David Ottaway, '"Free Angola Now" Call', *Guardian*, 13 August 1975. Addison, op. cit., p. 209, records that the censorship of news in the domestic South African media, relating to South African military activity in Angola, was introduced on 11 August 1975. Some weeks earlier, on 14 July, the SADF had again intervened in Angola and engaged in combat with both the MPLA and UNITA. The South African force had retreated and adopted a defensive position near the Ruacana Falls hydroelectric project. (The project was South African financed and still in the process of being built.)

37. 'Flight from Angola', *The Economist*, 16 August 1975, p. 36. South African spokespersons during this period regularly claimed that the SADF were engaged in 'hot pursuit' of SWAPO guerrillas.

38. 'South Africa Sends Troops into Angola to Protect River Project', *Financial Times*, 23 August 1975. For other reports on the South African intervention, see 'Angola Rivals Fighting to Control Port', *Washington Post*, 17 August 1975; David B. Ottaway, 'Angola's Grim Civil War Shakes Africa', *Washington Post*, 24 August 1975; Reuters, 'International Implication Seen in Angola Clashes', *Washington Post*, 31 August 1975; Dial Torgerson, 'Angola Invasion by Uniden-tified Force Reported', *Los Angeles Times*, 1 September 1975; 'Africa Service', BBC Radio, 2 September 1975: 'gave wide currency to reports of a movement of South African troops into Angola with armoured cars and helicopter cover'. (Gerald Shaw, op. cit., p. 1.)

39. Richard Gott and Antonio de Figueiredo, 'Uneasy Silence Over Angola's "Invaders"', *Guardian*, 4 September 1975.

40. Leslie H. Gelb, 'US, Soviet, China Reported Aiding Portugal, Angola', *New York Times*, 25 September 1975. See Basil Davidson, 'Report on Angola Now', *West Africa*, 29 September 1975, p. 1139, which included the prescient observation that 'South Africa's intervention … can now be made good only by a major invasion of South African troops'. During mid-September, 20 South African infantry corps instructors had arrived in Silva Porto. On 5 October, the South Africans and a UNITA force clashed with the MPLA. On 14 October,

the South African-commanded 'Zulu' column invaded Angola from Namibia.

41. 'Cuban Mercenaries Reported to be Helping MPLA to Keep its Grip on Angola until Independence', *The Times*, 24 October 1975. MPLA spokespeople had been condemning South Africa's invasion since August 1975. Neto announced the existence of the Zulu column during a speech on Radio Lisbon, 19 October 1975. (Legum and Hodges, op. cit., p. 15. See also 'South Africa Invades Angola, Seeking Guerrillas', *Africa News*, Vol. 5, No. 24 (20 October 1975), pp. 9–10.) *The Times*'s report was the first major reference to the Cubans in the international media.

42. 'Pretoria Silent on "Invasion"', *Guardian*, 25 October 1975. One exception was Richard Kershaw who interviewed Jonas Savimbi, in London, during this period: 'Kershaw: "It's been charged that South Africa has made a direct military intervention into the South of Angola ... Is that charge true or false?" Savimbi: "That is not true ... it is a false allegation".' ('Newsday', BBC 2, 28 October 1975.) See also Jane Bergerol, 'White Force Aiding Angola Guerrillas, say Portuguese', *Financial Times*, 31 October 1975; 'Angola's Quagmire', *Africa*, No. 50 (October 1975), pp. 80–81.

43. See David Martin, 'Mercenaries Head for Angola Battle', *Observer*, 2 November 1975: 'No one is sure who the mercenaries are. But a Portuguese captain who talked with them at Angola's southern port of Mocamedes ... says the column is led by English-speaking officers who, he believes, are South Africans.'

44. Bridgland, op. cit., p. 16. The only way for journalists to enter UNITA territory was to obtain a flight on Savimbi's Hawker-Siddeley 125 executive jet. The aeroplane had been loaned to Savimbi by Tiny Rowland and Lonhro.

45. Ibid., p. 129.

46. Fred Bridgland, *The War for Africa: Twelve Months that Transformed a Continent* (London, Ashanti, 1990), p. 6. See also Fred Bridgland, 'Angola-South Africans', *Reuters*, 15 November 1975.

47. Bridgland, *Jonas Savimbi*, p. 138.

48. Robert Moss, 'Behind the Lines', *Spectator*, 15 November 1975, p. 626.

49. Michael Nicholson, *A Measure of Danger: Memoirs of a British War Correspondent* (London, HarperCollins, 1991), p. 176.

50. Nicholson's and Bridgland's accounts differ in a number of important respects: both claim that they informed the other of the South African incursion; both claim that the film was shot in different places and at different times; and both cite different reasons for not announcing the existence of South African troops in Angola before 11 November. The version that follows is based upon interviews with Michael Nicholson, 13 February 1995; Fred Bridgland, 9 May 1995; Tony Hodges, 23 January 1995; and Andrew Jaffe, 18 April 1996; it tends to correspond relatively closely with the Bridgland version in *Jonas Savimbi*.

51. The pilots requested that Nicholson and Bridgland encourage Jaffe to leave the aeroplane. (Interview with Fred Bridgland, 9 May 1995.) See also Andrew Jaffe, 'Hot and Cold Warriors', *Newsweek*, 24 November 1975, p. 25: 'The British pilots ... shrugged when asked who had hired them. "You can say we work for MI6-and-a-half," one quipped.' Jaffe comments in retrospect: 'I was trying to convey that all around me were all those murky "spooks" [intelligence operatives]. I remember that when I got to Huambo ... I ended up lodging with four American "pilots". They were all armed to the hilt, they wouldn't tell me where they were from ... and when I started to get to know one of them and I said: "You're CIA aren't you?" ... he said: "Go easy on that".' (Interview with Andrew Jaffe, 18 April 1996.)

52. Bridgland, *War for Africa*, p. 8.

53. Bridgland, *Jonas Savimbi*, p. 139.

54. Nicholson, op. cit., p. 177.

55. Alan Downes' most famous film to date had been the ITN news report from Vietnam in 1972 which featured 'a naked Vietnamese girl, Kim Phuc, screaming in pain, on fire from napalm dropped by an American aircraft'. (Sandy Gall, 'Obituary: Alan Downes', *Independent*, 10 October 1996.)

56. Fred Bridgland, 'Angola-South Africans', Reuters, 15 November 1975.

57. Andrew Jaffe, 'Hot and Cold Warriors', *Newsweek*, 24 November 1975, p. 25. For a different version of Savimbi's comment, see Fred Bridgland, 'Angola-South Africans', Reuters, 15 November 1975.

58. 'First Report', ITN, 14 November 1975. Previous film reports by Michael Nicholson from Angola had been broadcast on ITN on 7, 9, 10, 12 and 13 November 1975.

59. Tony Hodges and David Martin, 'South African Troops Join Angola Civil War', *Observer*, 16 November 1975.

60. Andrew Jaffe, 'Hot and Cold Warriors', *Newsweek*, 24 November 1975, p. 25.

61. Bridgland, *Jonas Savimbi*, p. 142. AP and UPI appear to have been even more nervous than Reuters. The problem was the lack of an authoritative source.

62. Fred Bridgland, 'Angola-South Africans', Reuters, 15 November 1975. Versions of this report were published in *The Times*, 15 November 1975, *Los Angeles Times*, 16 November 1975 and the *Chicago Tribune*, 17 November 1975.

63. Fred Bridgland, 'Angola-Forces', Reuters, 21 November 1975.

64. Stockwell, op. cit., p. 202; Fred Bridgland, 'S. African Regulars Fight Inside Angola', *Washington Post*, 23 Nov. 1975, p. 18; This did not stop the CIA from trying to negate the Bridgland story. Indeed, Fred Bridgland, 'Angola-Forces', Reuters, 21 November 1975, had also noted that 'UNITA today reported it had taken 20 Soviet soldiers prisoner'. See David Ottaway, 'Angola group claims capture of 20 Russians, 35 Cubans', *Washington Post*, 22 November 1975; Reuters, 'Angola Unit Says it Holds Russians', *New York Times*, 22 November 1975.

65. 'Angola: Détente Under Fire', *Newsweek*, 19 January 1976, p. 6.

66. Editorial, 'Angola Intervention', *New York Times*, 26 November 1975.

67. See, for example, Len Clarke, Letter to the editor, *Guardian*, 29 November 1975. On Clarke, see Chapter 4.

68. Marsha Lynne Coleman, 'Prestigious American Newspapers' Coverage of African Political Crises Events', unpublished PhD dissertation, Massachusetts Institute of Technology, 1982, p. 2.

69. Bender in Lemarchand (ed.), op. cit., p. 99.

70. George M. Houser, 'Communism and the War in Angola', *New York Times*, 14 December 1975; Editorial, 'Angola', *Nation*, 27 December 1975, p. 676.

71. Oswald Johnston, 'Who Intervened First? US Move in Angola Seen as Spur to Russia', *International Herald Tribune*, 10 December 1975; Seymour M. Hersh, 'Angola-aid Issue Opening Rifts in State Department', *New York Times*, 14 December 1975; Seymour M. Hersh, 'Early Angola Aid by US Reported', *New York Times*, 19 December 1975; David Anable, 'American Involvement in Angola Deepens', *Christian Science Monitor*, 15 December 1975. See also 'Gulf Places in Special Fund $125 million due Angola to Bypass Warring Factions', *Wall Street Journal*, 23 December 1975; Editorial, 'Rethinking Angola ...', *New York Times*, 26 December 1975; Nigeria recognised the MPLA as the government of Angola on 27 November 1975.

72. See, for example, Conrad, 'The Battle over Angola', cartoon, *Los Angeles Times*, 17 December 1975: 'If you liked Vietnam, you'll love this one! Angola:

Produced and Directed by Henry Kissinger, starring the CIA at a cost of millions!'

73. The secret report of the Pike Committee was leaked and published as 'The CIA Report the President Doesn't Want You to Read', *Village Voice*, 16 February 1976. See p. 88, on the issue of US support for UNITA–FNLA: 'Mr Aspin: "And why are the Chinese backing the moderate group?" Mr Colby [Head of the CIA]: "Because the Soviets are backing the MPLA is the simplest answer." Mr Aspin: "It sounds like that is why we are doing it." Mr Colby: "It is".'

74. Anthony Lewis, 'No Questions, Please', *New York Times*, 15 December 1975; CBS television ran a week of nightly segments on 'Evening News', focusing on the question of Angola, hosted by Walter Cronkite, during the week of 14 December 1975. These programmes examined the similarities between the Vietnam war and the Angolan conflict. Cronkite stated that the series was designed 'to try to play our small part in preventing that mistake this time'. ('The Battle over Angola', *Time*, 29 December 1975, pp. 19–20.) NBC also provided heavy coverage of the Angolan war during the same week.

75. Leslie H. Gelb, 'There is no Basic Text with the Lessons of Vietnam', *New York Times*, 21 December 1975.

76. Editorial, 'Havana's Men in Angola', *Washington Post*, 30 December 1975. See also Editorial, 'The Wrong African Policy', *Washington Post*, 28 December 1975; John D. Marks, 'The Fallacy of our Angolan Involvement', *Los Angeles Times*, 17 December 1975; Editorial, 'The Courting of Disaster', *Los Angeles Times*, 28 December 1975.

77. Anthony Lewis, 'How to Arrange Disaster', *New York Times*, 15 January 1976.

78. Editorial, 'Dithering over Angola', *Wall Street Journal*, 19 December 1975.

79. Robert Keatley, 'Uneasy Choices in Angola', *Wall Street Journal*, 23 December 1975. In the weeks that followed, the *Wall Street Journal* carried two diametrically opposed commentaries on Angola: Karen Rothmyer, 'Angola and some African Memories', *Wall Street Journal*, 8 January 1976, posed the following question: 'Remembering my own ineptness, my own insensitivity, my own ignorance [on the subject of African life]. I wonder: How can the US know what is best for Angola … ?' Bowen Northrup, 'Jungle, Fighter: In South of Angola, Guerrilla with a PhD is Something of a God', *Wall Street Journal*, 22 January 1976, was possibly the most inept reporting of the war, it contains the following massive understatement: 'It's an odd civil war they're having in Angola.'

80. Murrey Marder, 'The Angolan Involvement: US, Soviets Caught in a Byzantine Conflict', *Washington Post*, 6 January 1976.

81. 1976 was a Presidential election year. With the primaries due in February and challenging candidate, Ronald Reagan promoting a proactive role on Angola, President Ford persisted with the belligerent language. Among the American columnists who remained unreservedly 'hawkish' was Patrick Buchanan, 'We're "Hip Deep in Pygmies"', *Chicago Tribune*, 23 December 1975: 'victory in Angola for Soviet arms and Cuban mercenaries will send a message to the world: the West has no "strategic reserve"'. See also James Burnham, 'The Protracted Conflict – Angola: The National Disinterest', *National Review*, 6 February 1976, p. 80.

82. Editorial, 'The Crucial Struggle for Africa', *Guardian*, 22 November 1975. See also Stockwell, op. cit., p. 194–95.

83. Editorial, 'Better Split than Twisted', *Guardian*, 16 December 1975.

84. M. Gumbo, Stobhill General Hospital, Glasgow, Letter to the editor, the *Guardian*, 6 January 1976.

85. Editorial, 'As Africa Casts its Vote', *Guardian*, 7 January 1976. Adrian Hastings,

Letter to the editor, *The Times*, 30 December 1975. Father Hastings also attracted criticism from Michael Nicholson, Letter to the editor, *The Times*, 6 January 1976: 'I can give him documented evidence that the Russians were sending in vast quantities of military aid to the MPLA as far back as April 1975.'

86. Interview with James MacManus, 16 October 1995. MacManus suggested that Richard Gott and Jonathan Steele were the 'prime movers' in this protest. Interviews with Richard Gott, 14 May 1996 and Geoffrey Taylor, 24 March 1996, reveal that Peter Niesewand was the leading protester. Niesewand had been born in South Africa and was imprisoned in Rhodesia/Zimbabwe in 1973 (see Peter Niesewand, *In Camera: Secret Justice in Rhodesia* (London, Weidenfeld & Nicholson, 1973)). He won the International Reporter of the Year award twice (1973 and 1977). Niesewand died in 1983. ('Obituary', *Guardian*, 7 February 1983.)

87. Editorial, 'Angola: The Aid that Helps Most', *Guardian*, 20 December 1975.

88. David Martin, 'Little Chance of OAU Deal on Angola', Observer Foreign News Service, 24 December 1976, p. 3.

89. Editorial, 'Innocence is not Enough', *Observer*, 21 December 1975.

90. Interview with David Martin, 4 September 1996.

91. Colin Legum, 'A Letter on Angola to American Liberals', *New Republic*, 31 December 1975, p. 16. See also Colin Legum, 'When the War is Over, What Next for Angola?', *New York Times*, 15 February 1976.

92. Peregrine Worsthorne, 'How Angola went East', *Sunday Telegraph*, 4 January 1976. See also Peter Simple, 'Way of the World: Paralysed', *Daily Telegraph*, 9 January 1976: 'Paralysed by guilt, accepting as an article of faith that South African apartheid is the most fiendish system of tyranny ever seen on earth ... we have made ourselves powerless to resist the advance in Africa ... of a system of tyranny a million times worse.'

93. Michael Harrington, 'Apartheid or Bloody Chaos?', *Daily Telegraph*, 16 January 1976. See also Ian Lloyd, Conservative MP, Letter to the editor, *The Times*, 22 January 1976, most notably his assessment of apartheid as 'a comparatively mild form of social failure'.

94. Max Hastings, 'The Bear Hug Wins in Africa Too', *Evening Standard*, 10 February 1976.

95. Bridgland, *Jonas Savimbi*. Bridgland covered Angola continuously until the late 1980s when he finally discovered UNITA's 'dark side'. (Interview with Fred Bridgland, 9 May 1995.) See Fred Bridgland, 'Savimbi: Fallen Idol on Angola', *Sunday Telegraph*, 12 March 1989; Fred Bridgland, 'Angola's Secret Bloodbath', *Washington Post*, 29 March 1992.

96. Nicholson, op. cit., p. 179.

97. A.J. McIlroy, 'When the Cubans Fight, They Use their Guns Well', *Daily Telegraph*, 19 January 1976.

98. A.J. McIlroy, 'Takeover of Off-shore Oilfields Planned by MPLA', *Daily Telegraph*, 2 February 1976.

99. Editorial, 'Defeat', *Daily Telegraph*, 7 February 1976. David Martin suggests that Kenneth Kaunda originally gave McIlroy the nickname. (Interview with David Martin, 4 September 1996.) For an example of the bizarre mix of cliché and fantasy in McIlroy's coverage, see A.J. McIlroy, 'Angola Threatens Shipping Lines', *Daily Telegraph*, 6 February 1976 wherein McIlroy confirms the prejudices of *Telegraph* readers when he notes that while he was being confined before his expulsion, 'One of the Africans masturbated openly.'

100. See Loudon's reports in *Daily Telegraph*, 5–8 December 1975.

101. For evidence of Loudon's ability to control a damaging story, see Father Adrian Hastings, 'Portuguese Massacre Reported by Priests', *The Times*, 10 July 1973;

Bruce Loudon, 'No Massacres, say Tete Tribesmen', *Daily Telegraph*, 13 July 1973; Bruce Loudon, 'Priests Do Not Know of Massacre', *Daily Telegraph*, 14 July 1973. For the impact of Loudon's efforts, see James J. Kilpatrick, 'The Portuguese Atrocity that Didn't Happen', *National Review*, 10 May 1974, pp. 525–27.

102. Interview with J.D.F. Jones, 3 November 1995.
103. 'Telegrafted Tales', *Time Out*, No. 308, 6 February 1976, p. 5.
104. Ibid., p. 5.
105. Bergerol's reports apparently became more radical as the war progressed. Her reports for BBC World Service were cancelled with no explanation during the spring of 1976. (Interview with Stanley Uys, 5 January 1995.) Bergerol remained in Angola for many years after the war, eventually abandoning journalism in order to study medicine. For allegations regarding other partial journalists of the liberal-left, see 'Letter from Angola', *Private Eye*, No. 418, 23 December 1977, p. 8.
106. Interviews with Bridget Bloom, 21 March 1995 and J.D.F Jones, 3 November 1995. Bergerol's retort is 'They were told to water it down ... The Foreign Office put pressure on the *Financial Times* on more than one occasion.' (Interview with Jane Bergerol (Wilford), 22 May 1995.)
107. Editorial, 'Russia's African Empire', *The Times*, 14 January 1976.
108. Notable exceptions include 'South Africa and Angola: The Reason Why', *Financial Times*, 29 December 1975; Nicholas Ashford, 'Marxist Slams "Africa Traitors"', *Sunday Times*, 11 January 1976; Nicholas Ashford, 'South Africa's Costly Blunder in Sending Troops to Angola', *The Times*, 2 February 1976; Jane Bergerol, 'Heading Towards the Thin White Line', *Financial Times*, 12 February 1976; Stanley Uys, 'UNITA Begged Vorster to Send Troops into Angola', *Guardian*, 16 February 1976.
109. Gerald J. Bender, 'Angola: A New Quagmire for US?', *Los Angeles Times*, 21 December 1975.
110. Stockwell, op. cit., p. 181.
111. 'Survival of the Fittest in the World's Scramble for Secrets', *To The Point*, 5 December 1975, p. 7.
112. Stockwell, op. cit., pp. 200–1.
113. Bernard Nossiter, 'Other Cloaks, Other Daggers II – Britain's Spies: Muddling Through', *Washington Post*, 22 December 1975. Some days later, Louis Heren (the foreign editor of *The Times*) appeared on 'Today', BBC Radio 4, to debunk the Nossiter report. ('London Diary', *New Statesman*, 16 January 1976, p. 66.) For information on the CIA's employment of journalists, see Miles Copeland, Letter to the editor, *New York Times*, 30 September 1977; Carl Bernstein, 'The CIA and the Media', *Rolling Stone*, No. 250 (20 October 1977), pp. 55–67.
114. Jonathan Bloch and Patrick Fitzgerald, *British Intelligence and Covert Action: Africa, Middle East and Europe since 1945* (Co. Kerry, Brandon Book Publishers, 1983), p. 194. See also *Private Eye*, No. 435, 18 August 1978, p. 4. During December 1975, Andrew Fraser, the youngest son of Lord Lovat, contributed two peculiar reports which suggested that Jonas Savimbi feared a South African plan to balkanise Angola. Fraser claimed that the South African intervention had been designed to destabilise UNITA: 'It is therefore South Africa's policy to weaken Savimbi with adverse publicity.' (Andrew Fraser, 'South Africa's Fear', *Spectator*, 13 December 1975, p. 758.) There is barely any evidence to supports this assertion. See also Andrew Fraser, 'Why Angola Needs Western Aid in the Fight for Stability', *The Times*, 8 December 1975.
115. The Club of Ten, 'The Free World Stands Today in Greater Danger ...', advertisement, *The Times*, 6 February 1976. See illustration.

116. Eschel Rhoodie, *The Real Information Scandal* (Pretoria, Orbis, 1983), p. 146.

117. 'Four Faces of Angola', *West Africa*, 2 February 1976, p. 130. See also Editorial, 'South Africa Loses', *New Society*, 19 February 1976, p. 370: 'For the first time since the Treaty of Vereeniging, 1902, white Afrikaner South Africa has lost a war.'

118. Benjamin Pogrund, 'A Gloomy Outlook for South Africa', *The Spectator*, 7 February 1976, p. 6. See also Editorial, 'Angola's Lesson for South Africa', *African Communist*, No. 65 (Second Quarter 1976), pp. 11–12: 'The era of the South African revolution has opened. *Are we ready for it?* ... If we fail to strike when the iron is hot, we may have to wait years for another chance.'

7

'The Children's Revolt', 1976

'I could take you down this street,' said a student whose home is in Soweto, 'and you'll find they all talk about Black Power. Vietnam will be nothing to this. Even with all the arms the white man has, I fear the day when the Africans take their revenge. The cruelty will be terrible. On the surface, it is quiet, but below there is a volcano.'[1]

Whatever is stirring in South Africa is taking place more among whites than the blacks. It is not revolution nor violence ... The two elements indispensable in any popular uprising are both missing in South Africa. One is a deep fury of resentment, and the other is freedom to strike at the governing system. There is no tension in South Africa today as the Middle East and Asia know it.[2]

Dan O'Meara has commented that 'Like "Munich" or "Suez", Soweto was one of those rare historical catalysts which irreversibly transform the political landscape, whose very name becomes a metaphor for lessons learned by an entire society.'[3] It is now accepted that the Soweto uprising represented a crucial juncture in contemporary South African history. In effect, the protest by African schoolchildren against the introduction of Afrikaans-language instruction, which developed into 18 months of intermittent unrest, signalled the end of 12 years of mainly muted African submission in the face of the repression of the South African state. The Soweto uprising inspired a resurgence of the industrial action already evident in 1972–73, and, eventually, the domestic reappearance of the ANC; it also possessed a millenarian quality which would reappear in the 1980s. 'Soweto' signified the emergence of a revitalised African agency and it sounded the first death knell for the apartheid regime.

This chapter examines the international media's coverage of the Soweto uprising and reveals that although the correspondents in South Africa and the commentators in Britain and the United States recognised the importance of the re-emergence of violent resistance in the Republic, the ensuing coverage demonstrated a profound ambiguity.

The cause of this ambiguity was the media's desire for an ordered resolution to the crisis in southern Africa and the conflict between this desire and the undisguised agency of the African students. The two widely differing assessments of African opinion in South Africa just before the uprising, at the head of this chapter, suggest that if a correspondent or commentator wished to discuss (and report on) African life in South Africa, it was advisable to talk to Africans. Neither writer was a 'liberal' but the first (Graham Turner) had visited Soweto and the second (Jerome Caminada) had not. The central lesson of the Soweto uprising for journalists in South Africa was that communication with Africans was essential. It would no longer be possible for a correspondent to depend on the domestic English-language press supplemented by occasional conversations with domestic workers and taxi-drivers. This chapter considers the coverage of the first ten days of the unrest; the importance of the photographic and television images of the struggle; the role played by African journalists in relaying the story through the structures of the South African press, and the international media's utilisation of that story; and the contradictions which emerged in the developing representation of the uprising. On 28 March 1960, Richard Dimbleby introduced the BBC's programme, 'Panorama', by drawing comparisons between the Sharpeville massacre and 'Guernica and Lidice, Belsen and Hola and Little Rock'.[4] The international media made no such comparison in 1976.

Although the signs that unrest was intensifying in the schools of Soweto had been apparent for some time, most of the correspondents and stringers were caught unprepared by the events of 16 June 1976.[5] The uprising, as it developed, represented an archetypal 'breaking story' during which the journalists' inability to witness the events made their dependence upon sources more than usually crucial. As these sources (the South African police and the African journalists) contradicted one another, the reports remained relatively confused. Nick Ashford, who had attempted unsuccessfully to see the unrest for himself, opened his first report with the police's version of events ('Police opened fire on the students who had started pelting them with stones ...'), before providing a degree of balance through a citation of Sophie Tema's account.[6] Robin Wright (*Washington Post*) quoted an unnamed but prescient Western diplomat who had commented: 'The damage has been done. This is an important signal of what the future may hold in store for South Africa. Blacks have shown they will actively protest government policy. This could be only the beginning.'[7] A number of other reports relayed the explanation provided by a police officer: 'We fired into them. It's no use firing over their heads.'[8]

The first editorial on the subject appeared in *The Times*. It focused on the wider ramifications of the language edict: 'It is in English that Africans can listen to the radio (east or west) and read the world's magazines and newspapers published in many countries ... [This is] precisely why the Afrikaners try to enforce their language. They do not wish to train the rising black generation to read the world's press or even the Johannesburg English press.'[9] The *Daily Telegraph* suggested that the world had changed since 1960 and that South Africa had failed to keep pace: 'the South African Government is in the wrong, both as to the cause of the riots and as to their handling'. However, the editorial also suggested that the riots 'may have been organised in the background by adults (and they must have been)' before enquiring why the South African police had not used water cannon instead of bullets.[10] In the American newspapers, only the *Christian Science Monitor* discussed the subject at this stage: 'it is just such instances as Soweto that could unify the usually passive black majority community into an all-out effort to take by force what it cannot obtain otherwise under the present system'.[11]

Coverage on the second day of the unrest continued to be limited by the inability of the foreign journalists to enter the townships. John Burns referred to the correspondents' dependence 'on information from the police and government officials'.[12] Resourceful journalists used the telephone to contact residents of Soweto.[13] On 19 June, a number of correspondents visited Alexandra township before the area was sealed off by the police. Peter Younghusband reported that he had witnessed police shooting into crowds: 'I saw police open fire on a group of black youths, who were clearly hostile, but not attacking – or, at that moment, doing any damage to property.'[14] However, the most detailed report was filed by Nicholas Ashford, who visited the northern perimeter of the township in the company of Stewart Dalby and Alain Cass of the *Financial Times*:

> One of the soldiers ran towards us. 'Go back, go back, or they will kill you', he cried. In fact, the Africans looked considerably less menacing than he did, so we decided to talk to them. When they heard we were British journalists they became friendly and talked openly to us, expressing their hatred of the system under which they were forced to live ... While we were talking we suddenly heard a burst of gunfire from the group of policemen who by that time were about 200 yards away down the road ... One of my colleagues saw one of the policemen fire, apparently unprovoked into a crowd of Africans. Certainly we saw no sign of any stones being thrown at the police.[15]

As if to balance Ashford's treatment, *The Times* also carried a report by a stringer, Richard Cecil, who had managed to enter Soweto on the same day. Cecil's report displayed little of the desire for accurate representation which dominated Ashford's and Dalby's work, preferring instead to rely on the clichés of traditional foreign correspondence: 'I narrowly escaped death from a mob of angry Africans in the heart of Soweto this morning. "If we slow down now we're both dead," said my driver, as we accelerated towards a group of African youths …'[16] Meanwhile, the *New York Times* demonstrated its irritation at not having been supplied with any interview material from its correspondent, John Burns, by carrying two reports directly from the news agency wires.[17]

The editorials in the American press were primarily mediated by the regional imperatives of the Cold War.[18] The *New York Times* argued that 'The deadly riots – the worst South Africa has ever known – underscore, however, that there is no hope for permanent order when the law does not promise justice and equality.'[19] The *Los Angeles Times* echoed the concern with order: 'the riots represent no triumph for the moderation and orderly change that should be the hallmarks for a just settlement of differences between southern Africa's blacks and whites'.[20] Meanwhile, in Britain, the *Sunday Express* launched the first tentative defence of the South African government's response to the uprising: 'no one should imagine that the rioting was spontaneous. It was clearly timed to sabotage Dr Vorster's meeting with the US Secretary of State, Dr Kissinger … There are evilly disposed individuals who do not want agreement in Southern Africa, who for their own political purposes are willing to sacrifice the blood and the lives of Africans.'[21]

In addition to the editorials, the columnists began to comment on the subject. Anthony Lewis, for example, contributed a detailed account of the restrictions imposed upon Africans in South Africa. His conclusion stands as an important stage in the rehabilitation of the reputations of previous African leaders:

> The situation is about as intractable and as dangerous as could be imagined, and it is made the worse by the absence of responsible black leadership. The natural black leaders have mostly been pinched [sic] off by the Government: Nelson Mandela in prison, Robert Sobukwe restricted to a remote town, many student leaders prosecuted or in detention.[22]

In contrast, Peregrine Worsthorne expressed his 'awed respect' at what he perceived to be a demonstration of white South African strength. Worsthorne continued: 'the South African whites are not like most of the rest of Western mankind, whose will to defend itself has been softened by liberal inhibitions, post-imperial guilt and the fear of thermonuclear destruction encapsulated in the phrase "better Red than dead". For them it is most emphatically not a case of "better black than dead".'[23]

Among the reports which summarised the week's events, Christopher Munnion's analysis depended the most closely on South African police sources. He suggested 'that some sections of the demonstrators were anticipating violence. Many groups of youths were carrying batons, shields and knives when they joined the march. And some groups of young blacks had started stoning cars and looting *before* the police arrived on the scene.'[24] No conclusive evidence to support this contention was ever presented. In the *Chicago Tribune*, reporters who had recently conducted a tour of southern Africa offered their explanation for the unrest: 'It's easy to understand what lay behind the flames and gunfire and looting. All you have to do is stroll around [Soweto] with your eyes open. It's a massive sprawling dump.'[25] Denis Herbstein attempted to extend the coverage to include the projected independence of the homelands. He suggested that 'If protests against Afrikaans can spark off a momentous rebellion like last week's there is one issue which could take it further still. When the Transkei becomes "independent" in October, all Xhosas living in white cities will become citizens of that homeland, whether they want to or not.'[26]

Keith Waterhouse, in the *Daily Mirror*, adopted a facetious tone in order to attack the apologists of South Africa: 'Just because there are black bodies lying about all over the township of Soweto, there is no need to get an isolated and highly publicised incident out of perspective. As anyone who has ever been to South Africa will tell you, you have got to go out there and see schoolchildren being shot at first hand before forming an opinion.'[27] Waterhouse's column may well have been directly aimed at the editorial which appeared in the *Daily Mail* on the same day. The editorial obliquely criticised the 'double standard' which rated the murder of schoolchildren (or 'black rioters') in Soweto above the slaughter in Cambodia. Paradoxically, the newspaper proceeded to suggest that the scale of the coverage was testament to the freedom of the press in South Africa. The conclusion of the editorial bears repetition for its logic:

> As we view with apprehension and sorrow the future for South Africa and all its people, we have one moral duty above all others. *Not to feed false hopes.* There is no virtue in encouraging the black bondsmen of South Africa to cast off their chains, if they are to exchange them for a well-aimed police bullet in the head. It would be as cruel and heartless as to ask the Czech people to rise up and take on the Soviet tanks ...

> The West must maintain its contacts with South Africa. Only through contact can pressure be exerted.[28]

The arrival of Michael Kaufman in South Africa, from Nairobi, had an immediate effect on the coverage in the *New York Times*. The newspaper's correspondent, John Burns, had previously relied upon official statements and media sources. Inspired by Kaufman, Burns engaged in 'dozens of conversations' with ordinary South Africans.[29] At a press conference on 20 June, Kaufman asked Jimmy Kruger, the Minister of Justice, why the police had not used rubber bullets. Kruger's reply that rubber bullets 'make people tame to the gun' became the first of his many widely-reported insensitive statements.[30] As the intensity of the unrest in South Africa decreased, the international media continued to publish articles which examined the background to and the potential consequences of the conflict.[31] Bernard Levin's comments were among the more extreme. He suggested that Kruger's remarks 'richly deserved wiping from the speaker's lips with a blow', and attacked the English-speaking whites of South Africa for what he considered to be their hypocrisy and selfishness:

> Many of the English there have been among the worst defenders of the vilest excesses of apartheid, and without even the mad ideology that is to be found somewhere embedded in Nationalist cruelty; for the English who live off apartheid while looking down on the uncouth Afrikaner there has rarely been anything more theoretical than selfishness involved. In the end, the black majority in South Africa will have to strike the shackles from its own wrists.[32]

Some representatives of the international media were allowed to re-enter the townships on 24 June as the South African police judged the unrest to have abated. Correspondents began to refer to the lack of obvious leadership amongst the students. In an article which compared the US race riots of the 1960s with the disturbances in South Africa, Michael Kaufman commented that the major difference was 'that while in American cities there were black organizations and individuals who articulated the feelings and motives of mobs and looters, none exist here'.[33] Robin Wright later expanded this point: 'no clear statement was made by any articulate spokesman during five days of violence, so it is difficult to understand what specifically the "minorities" would accept as interim steps in the "right" direction'.[34] Denis Herbstein used the opportunity provided by the apparent cessation in the unrest to attempt a refutation of South African police disinformation. In response to the police reports of random anarchic violence, Herbstein countered that only four homes had been attacked, and asserted: 'it is clear from the targets that the hatred was not mindlessly expressed'.[35] Christopher Munnion signalled the aftermath of the unrest by including a joke in the final paragraph of his report: 'An opposition spokesman in Parliament suggested that less trouble might be caused if black townships were given "English-style corner pubs" instead of large soul-less beer halls. Soweto wags now talk of meeting their friends down at the old "Clenched Fist" or popping over for a pint to "The Imperialist Running Dog".'[36] The *New Statesman*'s editorial acknowledged that the British media treatment of South Africa had shifted significantly since the Sharpeville massacre:

> Few developments have been more depressing over the past decade than the way in which racial oppression in South Africa has come to be accepted by the world community as a fact of life – uncomfortable, no doubt, but something we must all learn to live with in an unemotional way. The change has perhaps been most striking in Britain. Sixteen years ago there was no doubting the universal sense of outrage – uniting Left and Right alike – that greeted the Sharpeville massacre; this week Mr Vorster was to be heard from Germany not only actually quoting with approbation from the *Sunday Express* but also congratulating 'all the British newspapers' on the tone of their comments on the latest police carnage – a tone, he said, that he found 'an agreeable contrast' to the reaction of the press in his own country. The truth, sadly, is that even the British liberal conscience has long since put South Africa on the back-burner ... those on the Left are told today to 'face facts' and to 'come to terms with reality'. But what has happened in Soweto and Alexandra and the other townships over the past week should at least enable us to realise just what the 'reality' is that we are being asked to accept. For all the bland advertising of bodies like the 'Club of Ten', South Africa stands starkly revealed as being today just as ruthless a police state as it ever was in Dr Verwoerd's time.[37]

Stanley Uys, who had not been in the Republic during the first period of the unrest, suggested that 'the Western world acknowledges ... that control in South Africa is firmly in the hands of Mr Vorster's Afrikaner Government, that the Government has the capacity to wreak immense havoc in Southern Africa, and that the time has passed for the simplistic response of putting South Africa beyond the pale – that somehow it has to be brought within the reach of rational argument'.[38] Another reason for the shift in the coverage from 1960 to 1976 related to the concurrent decline in Western optimism regarding sub-Saharan

Africa. The fundamental difference between Sharpeville and Soweto, however, lay in the nature of the protests. In March 1960, African protest was non-violent and many of the protesters were shot in the back. Therefore, the international media represented the protest as passive. The schoolchildren in Soweto could not, and were not, considered to be passive; their agency was apparent for all to see. In effect, the juxtaposition of African agency and the challenge to order which the riots represented encouraged a contradictory and, in comparison to Sharpeville, muted response from the international media. As Eschel Rhoodie later informed Mervyn Rees, 'Had the riots lasted a week and been confined only to Soweto, the media would have dropped the matter.'[39] Indeed, South Africa's propagandists were relatively pleased with the 'interesting divergences and ambiguities' in the coverage of the initial unrest:

> Despite conventional Whitehall statements about deep shock to public opinion and opposition to apartheid, there is unexpected confusion in the British attitude. This confusion stems partly from Britain's image of John Vorster as statesman-realist who would put the screws on Rhodesia's Ian Smith ... From Washington it is reported that US officials are saying privately that every sovereign nation has the right to maintain civil order and that, regardless of ideology, any other Government would have had to operate the way South Africa did when the riots erupted.[40]

Modern historical events are nearly always accompanied by iconic images which stand as powerful but simplified versions of the incidents being reported. The Soweto uprising was no exception. As has been noted, few, if any, British or American reporters or photographers were present when the language protest erupted into violence. The first mediators in the struggle were the African photographers whose images came to symbolise the events of June 1976. The 'Today' programme on BBC Radio 4 commented, by way of introduction on the morning of 17 June: 'I don't know how many of you have had the chance yet to read your morning paper but most of them carry the somewhat horrifying pictures of schoolchildren in the South African town of Soweto being shot dead by South African police.'[41]

Three photographs, which were taken by African photographers and syndicated by the news agencies, were reproduced on the front pages of newspapers around the world.[42] Each image, however, offered a different interpretation of the conflict. The most famous of these photographs, Sam Nzima's picture of the dying Hector Pieterson, symbolised the brutality of the South African state and the passive (or victim-like) status of the schoolchildren. In this respect, Nzima's photograph portrayed Soweto as an extension of the Sharpeville massacre. He later recalled that although his colleagues and editors had been delighted with the photograph, informing him that 'You put *The World* on the map', he had also been subject to 'a lot of harassment from the police. They phoned my editor and said they wanted me because I had "sold" this bad image of South Africa to communist countries.'[43] Following months of such intimidation, Nzima abandoned photo-journalism in 1977. The second photograph, which he is also thought to have taken, was of African policemen shooting their handguns at a target which was not visible in the picture.[44] This image might be interpreted to represent the restoration of order, in the process acknowledging the brutality of the South African state while avoiding the issue of the agency of the African protesters. The fact that the policemen in the photograph were Africans led Mr Robert Stovall, an analyst with Reynolds Securities, to suggest that because of this 'black-on-black' image the New York Stock Exchange had not lost its confidence in the South African economy.[45]

The third photograph, Peter Magubane's treatment of the students running at the camera, represented them as active or, in the words under the original reproduction in the *Rand Daily Mail*, 'happy-go-lucky'.[46] However, the photograph was deeply ambiguous and could also be read as a representation of a violent and threatening mob. The Magubane picture was the antithesis of the Nzima–Pieterson image, symbolising strength and energy, where Nzima recorded misery and destruction. The decision to focus solely on the students and to dispense with the South African police transformed the photograph into a classic representation of black consciousness, or perhaps more accurately, black power. Alternatively, the image could be interpreted as symbolising the Soweto uprising as a race riot: black versus white. In effect, the three pictures represented differing instant interpretations of the Soweto uprising. Sam Nzima's portrait of the death of Hector Pieterson captured the last moments of the previously dominant representation of Africans as passive, docile, weak and defeated. Peter Magubane's treatment of the running students symbolised a new portrayal of active resistance, albeit interpretable as random, anarchic violence. The 'handgun' picture represented the violence of the state and the South African government's co-option of compliant Africans. It pointed towards the desperate attempts at the manipulation of existing tensions which would occur during August 1976.

Television had been introduced into South Africa during February 1976.[47] The Soweto uprising was one of the first major stories that the South African Broadcasting Corporation (SABC) had been called upon to cover. Erik Van Ees commented some weeks after the beginning of the unrest that 'television screens and newspaper photographs have given many whites their first look into Soweto, Mamelodi, Alexandra, and the other squalid communities where their employees and servants live'.[48] The vision that greeted them was brutal:

> The state-owned South African Broadcasting Corporation last night screened scenes from the Alexandra riots showing uniformed police, kneeling to take aim, firing at three rock-throwing blacks. After hurling one fist-sized stone at the police, a man in a blue sweater danced back and forward, found another rock, and was taking aim when his hand dropped to the sound of gunfire. He jolted sideways and keeled over … Scores of bleeding blacks were led away by police in the television films.[49]

Although it seems to run against the South African government's usual tendency to attempt to control the media, the SABC images of the violent unrest were supplied to the international media.[50] There are three possible explanations. The first contends that far from reflecting the media naivety of the SABC, graphic films were broadcast as an early stage in what Deborah Posel has called the 'battlefield of perceptions – an ideological contest between competing versions of events'.[51] By representing the African protesters as a leaderless, unthinking, mob, engaged in stone-throwing and destructive violence, the films could emphasise the opposition between 'supposedly "traditional"/"primitive" and "civilised" behaviour'. In this context, police violence could be interpreted as 'a reasonable, restrained defence against the barbarism of mindless mobs'.[52] A significant number of viewers in Britain and the United States, however, did not perceive either the unrest or the response of the police through the lens of a white South African's cultural experience. The South African government thus discovered that the 'battlefield of perceptions' was subject to ambiguous interpretation. Alternatively, the SABC may only have been fulfilling its contractual obligations with the international broadcasting networks, and earning revenue in the process.[53] Perhaps the most likely explanation is that the SABC genuinely believed its own version of events and failed to recognise that the films could be viewed differently.

The significance of the SABC footage lay only partly in its brutal images. The films also acted as a magnet for the international broadcasters. An article published in the *World* suggested that the US media were forced by the events in South Africa to undergo a rapid education in the subject: 'On a reference blackboard in the *New York Times* editorial offices are the boldly scrawled words: "Soweto" and "King Williamstown". In a television network's tape bank, a South African voice is on tap to pronounce "Soo-oo-leh-too", "Buhfootuhwanuh" and "Melkbawsstrunt".'[54] Although the international media did not establish bureaus in the Republic until 1977, a Thames Television film crew did manage to enter the country soon after the initial unrest and returned with a report which *Anti-Apartheid News* described as 'stark and straight, unembellished by balancing tricks in which "the other side" is represented. It seemed too short, but that is a comment which comes from gratitude.'[55] The documentary which had been made at a 'secret location' in South Africa 'showed the most graphic film footage yet of the scale of the township violence.'[56] The film also featured an extended interview with Tsietsi Mashinini, former executive member of the South African Students' Movement and president of the Soweto Students' Representative Council.

Mashinini's comments dramatised the passage of African passivity and the emergence of a confident agency: 'I really believe that five years will be too much. If South Africa does not change within the course of this year ... it means that South Africa will have riots as its daily meal and then it may change from riots to something more drastic. For now riots are centred in black townships. Some day or other the target will be made residential suburbs.'[57] In London, the complaints of Chris van der Walt (the Director of Information at the South African Embassy) fell on deaf ears. David Elstein, the producer of the programme stated: 'I hope they go ahead with their complaint to the IBA. The answer will be, I feel, that we fulfilled our professional role by getting this very important story and bringing it to the public even though our way was blocked by the censorial attitude of the South Africans. I would not hesitate to smuggle a crew in again if I had to.'[58] Within South Africa, the film also had a powerful impact. Both the *Rand Daily Mail* and the *World* published reports which included extensive quotations from Mashinini's interview.[59] In effect, British television had provided a method for bypassing the censorship regulations.

To what extent the coverage broadcast by the SABC and the reports published by the South African newspapers actually contributed to sustaining the protests remains an open question. On 17 June 1976, the *World* reported that 'When the CNA truck arrived with copies of *The World*, there was a free-for-all. Nobody bought papers. They were just grabbed and the streets were cluttered with papers flying in all directions.'[60] Six months later, Jim Hoagland started an article with the following cautionary tale:

> Standing quietly in the yard, the African workers gazed in through the living-room window at the new television set in the foreman's house,

where the white farmer's wife obligingly swept the curtains back for two hours each night. This nightly scene began on a large farm in the Eastern Cape Province a year ago, when the government finally permitted television here. It stopped abruptly in August after, as the foreman's wife said in a trembling voice to a friend, 'Soweto came to the farm.' Sheds on this and other white-owned farms in the region went up in flames that night.[61]

If this episode was being repeated more widely, perhaps, the 'people [who were] buying transistors, tape decks and television sets, as if suddenly eager to latch onto a few small pleasures in life' in the *Time* report of June 1977, *were* making a political purchase, despite William McWhirter's assessment that it was a sign 'of a new kind of life in Soweto, a spirit that is not limited to political consciousness'.[62]

African journalism in South Africa had a long and respectable history.[63] During the 1950s, *Drum* magazine served as a beacon for a particularly innovative new form of populist journalism. As Shaun Johnson has observed, 'Whilst retaining ... an element of thorough investigative reporting documenting black grievances, and nurturing some of South Africa finest writers, the magazine was a step away from the original pioneering black publications.'[64] Although repressed in the 1960s, African journalism once again embraced radicalism, in the form of the Black Consciousness Movement (BCM), during the 1970s. In 1971, 30 journalists in Johannesburg formed the Union of Black Journalists (UBJ). Harry Mashabela (an ex-*Drum* writer) was elected as the first president. The UBJ quickly formed a close bond with the South African Student Organisation (SASO). In 1973, Mashabela was replaced as president by Joe Thloloe. During 1975, the UBJ published its own tabloid periodical the *Bulletin*, which according to *Anti-Apartheid News* was 'an attempt to counter the "complete control" which ... whites have over the opinion-making machinery which conditions the attitudes of South African blacks'.[65]

Meanwhile, Percy Qoboza, appointed editor of the *World* and *Weekend World* in 1974, had been spending a year as a Nieman fellow at Harvard University. Towards the end of the period of his fellowship, Qoboza stated in an interview with the *Washington Post*: 'The Black journalist in South Africa must ask himself: "What comes first, my personal comfort or ... the broad black consciousness movement?" I have decided I am part of the struggle.'[66] Qoboza returned to South Africa on 8 June 1976 as the first African editor to be in complete control of a newspaper owned by the Argus Group; previous editors of the *World* had had their work overseen by a white editorial director. Seizing the opportunity, he moderated the *World*'s sensationalist tone and concentrated on providing a voice which could mediate between the African parents and students. Additionally, as Qoboza later commented, it had '[fallen] on the shoulders of black journalists to keep South Africa and the outside world informed about what was going on [in Soweto]'.[67]

During the first days of the Soweto uprising, African journalists found some sections of the British media were keen to publish their insights. The *Daily Express* started this process by commissioning a special report from the veteran [Johannesburg] *Star* reporter in South Africa, Langa Skosana.[68] Two days later, the *Sunday Times*, in place of an editorial, explained that 'We give our space and our comment today to a black reporter on the *Rand Daily Mail*, Nat Diseko.'[69] On the same day, the *Observer* carried a report by Alf Kumalo, a photographer on the [Johannesburg] *Sunday Times*.[70] The Soweto uprising had thus immediately transformed the significance of the African journalists. As Caryle Murphy commented some time later, 'black South African journalists had traditionally been consigned the role of "leg men", the unsung gatherers of facts who turned over their notes to white reporters who generally got the byline – and the credit – for the story'.[71] The events of 1976 and the inability or the unwillingness of white journalists to report from the townships led to a situation where 'many [representatives of the foreign media] turned to *The World* ... "The BBC was calling five times a day," recalled *World* editor Percy Qoboza. "I finally had to tell them I was also trying to run a newspaper".'[72] Although African journalists undoubtedly exerted a mediating influence on the international media's coverage, they paid a high price for this influence. At the end of July, the South African police detained Harry Mashabela.[73] At the time of his arrest, he had taken leave of absence from his job as a reporter on the [Johannesburg] *Star* to write a book about the unrest with fellow reporter, Graeme Addison. In Mashabela's account, which was eventually published 11 years later, he recalled that the first question he was asked by the police related to the book project.[74]

The second stage of violent unrest erupted on 4 August and the townships were immediately sealed, making entrance by white journalists virtually impossible.[75] The intimidation of their African contemporaries continued apace: a petrol bomb was thrown at Peter Magubane's house on 5 August.[76] Less than a week later, he suffered a compound fracture of the nose after being beaten by the South African police.[77] Nonetheless, African reporters continued to bring exceptional stories out of Soweto. Jan Tugwana (*Rand Daily Mail*), for example, reported that he had spent the night of 24 August hiding in a coal-box. While there he had overheard the following statement:

'We didn't order you to destroy the West Rand (Administration Board) property, Zulus ... You were asked to fight people only.'[78] The next day, another *Rand Daily Mail* journalist, Nat Serache, managed to slip inside Mzimhlope hostel disguised in 'Zulu dress': 'There I saw a policeman in a camouflage suit ... Through an interpreter, [he] said: "You are warned not to continue damaging the houses because they belong to the West Rand Administration Board. If you damage houses, you will force us to take action against you to prevent this. You have been ordered to kill only these troublemakers."'[79] The Tugwana–Serache stories were supported by reporters on other newspapers. The [Johannesburg] *Star*, for instance, reported that one of its journalists had overheard an African policeman instructing hostel dwellers to 'eat and drink well so they could "kill on full stomachs"'.[80]

A number of stringers and foreign correspondents duly relayed the story of the Zulu hostel dwellers' collusion with the South African police.[81] An equal number, however, found the traditional representation of 'the Zulu' too powerful to ignore.[82] Only Robin Wright felt that further explanation was needed: 'ironically, many of the residents who fought the Zulu migrant workers and a large share of the black police who tried to restore order were also Zulu'.[83] The American media, in particular, devoted a series of columns and editorials to the subject of 'black-on-black' violence. The liberal position was taken by Tom Wicker in the *New York Times*: 'Even police efforts to set one group of blacks against another, while producing more violence, did not succeed in bringing the boycott to an end.'[84] Conservative commentators barely acknowledged the link between the second mass 'stay-at-home' which had begun on 23 August and the encouragement of the migrant workers' retaliation. The *Chicago Tribune* suggested:

> South Africa's troubles are no longer simply a matter of blacks rioting and white police trying to restrain them. We now find blacks fighting blacks ... This is the clearest refutation yet of the myth of Black solidarity in South Africa. Those who call for early black majority rule there also insist on believing in this myth – for without it their prescription would mean an Angola-type civil war and chaos.[85]

The importance of the work of the African journalists can be gauged from the fact that equivalent examples of South African police collusion in Cape Town during Christmas 1976 were not reported in the Cape newspapers.[86] The reporters who worked for the *Rand Daily Mail*, however, continued to be subject to a humiliating degree of editorial interference. Serache, for example, felt that his copy was being 'butchered'.[87] Patrick Laurence claimed at the time that 'Blacks were less inclined to question eye-witness accounts and were more likely to give credibility to police brutality. White reporters in supervisory positions were more critical.'[88] Mike Dutfield later informed Les Payne that 'I collected the blacks' stories and wrote articles for the white edition [of the newspaper]. The black reporters were out in Soweto risking their necks and I was back in the office getting credit for the stories in the paper. For a while it was getting hostile. The blacks didn't like the set-up, and I don't blame them.'[89]

If the South African white newspapers failed to fully appreciate the exceptional talents of the African journalists, the South African police did not. The UBJ's periodical, the *Bulletin*, was banned and Peter Magubane was detained on 26 August.[90] The UBJ's president, Joe Thloloe was detained on 2 September, with Nat Serache and Jan Tugwana following him into custody on 3 and 9 September, respectively.[91] Clive Emdon, vice-president of the South African Society of Journalists, commented at the time: 'Black journalists who recorded the events in Soweto in the past weeks displayed amazing courage and performed a job in the greatest traditions of the Press. It was because they felt their reports and pictures were not properly used in the 'White-owned Press' that they saw the need for [a] bulletin which would tell the whole truth.'[92] During the uprising, however, African reporters experienced a transformation in their status within the townships. Journalism began to be perceived by young Africans as a possible avenue for resistance.[93] The dramatic increase in the *World*'s circulation from 105,000 to 200,000 copies, before the newspaper was banned in October 1977, demonstrated the importance of Qoboza and his staff's achievement. Recalling the transformation in 1978, Sophie Tema commented: 'In the past, people used to shun you, used to say, "Journalists, oh, they are liars," ... It's different now ... They will help you and even come and tell you things. But they also put more pressure on us, too. They demand to know more from us and want us to inform them.'[94] The mere fact that the international media's reports from South Africa were full of stories which originated with the African journalists was a testimony of a different type. By the autumn of 1976, diligent foreign correspondents slowly began to explain the role played by the African journalists in updating and authenticating the coverage of the Soweto uprising.[95]

The images of the unrest in South Africa and the reports of the African journalists served a useful function in moderating the coverage in the international media. However, for the British and American correspondents and commentators, the primary theme of the coverage was the dichotomy of order and disorder. This theme was one which affected the entire southern African region. The Cuban involvement in Angola, the burgeoning conflict in Rhodesia/Zimbabwe and the negotiations over South West Africa/Namibia had, in effect, been given priority over South Africa in Kissinger's post-Angola initiative. The fundamental problem, apartheid, was thus condemned, but not directly challenged. As the *Washington Star* observed in June 1976, 'The turmoil is an unwanted complication in the meeting planned in West Germany this week between Secretary of State Kissinger and South African Prime Minister John Vorster ... Increased pressure on South African apartheid, at this moment, could reduce the chance for détente and, with it, the incentive to promote a Rhodesian settlement.'[96] This impression that Vorster and the South African government were no more than supporting players in a sub-continental crisis was echoed in many of the cartoons of the period.[97]

The meetings between Kissinger and Vorster which framed the central period of the unrest in South Africa were treated by the international media as if they were only tenuously linked to the violence in the townships.[98] For students in South Africa, the American focus on southern Africa undoubtedly provided the greatest opportunity to publicise the iniquities of apartheid since the early 1960s. By organising demonstrations and strikes, which were normally met with police brutality, the protesters both willingly and unwillingly contributed to the representation of disorder. Although this was effective in 'destroy[ing] the impression of South African stability and invulnerability' and was a critical factor in the process of transforming the representation of the African population, it also assisted in the creation of an image of the protesters as a leaderless, amorphous mass, incapable of negotiation.[99]

The confusion engendered by the student protest had a particular effect on 'liberal' South African commentators. In August 1976, Stanley Uys commented that 'The attitude of many black youngsters is significantly different from that of their parents. They are patently not interested in improving their condition: they want an explosion, a catharsis.'[100] He picked up the theme two weeks later: 'Whereas the black militants of the 1950s and 1960s were united politically by their opposition to apartheid, today's young blacks are united emotionally by their hatred of whites. It's a subtle, but terrifying, difference.'[101] Benjamin Pogrund (writing from America) recognised the problem facing liberal journalists: 'the battle lines between whites and blacks are being drawn more sharply, and attitudes on both sides are hardening by the day. That is cause for deep despair among the liberals. Even while the need for their mediation becomes more vital, they are conscious of being made increasingly irrelevant.'[102] The tensions and fears bound up in this sense of increasing irrelevance exerted a powerful influence over the less experienced correspondents. John Burns, for instance, commented that 'Unlike Mr Mandela, who is the son of a tribal chief, most of the new leaders were born and peered [sic] in black townships. Most are in their 20's and their heroes are the heroes of American radicals – Mao Tse-Tung, Che Guevara, Malcolm X. Whereas Mr Mandela opted for violence only as a last resort, these young people speak calmly [of] terrorism against whites.'[103]

The Soweto uprising had, in effect, forced South African liberals to face the contradictions of their position. Alan Paton's widely syndicated assessment of the situation in the Republic was riddled with a terror of unrestrained African agency: 'I fear for the future of Afrikanerdom. I fear it is going to be destroyed ... I have my own fears too. If Afrikanerdom is destroyed, there will be no room here for any white person.'[104] Right-wing newspapers and commentators in Britain and the United States were equally concerned with the question of order, although they tended to perceive the problem only in relation to the South African government's ability to exercise control. The representation of African agency, far from instilling panic or philosophical angst in the commentaries of the international media, demonstrated the scale of the resistance to the apartheid system. As the unrest persisted, South Africa's natural sympathisers began a process of re-evaluation. In the *National Review*, James Burnham refuted South Africa's often-stated claims that 'the non-whites are satisfied with the system and the gradual improvement in their lot occurring under it, and ... the government chosen by the white electorate has things well in hand'.[105] The *Sunday Telegraph* acknowledged in an editorial that 'Mr Vorster's Government has given the impression of reacting to events rather than imperturbably controlling their course'.[106] Following the extensive bannings and detentions of African leaders, and the organisation of the second mass strike, the *Daily Telegraph*'s impatience with the Vorster administration was tangible:

> Outside observers of current events inside South Africa, however sympathetic to the cause and rights of white South Africans, could be excused for wondering whether the Nationalist Government of Mr Vorster is getting out of its depth. Has it a policy, other than that of sheer physical repression? ... Mr Vorster's Minister for Police, has expressed the view that the current unrest, of which there was more in Soweto yesterday, is due to agitators. Of course there are agitators, just as there were in Tsarist Russia, but they have a richly fertile ground in which to operate.[107]

By September, the *Daily Mail* had also come to terms with the need for fundamental change in southern Africa: 'The never-ending riots in the townships have exposed the pretence that the blacks accept apartheid ... Kissinger's timing is ruthless. It is also right. *For now, if ever, is the moment for white southern Africa to come to terms. Had he tried sooner, they would have felt too secure to listen. Later will be too late.*'[108] As the editorial position of the conservative media began to moderate, voices in support of the apartheid regime became somewhat isolated within the newspapers.[109] It rapidly became clear that the credit which Vorster had built up during the period of South Africa's détente with Black Africa had run out. One indication of this shift in tone was the *Guardian*'s decision to publish Richard Gott's polemical article in favour of the South African 'revolution': 'When I see photographs of the black radicals engaged in resistance in the townships, I fear for them. But I want them to win. I want them to destroy the evil system that the white man has created. I think they are going to be successful.'[110]

If the theme of order/disorder eventually inspired a degree of pragmatic comment in the international media, the overall commentary remained reactionary in comparison to that which had appeared following the Sharpeville massacre. The reactionary tone was, in part, a sluggish response to the widely-remarked upon African agency. In the immediate aftermath of the initial unrest, Robin Wright reported a conversation in Soweto as follows: '"Don't believe for a minute it's over," the handsome 23-year-old African declared, a smug smile across his face. "There's no way they can stop it now." They? "The whites." The white government? "No, every damn white. None of them mean anything."'[111] Three days later, Michael Kaufman quoted 'a young black salesman' as saying: 'There is a feeling that Soweto has showed that we are not quite so docile as the whites believed.'[112] Wright and Kaufman's reports symbolised two different transformations in the representation of Africans which would be employed in parallel by the international media during the months that followed June 1976. Wright's snide tone and her selective quotation of the '23-year-old' invoked an early twentieth-century representation of African confusion, irrationality, anger and ignorance. Her patronising description of the man as both 'handsome' and 'smug' would also have not been out of place 70 years earlier. Kaufman's 'salesman' is a completely different character who merely acknowledges the obvious, that the attribution of passivity to Africans and coloureds was inaccurate. The Soweto uprising had clearly destroyed that particular trope. As Percy Qoboza stated categorically some weeks later: 'the days of the good Kaffir and obedient Bantus belong to the ox-wagon era which is never to return'.[113] However, this did not stop the *Daily Telegraph*, for example, from suggesting that 'No doubt the rioters ... will retreat into a sullen passivity when enough of them have been killed'.[114]

Z. Nkosi observed in the *African Communist* that 'what died at Soweto ... was not the black hope of liberation but the white hope of pacification and eternal domination'.[115] The international media's interpretation of the uprising was fundamentally ambiguous. While the unrest had destroyed the South African government's reputation for authority, it had also inspired representations of African brutality, cruelty and primitivism. The shifts and fluctuations in the international media's coverage were, as we have seen, directly related to the complicated and contradictory representations which appeared in the domestic South African press. These representations were only partly balanced by the influence of the reports of the African journalists. The dependence of the foreign correspondents on the domestic media was of paramount importance in the development of the coverage.

Nadine Gordimer has remarked that 'Black children traditionally have been the object of white sentimentality; it is only after the girls grow breasts and the boys have to carry the passbook that chocolate suddenly turns black.'[116] The emergence of schoolchildren who were willing, in the words of June Goodwin, to 'vote with their lives', sent white South Africa's representations of African children, and by extension the representation of the African population, into flux.[117] This confusion unleashed the archaic colonial representations which were duly relayed by many within the international media. It also emphasised the simple but significant representational message that 'Passivity is gone.'[118]

NOTES

1. Graham Turner, 'Behind the Mask of Black South Africa', *Sunday Telegraph*, 28 March 1976.
2. Jerome Caminada, 'In South Africa, the Major Issue is Citizenship for the Blacks', *The Times*, 14 June 1976. See also Jerome Caminada, 'Looking for Answers in South Africa', *South Africa International*, Vol. 7, No. 2 (October 1976), pp. 95–100.
3. Dan O'Meara, *Forty Lost Years: The Apartheid State and the Politics of the National Party, 1948–1994* (Randburg, Ravan Press, 1996), p. 180.
4. Howard Smith, 'Apartheid, Sharpeville and "Impartiality": The Reporting of South Africa on BBC Television, 1948–1961', *Historical Journal of Film, Radio and Television*, Vol. 13, No. 3 (1993), p. 253.
5. Exceptions included Bridget Bloom, 'Potential Flashpoints in South Africa', *Financial Times*, 23 April 1976: 'By mid year it is thought that 8 per cent of the African workforce will be unemployed. It would not be surprising if this leads

to an escalation of unrest and protest among Blacks.'; Nicholas Ashford, 'Mr Vorster Rejects Dean's Plea', *The Times*, 15 June 1976: 'He feared South Africa might soon reach a point of no return beyond which nothing would stop events moving to a bloody denouement.'; Desmond Tutu, 'An Open Letter to Vorster', *Guardian*, 16 June 1976.

6. Nicholas Ashford, 'Six Die after South African Police Open Fire on Rioters', *The Times*, 17 June 1976. See also Sophie Tema, '"World" Car Rushes Shot Schoolboy Riot Victim to Clinic', *World*, 17 June 1976.

7. Robin Wright, 'S. Africa Blacks Riot, 23 Die', *Washington Post*, 17 June 1976.

8. Alain Cass and Stewart Dalby, 'Six Killed, 40 Injured in S. Africa Rioting', *Financial Times*, 17 June 1976.

9. Editorial, 'From Sharpeville to Soweto', *The Times*, 17 June 1976.

10. Editorial, 'South African Nemesis', *Daily Telegraph*, 18 June 1976.

11. Editorial, 'South Africa's Dark Cloud', *Christian Science Monitor*, 18 June 1976.

12. John Burns, 'South Africa Toll Rises to 58 Dead; Nearly 800 Hurt', *New York Times*, 18 June 1976.

13. Alain Cass and Stewart Dalby, 'Vorster Faces Storm in Cabinet as Riot Toll Mounts', *Financial Times*, 18 June 1976; 'Soweto', *Africa News*, Vol. 7, No. 2 (28 June 1976), p. 7.

14. Peter Younghusband, 'South Africa on the Brink', *Daily Mail*, 19 June 1976.

15. Nicholas Ashford, '"Go Back or They Will Kill You" Warning', *The Times*, 19 June 1976; Stewart Dalby, '"Time has Come for Bursting Out ..."', *Financial Times*, 19 June 1976. Alain Cass was the foreign news editor of the *Financial Times*, from 1976. See also Christopher Munnion, *Banana Sunday: Datelines from Africa*, second edition (Rivonia, William Waterman, 1995), p. 446.

16. Richard Cecil, 'Mobs Bring Terror to Soweto', *The Times*, 19 June 1976. Lord Richard Cecil, second son of the Marquis of Salisbury, had served with the Grenadier Guards and the SAS before turning to journalism. At this point, he was working as a stringer for *The Times*. Cecil would later contribute to the National Association for Freedom's (NAFF) newspaper, *Free Nation*. He was killed by African guerrillas in Rhodesia/Zimbabwe on 20 April 1978. See Munnion, op. cit., pp. 10, 384, 394–95; Ed Harriman, *Hack: Home Truths about Foreign News* (London, Zed Books, 1987), pp. 124–25; 'Tribute to Lord Richard Cecil', *Free Nation*, 28 April 1978, p. 3.

17. UPI and Reuters, 'Moments of Kindness in Blacks and Whites', *New York Times*, 19 June 1976.

18. An exception was the *Boston Globe*. During the summer of 1976, Benjamin Pogrund was on a work exchange between the *Boston Globe* and the *Rand Daily Mail*. Following the events in Soweto, he was requested to write articles and editorials on the subject. (Interview with Benjamin Pogrund, 12 September 1995.) See Editorial, 'Tragedy in South Africa', *Boston Globe*, 19 June 1976.

19. Editorial, 'Somber Warning', *New York Times*, 20 June 1976.

20. Editorial, 'A Signal, but No Triumph', *Los Angeles Times*, 20 June 1976.

21. Editorial, 'Folly', *Sunday Express*, 20 June 1976.

22. Anthony Lewis, 'South Africa's Apartheid, a Violence-prone Policy', *New York Times*, 20 June 1976.

23. Peregrine Worsthorne, 'Black Day for Black S. Africa', *Sunday Telegraph*, 20 June 1976. It appears as if the *Sunday Telegraph*'s sub-editors felt that Worsthorne's position required a degree of balance. Worsthorne's article was illustrated by a South African Tourist Corporation advertisement: a picture of wild animals with the words 'Discover South Africa' superimposed upon it; alongside the advertisement was a reproduction of Sam Nzima's photograph of

the dying Hector Pieterson with the same words superimposed. For the Nzima photograph, see illustrations.

24. Christopher Munnion, 'What One Man Knew about His Own Death', *Sunday Telegraph*, 20 June 1976. Munnion attempted to confirm the allegation some days later, 'independent corroboration ... came from a Johannesburg newspaper editor who found pictures of stone-throwing youths placed at his desk at about the same time the police fired their first shots'. (Christopher Munnion, 'Soweto's Troubles will Not Go Away', *Daily Telegraph*, 2 July 1976.)

25. James Yuenger and Clarence Page, 'Wheel of Hatred Turns, S. African Town Explodes', *Chicago Tribune*, 20 June 1976.

26. Denis Herbstein, 'Why a White Language Law Ignited a Black Powderkeg', *Sunday Times*, 20 June 1976.

27. Keith Waterhouse, 'Horses' Mouths', *Daily Mirror*, 21 June 1976.

28. Editorial, 'We Have a Duty Not to Feed False Hopes', *Daily Mail*, 21 June 1976.

29. Interview with Michael Kaufman, 9 September 1995. See John F. Burns, 'Despite alarm over racial violence, most White South Africans Seem to Support the Status Quo' and Michael T. Kaufman, '10 Reported Slain in Riots in Townships of Pretoria', *New York Times*, 22 June 1976.

30. Interview with Michael Kaufman, 9 September 1995. Chris Munnion incorrectly credits this question to Charles Mohr. (Munnion, op. cit., p. 426.) Kruger's insensitive statements multiplied in the 15 months that followed, culminating with his comment that Biko's death 'leaves me cold'. (Ray Kennedy, 'S. African Editor Demands Apology from Kruger', *Daily Telegraph*, 17 October 1977.)

31. Examples included Max Hastings, 'The Dream Factory Still Can't Smell Smoke', *Evening Standard*, 22 June 1976; Norman Sklarewitz, 'Soweto: A Preview of Things to Come?', *Los Angeles Times*, 22 June 1976; Donald Woods, 'Dress Rehearsal in South Africa', *New Statesman*, 25 June 1976, pp. 833–34; Nadine Gordimer, 'Apartheid, the "Agitator"', *New York Times*, 27 June 1976; See also Alan Paton, 'The Beloved Country Cries Again ...', *Daily Express*, 18 June 1976; Alan Paton, 'South Africa', *New York Times*, 24 June 1976, republished in the *Los Angeles Times*, 27 June 1976; 'South Africa: Black Explosion', *Time*, 28 June 1976, pp. 1, 10–13; Peter Younghusband, 'Sharpeville to Soweto', *Newsweek*, 28 June 1976, pp. 6–8.

32. Bernard Levin, 'A Lesson Still Unlearned as the Dead are Counted', *The Times*, 22 June 1976.

33. Michael T. Kaufman, 'The Tragedy of Soweto', *New York Times*, 25 June 1976.

34. Robin Wright, 'Change: Elusive Concept in S. Africa', *Washington Post*, 28 June 1976.

35. Denis Herbstein, 'S. Africa Bans Mass Burial of Soweto Schoolchildren', the *Guardian*, 25 June 1976.

36. Christopher Munnion, 'Minister Accuses Whites of Inciting Soweto Riots', *Daily Telegraph*, 25 June 1976. Munnion apparently included this fictional joke in the final paragraph of his report, expecting it to be removed by the sub-editor. (Interview with Chris Munnion, 10 May 1995.)

37. Editorial, 'Naught for Dr Kissinger's Comfort', *New Statesman*, 25 June 1976, p. 831. The *Sunday Express* responded to Vorster's comments, by demanding 'If Mr Vorster likes the style and fairness of the Sunday Express so much, why does he not take the advice given to him in that same leader? And stop trying to force the archaic Afrikaans language down the throats of Bantu children?' Editorial, 'End It', *Sunday Express*, 27 June 1976. The almost racist, anti-Afrikaner, tone of the *Sunday Express*'s editorial was a feature of much of the coverage of this period.

38. Stanley Uys, 'Why Dr K Plays Footsie Footsie', [Johannesburg] *Sunday Times*, 4 July 1976.

39. Mervyn Rees and Chris Day, *Muldergate: The Story of the Info Scandal* (Johannesburg, Macmillan, 1980), p. 186.

40. 'How Other Nations Reacted', *To The Point*, 2 July 1976, p. 60. See also 'The Riots: British Views' and 'US Responses', *The South Africa Foundation News*, Vol. 2, No. 7 (July 1976), p. 1: '[British] Coverage of events in Soweto has been wide and fair', 'American reaction to the black riots in South Africa has been relatively calm and unsensational'.

41. 'Today', BBC Radio 4, 17 June 1976.

42. For reproductions of the photographs see illustrations. Sam Nzima's photograph of the dying Hector Pieterson appeared first in the *World*, late edition, 16 June 1976, p. 1. It was then syndicated by AP. The *Los Angeles Times*, late edition, 16 June carried the picture on p. 2. On 17 June, the photograph appeared on the front page of *The Times*, *Guardian*, *Daily Telegraph*, *Sun*, *San Francisco Chronicle* and the *Chicago Sun-Times*. The *Chicago Tribune*, *New York Times*, *Daily Mirror* and *Daily Express* carried the picture on their inside pages. The *Sunday Telegraph* reproduced the picture to accompany Peregrine Worsthorne's article on 20 June and the *Financial Times* published the picture on 21 June to accompany an article by Bridget Bloom. The photograph of African policemen shooting their handguns did not appear in any South African newspaper, although it appears to be very similar to a picture in the *World*, morning edition, 17 June, p. 1. It was syndicated by AP. On 17 June, the 'handgun' picture was published on the front page of the *Washington Post*, *New York Times*, *Guardian*, *San Francisco Chronicle* and *Chicago Sun-Times*. The *Daily Express*, *Daily Mail* and *The Times* carried the picture on their inside pages. Peter Magubane's photograph of the students running at the camera appeared in the *Rand Daily Mail*, 17 June. It was syndicated by UPI. The Magubane picture was reproduced on the front pages of the *Daily Telegraph*, *New York Times* and the *Washington Post*. The *Daily Express* carried the picture on an inside page. *Newsweek* and *Time*, 28 June 1976, reproduced all three images. The international edition of *Time* devoted a cover-story to the unrest. The cover-picture featured John Vorster's head and shoulders superimposed upon the Magubane photograph. *Newsweek* displayed a tableau of all three images, the 'handgun' picture on the left, the Magubane picture in the centre and the Nzima photograph on the right. AP and UPI possessed long-standing agreements to share their material with the Argus Group and SAAN, respectively. The arrangement provided Argus and SAAN with access to the AP and UPI wire services, while AP and UPI retained the option to pick up stories or photographs from Argus or SAAN for a minimal fee. (Interview with Larry Heinzerling, 19 September 1995.) African photographers did not receive syndication bonus payments. (Interview with Peter Magubane, 20 May 1995.)

43. Mark Gevisser, 'Three Lives in Black and White,' *Observer* magazine, 17 April 1994, p. 32.

44. The provenance of the 'handgun' photograph is still uncertain. A number of people believe it was taken by Nzima. (Interviews with Nat Serache, 4 October 1996 and Don Mattera, 20 September 1996.)

45. 'Not a Sharpeville, say US Observers', [Johannesburg] *Star*, 18 June 1976.

46. 'The eemo that Boiled Over', *Rand Daily Mail*, 17 June 1976.

47. For the best study of the debates surrounding the introduction of television in South Africa, see Rob Nixon, *Homelands, Harlem and Hollywood: South African Culture and the World Beyond* (New York, Routledge, 1994), pp. 43–76.

48. Erik Van Ees (UPI), 'Riots Open Eyes in S. Africa', *Chicago Tribune*, 19 August 1976.
49. Denis Herbstein, 'Vorster Warns Africans as Riots Spread', *Guardian*, 19 June 1976.
50. 'TV Coverage Seen Abroad', *Rand Daily Mail*, 19 June 1976: 'The contribution was fed into the European news pool and all countries in Europe and in America had access to the film.'
51. Deborah Posel, 'Symbolising Violence: State and Media Discourse in Television Coverage of Township Protest, 1985–7', in N. Chabani Manganyi and Andre du Toit (eds), *Political Violence and the Struggle in South Africa* (Basingstoke, Macmillan, 1990), p. 154.
52. Ibid., pp. 161–65.
53. *Fortieth Annual Report of the South African Broadcasting Corporation: 1976* (Johannesburg, SABC, 1977), pp. 87–88.
54. 'South Africa is Right in the News', *World*, 13 September 1976.
55. Sadie Forman, 'Reviews', *Anti-Apartheid News*, October 1976, p. 11.
56. 'Embassy Slams Film of Hunted Student', *Rand Daily Mail*, 3 September 1976.
57. 'South Africa: There is No Crisis', 'This Week', Thames Television, 2 September 1976.
58. Ian Hobbs, 'SA Envoys to Hit Back at "Smear" Campaign in UK', *Rand Daily Mail*, 20 September 1976. See also 'The Law-breakers', 'World in Action', Granada Television, 6 December 1976.
59. 'Tsietsi speaks out', *World*, 3 September 1976; 'Embassy Slams Film of Hunted Student', *Rand Daily Mail*, 3 September 1976.
60. 'Free For All as Rioters Grab "World" from Van', *World*, 17 June 1976.
61. Jim Hoagland, 'Black Power vs. White Power: Whites Get Taste of Fear', *Washington Post*, 13 January 1977.
62. William McWhirter, 'Soweto: The Children Take Charge', *Time*, 27 June 1977, p. 18.
63. See Les Switzer and Donna Switzer, *The Black Press in South Africa and Lesotho: A Descriptive Bibliographic Guide to African, Coloured and Indian Newspapers, Newsletters and Magazines, 1836–1976* (Boston, G.K. Hall, 1979).
64. Shaun Johnson, 'An Historical Overview of the Black Press', in Keyan Tomaselli and P. Eric Louw (eds), *Studies on the South African Media: The Alternative Press in South Africa* (London, James Currey, 1981), p. 23.
65. 'Journalists Condemn SA Television', *Anti-Apartheid News*, December 1975, p. 5.
66. Steward Dill McBride (*Christian Science Monitor*), 'Editing a Black Newspaper in a White-ruled Country', *Washington Post*, 7 March 1976.
67. Percy Qoboza, 'The Press as I See It', *South African Conference on the Survival of the Press and Education for Journalism* (Grahamstown, Department of Journalism, Rhodes University, 1979), p. 4.
68. Langa Skosana, '50 Dead as Children's Fury Tears a Town Apart', *Daily Express*, 18 June 1976.
69. Nat Diseko, 'A Black Man in Soweto', *Sunday Times*, 20 June 1976.
70. Alf Kumalo, 'Children Who Died', *Observer*, 20 June 1976.
71. Caryle Murphy, 'S. Africa's Black Reporters Move Up', *Washington Post*, 28 July 1978.
72. Robin Wright, 'Black South African Newsmen Find Fame in Coverage, Jail' [sic], *Washington Post*, 20 October 1976.
73. 'S. African Journalists Held Under Terrorism Act', *The Times*, 30 July 1976.
74. Harry Mashabela, *A People on the Boil: Reflections on Soweto* (Johannesburg, Skotaville Publishers, 1987), p. 45.

75. Nicholas Ashford, 'Soweto in Grip of Violence for Third Day', *The Times*, 7 August 1976. Stanley Uys reported that 'A woman journalist who blackened her face and put on a wig to enter Soweto returned with her car windows smashed to say she had had a "terrifying" experience.' (Stanley Uys, 'Soweto Killings Raise the White Nightmare', *Guardian*, 5 August 1976.)
76. Nicholas Ashford, 'New Demonstrations in Soweto', *The Times*, 6 August 1976. A petrol bomb was thrown at Winnie Mandela's house on the same evening.
77. Helen Zille, '"Mail" Photographer Assaulted by Police', *Rand Daily Mail*, 11 August 1976.
78. Jan Tugwana, 'Stop Raid, Police Warned', *Rand Daily Mail*, 26 August 1976. Tugwana recalls that he spent the night in the coal-box because his parents lived close to the hostel and he was concerned for their safety. When he took the story to the *Rand Daily Mail*, '[they] couldn't believe it. They asked: "Are you sure?"' (Interview with Jan (Gabu) Tugwana, 20 September 1996.)
79. Nat Serache, 'Police Repulse 1000 on Hostel "Rescue Raid"', *Rand Daily Mail*, 26 August 1976. Serache, who was not Zulu, accepted that being in disguise was dangerous, however, he justified the risk because 'I needed that story.' (Interview with Nat Serache, 4 October 1996.)
80. 'Soweto Gangs Run Wild', [Johannesburg] *Star*, 26 August 1976. It is assumed that the uncredited journalist responsible for this piece was Langa Skosana. See also Marion Whitehead, 'The Black Gatekeepers: A Study of Black Journalists on Three Daily Newspapers which Covered the Soweto Uprising of 1976', unpublished BA (Hons) dissertation, Rhodes University, Grahamstown, 1978: '*The Star* ... omitted part of Langa Skosana's report on the Mzimhlope killings which referred to the police standing by while hostel dwellers attacked Soweto residents.'
81. See Stanley Uys, 'Soweto Zulus Defy Call to End Reprisals', *Guardian*, 26 August 1976. See also 'Strife between Zulu Workers and Strikers in Soweto is Declining', *New York Times*, 27 August 1976, wherein the reporter misquotes the *Rand Daily Mail*, and suggests that Serache rather than Tugwana had hidden in the coal-box.
82. See Christopher Munnion, 'Zulu Mob in Soweto Tribe War', *Daily Telegraph*, 26 August 1976: 'The Zulus, members of Africa's most renowned warrior tribe, took to the township streets ... yesterday, stoning, burning, raping and killing other Blacks in what one official described as "Soweto's civil war"'.
83. Robin Wright, 'Unity Eludes S. African Blacks', *Washington Post*, 27 August 1976.
84. Tom Wicker, 'Reaping the Whirlwind in Southern Africa', *New York Times*, 27 August 1976. See also Editorial (Benjamin Pogrund), 'African Black on Black', *Boston Globe*, 27 August 1976.
85. Editorial, 'Soweto Blacks against Blacks', *Chicago Tribune*, 27 August 1976.
86. Report by the Ministers' Fraternal of Langa, Guguletu and Nyanga, *Role of the South African Riot Police in Burnings and Killings in Nyanga, Cape Town, Christmas 1976*, United Nations Centre against Apartheid, Notes and Documents No. 6/77 (February) 1977. See Alan Brooks and Jeremy Brickhill, *Whirlwind Before the Storm: The Origins and Development of the Uprising in Soweto and the Rest of South Africa from June to December 1976* (London, IDAF, 1980), p. 143: 'None of the daily papers in Cape Town seemed to use black journalists who could work in the townships and report at first hand what they observed.' See also Andrew Silk, *A Shanty Town in South Africa: The Story of Modderdam* (Johannesburg, Ravan Press, 1981), pp. 98–100.
87. Interview with Nat Serache, 4 October 1996.
88. Whitehead, op. cit., p. 87.

89. Les Payne, 'Most Facts Off-limits to South African Press', *Newsday*, 6 February 1977.
90. Llewellyn Raubenheimer, 'From Newsroom to the Community: Struggle in Black Journalism', in Tomaselli and Louw, op. cit., p. 98; Peter Magubane, *Magubane's South Africa* (New York, Alfred A. Knopf, 1978), p. 13.
91. Nat Serache, 'Journalist Tortured by Security Police', *Anti-Apartheid News*, June 1977, p. 6. Following his period in detention, Serache was appointed President of the Black People's Convention. Following a further period of imprisonment, he fled the country in 1977. Detentions of African journalists continued apace through the autumn of 1976, see Nicholas Ashford, 'South African "Round-up" of Reporters Condemned', *The Times*, 25 September 1976; Nicholas Ashford, 'Black Journalists are Held Without Trial', *The Times*, 4 November 1976, '12 Black Journalists Now Held in South Africa', *The Times*, 9 November 1976.
92. Mike Ndlazi, 'Police Detain Leader of Black SA Journalists', *Rand Daily Mail*, Township edition, 2 September 1976. Copies of the *Bulletin* are now very difficult to find. Mike Norton, the first national organiser of the UBJ recalled that it 'carried some "brilliant" eyewitness accounts by young black journalists who could not get their copy used on other newspapers. One such reporter, Willie Bokala, was photographed trying to stem the flow of blood from someone's bullet wound by putting his finger in the bullet hole. The picture was carried on the front page of The Bulletin.' (Llewellyn Raubenheimer, 'A Study of Black Journalists and Black Media Workers in Union Organisation, 1971 to 1981', unpublished BA (Hons) dissertation, University of Cape Town, 1982.)
93. Chris More, for example, was a student in 1976. Following a period of detention, More started work as a journalist. During the early 1980s, he was employed by Joe Lelyveld (*New York Times*) as an interpreter and assistant. (Interview with Chris More, 27 May 1995.)
94. Caryle Murphy, 'S. Africa's Black Reporters Move Up', *Washington Post*, 28 July 1978.
95. See Graham Leach, 'Southern African Blacks', 'From our own correspondent', BBC Radio 4, 4 September 1976; Robin Wright, 'Black South African Newsmen Find Fame in Coverage, Jail' [sic], *Washington Post*, 20 October 1976. At the end of 1976, Peter Magubane became the first African journalist to be awarded the Stellenbosch Farmers Winery Press Award for enterprising journalism. Although in prison at the time of his award, Magubane was given the prize by Walter Cronkite upon his release in 1977. See also C. Gerald Fraser, 'A Black Photojournalist Depicts Apartheid Life', *New York Times*, 14 May 1978.
96. Editorial, 'The Afrikaans Complication', *Washington Star*, 20 June 1976.
97. See Garland, 'Now After Me, Balthazar', cartoon, *New Statesman*, 25 June 1976, p. 833; 'White Elephant', cartoon, *Christian Science Monitor*, 2 September 1976; Graysmith, 'Smith, Vorster and Apartheid', cartoon, *Time*, 20 September 1976, p. 25, originally published in the *San Francisco Chronicle*; Wright, 'South Africa', cartoon, *Time*, 27 September 1976, p. 12, originally published in the *Miami News*.
98. The Kissinger–Vorster meetings were held between 20–22 June in Bavaria, 4–6 September in Zurich and 17–20 September in Pretoria.
99. Editorial, 'South Africa's Horizon', *Daily Telegraph*, 14 August 1976.
100. Stanley Uys, 'Mr Vorster's Debt Throws', *Guardian*, 3 August 1976.
101. Stanley Uys, 'Is this the Start of the Final Phase in the Struggle for South Africa?', *Observer*, 15 August 1976.
102. Benjamin Pogrund, 'In South Africa, White Liberals Lose Hope', *Los Angeles Times*, 29 September 1976.

103. John F. Burns, 'White South Africans Seem Untouched by Black Strife', *New York Times*, 8 August 1976.

104. Alan Paton, 'Must Everything be Destroyed?', *New York Times* magazine, 19 September 1976, p. 18. An earlier version of Paton's article had been published as 'My African Nightmare', *Daily Express*, 17 August 1976. The syndicated article was also carried by the *Los Angeles Times*, 19 September 1976 and *Observer* magazine, 31 October 1976.

105. James Burnham, 'The Protracted Conflict: The Expendables', *National Review*, 23 July 1976, p. 776.

106. Editorial, 'Red over Black', *Sunday Telegraph*, 8 August 1976.

107. Editorial, 'Has Vorster got a Policy?', *Daily Telegraph*, 24 August 1976.

108. Editorial, 'Is this Kissinger's Last Odyssey?', *Daily Mail*, 2 September 1976. See also Editorial, 'Facing the Realities', *Daily Express*, 24 August 1976.

109. Examples include Peregrine Worsthorne, 'The Other South Africa', *Sunday Telegraph*, 19 September 1976; Honor Tracy, 'Personal View: In Praise of South Africa', *Daily Telegraph*, 10 September 1976; Both Worsthorne and Tracy blamed 'the media' for the negative representation of South Africa. The only equivalent in the US media was William A. Rusher, 'Cold Eyeball to Cold Eyeball on Southern Africa', *National Review*, 6 August 1976, p. 839: 'Let the Effete Clerks of Whitehall and Foggy Bottom Ring Down All the Curtains They Want To. "Inevitable"? Balderdash.'

110. Richard Gott, 'Rising Hopes', *Guardian*, 27 August 1976. See also A.J.P. Taylor, 'London Diary', *New Statesman*, 27 August 1976.

111. Robin Wright, 'Soweto: Defiance Amidst the Ruins', *Washington Post*, 25 June 1976.

112. Michael T. Kaufman, 'Witnesses Tell What They Saw When Riots Came to Soweto', *New York Times*, 28 June 1976.

113. Nicholas Ashford, 'Springbok Victory Shines in Darkening S. African Scene', *The Times*, 7 August 1976. See also Editorial, 'Change in South Africa', *New York Times*, 17 September 1976: 'the once-docile "coloreds" ... have taken up with courage and ingenuity the revolt begun by Soweto blacks'.

114. Editorial, 'South Africa's Horizon', *Daily Telegraph*, 14 August 1976.

115. Z. Nkosi, 'The Lessons of Soweto', *African Communist*, No. 68 (First Quarter 1977), p. 18.

116. Nadine Gordimer, 'The Children who Face Bullets', *Observer*, 12 December 1976.

117. June Goodwin, 'South Africa after Soweto Riots', *Christian Science Monitor*, 26 July 1976.

118. Jim Hoagland, 'Young Black Power Leads the Battle Against Apartheid', *International Herald Tribune*, 28 January 1977. This observation was added by a sub-editor, as a sub-heading, during the reproduction of Hoagland's article, which had originally appeared in the *Washington Post*, 12 January 1976.

8

Dependency and Manipulation

If we in the West as a result of a bovine obsession with racial equality pressurise South Africa and Rhodesia into a debased form of our own democracy, we will see not liberal democracy but a black tyranny replacing a white one ... The truth is that South Africa, for all its faults, is part of the West. And its enemies are after a system which will take South Africa out of this community. Surely we are not so gutless as to refuse to stand up and fight against our enemies? The South Africans have got the guts. They will take the guilt upon their sturdy shoulders. What kind of men are we who condemn them, not for their cowardice but for their courage?[1]

I found all [the correspondents] without a single exception, to possess either a rank colonialist outlook or a rank American racist outlook.[2]

This book has examined the forces which attempted to influence the media coverage of South Africa during the 1970s. The three case-studies have demonstrated the confusion, contradictions and ambiguous representations inherent in the reports that ensued. This penultimate chapter will examine the dependence of the British and American correspondents on the South African domestic English-language press; the transformations in the working conditions of the foreign journalists during the decade; and the allegations of media manipulation and the examples of the expulsion of reporters.

At the beginning of the 1970s, more than half of the reports which emerged from South Africa were written by South African stringers employed by the British and American media. There were a number of reasons for this state of affairs, not the least being the obduracy of South Africa's Department of Information in refusing to permit foreign news organisations to establish bureaus in the country.[3] While South African citizens could be 'banned', they could not be expelled, refused entry to the country or be denied visas or work permits, like a staff correspondent. Local 'hires' were also significantly less expensive, usually being employed by the news organisations for little more than a monthly retainer. However, South African stringers carried with them their own prejudices and perspectives. These were particularly problematic because not only were white South African journalists, however liberal, the purveyors of a white interpretation of events, their reports for the foreign press were also subject to the shifting domestic censorship regulations.[4] The white South African perspective continued to exert a powerful mediating influence over the news from the Republic throughout the decade.

Benjamin Pogrund described the inherent contradictions in the South African press, in 1975, in the following terms: 'The press is free and yet unfree. It is a press choked by restrictions imposed by the Afrikaner Nationalist government yet it enjoys an extraordinary degree of freedom. It is often a courageous press; it is also often cowardly.'[5] In effect, the South African press was fundamentally ambiguous. This ambiguity was in part a response to the complexities of the South African system of press controls. It was also due to the complicity of many South African journalists who practised self-censorship in order to avoid government harassment. Peter Bernstein, an American student who spent six months during 1974 working for the *Pretoria News*, the *Cape Argus* and the *Cape Herald*, described the legal difficulties of writing any story, which addressed the lives of the African population, as being similar to 'a kaleidoscopic picture ... it is an exacting job to surmount all the fractured obstacles and forge a coherent image. The pieces and the parts are always changing. The picture is never the same, but it is always similar.'[6]

In addition to the state's attempts to control the press, the South African English-language newspapers were also subject to another form of control: that coming from the owners of the press groups. In 1972, the Argus Printing and Publishing Company had, amongst its directors, nominees of the Rand Mines Group, the Johannesburg Consolidated Investment Company, the Barclays and Standard Banks and the Anglo-American Group.[7] South African Associated Newspapers (SAAN)'s majority shareholder was the Abe Bailey Trust and Estate. Despite a *Rand Daily Mail*–[Johannesburg] *Sunday Express* exposé into corruption in the Department of Information, which eventually led to the resignation of a number of the Republic's leaders, no English-language newspaper engaged in equivalent investigations into the operations of the mining companies in South Africa. South African journalists were, in effect, subject to two slightly different forms of control: on the one hand, there were the encroaching restrictions of the apartheid state, and on the other, the corrupting sponsorship of the English capital interests. These dual forces of influence were replicated in the two propaganda agencies which spoke for South

Africa: the Department of Information and the South Africa Foundation. Paradoxically, the South African English-language print media, despite these almost intolerable pressures, was a dynamic force during the 1970s. In some respects, this was due to the legacy of Laurence Gandar, the *Rand Daily Mail*'s editor between 1957 and 1966.[8] Martin Walker suggests that Gandar:

> inspired a new generation of South African journalists: Allister Sparks, later editor of the [*Rand Daily Mail*]; Rex Gibson, later editor of the *Sunday Express*; Harry O'Connor, later editor of the *Eastern Province Herald*; and his own successor, Raymond Louw. This team of politically liberal (if not all Progressive) journalists was exhilarated by the changes that Gandar introduced to the South African press. Hitherto, there had been no combative editorials, no philosophizing in the leaders, no firm statements that the press had a right and a duty to lead South African political thinking, rather than just comment on the thoughts of the politicians. 'It had a galvanizing effect on those of us who worked for him. It seemed the first injection of intellectual content into the political debate. Newspapers suddenly seemed to stand for a lot more than just the news,' Allister Sparks said.[9]

During the 1970s, Gandar's protégés and a number of other South African journalists, such as Donald Woods, Tony Heard and the veteran commentator, Stanley Uys, struggled to introduce a genuinely critical component to the domestic South African press. They were, however, a tiny, if powerful, minority. The majority of South Africa's journalists were journeymen and women with little real commitment to either a free press or a free South Africa. As Martin Schneider, the political editor of the *Rand Daily Mail* observed in *More* magazine: 'The *Rand Daily Mail* has gained a considerable international reputation for its exposure of government malpractices and cruelties in the implementation of *apartheid*. But, like the other English-language newspapers, it has seldom made any practical commitment to its strong editorial stand against discrimination.'[10]

Eschel Rhoodie believed that the South African English-language press was directly responsible for the negative international image of South Africa. In his memoir, he insisted that 'The foreign press corps in South Africa lived on the *Rand Daily Mail*. Some foreign journalists hardly bothered to change a word. The opinion of millions of people in two dozen countries were [sic] being shaped not by the independent observation of the foreign press in South Africa but by the *Rand Daily Mail*.'[11] On this, if nothing else, the ANC journal, *Sechaba*, was in agreement with the Department of Information: 'The news published in newspapers outside the country, at least in the West, is all culled from the local newspapers with the result that the international media is as guilty of omission and distortion as newspapers like the *Rand Daily Mail*.'[12] There was some truth in these accusations but there was also a degree of hyperbole. Foreign correspondents naturally read the domestic press; they were expected to gravitate to the best possible source of news. In South Africa, where the restrictions of apartheid complicated the development of African contacts, the *Rand Daily Mail* served as a useful short cut. The newspaper's influence actually spread far further than being a source for stories; it was a central location on the 'liberal tour' which so many foreign commentators and visitors to South Africa embarked upon.[13] Before the emergence, in 1976, of the *World* as a more authentic African voice, the *Rand Daily Mail* also supplied African journalists as guides to visiting foreign journalists.[14]

However, the correspondents in the Republic were also concerned about their dependence on the domestic English-language press. This concern was focused upon the problem of gaining access to leading National Party politicians. In 1977, Gerry Suckley, the chairman of the Foreign Correspondents' Association (FCA), wrote to the Prime Minister:

> This Association, representing virtually the entire foreign press corps in the Republic, respectfully draws to your attention the generally poor level of co-operation extended to our members by various departments of your Government, and appeals to you to take steps to improve the situation. Due to this lack of co-operation and access to news information, our members are being compelled to rely to an increasing extent on reports in the South African newspapers, and since few of our members have fluent command of Afrikaans, being, in the main, on fairly short-term assignments to SA, these newspapers tend to be the English-language ones. This state of affairs, we are sure you will agree, is unsatisfactory for all concerned.[15]

Despite the FCA's concern, in practice the *Rand Daily Mail* had come to represent a sort of totem for foreign correspondents in South Africa. In this respect, it was not dissimilar to the role played by Alan Paton, the celebrated 'liberal' author of *Cry, The Beloved Country*.[16] Although Paton had once been an anti-apartheid campaigner, by the 1970s and in old age, he had become distinctly right-wing and fatalistic. His opinions on the events in South Africa, however, continued to be regularly published, particularly in American newspapers and news-magazines. During April 1977, for example, the *Los Angeles Times* carried an article based upon an interview with Paton conducted by Barbara Hutmacher:

Everybody, it seems, is urging change upon South Africa. I, too, would like to see some change: a common society, for instance, instead of the separate societies we have now. But I don't think this will ever come about, not without armed revolution, resistance to the revolution and, ultimately, the desolation of the entire country. The black radical would say: 'The hell with it. Let's smash everything. What does it matter? Everything is rotten. Let's knock it all down and start again.' But, of course, I'm not black and I'm not radical and I couldn't possibly bring myself to agree with that position – much less advocate it.[17]

Paton, the elder statesman, demonstrated the paternal nature of his position in his willingness to put words into the imaginary black radical's mouth; some younger South African journalists were, however, becoming aware of the importance of allowing Africans to speak for themselves. During 1978, Donald Woods was questioned by Paula Giddings about the Black Consciousness Movement in South Africa: 'Woods said he could not speak for them but could relay what they have told him.'[18] This was a small but significant step in the South African context.

The Department of Information's belief that the foreign media were completely dependent upon stories published in the South African press eventually served to justify the establishment of a pro-government English-language newspaper, the *Citizen*, which it was hoped would go some way to balance the perceived liberalism of the *Rand Daily Mail*. Before the exposure of the *Citizen* as a secret government-funded project in 1978, the newspaper had little impact on the coverage of the Republic, offering as it did neither insight into the vagaries of the Afrikaner polity nor a short cut to the previously smothered African voice. Translations of editorials and significant articles in the Afrikaans press had long been available through the South African Press Association (SAPA) or, from 1974, in the Department of Information publication, *Comment and Opinion*.[19] In January 1978, Doreen Nussey, the wife of Wilf Nussey, an ex-editor of the *Pretoria News* and Argus Africa News Service, instigated a daily summary and translation of the news in *Die Vaderland, Beeld, Die Transvaler* and *Rapport* as a commercial venture. 'From the Afrikaans Press' normally stretched to between five and eight pages of densely-packed text.[20] The majority of the staff correspondents became subscribers.

The foreign press showed little interest in the Afrikaans-language newspapers for the simple reason that they were searching for an opposition viewpoint. While Afrikaner newspaper editors such as Piet Cillie were familiar figures on the government-organised tours of the country, few foreign journalists felt the need, as Peregrine Worsthorne did, to publicise the role of the Afrikaner journalist.[21] The crucial influence of the English-language press was in the area of self-censorship. Cultures of deception and restriction are insidiously infectious, and there can be little doubt that foreign correspondents in South Africa were rapidly and sometimes subconsciously instilled with the fears and concerns of the local journalists. As an anonymous correspondent informed Richard Pollak in 1978, 'There is also the problem of self-censorship ... A good deal of it goes on all the time, no doubt about it.'[22] In 1952, Horace Flather, the editor of the [Johannesburg] *Star*, described the problems of editing a newspaper, under the South African press restrictions, as being 'like walking blindfold through a minefield'.[23] To extend the metaphor, the problems of utilising the English-language print media, which all the foreign correspondents did to one degree or another, was something akin to handling a live mine.

At the beginning of 1972, the news from South Africa in the international media was produced by a dozen reporters, all of whom were white and male; more than half were South Africans. By the end of the decade, the FCA listed 65 members, of whom the majority were British or American, and eight were women.[24] In the interim, South Africa had developed from being a location from which correspondents travelled to cover other African countries, to being 'a country no longer at peace and not yet at war'.[25] The quality of life in the Republic had also changed for the correspondents. In 1973, Virginia Waite observed that 'The professional and social links between [the staff-writers] seem far stronger in South Africa, perhaps because they are such a small, exclusive group.'[26] Waite demonstrated the closeness of these links, on the final page of her colour supplement article, when she revealed that she was married to John Osman, the BBC's radio correspondent. By the end of the decade, the escalation of people employed by the news agencies, the establishment of television news bureaus, the arrival of American journalists (there had only been one American correspondent in the Republic in 1972) and the emergence of independent freelance reporters had destroyed the correspondents' previously cosy culture of exclusivity.

The experiences of the correspondents and stringers who reported from South Africa during the decade were as varied as one might imagine possible amongst a group of 100 people. Some reporters were careerists, perceiving South Africa as no more than one step in their journey up the journalistic ladder; others were iconoclasts, happy to operate with some distance between themselves and their news organisations. Some of the journalists were lazy; others were gifted.

Some became politically engaged by the struggle against apartheid; others enjoyed the racially privileged life of the white population of South Africa. Some reporters were alcoholics; others were adulterers or homosexuals. There is no particular significance in this, beyond demonstrating that the correspondents and stringers were normal human beings, subject to normal human frailties.[27] The majority of them were in their mid-30s and a significant number of the staff correspondents who had arrived in South Africa between 1975 and 1977 went on to become senior figures on their newspapers and news organisations in the years that followed. However, there was one particular attribute which none of the journalists possessed: they were not black.

Michael Knipe recalled of his period in South Africa (1972–75) that 'It wasn't easy to talk to Africans ... There was no natural source of African opinion.'[28] On BBC radio in December 1977, Bridget Bloom (the Africa editor of the *Financial Times*) acknowledged that South Africa 'is an extremely difficult country to try to report [from], in that you are only really seeing the white side ... There is no black voice that it is easy to go and talk to.'[29] Three years later, Michael Beaubien commented in *Southern Africa* 'that one way to overcome the Africans' natural hesitance to talk freely with Europeans would involve a greater use of African stringers or the employment of more African-Americans as correspondents in southern Africa'.[30] Between 1972 and 1979, none of the British or American newspapers, news agencies, broadcasting companies or news-magazines stationed (or, to the best of my knowledge, attempted to station) an African-American or an Afro-Caribbean correspondent in South Africa. Indeed, only one news organisation, the BBC World Service, employed an African stringer in the Republic during the entire period.

While the racial oppression of the South African state was severe, the failure of the international media to attempt to breach the racial divide was by no means the sole responsibility of the Department of Information. During 1976, for example, three African-American reporters were granted visas to enter the Republic.[31] The third of these reporters was Les Payne, a Pulitzer prizewinner employed by *Newsday*.[32] Having gained editorial approval for his application to visit South Africa, Payne appealed to the tennis player, Arthur Ashe, who had visited the country some years earlier, to mediate with the South African government Minister, Piet Koornhof, on his behalf. Payne's visa application was successful and he spent three months in the Republic in the autumn of 1976. During his time in South Africa, he was often accompanied by Andrew Hatcher, an African-American who was employed by the Department of Information through its contract with the American public relations company, Sydney S. Baron. Payne recalls that 'I found my colleagues ... were very resistant to my presence there as an African-American journalist.'[33] He felt that some of the correspondents were concerned about his competitive advantage; Payne could easily slip into the townships without being noticed. In one of the (11-part series of) articles which he wrote upon his return to the United States, Payne discussed:

> [the] prize-winning foreign correspondent for a large East Coast paper [who] gleaned anecdotes from conversations between blacks and usually, without the aid of notes, misreconstructed accounts for his paper. Before we talked about the treatment of Africans, he was prepared – after the Soweto riots – to file a series detailing how much racial progress South Africa had made since he last visited the country in 1971: 'Blacks couldn't ride the elevators back then,' he said.[34]

Jim Hoagland, who appears to have been the beneficiary of Payne's information, told *More* magazine, one year later, that '"When I arrived in late October, I realized that [Soweto] had been an essentially unreported story ... I asked wire-service people if they had ever gone into Soweto, but they hadn't." Hoagland also noted that no American newspapers, to his knowledge, employed black stringers who might have had greater access to the townships.'[35] Nat Serache (*Rand Daily Mail*) had the honour of being the first African stringer hired by the international media. In 1975, Graham Mytton, of the BBC World Service, had arrived in South Africa, hoping to interview Winnie Mandela. He asked the *Rand Daily Mail* to supply an African journalist who could facilitate an introduction. Serache recalls that Mrs Mandela 'was very selective about who [she] would [let] bring people to her. You had to be politically acceptable to her, to bring a journalist to her.'[36] Following Mytton's successful interview, he offered Serache work as a stringer for the BBC World Service. Serache continued to report regularly for the BBC during the next year. In 1976, following his arrest and detention, the BBC string was passed on to Serache's fellow *Rand Daily Mail* journalist, Jan (Gabu) Tugwana.[37]

When questioned, correspondents and editors of the newspapers and news-magazines that covered South Africa during the 1970s provided two reasons for their unwillingness to employ African stringers. The majority stated that they had been concerned that the employment of an African might endanger the person and attract unwanted police attention. Bearing in mind that Serache was a BBC stringer for a year before his arrest, and that his arrest was directly related to his work for the *Rand Daily Mail*, not the international media, this defence does not hold up. The second reason was the belief that 'While African journalists were good at getting the news, they were bad at writing.'[38] This disdain for the abilities of African reporters was one of the more pernicious legacies of the influence of the domestic press. As a perpetuation of South African racism, it was possibly the most significant failing of the international media in the Republic during the decade. As this book has demonstrated, those foreign journalists who interviewed Africans often discovered fascinating insights into the struggle. Some reporters, however, did not consider it necessary to talk to Africans. As Geoffrey Taylor explained, when asked why he had not quoted any Africans in his four-part series on South Africa: 'The Africans were at that point powerless and ... it was more important to know if there were any changes in the solid opposition to African aspirations, than in listening to the aspirations, which you could get in London anyway by listening to the ANC.'[39]

There were many changes in the working practices of the correspondents and stringers during the period in question. In 1972, *The Times* and *Daily Telegraph* staff correspondents were based in Cape Town, primarily in order to report the news from the South African Parliament. As the decade progressed and more news organisations arrived in the country, bureaus tended to be moved to Johannesburg which was then thought to be the epicentre of the crisis in South African race relations. Traditionally, British journalists had been allowed to enter South Africa without being required to apply for any documentation. One of Rhoodie's innovations was that, from 1973, British correspondents had to apply for six-monthly work permits. Other international journalists were also forced to apply for visas, which normally covered a three-month period. If they wished to stay in the country, they then had to apply for a multiple re-entry visa. In addition they required a six-month work permit and a police press card. If granted, the multiple re-entry visa had to be renewed annually and the work permit was subject to reconsideration every six months.[40] The system, of course, was a subtle form of intimidation which probably encouraged some journalists to be over cautious in their coverage. There was one bonus, however: journalists who operated in South Africa on a visa or a work permit basis either did not pay any tax, or paid tax at a reduced rate. In his book, *Banana Sunday*, Christopher Munnion recalled broaching the subject of the work permit renewals with Eschel Rhoodie:

> there was this tedious business of regular renewal of work permits, a process that took sometimes several days of valuable time. Could it not be speeded up? The real Eschel Rhoodie was suddenly before me. He scowled. 'You'll just have to live with that,' he snapped. 'It's all to do

with this double taxation business.' If there's one word that will stop any foreign correspondent in his tracks it is 'tax'. My new friend had just mentioned 'double tax'. I made my excuses and left.[41]

Journalists in South Africa during the 1970s also faced other forms of intimidation, perhaps the most significant of which was related to the activities of BOSS. Patrick Keatley, the diplomatic correspondent of the *Guardian*, noted in 1976 that he was 'careful never to cross [the South African] frontier carrying anything as naive as an address book, or even a sheet of paper with names of prospective contacts ... this is standard practice for all correspondents bound for South Africa'.[42] Few reporters, however, bothered to comment upon the subject. There can be only two reasons for this silence. Either the degree of intimidation was no more than 'the routine, mild harassment that reporters come across in all such states', as John Humphrys suggests, or the lack of coverage demonstrated the success of the intimidation; journalists do not like to draw attention to their weaknesses or the factors which directly restrict their work.[43] The correspondents who did comment on the subject tended to be those whose liberal positions were well-known. Caryle Murphy, for instance, wrote a humourous article in 1978 which recounted her experience of being 'tailed' by the security police throughout a visit to East London. Her article concluded:

> Whites and blacks who live in these small towns and who consistently show opposition to South African government policies are used to these experiences. They never say anything important on the telephone, confidential conversations are held outdoors, out of range of listening devices ... With mixed emotions I returned to the freer atmosphere of cosmopolitan Johannesburg, where most foreign correspondents in this security-conscious country are based. On the one hand, I was relieved since the security police here – outside of routinely bugging phone calls – do not have the time to regularly follow the moves of all foreign reporters. On the other hand, I missed all the attention I was getting.[44]

Continuous pressure from BOSS was complemented by the fear that the South African government might institute some form of censorship of the correspondents' work. This fear intensified in the period following the South African government's clampdown in October 1977. However, the situation was, as always, contradictory. Gerry Suckley observed in his chairman's report to the FCA: 'There may be members who believe as I do that pressures will mount against foreign correspondents. (Conversely, with the recent banning of people, organisations and newspapers with total disregard to the country's image, one may feel that the authorities will not be too concerned about what these correspondents write.)'[45] The sense of relief in the next annual chairman's report was profound: 'Finally I would say that we may not have had a good year but we have survived, which is more than we can say for Dr Rhoodie and his Department of Information.'[46]

As it became clear that South Africa would become one of the running stories of the 1980s, an additional burden was added to the correspondents' shoulders. In effect, they needed to protect their news organisations' 'investment' in the country. In March 1978, for example, *Time* magazine organised a 'news tour' of the Republic, during which it 'took thirty-one high level American businessmen to South Africa, where they met with among others, the ... Prime Minister, John Vorster, and five members of his Cabinet'.[47] Both the *Time* correspondent, William McWhirter, and the magazine's stringer, Peter Hawthorne, were very impressed by this demonstration of institutional power.[48] It is, perhaps, no surprise that McWhirter did not view the risk of expulsion as being beneficial to his career:

> We were well past the point where people who were expelled from their beats were regarded as domestic heroes for bravery and courage. That disappeared when we started making accommodations with Moscow and China. No editor who can not even watch or monitor you in a place like South Africa wants you to screw things up over things that he doesn't know and can't defend. You become an administrative embarrassment – You become a competitive disadvantage ... and then ... they've got to go around and kiss ass for six months with the South Africans and send somebody else in on a weaker basis ... No one gets points for being expelled.[49]

In comparison to the 1960s and the 1980s, the South African government did not expel very many journalists during the 1970s. This can be partly explained by the fact that certain correspondents were already placed on a prohibited list and others were banned after they had left the Republic.[50] Stanley Uys felt that the Department of Information was 'always very sensible. [They would] look at what the reaction was going to be – if they thought it was going to [cause] too much trouble outside ... they'd keep their hands off you.'[51] There is little doubt that being accredited to a major news organisation, or being a well-known figure such as Uys himself, provided a degree of security from South African government pressure which freelancers and casual stringers did not possess. Following the establishment of the FCA in November 1976, members could call upon the support of the Association. However, the records indicate that the FCA's assistance was very limited.[52]

In 1976, Arnaud de Borchgrave, *Newsweek*'s senior foreign cor-respondent, was expelled from South Africa following the publication of an article in which he had suggested that 'key officials' in BOSS favoured a more radical approach to South Africa's problems than that being currently practised by John Vorster. The article concluded: 'Will the boss [Vorster] listen to BOSS? Many observers conclude that he will not. Such a display of leadership and imagination, they believe, is beyond him.'[53] De Borchgrave's source for the article had been an off-the-record briefing by Hendrik van den Bergh, the head of BOSS.[54] Van den Bergh later informed *To The Point* magazine that 'de Borchgrave must have been dreaming, or off his rocker'.[55] Six months earlier, de Borchgrave had published an interview with John Vorster in which he had asked the Prime Minister: 'Would it also be accurate to say you received a green light from Kissinger for a military operation in Angola ...?' He quoted Vorster, as replying, 'If you say that of your own accord, I will not call you a liar.'[56] De Borchgrave accepts that it is possible that the Prime Minister's office had asked for this sentence to be struck from the published version of the interview, but he had felt that the answer was too significant to be subjected to South African censorship.[57] Following his expulsion, de Borchgrave's photograph was included, with those of Donald Woods, Eric Marsden and Philip Jacobson, in a *Sunday Times* report on relations between the foreign press and the Department of Information. De Borchgrave later commented: 'I was a little shocked to find my picture with those people because I had nothing in common with their approach.'[58]

During November 1976, Eric Abraham, a South African citizen, anti-apartheid campaigner and BBC stringer, was banned and placed under house arrest. He had returned to the Republic in 1975 in order to establish the Southern African News Agency (SANA), having worked for Amnesty International in England for a number of years. He later explained:

> [SANA] grew out of what I perceived as the need for an in-depth and factual information service to reflect the views and opinions of the 18 million blacks ... The local press and the Western Agencies seemed to have neglected the fact that threequarters of the South African population was black. It was, and still is, far too easy for foreign correspondents to rely on the validity of the communiqués from the South African politicians and the Nationalist Government's Ministries of Information, Justice and Police ... During the first half of 1976 every SANA bulletin was banned as prejudicial to State security.[59]

Although effectively silenced, Abraham and SANA established links with a number of African journalists and photographers, such as Peter

Magubane, Nat Serache and Thenjiwe Mtintso.[60] Following unsuccessful appeals to the South African government to lift his banning order and permit him to leave the country, Abraham fled through Botswana at the beginning of 1977. In almost every respect the South African state's treatment of Abraham, and his ensuing departure into exile, anticipated Donald Woods' experiences 12 months later. A completely different case was that of Daniel Drooz, an Israeli citizen, who had arrived in South Africa in 1976 and claimed to be stringing for the *Chicago Sun-Times, US News and World Report* and *Maariv*.[61] Drooz was a somewhat mysterious figure who was either not a particularly able journalist, or was involved in intelligence activity.[62] *The Times*'s report recording his expulsion in August 1978 noted that 'he had run into trouble over three stories published abroad – one on Israeli arms sold to South Africa, one on black education and a third on the scandal within the Department of Information'.[63]

The most dramatic example of South African attempts to manipulate the media, beyond those discussed in Chapter 3, occurred in London in 1976. During a period of three days, the *Guardian* and the BBC were both victims of elaborately hoaxed reports which eventually left both news organisations wary of publishing or even investigating anti-South African stories. The two hoaxes were directly related to the current Jeremy Thorpe scandal and Harold Wilson's related statement to the Parliamentary Press Gallery, on 12 May 1976, that 'Overseas anti-democratic forces have conspired for years to undermine the political situation of individuals and parties that have opposed arms to South Africa.'[64] Three days later, the *Guardian*'s front page carried a story which claimed that a South African diplomat had attempted to purchase a pornographic film which featured a British politician.[65] The source for the story, Andre Thorne, later confessed to the *Sunday People* that the entire story had been fiction.[66] Meanwhile, the BBC 'Nine O'clock News', on 18 May, broadcast an interview with a 'Colonel' Cheeseman who claimed that he had seen evidence in South Africa relating to the campaign against senior Liberal politicians.[67] Within days it was established that Cheeseman was also a hoaxer.[68]

As the *Sunday Times* commented in an editorial: 'It has been a good week for South Africa and especially for BOSS ... the discrediting of South Africa's critics could hardly have been better managed if BOSS itself had been manipulating it.'[69] The investigations into what William Raynor and Geoff Allen later called 'the English Watergate' were dealt a deathblow by the Thorne and Cheeseman hoaxes.[70] In the years that followed, the majority of investigations into Harold Wilson's allegations against the South Africans concluded that they had no substance.[71] This is particularly strange because both Thorne and

Cheeseman later retracted their retractions.[72] Indeed, Peter Deeley recalled at the time that, during an investigation into BOSS organised by the *Observer* in 1971, 'Three times in as many weeks we were "fed" false information which, if it had been published, would have destroyed the credibility of the case we had built up.'[73] Ian Wright (the *Guardian*'s foreign editor in 1976) recalls that the newspaper was 'deeply, deeply scarred by [the experience]. I thought we've got to be careful with these bastards.'[74]

The South African government possessed other methods for manipulating foreign correspondents in the Republic. Many South African journalists believe that the late Tertius Myburgh, the editor of the [Johannesburg] *Sunday Times*, colluded with BOSS, during the 1970s, and its successor intelligence agencies in the 1980s. There is undoubtedly considerable evidence to support this supposition.[75] If true, Myburgh would have been in a particularly powerful position to manipulate both news and opinion. As the editor of South Africa's largest-selling and only genuinely national newspaper, he was the country's leading newspaperman. As a Nieman fellow and occasional stringer for the *New York Times*, he could exert a powerful influence in the United States. He was also apparently a likeable fellow who was regularly approached by foreign journalists who were delighted to gain access to the thoughts of a 'liberal' Afrikaner. The *Washington Post* correspondent, Sanford Ungar, paid tribute to Myburgh's influence in the acknowledgements section of his book, *Africa*: 'I was introduced to one part of Africa by Tertius Myburgh ... without [him] this book truly would not have been possible.'[76]

Although South Africa's media manipulation was rarely successful at diverting the international media's coverage of African issues, it does appear to have steered both the correspondents inside the country and the editorial staff of the news organisations in Europe and North America away from the subject of South African 'dirty tricks'. In 1978, when the Information scandal began to emerge, no foreign correspondents in South Africa engaged in research in support of the *Rand Daily Mail* and the [Johannesburg] *Sunday Express*'s investigations. To a certain extent this was because the domestic exposés were difficult to expand upon or even to get verified. However, one would have imagined that the foreign correspondents would have been interested in developing a story that dealt, in part, with attempts to corrupt foreign journalists and their news organisations. As Anthony Sampson, one of the few commentators genuinely to engage with the story, observed: 'Journalists, who are so active in investigating other businesses, are often oddly ignorant of the control of their own.'[77]

There is little evidence to suggest that any of the British or American correspondents and stringers in the Republic were actively funded by the Department of Information but it does seem possible that a number of reporters may have been compromised through contact with South African government money. Richard West, for instance, commented in the *Spectator* that 'The Department ... offered each journalist a first-class return ticket [to the Transkeian independence celebrations] and some £1,000 in cash for expenses.'[78] While it proved impossible to find any correspondent who would admit to accepting such a 'gift', Larry Heinzerling (AP) did recall that his first thought on hearing of the Information scandal was 'thank God I didn't take the money to go to the Transkei'.[79] Whether journalists were actually bribed, as West suggested, remains unproved. However, bearing in mind the large amount of money expended by the Department of Information and the scale of secret front-organisations in operation, there seems little doubt that a number of reporters and commentators had been the innocent recipients of South African largesse.[80] With a few rare exceptions, the various investigations into the Information scandal by British and American-based freelance journalists and staff writers received little support from the mainstream international news organisations.[81] Muldergate remains a riddle awaiting re-examination.

NOTES

1. Editorial, 'The Decadence of Western Politics', *Daily Express*, 25 October 1977.
2. Interview with Les Payne, 8 November 1996.
3. Other reasons included the fact that many news organisations did not view South Africa as a particularly dynamic news story, especially as internal resistance had been relatively quiet since the mid-1960s.
4. For a list of the laws affecting the press in South Africa, see 'The South African Press: And the Laws that Govern It', *Sechaba*, Vol. 7, No. 1 (January 1973), pp. 13–14. On the continuing threats, during the 1970s, made by the South African government against the domestic press, see William A. Hachten and C. Anthony Giffard, *The Press and Apartheid: The Role and Plight of the Press in South Africa* (London, Macmillan, 1984), pp. 66–75.
5. Benjamin Pogrund, 'The South African Press', *Index on Censorship*, Vol. 5, No. 3 (Autumn 1976), p. 10.
6. Peter Bernstein, 'Reporting in Pretoria', *Index on Censorship*, Vol. 4, No. 3 (Autumn 1975), p. 48.
7. Frene Ginwala, *The Press in South Africa*, United Nations Unit on Apartheid: Notes and Documents, No. 24/72 (November 1972), p. 12.
8. Following the publication of a series of articles by Benjamin Pogrund on the conditions inside South African prisons (July 1965), Gandar was effectively removed from the editorship of the newspaper.
9. Martin Walker, *The Powers of the Press: The World's Great Newspapers* (London, Quartet Books, 1982), p. 324.
10. Martin Schneider, 'Truth Victim of Press Laws', *More*, December 1977, p. 14.
11. Eschel Rhoodie, *The Real Information Scandal* (Pretoria, Orbis, 1983), p. 314.

12. 'The Press in SA', *Sechaba*, April 1980, p. 19.
13. Beyond the *Rand Daily Mail*, visitors on the 'liberal' tour normally spoke with Helen Suzman, Robert Sobukwe, Gatsha Buthelezi, Donald Woods, Alan Paton and Laurence Gandar.
14. Interview with Nat Serache, 4 October 1996.
15. G.A. Suckley, Letter to John Vorster, 8 August 1977. (FCA Archive, now held at the Institute of Commonwealth Studies, University of London.)
16. Alan Paton, *Cry, The Beloved Country* (London, Jonathan Cape, 1948). A similar iconic figure of South African letters was Laurens van der Post. See Laurens van der Post, 'Last Liner from the Cape' and 'The Human Face of South Africa that Need Not Fear the Rest of the World', *The Times*, 24 September and 21 November 1977. See also Edwin N. Wilmsen, 'Primitive Politics in Sanctified Landscapes: The Ethnographic Fictions of Laurens van der Post', *Journal of Southern African Studies*, Vol. 21, No. 2 (June 1995), pp. 201–23.
17. Barbara Hutmacher and Alan Paton, 'While Novelist Alan Paton Suggests Change (for the Better)', *Los Angeles Times*, 21 April 1977.
18. Paula Giddings, 'Exile with a Mission', *Encore American and Worldwide News*, 20 March 1978, p. 18.
19. SAPA, through its relationship with all the newspapers of South Africa, republished (in English) the first news reports it received, regardless of whether the report had originated with an English-language or an Afrikaans publication. *Comment and Opinion* was incorporated within *SA Digest* in 1976.
20. The 'From the Afrikaans Press' archive is stored at the University of the Witwatersrand.
21. Worsthorne wanted to publicise the Afrikaner cause through the medium of the Afrikaner journalist, 'just as Anthony Sampson did it with *Drum* for the black journalists'. (Interview with Sir Peregrine Worsthorne, 15 January 1996.) See also Peregrine Worsthorne, 'The Other South Africa', *Sunday Telegraph*, 19 September 1976: 'almost all visitors – and none more than journalists – find it so much easier in South Africa to listen to the voice of opposition than to the voice of government, to the voice of dissent, criticism and despair, than to that of agreement, commendation and hope, since the former is in English, which almost everyone can understand, while that of the latter is in Afrikaans, a language totally incomprehensible except to the Afrikaners themselves'. See also P.J. Cillie, 'The Case for Africa's White Tribe', *New York Times* magazine, 12 December 1976, pp. 34–124, republished in *Saturday Evening Post*, March 1977, pp. 90–103.
22. Richard Pollak, *Up Against Apartheid: The Role and Plight of the Press in South Africa* (Carbondale and Edwardsville, Southern Illinois University Press, 1981), p. 89.
23. 'The South African Press: And the Laws that Govern It', *Sechaba*, Vol. 7, No. 1 (January 1973), p. 14.
24. In 1972, there were only two foreign journalists representing the non-Anglophone media in South Africa. By the end of the decade, Chinese, Dutch, Swedish, Canadian, Japanese, German and French reporters covered the Republic for more than a dozen news organisations.
25. David Halberstam, 'The Fire to Come in South Africa', *Atlantic Monthly*, May 1980, p. 87.
26. Virginia Waite, 'Men Who Write Us Up', [Johannesburg] *Sunday Times* magazine, 18 November 1973, p. 30.
27. The extent to which these frailties left the journalists vulnerable to manipulation or blackmail by the Department of Information or BOSS is very difficult to assess.
28. Interview with Michael Knipe, 12 April 1995.

29. 'Between the Lines', BBC Radio 4, 10 December 1977. It is notable that Bloom was one of the relatively few journalists who made the effort to develop, as opposed to exploit, African sources.

30. Michael Beaubien, 'Telling It Like It Isn't: US Press Coverage of Zimbabwe', *Southern Africa*, July–August 1980, p. 3.

31. Paula Giddings visited during the spring of 1976, see Paula Giddings, 'Inside South Africa Today', *Encore American and Worldwide News*, 2 August 1976, pp. 16–20. Clarence Page visited South Africa some weeks later, for the *Chicago Tribune*.

32. *Newsday*, at this time, had no overseas bureaus.

33. Interview with Les Payne, 8 November 1996.

34. Les Payne, 'White Power, Black Rage – A Report from South Africa: Reporter's Notebook', *Newsday*, 30 January 1977. The series ran in *Newsday* from 30 January–9 February 1977.

35. Cited by Daniel Schechter, 'Media Myopia', *More*, December 1977, p. 30.

36. Interview with Nat Serache, 4 October 1996.

37. Tugwana and Serache had jointly exposed police collusion with the Zulu hostel dwellers in August 1976 (see Chapter 7). Following Tugwana's arrest and detention, the string was passed to Thami Mazwai.

38. Interview with Colin Legum, 15 June 1995. Legum explained that this was 'because of the lack of training given to African journalists' by the domestic South African press. Peter Gregson (Reuters) suggests that 'It was actually a problem because they could write about the townships but they wrote in a different way to an international news agency – they wrote for a different audience.' (Interview with Peter Gregson, 26 May 1995.) Raymond Louw, the editor of the *Rand Daily Mail* until 1976, referred to 'errors of language' in the African journalists' copy. (Interview with Raymond Louw, 20 September 1996.)

39. Interview with Geoffrey Taylor, 24 March 1996. See Geoffrey Taylor, 'Afrikanerdom in a Sea of Change', *Guardian*, 15–18 November 1976. While journalists in London might have been 'listening' to the ANC, very few reported the ANC's viewpoint (see Chapter 4).

40. Pollak, op. cit., pp. 79–80. British correspondents and stringers did not require a visa.

41. Munnion, *Banana Sunday: Datelines From Africa*, second edition (Rivonia, William Waterman, 1995), pp. 447–48.

42. Patrick Keatley, 'Living with the Boss-eyed Monster', *Guardian*, 11 March 1976.

43. Letter from John Humphrys, November 1995.

44. Caryle Murphy, 'Letter from Johannesburg: Keeping a Watch on South Africa's Security Policemen', *Washington Post*, 8 March 1978. June Goodwin was also followed when she visited East London (Pollak, op. cit., p. 86). For evidence of the security police's intimidation of foreign correspondents, see Paul Erasmus, 'Nocturnal Paint Bombs – Gun-toting Neighbours', [Weekly] *Mail & Guardian*, 30 June 1995.

45. Gerry Suckley, Chairman's Report, December 1977 (FCA Archive).

46. Peter Hawthorne, Chairman's Report, 22 November 1978 (FCA Archive).

47. E.J. Kahn Jr, 'Annals of International Trade: A Very Emotive Subject', *New Yorker*, 14 May 1979, p. 121.

48. Interviews with William McWhirter, 6 April 1996 and Peter Hawthorne, 16 May 1995.

49. Interview with William McWhirter, 6 April 1996. See Mort Rosenblum, *Coups and Earthquakes: Reporting the World for America* (New York, Colophon Books, 1981), p. 95: 'An expulsion is not necessarily a badge of honour.' See also interview with Bill Nicholson, 9 April 1996: 'We're there for the long haul. Its not up to us to be on a mission … we're there to cover the news.'

50. Colin Legum (*Observer*) was on the prohibited list throughout the decade. Adam Raphael (*Guardian*) was banned from returning to South Africa, following his wage starvation exposé in 1973.
51. Interview with Stanley Uys, 22 September 1994.
52. See the variety of appeals in the FCA Archive.
53. Arnaud de Borchgrave, 'The Way the BOSS Sees It', *Newsweek*, 25 October 1976, p. 20.
54. Interview with Arnaud de Borchgrave, 14 November 1996.
55. Carol Birkby, 'Vorster on Journalist: "Blow Him Sky-high"', *To The Point*, 29 October 1976, p. 59. Vorster dismissed de Borchgrave as 'an untrustworthy journalist' and 'a liar'.
56. Arnaud de Borchgrave, 'We Can Trump Russia', *Newsweek*, 17 May 1976, p. 23.
57. Interview with Arnaud de Borchgrave, 14 November 1996.
58. Ibid. See also Denis Herbstein, 'South Africa Turns Screw on Pressmen', *Sunday Times*, 31 October 1976. Herbstein's application for a work permit extension was refused a few week later and he was forced to return to Britain.
59. Eric Abraham, 'Flight from a Coming Race War', *Guardian*, 10 January 1977.
60. During March 1976, Abraham interviewed Mrs Winnie Mandela. The interview was later published as 'Profile in Courage: Mrs. Winnie Mandela', *Objective: Justice*, Vol. 10, No. 1 (Spring 1978), p. 32.
61. Drooz was registered as a founding member of the FCA (FCA Archive). His strings were listed in 'South Africa Orders Out US Journalist', *The Times*, 30 August 1978. However, there is no evidence in the *Chicago Sun-Times* or *US News and World Report* of Drooz having ever written for these newspapers.
62. In 1977, Drooz had been accused by a South African government official 'of spying for both the Central Intelligence Agency and the Israelis'. (Pollak, op. cit., p. 87.) Larry Heinzerling recalls Drooz 'fishing for information', he felt that Drooz was probably an intelligence man, using journalism as a cover. (Interview with Larry Heinzerling, 19 September 1995.)
63. 'South Africa Orders Out US Journalist', *The Times*, 30 August 1978.
64. Julian Burgess, Esau du Plessis, Roger Murray, Peter Fraenkel, Rosanne Harvey, John Laurence, Peter Ripken and Barbara Rogers, *The Great White Hoax: South Africa's International Propaganda Machine* (London, Africa Bureau, 1977), p. 39. Jeremy Thorpe was the leader of the Liberal Party. In 1976, the press revealed that ten years earlier he had been involved in a homosexual relationship.
65. Peter Hillmore, 'South Africa's Man and the Dirty Story', *Guardian*, 15 May 1976.
66. Terry Lovell and William Dorran, 'I Lied about that Blue Film', *Sunday People*, 23 May 1976.
67. 'Nine O'clock News', BBC 1, 18 May 1976.
68. Norman Luck and Don Coolican, 'Colonel Bogus: "I Admit It – Spy Tale Was All Lies"', *Daily Express*, 20 May 1976.
69. Editorial, 'The Real Scandal', *Sunday Times*, 23 May 1976.
70. William Raynor and Geoff Allen, 'Smear: The Thorpe Affair', unpublished book, p. 1.
71. See, for example, Peter Kellner and Tony Rocca, 'Insight: The Plot that Never Was', *Sunday Times*, 15 May 1977; Barrie Penrose and Roger Courtiour, *The Pencourt File* (London, Harper & Row, 1978); and the BBC's unbroadcast documentary investigating the subject: 'It showed beyond doubt that the South African allegations were baloney.' ('The Tale of Jeremy Fishier', *Private Eye*, No. 413, 14 October 1977, p. 18.)
72. 'Thorne's Porn "Set-up"', *Time Out*, No. 333, 6 August 1976, p. 5: 'The South Africans asked me to set up the *Guardian*.' Raynor and Allen, 'Smear', p. 162:

'[Cheeseman] said that it had been necessary to "stop the train," of the smear story to normalise Anglo-South African relations before the first Kissinger Vorster meeting ... [Cheeseman] acknowledged, "It was a brilliant manipulation of the press".' See also David Norris and Nicholas Roe, 'South African "Plot to Discredit BBC"', *Sunday Telegraph*, 23 May 1976; Gordon Winter, *Inside BOSS: South Africa's Secret Police* (Middlesex, Penguin, 1981), pp. 468–72; Peter Hain, *Sing the Beloved Country: The Struggle for the New South Africa* (London, Pluto Press, 1996), pp. 111–12: 'A former British Intelligence officer, Colin Wallace, told me in 1987: "The Colonel Cheeseman saga is known in intelligence circles as the 'double bubble' because it contains a second dimension in deception and not only deflects attention from the main target, but also 'bursts', leaving the investigator doubting everything he has uncovered so far."'

73. Peter Deeley, Letter to the editor, *The Times*, 22 May 1976.
74. Interview with Ian Wright, 26 October 1994.
75. 'In 1976 H.J. van den Bergh told me that BOSS had thirty-seven South African journalists on its payroll. Three of these were parliamentary correspondents, one was an editor in chief, and eight worked on news desks in one capacity or another.' (Winter, op. cit., p. 578); 'I confronted the editor who was most mentioned in the rumours, and he said: "Tony when I die and they look at my papers, they will find that I was on the level." He warned that he would sue anyone repeating the rumour.' (Tony Heard, *The Cape of Storms: A Personal History of the Crisis in South Africa* (Johannesburg, Ravan Press, 1990)); Interviews with Tony Heard, 23 September 1996; Raymond Louw, 20 September 1996; Stanley Uys, 19 January 1996. See also June Goodwin and Ben Schiff, interview with John Horak, 4 May 1992. (Unpublished extract from June Goodwin and Ben Schiff, *The Heart of Whiteness: Afrikaners Face Black Rule in the New South Africa* (New York, Scribner, 1995).)
76. Sanford Ungar, *Africa: The People and Politics of an Emerging Continent* (New York, Simon & Schuster, 1985), p. 7. Bill Deedes also commented upon his friendship with Myburgh. (Interview with Lord Deedes, 16 November 1995.)
77. Anthony Sampson, 'The General's White Lies', *Observer*, 21 January 1979.
78. Richard West, 'A Family Affair', *Spectator*, 24 June 1978, p. 8. See also Ray Kennedy, 'South Africa Offered Journalists Money', *The Times*, 17 April 1978.
79. Interview with Larry Heinzerling, 19 September 1995.
80. See, for example, *Supplementary Report of the Commission of Inquiry into Alleged Irregularities in the Former Department of Information* (Pretoria, Government Printer, 1979), chapter 5.42 and 5.43, p. 18, which reported that Hennie Serfontein had received money from the Foreign Affairs Association (a Department of Information front-organisation) as payment for a book on John Vorster's détente with black Africa. Serfontein, who had worked for the [Johannesburg] *Sunday Times* and the *Rand Daily Mail* and was an occasional stringer for the *Observer* (1978–79) and *Africa*, recalls that as a freelance journalist he accepted funds without asking too many questions. He did not, however, suspect that the money originated with the Department of Information. The projected book was never completed. (Interview with Hennie Serfontein, 3 October 1996.) See also Patrick Laurence, 'Botha Scraps SA Front', *Guardian*, 23 November 1978, which revealed that Lord Chalfont had been a guest of the Foreign Affairs Association (FAA). Chalfont claims that he had no idea that the FAA was financed by the South African government. (Interview with Lord Chalfont, 12 March 1996); Nicholas Ashford, 'Freedom Foundation Named as Pretoria Funded Front', *The Times*, 25 November 1978, revealed that Robert Moss had been a guest of another Information front-organisation, the South African Freedom Foundation.

81. For examples of the international media's investigative research into the Information scandal, see Anthony Sampson, 'The General's White Lies', 'The Spymaster and the Playboy' and 'The Long Reach of the Arms Men', *Observer*, 21 January–4 February 1979; David Dimbleby, Interview with Eschel Rhoodie, 'Tonight Special', BBC 1, 21 March 1979; Anthony Sampson, 'South Africa's Scandal Spreads to the West' and Bernard D. Nossiter, 'South Africa PR is a $650,000 Plum', *Washington Post*, 25 March 1979; Anthony Sampson, 'Pretoria's Scandal: Special Report', *Newsweek*, 2 April 1979, pp. 1, 20–24; Anthony Sampson, '"Muldergate" and Zurich', *New York Times*, 8 April 1979; Peter H. Stone, 'Muldergate on Madison Avenue' and Karen Rothmyer, 'Apartheid Trib', *Nation*, 14 April 1979, pp. 390–93; David Beresford, 'The Disastrous Course of South Africa's Flying Propaganda Circus' and 'How Pretoria Planned its Undercover Operations', *Guardian*, 7–8 August 1979; Karen Rothmyer, 'The McGoff Grab', *Columbia Journalism Review*, November/December 1979, pp. 33–39; Donald K. Thrasher and James G. Newland Jr, 'South African Story Involves SerVaas, "Post"' (five-part series), *Indianapolis Star*, 23–27 March 1980; Karen Rothmyer, 'The South African Lobby', *Nation*, 19 April 1980, pp. 455–58; Jonathan Bloch and Andrew Weir, 'The Adventures of the Brothers Kimche', *Middle East,* No. 90 (April 1982), pp. 25–26; Derek Knight, *Beyond the Pale: The Christian Political Fringe* (Lancashire, Caraf Publications, 1982).

9

Interpretation

The previous chapters of this book have attempted to demonstrate that the international media treatment of South Africa during the 1970s was influenced by (and mediated through) many opposing forces. These included South Africa's propagandists, the anti-apartheid movements, the British and American governments and intelligence agencies, the South African press and the legacy of historicised representations. The ensuing coverage of the Republic reflected the struggle for representation of these influential voices.

The coverage of the eight years between 1972 and 1979 can, in retrospect, be divided into four stages. In the first, between January 1972 and April 1974, the news from South Africa was relatively quiet, punctured only by the occasional dramatic event such as the Durban strikes (February 1973) or the shooting of African miners at the Western Deep Level mine, Carletonville (September 1973).

The South African story returned to prominence in April 1974 following the collapse of the Portuguese empire. As a prescient editorial in the *New York Times* suggested, 'After April 25, things may never be the same again, not only in Portugal's African territories but in Spain, Greece, Rhodesia and South Africa.'[1] However, during the 26 months up to June 1976, the coverage of the Republic was primarily concerned with the apartheid regime's relations with its newly liberated neighbours (Angola and Mozambique) and its potential role in the resolution of the crisis in Rhodesia/Zimbabwe. The most significant domestic South African story was perceived by the international media to be John Vorster's promise to introduce reforms.[2] Following the Angolan war, American newspapers began to establish bureaus in South Africa in the expectation that the region would become the site of military action in the years that followed.[3]

The Soweto uprising came as a major shock to most correspondents and ushered in the third period of coverage in this study.[4] Between June 1976 and December 1977, the rioting and unrest in South Africa attracted exceptional attention in the British and American media. This coverage intensified following Henry Kissinger's visit to the

Republic (September 1976) and the election of President Jimmy Carter (November 1976). During 1977, and in the light of an increasing number of deaths in South African prisons, the country became one of the testing grounds of President Carter's commitment to human rights. As the demand for news from the Republic increased, so the international news agencies expanded their staff and the television companies established bureaus in the country. However, following the murder of Steve Biko in police custody (September 1977) and the ensuing election victory of the National Party in December 1977, reporting from South Africa tended to dampen down. This was particularly apparent in the US media, where the extraordinary attention given to the Biko inquest and the abandonment of the South African story happened in a matter of weeks. In November 1977, American columnist, Nicholas von Hoffman, observed that 'The spigot has been turned on and the mass media ... has kept us up to date on every lie and evasion concerning the murder of Steve Biko ... Prime Minister Vorster ... can be seen almost every weekend, repeating his intransigencies on the public affairs programmes.'[5]

Yet, by the beginning of 1978, Michael Kilian opened an article for the *Chicago Tribune* by asking: 'Whatever happened to South Africa?'[6] There were a number of reasons for the decline in coverage during the fourth period of this study (1978–79) but the primary cause was undoubtedly the decline of violent unrest in South Africa. This led many reporters to shift their attention to the transformation of Rhodesia into Zimbabwe which was rapidly perceived as a more significant story. As Bill Nicholson, the Chairman of the FCA, commented at the beginning of 1980: 'I am entertaining ideas that we change our name to the Zimbabwe Foreign Correspondents' Association, because so many of us seem to be spending so much time there.'[7] The sheer number of journalists who were now technically based in South Africa, however, meant that incidents such as the Crossroads squatter-camp clearance (1978) and the Information scandal (October 1978–June 1979) received substantial coverage.

Although the central thrust of the Department of Information's programme of manipulation was aimed at the US media, Britain remained 'in terms of psychology if not so much in real terms of the greatest importance to South Africa'.[8] Indeed, on Fleet Street, South Africa was the subject of continuing fascination for many journalists and columnists. Apartheid, however, was often handled in a style which refused to permit linkage with race issues in Britain. In effect, South Africa was treated as a decolonisation story that had somehow gone wrong. William Davis commented in an editorial for *Punch* in 1977: 'The plain fact is that men like Kruger have nothing but contempt for Western liberal opinion. So for that matter, has Idi Amin, but somehow we can't quite bring ourselves to accept reality: we *want* to believe that white tribes have more sense. They are decent chaps *because* they are white, or so we like to think.'[9] Although South Africa had been forced to leave the Commonwealth in 1961, its white population was consistently portrayed in the British media as being, to a certain extent, the responsibility of Great Britain. British commentators were the most vociferous members of the international media in their resistance to sanctions and in their encouragement of dialogue with the South African government, even though the Afrikaners were often represented as a peculiar African 'tribe'. For the most part, the British media fluctuated between a form of paternalist panic and post-colonial ennui on the subject of South Africa and apartheid throughout the decade.

The American media reflected a number of different concerns. There was a profound sense in the United States that the South African story had gone unreported for too long. Tom Wicker, for example, recalling his visit to South Africa in 1978 and 1979, felt that 'It was such virgin territory. People hadn't written about this, they hadn't been down there (at least not many that I knew of) and interviewed black school teachers and so forth.'[10] The magazine, *Town and Country*, introduced a 24-page article on the Republic in June 1977 with an assessment that: 'What we hear or read about South Africa is always secondhand, based largely on various interpretations of political action. We know little, if anything, of what that country's people really think about their land and its problems.'[11] The American interest in South Africa was triggered by two key factors: the Angolan war and its role as a microcosm of the Cold War, and the re-emergence of violent African unrest (or agency) during the Soweto uprising. In 1973, before these events had occurred, Ken Whiting (AP, 1967–74, and the only American resident reporter in the Republic) observed that during his term in South Africa:

> I haven't seen as many political changes as you might expect, and putting over trends about a party that has been entrenched for 25 years isn't easy to readers accustomed to elections with landslides one way or the other. In any case, there isn't that much interest in the States about South Africa. American editors remain interested in Indo-China, Europe, problems in the Middle East and South America. I guess Africa comes after all that lot.[12]

American reporters and commentators during the second half of the 1970s permitted their coverage to be mediated, in part, through the British interpretation of the Republic. Sanford Ungar, in his study of the differences between the British and American 'reactions' to the subject, acknowledged that 'South African developments are covered more regularly, in greater detail, and in more depth in the British than in the American press. Americans who follow South African affairs feel obliged to read serious British newspapers and other periodicals.'[13] The fundamental difference between the coverage of the two countries, however, lay in the American journalists' references to race relations in the US. The treatment presented to the American reader demonstrated few of the variations on colonial paternalism or ennui common in the British media; instead, in general, the US media represented the South African story as a metaphor for the racial problems of the United States. In 1977, the anti-apartheid campaigner, E.S. Reddy, acknowledged that the central difficulty for the United Nations with regard to southern Africa was 'the intertwining of colonialism and racism'.[14] In recognition of their own respective histories, the British and American media divided upon the importance of these two subjects. Beyond these racial and colonial contexts, there was little dramatic difference between the British and American representations of apartheid. Ungar's conclusion in his analysis of the portrayal of South Africa in the US media is equally applicable to the British press:

> It is safe to say that most American news organizations have and convey a negative perception of South Africa ... There is an abhorrence of apartheid, a distrust and mockery of the homelands policy and other South African attempts to put a euphemistic face on its social order, and an impatience for the time when South Africa will finally begin to move in the direction of one-man, one-vote. But while this basic establishment view rejects the South African government's handling of the country's racial situation, it also tends to reject violent solutions. The mainstream press holds a persistent – perhaps naive – view that peaceful change is still possible in South Africa and that it is the role of the United States to help promote it.[15]

The international media's coverage, as described by Ungar, often tended to become confused through its continuing dependence on the voices of white South Africa. Daniel Schechter, an anti-apartheid campaigner, noted in 1977 that the American newspapers' 'stance towards the country's white minority is schizophrenic. Despite a clearly pervasive anti-apartheid bias, the dictates of professional neutrality often appear to lead to reports which equate the Afrikaner position with majority claims.'[16] The fact that South Africa was a partial democracy offering freedom within limits to members of the white population complicated the story for foreign reporters. As the previous chapters have explained, correspondents and visitors to the country could be relatively easily misled by the duality of South Africa under apartheid. John Burns (*New York Times*) recalls, perhaps with some degree of hindsight:

> South Africa was ... extremely misleading. Every morning you could get up and there were newspapers which looked pretty much like the newspapers we read at home. The country worked. If you could simply forget the eighteen million blacks, you could imagine yourself to be in New Zealand ... I think to be properly prepared for all of this you really had to understand just how much of a deceit all of that was and how much more significant than the fact [that] they had a National Assembly ... was the fact that they had a secret police which was on every measure as devious and evil as the KGB ever was.[17]

It is also useful to compare the international media's consensus on South Africa with the existing public opinion polls on the subject. In December 1977, a Harris Survey of 1,498 adults in the United States found that while 63 per cent of people polled felt 'that the system of apartheid ... [was] "unjustified"', 76 per cent opposed 'the US "urging blacks inside South Africa to engage in guerrilla warfare against the white government"'. On the question of American investment, the polling organisation found that while 51 per cent of those polled opposed 'any move "to force all US businesses now in South Africa to close their operations there"', 46 per cent favoured 'getting US companies now in business in South Africa to put pressure on the South African government'. As Louis Harris noted in his conclusion to the evidence in the poll, 'To a remarkable degree, public opinion in this country directly parallels that of the Carter administration.'[18] The only guide to British public opinion on South Africa during the 1970s was a BBC radio programme entitled 'You the Jury'. Following a debate between Donald Woods and the Conservative MP, Eldon Griffiths, on the proposition that Britain should cease trading with South Africa, the 100 members of the 'jury' returned a verdict of 45 per cent in favour, 54 per cent against, with one person undecided.[19]

The two opinion polls appear to demonstrate that the range of the consensus in the British and American media coverage of South Africa matched British and American public opinion quite neatly. Whether the same can be said of the representations constructed by the international media is less simple to assess. The case-studies in this book have shown that the representations of South Africa and South Africans constructed by the Western journalists did not emerge from an historical vacuum. Indeed, the 200-year history of the racial 'other' continued to exert a powerful influence on the construction of news and news-features in South Africa in the 1970s. The similarity between the interpretations, and the methods of interpretation employed by foreign correspondents and visiting staff writers and those of white travellers to Africa in the nineteenth century, suggests that although 'the imperial gaze' might have become blurred (or, perhaps, been averted) in the immediate post-independence period of the 1960s, by the 1970s it was being re-applied with vigour. In his seminal work, *Orientalism*, Edward Said discussed the shifting image of 'the Arab' in American popular culture since the Second World War. The international media's coverage of South Africa during the 1970s demonstrated that 'the African' *and* 'the Afrikaner' were equally able 'to accommodate the transformations and reductions – all of a simply tendentious kind – into which [s/]he is continually being forced'.[20]

The consensus on South Africa which emerged within the international media demonstrated many of the contradictions of liberalism. An examination of these contradictions exposes a multitude of ideological tensions. It also demonstrates that the international media treatment of South Africa reveals at least as much about the international media as it does about South Africa. Adam Gopnik recently commented in the *New Yorker*:

> The funny thing about a free press is that it is not really very good at its manifest role but it is terrific at a lot of its latent roles. Journalism has been bad at history, since it can paint only quickly and in very broad strokes. ... The press is also a poor tribunal and a worse department of justice – its standards of evidence are too low, and its amnesia is too sudden. But it can make a surprisingly good guardian of the public's compassion and sense of proportion. A free press, more than any other institution – more than schools or parliaments or scholars – protects public decency. It does this, like it or not, by making a distinction between the middle and the margins.[21]

During the 1970s, the British and American print and broadcast media judged both apartheid *and* anti-apartheid to be on 'the margins'. The 'middle' that existed in South Africa was confusing and contradictory. So was the international media treatment of South Africa in the 1970s.

NOTES

1. Editorial, 'Tremors from Lisbon ...', *New York Times*, 28 April 1974.
2. See Michael Knipe, 'Mr Vorster Asks the Press for a Year's Grace to Realize his Internal and External Reform Plans', *The Times*, 7 November 1974.
3. In 1975, a number of correspondents were moved directly from Vietnam to South Africa. It is clear that some foreign editors believed that southern Africa might

develop as the next epicentre of the Cold War.

4. See, for example, Chris Munnion, *Banana Sunday: Datelines From Africa*, second edition (Rivonia, William Waterman, 1995), p. 445: 'When the youngsters of Soweto took to the streets on June 16th, 1976 ... I was on a besieged farm in the north-eastern area of Rhodesia.'

5. Nicholas von Hoffman, 'The Energy Hotch-potch', *Spectator*, 12 November 1977, p. 9.

6. Michael Kilian, 'For Carter, South Africa Got So Big It Vanished', *Chicago Tribune*, 3 January 1978.

7. Bill Nicholson, Letter to members of the FCA, 7 February 1980 (FCA Archive).

8. Roy Macnab, 'Foreign Report: London', *South Africa International*, Vol. 5, No. 2 (October 1974), p. 107.

9. Editorial, 'Vorster's Laager', *Punch*, 23 November 1977, p. 967.

10. Interview with Tom Wicker, 19 September 1995.

11. Stephen R. Conn, 'Apartheid from the Top', *Town and Country*, June 1977, p. 47. The 'country's people' interviewed in Conn's article included Gatsha Buthelezi, Harry Oppenheimer, Piet Cillie, Jan S. Marais, Jimmy Kruger, Helen Suzman, Gary Player, Dr Christiaan Barnard, J.N. Reddy (chairman of the South African Indian Council), Richard Maponya (an African businessman), Des and Dawn Lindberg (South African folk singers), Franklin Sonn (the coloured President of the Cape Teachers Professional Association) and Alan Paton.

12. Virginia Waite, 'Men Who Write Us Up', [Johannesburg] *Sunday Times* magazine, 18 November 1973, p. 34.

13. Sanford Ungar, 'The American Scene: An Overview', in Alfred O. Hero Jr and John Barratt (eds), *The American People and South Africa: Publics, Elites and Policymaking Processes* (Massachesetts, Lexington Books, 1981), p. 171. The breadth of the debate in the British newspapers was significantly larger than that available in the US media. See for example the following polemical positions adopted during the Soweto uprising: Peregrine Worsthorne, 'Black Day for Black S. Africa', *Sunday Telegraph*, 20 June 1976; Richard Gott, 'Rising Hopes', *Guardian*, 27 August 1976. (See Chapter 7.) Columnists and commentators in the British media also appear to have been quicker than the Americans at recognising and instigating shifts in representation.

14. Enuga S. Reddy, 'The United Nations and the International Campaign against Apartheid', *Objective: Justice*, Vol. 9, No. 4 (Winter 1977/78), p. 9.

15. Sanford Ungar, 'South Africa in the American Media', in Hero and Barratt (eds), op. cit., pp. 42–43.

16. Daniel Schechter, 'Media Myopia', *More*, December 1977, p. 31.

17. Interview with John Burns, 19 November 1996.

18. Louis Harris, 'Harris Survey: US Public Opposes Apartheid', *Chicago Tribune*, 12 December 1977. The full figures were: on the justification of apartheid: 63 per cent to 12; on urging violent African resistance, 76 per cent to 4; on the withdrawal of US companies, 51 per cent to 21; on US companies applying pressure to the South African government, 46 per cent to 28.

19. 'You the Jury', BBC Radio Four, 22 February 1978. The witnesses in the debate in favour of the proposition were Abdul Minty and Neil Wates. Peter Adler (a petroleum technician and active member of the ASTMS union) and Justus Tshungu (an African South African) argued against withdrawal. Before the 'trial', the jury was divided 42 per cent in favour, 56 per cent against, with 2 per cent undecided.

20. Edward W. Said, *Orientalism* (London, Penguin, 1978), p. 285.

21. Adam Gopnik, 'A Critic at Large: Read All About It', *New Yorker*, 12 December 1994, pp. 101–2.

Appendix A

The list of correspondents and stringers that follows is by no means comprehensive. If one included all the journalists employed by the news agencies and the freelance reporters who covered South Africa during the 1970s, the number would stretch to more than 100 people. The 36 journalists whose brief biographical details appear below were amongst the most regularly published. All unspecified quotations are from the interviews conducted for this book. Other stringers or visiting staff-writers are provided with supporting biographical data within the relevant chapters. The chart which follows this biographical index lists the bureau chiefs of the news agencies and American broadcasting companies, the Africa correspondents of the *Christian Science Monitor*, the stringers of the *Wall Street Journal* and the *Financial Times*, and the BBC radio correspondents.

Nicholas Ashford. *The Times*, from 1975. Resident staff correspondent, southern Africa.
Ashford was certainly amongst the most gifted of the correspondents who covered the Republic during the mid-1970s. Within a few months of arriving in the country, he interviewed Robert Sobukwe, who was subject to a banning order. The ensuing article, 'The Silent Triumph of a Black South African', *The Times*, 27 October 1975, 'conveyed the flavour of banishment [in Kimberley, and] was an accurate summation of the thinking of a man whom the government wanted to consign to political oblivion. It was a report which no one else had dared write, and yet Nick did it – and with such skill that he could not be accused of flouting the banning restrictions' (Benjamin Pogrund, 'Obituary: Nicholas Ashford', *Independent*, 12 February 1990). During the extended strike at *The Times* (1978–79), Ashford contributed articles to the *Spectator*. Ashford left South Africa in 1981 to take up the post of Washington correspondent. He died in 1990.

Bridget Bloom. *Financial Times*. Visiting staff correspondent, Africa.
Bloom made her reputation reporting the Biafran war. In 1968, she

joined the *Financial Times*. In 1969, she started a 12-year term as Africa editor for the newspaper. She recalls that she did not turn her attention to South Africa until 1973. However, in the years before the *Financial Times* placed a correspondent in the country (1977), Bloom visited the Republic regularly. She felt that the newspaper's dependence upon stringers from the [Johannesburg] *Financial Mail* occasionally led to timid reports: 'While they were very good, they were much like the *FT* at that time – rather cautious.' Bloom worked closely with Stewart Dalby while he was resident in South Africa. Her relationship with John Vorster was particularly difficult. The South African prime minister once walked out halfway through an interview that Bloom was conducting with him.

John Burns. *New York Times*, from 1976. Resident staff correspondent, southern Africa.

Burns was a Canadian who had been educated in England. He had previously covered China for the *Toronto Globe and Mail*. He joined the *New York Times* in 1974 and in 1976 was sent to South Africa as the first *New York Times* resident correspondent in the Republic since the expulsion of Joseph Lelyveld, ten years earlier. Burns ran into trouble immediately following his arrival in the country when the veracity of an article in which he had quoted Eschel Rhoodie (John Burns, 'South African Aide Bars Military Role in Rhodesia', *New York Times*, 14 May 1976) was challenged by the aforesaid Secretary for Information. Burns understood his (and the *New York Times*'s) message to the South African government to be: 'We are not South Africa's enemy. Our job is to tell South Africa's story, black and white – on both sides, as fully as we possibly can.' During an average year, Burns would spend up to one-third of his time in Rhodesia/Zimbabwe and other southern African countries. He was the only foreign correspondent to publish an interview with Steve Biko before his death (John F. Burns, 'A Jailed Black Relays Warning to Kissinger', *New York Times*, 19 September 1976). However, Burns was described by one anti-apartheid activist as 'sound[ing] like a public relations man for the South African government ... he rarely interviews [Africans] unless the man is seated in an office wearing a coat and tie ... Burns might easily win an award for the worst continuing coverage of South Africa' (Karen Rothmyer, 'US Press: Telling It Like It Isn't', *Southern Africa*, December 1978, p. 26). Burns recalls that the South African government 'never allowed me to forget that the axe was not far away'.

Stewart Dalby. *Financial Times*, **1975–76. Resident stringer, southern Africa.**
Dalby had previously covered the Vietnam war, remaining in the country after the fall of Saigon. He was sent to southern Africa by the *Financial Times* because the newspaper expected the region to be a suitable location for a war correspondent. Dalby was unhappy in South Africa and returned to London within twelve months. He recalls that while in the Republic, he had personal problems, which were a form of delayed reaction to the amount of time that he had spent in war-zones.

Jack Foisie. *Los Angeles Times*, **from 1976. Resident staff correspondent, southern Africa.**
Foisie was a veteran reporter who started his journalistic career during World War II and served extended terms in Vietnam and the Middle East. He arrived in South Africa in the midst of the Soweto uprising. He tended to spend two-thirds of the year in the Republic, and one-third elsewhere. David Lamb (*Los Angeles Times* correspondent in Nairobi, from 1976) describes Foisie thus: 'Jack wasn't a political reporter ... [he] was more of a street reporter – he was comfortable with average people – on the street, in the bush – and not necessarily in government offices.' Foisie, feels, in retrospect, that it took him some time to get on top of the South African story. He recalls, in particular, that 'I wasn't as good as I should have been at cultivating black sources.' In 1979, Foisie was criticised for writing like a nineteenth-century commentator in his coverage of the war in Shaba (Robert Cuddy, 'An Analysis of *Los Angeles Times* Coverage', *Ufahamu*, Vol. 9, No. 1, 1979, p. 20).

June Goodwin. *Christian Science Monitor*, **1976–79. Resident staff correspondent, Africa.**
June Goodwin was a Christian Scientist (as indeed were the other *Christian Science Monitor* correspondents of the period). She recalled that she was naive about the subject of apartheid before arriving in the country: 'Before I left Nairobi ... I told my roommate, a black American, "Look, I'm going to be very objective about South Africa. Those white people must have reasons for what they do and I want to find out what they are"' (June Goodwin, *Cry Amandla! South African Women and the Question of Power*, New York, African Publishing Company, 1984, p. 3). Goodwin was one of the few correspondents who became politically engaged by the struggle in South Africa. By the end of her term in South Africa, she was later told that 'one of the editors at the *Monitor* said that I was becoming too involved'. As a

journalist who had interviewed Steve Biko (although the interview was not published until after his death), she recalls her amazement at the discovery that the Reuters chief correspondent had never heard of the African leader. In 1977, Goodwin was given the Overseas Press Club Madeline Dane Ross award for international reporting that showed a concern for humanity. During the same year, she also developed a productive friendship with Thenjiwe Mtintso, an African political activist and journalist on the (East London) *Daily Dispatch* (for details on Goodwin's relationship with Mtintso, see Goodwin, *Cry Amandla*, pp. 4–6, 13–23, 199–200). In 1978, Karen Rothmyer suggested that 'June Goodwin ... would be a strong contender for an award for the best [continuing coverage of South Africa]' (Karen Rothmyer, 'US Press: Telling It Like It Isn't', *Southern Africa*, December 1978, p. 26).

Peter Hawthorne. *Time*, *Daily Express*, *New York Times* **and BBC. Resident stringer, southern Africa.**
After concluding his national service in Kenya during the 1950s, Hawthorne (a British citizen) joined the South African Argus Company and proceeded to report from various African countries. In 1962, in the aftermath of the exclusion of many news organisations from South Africa, Hawthorne began to collect the various remunerative strings which would later provide his income. In 1964, he ended his relationship with the [Johannesburg] *Star*, to concentrate on his stringing activities. Two years later, he was appointed by Joseph Lelyveld to operate as a stringer for the *New York Times*, during the newspaper's exclusion from the country. Following a short period, in which (in conjunction with Ray Kennedy), Hawthorne appears to have been responsible for the majority of print reports emerging from South Africa, he settled down to the four strings listed above. He summarises the style and subject matter of the reports which were required as follows: BBC: brief and concise – 150 words or one-and-a-half minutes; *Time*: a detailed report; *Daily Express*: a concentration on sensational racial stories; *New York Times*: 'I'd make it read like my insurance policy ... because [the *New York Times* was] so dull ... just let it run and run.' The telegram which was sent to him by the BBC on 16 June 1976 read: 'Interested in Agency Reports that 10,000 school-children rioted in Soweto.' Hawthorne felt that some of the innovations in press relations introduced by the Department of Information during the 1970s were beneficial: 'Suddenly for the first time we were recognised as a resident force to be acknowledged.' He also believed that television coverage of the Republic transformed the nature of the story: 'both the British and American press were absolutely captives of television. News editors saw pictures on television

and they wanted a story that was the same sort of picture'. Hawthorne continues to live in South Africa and report for *Time* magazine.

Denis Herbstein. *Sunday Times*, *Guardian* and BBC, 1975–76. Resident stringer, southern Africa.
Herbstein, who had been born in South Africa, worked for the *Cape Times* during the 1960s, before joining the *Sunday Times* in London in 1968. In 1975, he took leave from the newspaper in order to spend a year reporting from southern Africa. Although he was the recipient of a small retainer from the *Sunday Times*, he also arranged to string for the *Guardian* and the BBC. After 12 months in South Africa, he applied to have his South African passport renewed – this request was denied because he had taken up British nationality in 1974. Herbstein was instructed that from henceforth he would need to make a standard application to visit the country (Denis Herbstein, 'Why Vorster is Kicking Me Out', *Sunday Times*, 7 November 1976). In Britain, he continued to write reports which publicised the activities of the Anti-Apartheid Movement. Herbstein recalls that 'I never wanted the [white] South African point of view ... I am afraid I was a pretty subjective reporter. I just hated apartheid.'

John Humphrys. BBC, from 1977. Resident staff correspondent, Africa.
Humphrys had previously been the BBC's correspondent in the United States, where he had covered the Watergate scandal. He recalls that his term in southern Africa was dominated by the story in Rhodesia/Zimbabwe. He felt that the situation in the Republic was heading towards an apocalyptic conclusion: 'There is a temptation, after one's initial exposure to the South African system, to curse the government for its stupidity as much as its brutality in removing from circulation so many men who might – just might – help reduce the risk of confrontation in favour of consultation. The bannings must end scream the instant experts. Nelson Mandela and company must be released if there is to be any hope of avoiding the bloodshed. Perhaps, but, after three years in South Africa, I am coming to believe that such a reaction – however well-meaning – misses the point. The purpose of discussion is to reach a compromise. I do not believe that the South African government is in search of such a compromise' (John Humphrys, 'Farewell to South Africa: 'A Country Not Yet at War, but no Longer at Peace', *Listener*, 7 August 1980).

Ray Kennedy. AP (to 1975), *The Times, Daily Telegraph* **and** *Sunday Telegraph* **and** *Daily Mirror.* **Resident stringer, South Africa.**
Kennedy, who was British, had worked for the *Daily Mail* in London during the early 1960s. He met and married a South African woman and emigrated to the Republic in the mid-1960s. Having worked for both the *Rand Daily Mail* and the [Johannesburg] *Sunday Express* and become disenchanted with the quality of South African journalism, Kennedy decided to work with Peter Hawthorne as a stringer. After one year, Kennedy left Hawthorne to work on his own. He took the *Daily Telegraph* and *Daily Mirror* strings with him. Michael Knipe later invited him to string for *The Times*. During the 1970s, his specialities included mining and South West Africa/Namibia.

Michael Knipe. *The Times,* **to 1975. Resident staff correspondent, southern Africa.**
Based in Cape Town, where he worked in the same building as Stanley Uys and David Loshak, Knipe was the second *Times* correspondent to report from South Africa following the re-opening of the newspaper's bureau in 1968. His previous posting had been New York (1969–71). The first *Times* correspondent in South Africa had been Dan van der Vat, who was not an Afrikaner but a Briton of Dutch extraction. Following his three years in South Africa, Knipe became *The Times* correspondent in Rhodesia/Zimbabwe (1975–77).

Tom Lambert. *Los Angeles Times,* **1974–76. Resident staff correspondent, southern Africa.**
Lambert was a veteran correspondent who had served in World War II. After the war, he worked for AP, *Time* and the *New York Herald-Tribune*, covering the Chinese revolution, the Korean war, West Germany and the Soviet Union. He joined the *Los Angeles Times* in 1963 and served as diplomatic correspondent and bureau chief in Tel Aviv and London. He arrived in South Africa in 1974 to open the *Los Angeles Times* bureau before his retirement in 1976. Lambert died in 1996, aged 83.

Patrick Laurence. *Guardian,* **from 1977. Resident South African stringer.**
In 1973, Laurence received a suspended jail sentence for quoting a banned person (Robert Sobukwe) in an article which he had attempted to smuggle out of South Africa for publication in the *Observer* (Stanley Uys, 'S. African Journalist Sentenced', *Observer*, 5 August 1973). By 1976, he had moved from the [Johannesburg] *Star* to the *Rand Daily Mail*, where his primary function was to rewrite the copy of African

reporters. As he informed Marion Whitehead: 'Blacks were less inclined to question eye-witness accounts and were more likely to give credibility to police brutality. White reporters in supervisory positions were more critical and subjected news reports to tests, for example, talking to the reporters, getting police comment and comparing the two reports' (Marion Whitehead, 'The Black Gatekeepers: A Study of Black Journalists on Three Daily Newspapers which Covered the Soweto Uprising of 1976', unpublished BA thesis, Rhodes University, Grahamstown, 1978, p. 87). Laurence inherited Stanley Uys's *Guardian* string in 1977, although he was far less prolific in his output. Richard Gott, the *Guardian*'s foreign news editor at the time, recalls that Laurence was 'a very nice guy but his copy didn't sing'.

Colin Legum. *Observer*. Staff correspondent, Africa.

Legum was born in South Africa and emigrated from the country following the election of the National Party in 1948. He had previously been active in the South African Labour Party. In Britain, Legum joined the *Observer*, where he was eventually appointed to the post of Commonwealth correspondent. He also had a long association with the Africa Bureau. By the 1960s, Legum was considered by some to be 'the doyen of Western African correspondents, making the *Observer* an unrivalled centre of intelligence and enterprise on African issues' (Richard Cockett, *David Astor and The Observer*, London, 1991, Andre Deutsch, p. 182). Although Legum was opposed to apartheid, the scale of his influence over the coverage of Africa, attracted some criticism from younger journalists and anti-apartheid campaigners. In addition to his work for the *Observer*, Legum also edited the annual *Africa Contemporary Record*. He was a passionate anti-communist.

David Loshak. *Daily Telegraph* and *Sunday Telegraph*, to 1974. Resident staff correspondent, South Africa.

Loshak's previous postings had been as a 'fireman' (1965–69) and India (1969–72). He did not find covering South Africa a particularly happy experience, owing to the sense of cultural isolation in the Republic. Loshak recalls that his stringer, George Aschman, and Stanley Uys exercised a benevolent influence over his work at the time. He returned to London to become the *Daily Telegraph*'s Health correspondent.

Bruce Loudon. *Daily Telegraph* and *Sunday Telegraph*, from 1975. Resident stringer, southern Africa.

During the early 1970s, Loudon was the *Financial Times* and *Daily* and *Sunday Telegraph* stringer in Portugal (and the Portuguese colonies). Having being dismissed from the *Financial Times*, Loudon reported from Angola for the *Telegraph*. He arrived in South Africa in 1976 and continued to supply reports to the *Telegraph* when Christopher Munnion or A.J. McIlroy were not available. Loudon also worked for the [Johannesburg] *Sunday Times*, under the editorship of Tertius Myburgh. A number of my interviewees have suggested that Loudon was born in South Africa. He is also thought to have been closely involved with a number of intelligence agencies. Bruce Loudon declined to be interviewed for this book.

James MacManus. *Guardian*, from 1974. Visiting staff correspondent, Africa.

Having reported on the activities of BOSS agents in London ('Campus Spy Returns to South Africa', *Guardian*, 26 March 1973), MacManus was refused a work permit to enter South Africa in 1975, following his appointment as Africa correspondent by the *Guardian*. In the spring of 1977, MacManus was allowed to enter South Africa and he returned regularly over the next two years. MacManus travelled widely throughout Africa during the late 1970s.

Eric Marsden. *Sunday Times*, from 1977. Resident staff correspondent, southern Africa.

Marsden was appointed staff correspondent in South Africa by the *Sunday Times* during the autumn of 1976. Between 1957 and 1970, Marsden had worked for the *East Africa Standard*, ending his association with the newspaper as deputy-editor. From 1970 to 1976, he was the Middle East correspondent of the *Sunday Times*. Marsden's first attempt to enter South Africa was, however, thwarted by the Department of Information, who refused his application for a work permit. He finally settled in the Republic in 1977. He recalls: 'What I found in South Africa was that whatever I wanted to do, there were red hot local reporters and foreign correspondents who were already ahead of me. It wasn't the kind of situation where you could unearth something that nobody was going for and so I was much less effective in South Africa than I wanted to be, or than I had been in the Middle East.'

David Martin. *Observer* and BBC, from 1974. Staff correspondent, Africa.

Martin, a British citizen, had been resident in Africa since 1964, during which time he had reported for a number of different news organisations. From 1974, he reported for the *Observer* and the BBC's Africa Service. During the Angolan War, Martin reported from both

MPLA and UNITA territory. However, his coverage of South Africa was limited by the fact that he remained banned from entering the Republic throughout the 1970s. There was one exception to this banning: Martin was allowed to accompany David Owen, during the British Foreign Secretary's tour of South Africa. Although not permitted to enter the country on other occasions, Martin still managed to break a number of South African-related stories from Lusaka and London.

A.J. McIlroy. *Daily Telegraph* **and** *Sunday Telegraph*, **from 1976. Visiting staff correspondent.**
McIlroy was a *Telegraph* 'fireman', whose basic job description appears to have been to be available to cover disparate stories at a moment's notice. In 1973, McIlroy had reported from Nairobi. During the Angolan war, he covered the conflict from Luanda until he was expelled in January 1976. He reported from South Africa on a number of occasions during the late 1970s, when Christopher Munnion was on vacation or in Rhodesia/Zimbabwe. McIlroy later covered the Falklands War. A.J. McIlroy declined to be interviewed for this book.

William McWhirter. *Time*, **from 1977. Resident staff correspondent, southern Africa.**
McWhirter arrived in South Africa in 1977 to re-open the *Time* bureau, 15 years after the news-magazine had been excluded from the country. He had previously covered the war in Vietnam. He felt that life in Sandton was too distant from the South African story and relocated to a five-star hotel in the centre of Johannesburg. He found that his hotel accommodation made him more accessible to visiting celebrities and African sources. He recalls that 'everybody knew what I was saying and saying in a journal that went outside South Africa'.

Charles Mohr. *New York Times*, **to 1975. Visiting staff correspondent, Eastern and southern Africa.**
Refused a residency visa for South Africa, Mohr covered the Republic on an annual or twice-yearly basis. His previous career had involved a stint for *Time* in Vietnam (1962–63) following which, he left in protest at the magazine's editorial position. (David Halberstam, 'Time Inc.'s internal war over Vietnam', *Esquire*, January 1978, pp. 94–131). He then returned to Vietnam for the *New York Times*. Mohr was apparently offered the opportunity to be the *New York Times*' correspondent in South Africa (1975), but the Department of Information were not willing to permit him to be accompanied by his adopted Vietnamese daughter. He died in 1989.

Christopher Munnion. *Daily Telegraph* and *Sunday Telegraph*, from 1974. Resident staff correspondent, southern Africa.

Like David Loshak, with whom he had competed for postings, Munnion was one of the 'rising stars' of the *Daily Telegraph* during the late 1960s. Munnion had also specialised in 'fireman' reporting: brief visits to 'trouble-spots'. His first visit to Africa had been in 1967. He recalls that he barely covered South Africa before the unrest of 1976: 'The *Telegraph*'s priority was Rhodesia.' His position on South Africa was broadly in line with that of the *Telegraph* (see, for example, Munnion's articles in favour of Vorster's policies following the South African prime minister's 'give me six months' speech in 1974: 'Christopher Munnion, 'Vorster's Long Trek to Realism', and 'South Africa's Path to Dignity', *Daily Telegraph*, 18 March and 5 May 1975). In 1977, Munnion began to write a 'quickie' book on Biko with James MacManus (*Guardian*). The book was abandoned when Donald Woods's account of the murdered black consciousness leader was published. Munnion continued to be the *Telegraph*'s correspondent in South Africa throughout the 1980s. In 1993, he wrote *Banana Sunday: Datelines From Africa*, a humorous discourse on the decline of the traditional foreign correspondent. Munnion continues to live in Johannesburg.

Caryle Murphy. *Washington Post*, from 1977. Resident stringer, southern Africa.

Caryle Murphy started her journalism career by settling in Angola in 1974 and learning to speak Portuguese. Peter Younghusband encouraged her to remain in Luanda because he thought Angola was going to become a major story. She reported for the *Washington Post* throughout the Angolan war, as a stringer, until she was expelled from the country in August 1976. The *Washington Post* brought her back to the United States for one year's training before dispatching her to South Africa to take over from Robin Wright. Murphy was upgraded to correspondent status some years later. Her first reports from the Republic dealt with the inquest into Steve Biko's death. Murphy recalls that when she arrived in South Africa, 'the black confrontation ... was happening in the streets, in the newspapers, you could meet the people – you could talk to them – it had drama! After the inquest into Biko's death and because of all the bannings and the fear and the repression, things quietened down.' By 1980, 'it was almost as if black resistance had received a lobotomy'. Murphy continued to focus her attention on the iniquities of apartheid and became the subject of some attention from BOSS; in 1980, her application to renew her work permit was refused.

Michael Nicholson. ITN, from 1977. Resident staff correspondent, Africa.
Nicholson had been an ITN war correspondent since 1968. In the years before 1977, he had functioned mainly as a 'fireman' in countries as varied as Nigeria, Jordan, India, Israel, Cyprus, Vietnam, Cambodia and Angola. He opened the ITN bureau in Johannesburg in 1977, although the bulk of his coverage was concerned with Rhodesia/Zimbabwe. Nicholson later wrote an account of his years as a war correspondent, *A Measure of Danger: Memoirs of a British War Correspondent* (London, HarperCollins, 1991). Only a handful of pages are devoted to his days in South Africa. He recalls with some regret, however, that the television representations requested by ITN's editors were loaded with stereotypes. If 'you interviewed the whites in South Africa, you always interviewed them by the [swimming] pool'. In the case of Africans, 'you'd go to the worst part of Soweto and sit them outside a pile of garbage'.

Roger Omond. *New Statesman*, 1977–78. Resident South African stringer.
During the 1970s, Omond worked as an editorial writer and assistant editor for the (East London) *Daily Dispatch*, the newspaper he had joined as a graduate in the 1960s. He began to write regularly for the international media in 1976. In 1978, he followed the *Daily Dispatch*'s editor, Donald Woods, into political exile in Britain: 'It looked as though we were back into post-Sharpeville.' He continued to write and campaign against apartheid. Omond died in 1996.

David Ottaway. *Washington Post*, from 1974. Visiting staff correspondent, Africa.
Ottaway had covered the Algerian war during the early 1960s. He returned to Africa, as the *Washington Post*'s successor to Jim Hoagland in 1972. Two years later he was upgraded to staff correspondent status. Ottaway's experiences with South African visa and work permit regulations were very similar to James MacManus's. He was finally permitted a multi-entry visa in 1976. While Ottaway was visiting South Africa, his reports tended to take priority over the work of the *Post*'s stringers, Robin Wright and Caryle Murphy.

Quentin Peel. *Financial Times*, from 1977. Resident staff correspondent, southern Africa.
Johannesburg was Quentin Peel's first overseas posting for the *Financial Times*. In the Republic, he retained the assistance of the *Financial Mail* reporter, Bernard Simon, while relinquishing the

majority of the other local *Financial Times* stringers. Unlike his predecessor, Stewart Dalby, Peel was a full staff correspondent. Visits from Bridget Bloom (the Africa editor) and the foreign editor declined accordingly. Unlike a number of his contemporaries, Peel concentrated his attention on the Republic, although Rhodesia/Zimbabwe was also a prime concern. He also widened the focus of the *Financial Times*'s coverage, adding a variety of political and social stories to the usual economic analysis (see, for example, Quentin Peel, 'Condemned to Silence', *Financial Times*, 28 November 1977).

Benjamin Pogrund. *Sunday Times*, to 1976; *Boston Globe* and *New Republic*, from 1976. Resident South African stringer.
Pogrund possesses the distinction of being the first 'African Affairs reporter' to be appointed by any newspaper in South Africa. This historic event occurred during the 1950s when Pogrund was employed by Laurence Gandar of the *Rand Daily Mail*. In the mid-1960s, Pogrund was prosecuted during the infamous prisons trial. Although he was not imprisoned, his passport was withdrawn for a number of years. By the early 1970s, he was the night editor of the *Rand Daily Mail* and stringer for the *Sunday Times*. Pogrund recalls that 'either [the *Sunday Times*] would send me a request, but more often, I made the running – I made an offer – I promoted the story'. In addition to his work for the *Sunday Times*, he also contributed the occasional article to a multitude of publications from the *Spectator* and *The Economist* to *Africa Report* and the *Atlantic Monthly*. In 1972, Pogrund was given a nine-month suspended sentence for possessing copies of banned publications which he needed for an academic thesis on which he was working. Four years later, while on a work-exchange between the *Rand Daily Mail* and the *Boston Globe*, Pogrund found himself interpreting the Soweto uprising for Boston. For six months he explained the situation in the Republic to television viewers, Nieman fellows and the readers of the *Boston Globe*. He later recalled that there was almost 'total ignorance of South Africa' in the US. Returning to South Africa in 1977, he was appointed deputy editor of the *Rand Daily Mail*. He continued to write for American publications, although as he remembers: 'with the *Globe*, I usually had to do a harder sell [than with the *Sunday Times*].'

Andrew Silk. *Nation*, 1976–78. Resident stringer, South Africa.
Andrew Silk was the son of Leonard Silk, an economics specialist on the editorial board of the *New York Times*. Silk visited South Africa for one year in 1974, where he worked as a visiting reporter on the *Pretoria News* and the *Rand Daily Mail*. Having completed his degree

in the United States, he returned to South Africa on a Thomas J. Watson fellowship. In the Republic, Silk researched working and housing conditions of African migrant workers in Modderdam, near Cape Town. During his research visit to South Africa, Silk contributed a number of exceptional articles to *Nation*. He left the country in September 1977 following his arrest for being in Guguletu township without a permit. He continued to write on the subject of apartheid for the *Nation*. In 1980, his book, *A Shanty Town In South Africa: The Story of Modderdam* was published by Ravan Press, Johannesburg. Silk died in 1981, aged 28.

Allister Sparks. *The Economist*. Resident South African stringer.
Sparks had a long track history as a political columnist in the South African press, in which he had made his name in the 1950s and 1960s. He was *The Economist*'s chief contributor throughout the 1970s. He rarely wrote for any other foreign publication at this time, concentrating his attentions on editing the [Johannesburg] *Sunday Express* (1976–77) and the *Rand Daily Mail* (from 1977). While at the *Rand Daily Mail*, he bore the brunt of the opprobrium which was associated with publishing the details relating to the Information scandal.

Humphrey Tyler. *Christian Science Monitor*. Resident South African stringer.
Tyler gained recognition when he was the first journalist to report the Sharpeville massacre (March 1960). At the time he was writing for *Drum*. By 1962, he was the editorial director of the African newspaper, the *World*. His recollections of these days have been published as *Life in the Time of Sharpeville – And Wayward Deeds of a New South Africa* (Cape Town, Kwela Books, 1995). During the 1970s, Tyler divided his time between being assistant editor of the *Argus* [Cape Town] and the chief stringer for the *Christian Science Monitor*. As the *Monitor* rarely had a staff correspondent resident in South Africa until 1976, Tyler's observations of the news in South Africa were carried relatively regularly by the newspaper.

Stanley Uys. *New Statesman* (to 1976), *Guardian*, *Observer*, BBC and ITN. Resident South African stringer.
Uys was somewhat of a legend amongst journalists in South Africa. His multitude of strings, which had been more extensive during the 1960s, was only equalled by Peter Hawthorne. Uys was a liberal Afrikaner who had been appointed political correspondent of the [Johannesburg] *Sunday Times* in 1949. During the 1950s, he had been the stringer for the *News Chronicle*. His speciality in South Africa was

the study of the vagaries of Afrikaner politics; he was, in effect, a South African version of a 'Kremlinologist'. Uys's foreign editors on the liberal British publications viewed him as something more than a mere stringer because the newspapers in question were not permitted to employ a staff correspondent in the country. Uys also wrote and broadcasted extensively for the Irish, New Zealand, Australian and Indian media. He left South Africa in 1977, in order to become the SAAN bureau chief in London. Uys continued to write a column in the *Rand Daily Mail*, and comment on South Africa in the British media.

Donald Woods. *New Statesman* and *Observer*, 1976–77. Resident South African stringer.
Woods was, thoughout the first half of the 1970s, the editor of a regional South African newspaper: the [East London] *Daily Dispatch*. He began to report for the foreign press following the Soweto uprising. However, judging by the small number of articles which appeared under his byline during the sixteen months until his banning in October 1977, it would be an accurate assessment to conclude that Woods was not particularly concerned with 'selling the story'. He recalls that writing for the foreign press was a minor consideration. One article on Steve Biko, however, was widely syndicated by the international media: 'By normal standards, I am a fairly conservative sort of bloke, not unduly naive and not easily impressed by politicians. But I'll tell you one thing – make a note of the name Steve Biko and remember it well. One way or another it will be writ large in the South Africa of tomorrow' (Donald Woods, 'Remember the Name Well', *Rand Daily Mail*, 27 August 1976). Woods played a very important role in facilitating links between African journalists and the international media and introducing Steve Biko to the foreign press; he arranged John Burns's meeting with Biko, for example. Following the murder of Steve Biko in September 1977, Woods abandoned the constraints of journalism: 'On 12 September [1977], I stopped being a journalist and became an activist.' Woods published *Biko* (London, 1978).

Robin Wright. *Washington Post*, 1974–77, *Christian Science Monitor*, 1975–76 (Angola and Mozambique) and CBS, from 1976. Resident stringer, southern Africa.
In 1974, Wright (an American citizen) went to southern Africa on a grant from the Alicia Patterson Foundation. Originally she operated as a stringer for the *Argus* [Cape Town], before taking over Peter Younghusband's *Washington Post* string. In 1975, Wright gained a

degree of recognition for her work in Mozambique and Angola, which was published in the *Christian Science Monitor*. In 1976, she applied for the post of correspondent for the *Christian Science Monitor* but was unsuccessful. During the same year, she began stringing for CBS radio and television. In 1977, she was replaced as stringer for the *Washington Post* by Caryle Murphy, whereupon she concentrated her efforts on work for CBS. She regularly worked in both South Africa and Rhodesia/Zimbabwe. Wright was heavily criticised by an anti-apartheid activist, Lynne Watson, in a letter to a member of the *Washington Post* foreign staff: 'too often she gives readers the dubious generality, followed by a quote from a Rhodesian white. She appears never to ask a Rhodesian or South African official a tough question. Her coverage is marked by paternalism toward blacks and neglect of black opinion (in Rhodesia especially), superficiality of political analysis, and cultural chauvinism.' (Lynne Watson, Unpublished letter to Julian Ross, 9 April 1977.)

Peter Younghusband. *Washington Post* (to 1974), *Newsweek* and *Daily Mail*. Resident South African stringer.
Younghusband was an Afrikaner who adopted the nom de plume of a famous correspondent from the nineteenth century. Following an extended period as the *Daily Mail*'s representative in Africa, Younghusband added the *Newsweek* and *Washington Post* strings to his workload. Christopher Munnion's book, *Banana Sunday* recollects a number of Younghusband's amusing adventures. Within South Africa, he attracted the venom of the Department of Information. Although as Younghusband recalls: 'There was nothing [Rhoodie] could do about me because I was a South African. He couldn't deport me. I had, in effect, become *Newsweek*'s Trojan Horse.' Younghusband, was perhaps most renowned amongst the correspondents and stringers in South Africa for possessing an ability to stretch any story to its maximum number of words. His political position might best be described as apolitical.

	BBC Radio Correspondents	AP Bureau Chiefs	UPI Bureau Chiefs	Reuters Correspondents	*Wall Street Journal* Stringers
1972	Angus McDermid	Kenneth Whiting	Mike Keats	Bill Humphries	Neil Behrmann
1973	John Osman				
1974					
		Larry Heinzerling	John Platter		
1975	Clive Small				
				Peter Mosley	
1976					Stephen Mulholland
	Graham Leach				
1977					
	John Simpson				
1978					
	David McNeil	Bill Nicholson	Nat Gibson		
1979					

	Christian Science Monitor Africa Correspondents	CBS Bureau Chiefs	ABC Bureau Chiefs	NBC Bureau Chiefs	*Financial Times* Chief Stringers
1972	Frederic Hunter			Graham Hatton	
1973	Henry Hayward				
1974					
1975					
1976					
	June Goodwin				
1977			Rex Ellis	Tom Ackerman	Bernard Simon
		Douglas Sefton			
1978			Howard Tuckner		
		Robert Harris		Martin Fletcher	
1979	Gary Thatcher				

Appendix B

In April 1978, Dr Connie Mulder (the Minister of Information) sent a list of projected secret Department of Information projects for the year 1978–79 to the Minister of Finance, Owen Horwood. Mulder requested that Horwood 'sign every page of this presentation so that the projects may be proceeded with'. Horwood duly did this. The approved budget was R14.8 million. One year later, Eschel Rhoodie appeared on the BBC where he used this list to prove that Horwood was fully cognisant of the Department's activities. During the same month (March 1979), the *Interim Report of the Commission of Inquiry into Alleged Irregularities in the Former Department of Information* (Pretoria, Government Printer, 1979), Annexure A, pp. 1–7, reproduced the documents, in Afrikaans, with the titles of the secret projects removed. See also ' "Uiters Geheim" ... the Secret Papers', *Rand Daily Mail*, 3 April 1979.

In 1981, the documentation was leaked to the South African press with the names of the majority of the projects included. (Mike O'Sullivan and Anthony Duigan, 'The Full List of "Info" Secret Projects', [Johannesburg] *Star*, 11 April 1981.) In 1983, Eschel Rhoodie published the same list that had appeared in the *Star* in Rhoodie, *Real Information*, pp. 761–69. The descriptions of 26 of the projects, however, remained unknown 'because they are either ongoing or it is not in the national interest that they should be revealed'. The translation reproduced here, which includes the missing projects, was found in the archives of *Africa News* (North Carolina). An equivalent British translation was also provided by David Pallister (*Guardian*). The cost of the secret projects is listed in South African rand.

	Project	1978/79
G.2	African comics project in SA and SWA	400,000
G.2A	Publication of monthly journal 'Hit' and supplement	1,000

G.2E	Purchase and expansion of 'Drum Weekend' (nominal)	1,000
G.2G	Purchase costs for the establishment of a black newspaper	1,000
G.5 and G.16D	Count Donhoff, Germany and fellow workers	13,000
G.6	Club of Ten, London	300,000
G.7	Committee for Fairness in Sport	150,000
G.8A	Don deKiefer and Associates, Washington	250,000
G.8B	Heinz Behrens liaison programme in Latin America	20,000
G.8C	Hennenhoffer liaison programme in Germany	470,000
G.8D	Liaison programme in Germany	215,000
G.8E	Special Jewish liaison programme in USA, especially with regard to Senators and academics	20,000
G.9	External news bureau (C. Breyer)	30,000
G.10	Special covert advertisements, e.g. via *To The Point* and *Business Week*	100,000
G.11A and 11B	Ad hoc church actions. NGK special overseas action programme	60,000
G.11C	Christian League of SA and actions in Britain and US	320,000
G.11D	Church actions in Germany	—
G.12	African Development magazine in London for Southern and East Africa	—
G.14	Covert opinion surveys and market analyses	—
G.15	African American Affairs Association in New York	10,000
G.16A	Ad hoc secret co-workers	25,000
G.16F	Tom Stacey Publishers, London	6,000
G.16H	Special news bureau in Nairobi for African news (van Zyl Alberts)	20,000
G.16K	Jean Abadie in France	—
G.16L	Dr W. Breytenbach	6,000
G.16M	AAT Kaptein in the Netherlands	—
G.16N	A. de St Agnes in France	—
G.16O	G. Lorraine in London	—
G.16P	W. de Boer in the Netherlands	500
G.16Q	Gary Player (nominal)	1,000
G.17A	Bantu Films Production	500,000
G.17B	Distribution of films to black population	500,000
G.18	Case Studies in Human Rights – central manuscript	50,000

G.19	Institute for the Study of Plural Societies	100,000
G.20A	Special conferences in US	150,000
G.20B	Special conferences in Germany	60,000
G.20C	Special conferences in South Africa	1,000
G.20D	Special conferences in London	1,000
G.20G	Special conferences in Frankfurt	1,000
G.20H	Ad hoc contribution for special conferences which must still be arranged	75,000
G.21A	La Monde Modern, France	30,000
G.21D	*France Eurafrique* – monthly journal	—
G.21F	*University Libre* magazine in Paris	13,000
G.22	A guarantee for books about South Africa worldwide	200,000
G.23	Del Film Production companies in Switzerland	200,000
G.25	*To The Point*	300,000
G.26A	Front organisations: Ad hoc – aksies	—
G.26B	NZAW	19,000
G.26C	South African Society, London	6,000
G.26D	OESAC – Austrian Action	5,500
G.26E	AGNETA (Sweden)	12,000
G.26F	*Plural Studies Journal* in the Netherlands	21,000
G.26G	Foundation Control Centre, the Netherlands	13,000
G.26H	Israel – South African Chamber of Commerce	11,000
G.26J	Centre for International Politics, Potchefstroom	25,000
G.26X	Institute for Strategic Studies, University of Pretoria	10,000
G.26L	German–South African Association, Germany	105,000
G.26M	Institute for African Studies	4,000
G.26N	Netherlands–South African Association visits to the Netherlands	7,000
G.26O	Japanese–South African Association, Tokyo	5,000
G.26P	Human Rights Foundation, London	—
G.26R	Human Rights Research Institute, South Africa	—
G.27	Legal actions in the US, Britain, Netherlands and Germany	70,000
G.28	Bernard Lejeune: Salary, Travelling and Subsistence	45,000
G.29	Co-worker Ya'acov Yannay in Israel	42,000
G.30	Anonymous co-workers	25,000
G.31	Ad hoc travel and subsistence of officials and other visitors	100,000
G.32	Foreign guests of front organisations	200,000

G.33	Purchase of special equipment, e.g. tape recorders, telephone scramblers, etc.	5,000
G.34A	Valiant Publications – book publishing company	160,000
G.34D	Production Editoriale book publisher, France	5,000
G.34E	SA Freedom Foundation	130,000
G.35	Special SWA actions against Swapo	20,000
G.36	Special secret administration costs (nominal)	2,000
G.42	Emergency Fund	—
G.43	Communal actions together with the Israeli Government (nominal)	5,000
G.44A	Ad hoc contributions for pro-South African actions	—
G.44B	French South African Association, Johannesburg and Paris	100,000
G.44C	SA Railways re *To The Point*	12,500
G.44E	Satoer for providing cover for operations of Ya'acov Yannay in Israel	12,000
G.44G	French South Africa Association's actions in France	20,000
G.45	Foreign Affairs association (academic study organisation, organised seminars as well as publishing academic papers)	153,000
G.47	Operations in Far East	5,000
G.48	British Parliament members' visit to SA	10,000
G.52	Guard: Foreign Policy Institute, London	120,000
G.61	Special radio cassette programmes in African countries (nominal)	5,000
G.62	Political studies and evaluation in Africa	5,000
G.65	Thor Communicators – upkeep costs of company and replacement by Homerus Finance Corporation for channelling of funds to foreign countries (single)	6,000
G.73	Management budget for British, French and SA operations, including offices in Johannesburg, Paris and London	200,000
G.75	Prescon Business News – financial news service to the world	37,000
G.76	Americans Concerned for South Africa Operations in the USA	50,000
G.77	Internal actions in the black residential areas	25,000
G.78	External news-picture service	1,000
G.79	Ad hoc printing and distribution, e.g. Rotarians and Lions	25,000

G.80	Special bursary programme for foreigners tied in with ... Ian Player	30,000
G.81	Confidential French newsletter	1,000
G.82	S/project (Axel Springer), Berlin	28,000
G.83	International article service (nominal)	10,000
G.84	Letter writing campaign in different countries	500
G.85		
G.86	Special research programme re the *World*, the *Rand Daily Mail* and other projects	1,000
G.87	Action programme in Rhodesia for the benefit of moderate political parties (a one shot programme)	400,000
G.88	National Freedom Association, British (60,000 members)	200,000
G.89	Purchase of *Investors Review*, London and extension programme	—
G.90	Senate actions via Jewish groups	30,000
G.91	Purchase of *Marie Novelle* journals in France (passports from the Bureau)	—
G.92	Purchase of French municipal journals (two cabinet ministers)	—
G.93	Establishment of the Atlantic Council branch for South Africa as well as the establishment of the head office in London and branch office in USA	280,000
G.94	Actions in Scandinavia	10,000
G.95	Special action programme for trade unions in Britain, Germany, Belgium and the US (nominal)	1,000
G.96	Purchase of special space in newspapers and magazines in Europe, Australia and US by means of the so-called 'sailor' system whereby sympathetic journalists are involved (nominal)	1,000
G.97	Special movie programmes, e.g. the movie of Dr Beurt SerVaas of the *Saturday Evening Post* about South Africa (nominal)	1,000

Select Bibliography

PUBLISHED SOURCES

British newspapers

The Times; *Guardian*; *Daily Telegraph*; *Financial Times*; *Sunday Times*; *Observer*; *Sunday Telegraph*; *Daily Express*; *Daily Mail*; *Daily Mirror*; *Sun*; [London] *Evening Standard*; [London] *Evening News*; *Morning Star*; *Sunday Express*; *Sunday Mirror*; *Sunday People*; *News of the World*; *Independent*.

US newspapers

New York Times; *Washington Post*; *Los Angeles Times*; *Christian Science Monitor*; *Wall Street Journal*; *Chicago Tribune*; *International Herald Tribune*; *Washington Star*; *Boston Globe*; *Philadelphia Inquirer*; *Chicago Sun-Times*; *San Francisco Chronicle*; *Newsday*; *Sacramento Union*, 18 July 1979; *Indianapolis Star*, 23–27 March 1980.

South African newspapers

Rand Daily Mail; [Johannesburg] *Star*; [Johannesburg] *Sunday Times*; [Johannesburg] *Sunday Express*; *World*; *Weekend World*; *Citizen*; [East London] *Daily Dispatch*; [Weekly] *Mail and Guardian*.

British magazines

The Economist; *New Statesman*; *Spectator*; *New Society*; *Listener*; *Time Out*; *London Review of Books*; *Private Eye*; *Africa*; *New African*; *West Africa*; *Africa Confidential*; *Africa Research Bulletin*; *Anti-Apartheid News*; *Southern Africa Information Service*; *Focus on Political Repression in Southern Africa: News Bulletin of the International Defence & Aid Fund*.

US magazines

Time; *Newsweek*; *US News and World Report*; *Business Week*; *Nation*; *New Republic*; *New Yorker*; *Harper's Village Voice*; *National Review*; *Esquire*; *Atlantic Monthly*; *Encore American and Worldwide News*; *New York Review of Books*; *Commonweal*; *Commentary*; *Progressive*; *Saturday Evening Post*; *Ramparts*; *More: A Journalism Review*; *Africa Report*; *Government Executive*; *Southern Africa*; *Washington Notes on Africa*; *American Committee on Africa Action News*; *Objective: Justice* (UN).

South African magazines

Financial Mail; *Southern Africa Record*; *To The Point*; *To The Point International*; *South Africa International*; *South Africa Foundation News*; *Sechaba*; *The African Communist*; *South African Panorama*; *South African Digest* (later, *SA Digest*); *Comment and Opinion*.

News agency reports

Reuters; Associated Press; Observer Foreign News Service; Africa News.

Broadcast media

BBC television and radio; ITN television; Granada television; London Weekend Television; CBS television; SABC television.

'Press Perverts Rights Picture', *Accuracy In Media Report*, Vol. 8, No. 3 (1 February 1979).

Louis Althusser, *Essays on Ideology*, Verso, London, 1984.

Manuel Alvarado and John O. Thompson (eds), *The Media Reader*, BFI Publishing, London, 1990.

American Committee on Africa, *Annual Reports: 1972–79*, ACOA, New York, 1973–80.

Amnesty International, *Repression Against Opponents of Apartheid (1974–1976)*, United Nations Centre against Apartheid, Notes and Documents No. 18/76 (August 1976).

Anti-Apartheid Movement, London, *The Nature and Techniques of South African Propaganda*, A/AC.115/L.226/Add.1, United Nations Special Committee on the Policies of Apartheid of the Government of the Republic of South Africa, 5 July 1968.

Anti-Apartheid Movement, *Annual Reports, 1971–80*, A-AM, London, 1972–80.

Guy Arnold, *The Last Bunker: A Report on White South Africa Today*, Quartet Books, London, 1976.

Kadar and Louise Asmal, *Anti-Apartheid Movements in Western Europe (with special reference to their role in support of United Nations action against apartheid)*, United Nations Unit on Apartheid, Notes and Documents No. 4/74 (March 1974).

'International Editor of the Year', *Atlas World Press Review*, Vol. 26, No. 6 (June 1979), pp. 6–7.

James Barber, 'BOSS in Britain', *African Affairs*, Vol. 82, No. 328 (July 1983), pp. 311–28.

James Barber and John Barratt, *South Africa's Foreign Policy: The Search for Status and Security, 1945–1988*, Cambridge University Press, Cambridge, 1990.

Howard Barrell, 'The Turn to the Masses: The African National Congress' Strategic Review of 1978–79', *Journal of Southern African Studies*, Vol. 18, No. 1 (March 1992), pp. 64–92.

Edward Behr, *'Anyone Here Been Raped and Speaks English': A Foreign Correspondent's Life Behind the Lines*, New English Library, Sevenoaks, 1982.

Carl Bernstein and Bob Woodward, *All The President's Men*, Quartet Books, London, 1974.

Carl Bernstein, 'The CIA and the Media', *Rolling Stone*, No. 250 (20 October 1977), pp. 55–67.

Hilda Bernstein, 'Two South Africans from the Island', *In These Times*, 18–24 January 1978, pp. 9–10.

Hilda Bernstein, *No 46 – Steve Biko*, International Defence and Aid Fund for Southern Africa, London, 1978.

Peter Bernstein, 'Reporting in Pretoria', *Index on Censorship*, Vol. 4, No. 3 (Autumn 1975), pp. 44–48.

Geoff Berridge, *Economic Power in Anglo-South African Diplomacy: Simonstown, Sharpeville and After*, Macmillan Press Ltd, London, 1981.

John Blashill, 'The Proper Role of US Corporations in South Africa', *Fortune*, July 1972, pp. 48–91.

Jonathan Bloch and Patrick Fitzgerald, *British Intelligence and Covert Action: Africa, Middle East and Europe since 1945*, Brandon Book Publishers Ltd, Co. Kerry, 1983.

Arnaud de Borchgrave and Robert Moss, *The Spike*, Weidenfeld & Nicolson, London, 1980.

BOSS: The First Five Years, International Defence and Aid Fund, London, 1975.

Richard Bourne, *News on a Knife-edge: Gemini Journalism and a Global Agenda*, John Libbey & Company Ltd, London, 1995.

Oliver Boyd-Barrett, Colin Seymour-Ure and Jeremy Tunstall, *Studies on the Press: Royal Commission on the Press Working Paper Number 3*, Her Majesty's Stationery Office, London, 1977.

Oliver Boyd-Barrett, *The International News Agencies*, Constable, London, 1980.

Ben Bradlee, *A Good Life: Newpapering and Other Adventures*, Simon & Schuster, New York, 1995.

Fred Bridgland, *Jonas Savimbi: A Key to Africa*, Mainstream Publishing, Edinburgh, 1986.

Fred Bridgland, *The War for Africa: Twelve Months that Transformed a Continent*, Ashanti Publishing Ltd, London, 1990.

Alan Brooks and Jeremy Brickhill, *Whirlwind before the Storm: The Origins and Development of the Uprising in Soweto and the Rest of South Africa from June to December 1976*, International Defence and Aid Fund for Southern Africa, London, 1980.

Douglas Brown, *Against the World: A Study of White South African Attitudes*, Collins, London, 1966.

Trevor Brown, 'Did Anybody Know His Name? US Press Coverage of Biko', *Journalism Quarterly*, Vol. 57 (Spring 1980), pp. 31–38.

Julian Burgess, Esau du Plessis, Roger Murray, Peter Fraenkel, Rosanne Harvey, John Laurence, Peter Ripken and Barbara Rogers, *The Great White Hoax: South Africa's International Propaganda Machine*, Africa Bureau, London, 1977.

Kenneth M. Cameron, *Africa on Film: Beyond Black and White*, Continuum, New York, 1994.

Centre for Contemporary Cultural Studies, *The Empire Strikes Back: Race and Racism in 70s Britain*, Routledge, London, 1992.

Zdenek Cervenka and Barbara Rogers, *The Nuclear Axis: Secret Collaboration between West Germany and South Africa*, Julian Friedman Books, London, 1978.

Chenhamo C. Chimutengwende, *South Africa: The Press and the Politics of Liberation*, Barbican Books, London, 1978.

Christian Concern for Southern Africa, *British Companies in South Africa*, CCSA, London, 1974.

CIA: The Pike Report, Spokesman Books, Nottingham, 1977.

Richard Cockett, *David Astor and The Observer*, Andre Deutsch, London, 1991.

Christopher Coker, *The United States and South Africa, 1968–1985: Constructive Engagement and Its Critics*, Duke University Press, Durham, NC, 1986.

Linda Colley, *Britons: Forging the Nation, 1707–1837*, Yale University Press, New Haven, CT, and London, 1992.

John and Jean Comaroff, *Ethnography and Historical Imagination*,

Westview Press, Boulder & London, 1990.

Stephen R. Conn, 'Apartheid from the Top', *Town & Country*, June 1977, pp. 47–116.

Counter-Information Services, *The Rio-Tinto Zinc Corporation Limited Anti-Report*, CIS, London, 1972.

Counter-Information Services, *The General Electric Company Limited Anti-Report*, CIS, London, 1972.

Counter-Information Services Anti-Report, No. 17, *Black South Africa Explodes*, London, 1977.

Timothy Crouse, *The Boys on the Bus*, Ballantine Books, New York, 1973.

Brian Crozier, *Free Agent: The Unseen War, 1941–1991*, Harper-Collins, London, 1993.

Jennifer Crwys-Williams (ed.), *South African Despatches: Two Centuries of the Best in South African Journalism*, Ashanti Publishing, Johannesburg, 1989.

Robert Cuddy, 'An Analysis of the Los Angeles Times Coverage', *Ufahamu*, Vol. 9, No. 1 (1979), pp. 6–55.

James Curran, Michael Gurevitch and Janet Woollacott (eds), *Mass Communication and Society*, Edward Arnold, London, 1977.

Anne Darnborough, *Labour's Record on Southern Africa: An Examination of Attitudes before October 1964 and Actions since*, Anti-Apartheid Movement, London, 1967.

Robert Darnton, 'Writing News and Telling Stories', *Daedalus*, Spring 1975, pp. 175–94.

Robert Darnton, *The Kiss of Lamourette: Reflections in Cultural History*, Faber & Faber, London, 1990.

Nathaniel Davis, 'The Angola Decision of 1975: A Personal Memoir', *Foreign Affairs*, Vol. 57, No. 1 (Fall 1978), pp. 109–24.

William Davis, 'Vorster's Laager', *Punch*, 23 November 1977, pp. 967–71.

Greg Dening, *History's Anthropology: The Death of William Gooch*, University Press of America, Lanham, 1988.

Department of Information, *Reports for the Period 1 January 1972 to 31 December 1977*, Government Printer, Pretoria, 1973–78.

Charles C. Diggs Jr, 'Action Manifesto', *Issue*, Vol. 2, No. 1 (Spring 1972), pp. 52–60.

Stephen Dorril and Robin Ramsay, *Smear! Wilson and the Secret State*, Fourth Estate, London, 1991.

Donald B. Easum, 'United States Policy toward South Africa', *Issue*, Vol. 5, No. 3 (Fall 1975), pp. 66–72.

'Best in the USA: Top 15 Dailies Picked by 610 News Leaders', *Editor & Publisher*, 11 June 1983, p. 11.

Ruth Dudley Edwards, *The Pursuit of Reason: The Economist, 1843–1993*, Hamish Hamilton, London, 1993.

John Eldridge (ed.), *Getting The Message: News, Truth and Power*, Routledge, London, 1993.

Stephen Ellis and Tsepo Sechaba, *Comrades Against Apartheid: The ANC and the South African Communist Party in Exile*, James Currey Ltd, London, 1992.

William S. Ellis, 'South Africa's Lonely Ordeal', *National Geographic*, June 1977, pp. 780–819.

Michael Emery and Edwin Emery, *The Press and America: An Interpretive History of the Mass Media*, 6th edition, Prentice Hall, New Jersey, 1988.

Dagmar Engels and Shula Marks (eds), *Contesting Colonial Hegemony: State and Society in Africa and India*, British Academic Press, London, 1994.

Edward Jay Epstein, *News from Nowhere: Television and the News*, Vintage Books, New York, 1973.

Harold Evans, *Good Times, Bad Times*, Weidenfeld & Nicolson, London, 1983.

Ruth First, Jonathan Steele and Christabel Gurney, *The South African Connection: Western Involvement in Apartheid*, Temple Smith, London, 1972.

Ruth First, *Foreign Investment in Apartheid South Africa*, United Nations Unit on Apartheid, Notes and Documents No. 21/72 (October 1972).

Ruth First, 'The South African Connection: From Polaroid to Oppenheimer', *Issue*, Vol. 3, No. 2 (Summer 1973), pp. 2–6.

Jack Foisie, 'A New Broom or an Old Hand?', *Nieman Reports*, Winter 1985, pp. 15–16.

John Forester (ed.), *Critical Theory and Public Life*, MIT Press, Cambridge, MA, 1985.

Roger Fowler, Bob Hodge, Gunter Kress and Tony Trew, *Language and Control*, Routledge & Kegan Paul, London, 1979.

Julie Frederikse, *None But Ourselves: Masses vs. Media in the Making of Zimbabwe*, Zimbabwe Publishing House, Harare, 1982.

Julie Frederikse, *South Africa: A Different Kind of War*, James Currey, London, 1986.

Simon Freeman and Barrie Penrose, *Rinkagate: The Rise and Fall of Jeremy Thorpe*, Bloomsbury Publishing, London, 1996.

Steven Friedman, *Building Tomorrow Today: African Workers in Trade Unions, 1970–1984*, Ravan Press, Johannesburg, 1987.

L.H. Gann and Peter Duignan, *Why South Africa Will Survive: A Historical Analysis*, Croom Helm, London, 1981.

Herbert J. Gans, *Deciding What's News: A Study of CBS Evening News, NBC Nightly News, Newsweek and Time*, Pantheon Books, New York, 1979.

Deon Geldenhuys, *The Diplomacy of Isolation: South African Foreign Policy Making*, Macmillan, Johannesburg, 1984.

Sean Gervasi, *Continuing Escalation in the Angola Crisis*, The Africa Fund, New York, 1975.

Rex Gibson and Allister Sparks, 'South Africa after Muldergate', *Atlas World Press Review*, Vol. 26, No. 8 (August 1979), pp. 17–20.

Frank Giles, *Sundry Times*, John Murray, London, 1986.

Frene Ginwala, *The Press in South Africa*, United Nations Unit on Apartheid, Notes and Documents No. 24/72 (November 1972).

Frene Ginwala, *African Workers Strike Against Apartheid*, United Nations Unit on Apartheid, Notes and Documents No. 14/73 (June 1973).

Frene Ginwala, 'The Press in South Africa', *Index on Censorship*, Vol. 2, No. 3 (Autumn 1973), pp. 27–43.

Todd Gitlin, *The Whole World is Watching: Mass Media in the Making and Unmaking of the New Left*, University of California Press, Berkeley, CA, 1980.

Glasgow University Media Group (Peter Beharrell, Howard Davis, John Eldridge, John Hewitt, Jean Oddie, Greg Philo, Paul Walton and Brian Winston), *Bad News*, Routledge & Kegan Paul, London, 1976.

Glasgow University Media Group (Peter Beharrell, Howard Davis, John Eldridge, John Hewitt, Jean Oddie, Greg Philo, Paul Walton and Brian Winston), *More Bad News*, Routledge & Kegan Paul, London, 1980.

Piero Gleijeses, 'Havana's Policy in Africa, 1959–76: New Evidence from Cuban Archives', *Cold War International History Project Bulletin*, No. 8/9 (1997), pp. 5–18.

Peter Godwin and Ian Hancock, *'Rhodesians Never Die': The Impact of War and Political Change on White Rhodesia, c.1970–1980*, Oxford University Press, Oxford, 1993.

June Goodwin, *Cry Amandla! South African Women and the Question of Power*, Africana Publishing Company, New York, 1984.

June Goodwin and Ben Schiff, *Heart of Whiteness: Afrikaners Face Black Rule in the New South Africa*, Scribner, New York, 1995.

Nadine Gordimer, *My Son's Story*, Penguin Books, London, 1990.

Antonio Gramsci, *Selections from Prison Notebooks*, Lawrence & Wishart, London, 1971.

Graham Greene, *The Human Factor*, Penguin Books, London, 1978.

Dennis Griffiths (ed.), *The Encyclopedia of the British Press,*

1422–1992, Macmillan Press, London, 1992.

John Grigg, *The History of The Times, Volume VI: The Thomson Years, 1966–1981*, Times Books, London, 1993.

William A. Hachten, 'Black Journalists under Apartheid', *Index on Censorship*, Vol. 8, No. 3 (May/June 1979), pp. 43–48.

William A. Hachten and C. Anthony Giffard, *The Press and Apartheid: The Role and Plight of the Press in South Africa*, Macmillan Press, London, 1984.

Peter Hain, *Don't Play with Apartheid: The Background to the Stop The Seventy Tour Campaign*, George Allen & Unwin, London, 1971.

Peter Hain, *A Putney Plot?*, Spokesman, Nottingham, 1986.

Peter Hain, *Sing the Beloved Country: The Struggle for the New South Africa*, Pluto Press, London, 1996.

David Halberstam, *The Powers That Be*, Alfred A. Knopf, New York, 1979.

Stuart Hall, Chas Critcher, Tony Jefferson, John Clarke and Brian Roberts, *Policing the Crisis: Mugging, The State and Law and Order*, Macmillan, London, 1978.

Robin Hallett, 'The South African Intervention in Angola', *African Affairs*, Vol. 77, No. 308 (July 1978), pp. 347–86.

Daniel C. Hallin, *The 'Uncensored War': The Media and Vietnam*, Oxford University Press, New York, 1986.

Ed Harriman, *Hack: Home Truths about Foreign News*, Zed Books Ltd, London, 1987.

David Harrison, *The White Tribe of Africa: South Africa in Perspective*, British Broadcasting Corporation, London, 1981.

Duff Hart-Davis, *The House that the Berrys Built: Inside The Telegraph, 1928–1986*, Hodder & Stoughton, London, 1990.

Paul Hartman and Charles Husband, *Racism and the Mass Media*, Davis-Poynter Ltd, London, 1974.

Tony Heard, *The Cape of Storms: A Personal History of the Crisis in South Africa*, Ravan Press, Johannesburg, 1990.

Peter Hennessy, *What the Papers Never Said*, Portcullis Press, London, 1985.

Nat Hentoff and Laurence I. Barrett , 'Woodward, Bernstein and "All the President's Men"', *Columbia Journalism Review*, July/August 1974, pp. 10–15.

Alex Hepple, *Press Under Apartheid*, International Defence and Aid Fund, London, 1974.

Denis Herbstein, *White Man, We Want to Talk to You*, Africana Publishing Co., New York, 1979.

Edward S. Herman and Noam Chomsky, *Manufacturing Consent: The*

Political Economy of the Mass Media, Pantheon Books, New York, 1988.

Alfred O. Hero and John Barratt (eds), *The American People and South Africa: Publics, Elites and Policymaking Processes*, Lexington Books, Lexington, MA, 1981.

Stephen Hess, *International News and Foreign Correspondents*, (Newswork 5), The Brookings Institution, Washington DC, 1996.

Alaistair Hetherington, *Guardian Years*, Chatto & Windus, London, 1981.

Baruch Hirson, *Year of Fire, Year of Ash: The Soweto Revolt: Roots of a Revolution?*, Zed Press, London, 1979.

Jim Hoagland, *South Africa: Civilisations in Conflict*, George Allen & Unwin Ltd, London, 1972.

Dr Ferry A. Hoogendijk, 'Muldergate: The Eschel Rhoodie Story', *Elseviers*, 28 July–18 August 1979, news agency transcript.

Muriel Horrell, Dudley Horner, John Kane-Berman and Robin Margo, *A Survey of Race Relations in South Africa, 1972*, SAIRR, Johannesburg, 1973.

Muriel Horrell and Dudley Horner, *A Survey of Race Relations in South Africa, 1973*, SAIRR, Johannesburg, 1974.

Muriel Horrell, Dudley Horner and Jane Hudson, *A Survey of Race Relations in South Africa, 1974*, SAIRR, Johannesburg, 1975.

George M. Houser, 'Meeting Africa's Challenge: The Story of the American Committee on Africa', *Issue*, Vol. 6, No. 2/3 (Summer/Fall 1976), pp. 16–26.

George M. Houser, *No One Can Stop the Rain: Glimpses of Africa's Liberation Struggle*, The Pilgrim Press, New York, 1989.

Ernest Marshall Howse, *Saints in Politics: The 'Clapham Sect' and the Growth of Freedom*, George Allen & Unwin Ltd, London, 1953.

Russell Warren Howe and Sarah Hays Trout, *The Power Peddlers: How Lobbyists Mold America's Foreign Policy*, Doubleday & Co., New York, 1977.

Tami Hultman, Reed Kramer and Don Morton, *The Changing Situation in Southern Africa*, United Nations Unit on Apartheid, Notes and Documents No. 14/75 (April 1975).

Derek Humphry, *The Cricket Conspiracy*, National Council for Civil Liberties, London, 1975.

Barbara Hutmacher, *In Black and White: Voices of Apartheid*, Junction Books, London, 1980.

Interim Report of the Commission of Inquiry into Alleged Irregularities in the Former Department of Information, Government Printer, Pretoria, March 1979.

'South Africa's Secret Scheme: Selling Apartheid in the US', *The*

Internews International Bulletin, Vol. 6, No. 5 (12 March 1979), pp. 1–3.

'South Africa' (survey), *Investors Chronicle*, 5–11 December 1975, pp. 1–32.

'Organizational Initiatives: Liberation in Southern Africa', *Issue*, Vol. 2, No. 4 (Winter 1973), pp. 43–53.

Henry F. Jackson, *From the Congo to Soweto: US Foreign Policy toward Africa since 1960*, William Morrow & Company, New York, 1982.

Gordon Jackson, *The 'Prison Exposés' and 'Muldergate': A Case Study in Changing Government–Press Relations in South Africa*, Bloomington, IN, 1980.

Lewis James, 'The Fund's Report on South Africa: The IMF Advises South Africa to Unpeg the Rand', *Euromoney*, June 1978, pp. 169–71.

R.W. Johnson, *How Long will South Africa Survive?*, Macmillan Press, London, 1977.

Frederick A. Johnstone, 'White Prosperity and White Supremacy in South Africa Today', *African Affairs*, Vol. 69, No. 275 (April 1970), pp. 124–40.

John Kane-Berman, *South Africa: The Method in the Madness*, Pluto Press, London, 1979.

Ryszard Kapuscinski, *Another Day of Life*, Pan Books, London, 1987.

Thomas Karis and Gwendolen M. Carter (eds), *From Protest to Challenge: A Documentary History of African Politics in South Africa, 1882–1964*, Gail M. Gerhart and Thomas Karis, *Volume 4: Political Profiles 1882–1964*, Hoover Institution Press, Stanford, 1977.

The Kissinger Study of Southern Africa, Spokesman Books, Nottingham, 1975.

Helen Kitchen (ed.), *Africa: From Mystery to Maize*, (Critical Choices for Americans, Volume 11), Lexington Books, Lexington, MA, 1976.

Derek Knight, *Beyond the Pale: The Christian Political Fringe*, Caraf Publications, Lancashire, 1982.

Phillip Knightley, *The First Casualty. From the Crimea to the Falklands: The War Correspondent as Hero, Propagandist and Myth Maker*, Pan, London, 1989.

Phillip Knightley, 'The Inside Story of Philby's Exposure', *British Journalism Review*, Vol. 9, No. 2 (1998), pp. 35–40.

Andrew Kopkind, 'MacNeil/Lehrer's Class Act', *Columbia Journalism Review*, September/October 1979, pp. 31–38.

Thomas S. Kuhn, *The Structure of Scientific Revolutions*, Second Edition, The University of Chicago Press, Chicago, 1970.

David Kynaston, *The Financial Times: A Centenary History*, Viking Penguin, London, 1988.

Zaki Laidi, *The Super-Powers and Africa: The Constraints of a Rivalry, 1960–1990*, University of Chicago Press, Chicago, 1990.

John Laurence, *The Seeds of Disaster*, Victor Gollancz, London, 1968.

John Laurence, *Countering South Africa's Misleading Racial Propaganda*, United Nations Unit on Apartheid, 18 March 1972.

John C. Laurence, *Race, Propaganda and South Africa*, Victor Gollancz, London, 1979.

John Laurence, 'Censorship by Skin Colour', *Index on Censorship*, Vol. 6, No. 2 (March/April 1977), pp. 40–43.

John Laurence, *South Africa's Propaganda: How the Contagion of Racism is Spread*, United Nations Centre against Apartheid, Notes and Documents No. 15/82 (August 1982).

Colin Legum and Tony Hodges, *After Angola: The War over Southern Africa*, Rex Collings, London, 1976.

David Leigh, *The Wilson Plot: The Intelligence Services and the Discrediting of a Prime Minister, 1945–1976*, Heinemann, London, 1988.

Joseph Lelyveld, *Move Your Shadow: South Africa Black and White*, Michael Joseph, London, 1985.

Rene Lemarchand (ed.), *American Policy in Southern Africa: The Stakes and the Stance*, University Press of America, Washington, DC, 1978.

A.J. Liebling, *The Press*, Ballantine Books, New York, 1961.

Walter Lippmann, *Public Opinion*, The Macmillan Company, New York, 1947 (originally published in 1922).

Tom Lodge, *Black Politics in South Africa since 1945*, Longman Group UK Ltd, London, 1983.

G.H.G. Lucas and G.J. De J. Cronje, *The Marketing of the International Image of South Africa*, University of South Africa, Pretoria, 1978.

James McCartney, 'The Washington "Post" and Watergate: How Two Davids Slew Goliath', *Columbia Journalism Review*, July/August 1973, pp. 8–22.

Peter Magubane, *Magubane's South Africa*, Alfred A. Knopf, New York, 1978.

N. Chabani Manganyi and Andre du Toit (eds), *Political Violence and the Struggle in South Africa*, Macmillan, Basingstoke, 1990.

John A. Marcum, *The Angolan Revolution, Volume II: Exile Politics and Guerrilla Warfare (1962–1976)*, MIT Press, Cambridge, MA, 1978.

Shula Marks, 'Ruth First: A Tribute', *Journal of Southern African Studies*, Vol. 10, No. 1 (October 1983), pp. 123–28.

Shula Marks and Stanley Trapido (eds), *The Politics of Race, Class and Nationalism in Twentieth Century South Africa*, Longman Group UK, Essex, 1987.

Gabriel Garcia Marquez, 'Operation Carlota', *New Left Review*, No. 101–102 (February–April 1977), pp. 123–37.

David Martin and Phyliss Johnson, *The Struggle For Zimbabwe: The Chimurenga War*, Faber & Faber, London, 1981.

Harry Mashabela, *A People on the Boil: Reflections on Soweto*, Skotaville Publishers, Johannesburg, 1987.

Piet Meiring, *Inside Information*, Howard Timmins, Cape Town, 1973.

John C. Merrill and Harold A. Fisher, *The World's Great Dailies: Profiles of Fifty Newspapers*, Hastings House, New York, 1980.

Joel Mervis, *The Fourth Estate: A Newspaper Story*, Jonathan Ball Publishers, Johannesburg, 1989.

Ministers' Fraternal of Langa, Guguletu and Nyanga, *Role of the South African Riot Police in Burnings and Killings in Nyanga, Cape Town, Christmas 1976*, United Nations Centre against Apartheid, Notes and Documents No. 6/77 (February 1977).

William Minter, *King Solomon's Mines Revisited: Western Interests and the Burdened History of Southern Africa*, Basic Books Inc, New York, 1986.

William Minter (ed.), *Operation Timber: Pages from the Savimbi Dossier*, Africa World Press Inc., New Jersey, 1988.

Kenneth Mokoena (ed.), *South Africa and the United States: The declassified history (A National Security Archive Documents Reader)*, The New Press, New York, 1993.

Jan Morris, 'States in Siege: Part 1 – South Africa, *Rolling Stone*, No. 240 (2 June 1977), pp. 46–53.

Roger Morris, 'A Rare Resignation in Protest: Nat Davis and Angola', *Washington Monthly*, Vol. 7, No. 12 (February 1976), pp. 22–32.

David E. Morrison and Howard Tumber, 'The Foreign Correspondent: Date-line London', *Media, Culture and Society*, Vol. 7, No. 4 (October 1985), pp. 445–70.

David E. Morrison and Howard Tumber, *Journalists at War: The Dynamics of News Reporting during the Falklands Conflict*, Sage Publications, London, 1988.

Robert Moss, *Chile's Marxist Experiment*, David & Charles, Newtown Abbot, 1973.

Robert Moss, *The Collapse of Democracy*, Temple Smith Ltd, London, 1975.

Robert Moss, 'Friends In Need: Five Good Reasons for Standing by

South Africa', *Politics Today*, No. 3 (May/June 1978), pp. 22–49.

Mrs. Winnie Mandela: Profile in courage and defiance, United Nations Centre against Apartheid, Notes and Documents No. 1/78 (February 1978).

Chris Munnion, *Banana Sunday: Datelines From Africa*, William Waterman Publications, Rivonia, 1993.

Chris Munnion, *Banana Sunday: Datelines From Africa*, second edition, William Waterman Publications, Rivonia, 1995.

Prexy Nesbitt, *Anti-Apartheid Activities in the United States of America: A rising tide*, United Nations Centre against Apartheid, Notes and Documents No. 32/77 (December 1977).

The Editor, 'The Percy Qoboza Case', *Nieman Reports*, Winter & Spring 1978, pp. 34–37.

The Editors, 'The Percy Qoboza Case: Continued', *Nieman Reports*, Summer 1978, pp. 46–49.

Herman Nickel, 'The Case For Doing Business in South Africa', *Fortune*, 19 June 1978, pp. 60–74.

Michael Nicholson, *A Measure of Danger: Memoirs of a British War Correspondent*, HarperCollins, London, 1991.

Peter Niesewand, *In Camera: Secret Justice in Rhodesia*, Weidenfeld & Nicolson, London, 1973.

Rob Nixon, *Homelands, Harlem and Hollywood: South African Culture and the World Beyond*, Routledge, New York, 1994.

James North, *Freedom Rising*, New American Library, New York, 1986.

'Dr Rhoodie talks about "South Africa's Biggest Secret"', *Noseweek*, No. 2 (July 1993), pp. 4–6.

Observance of Nelson R. Mandela's Sixtieth Birthday, United Nations Centre against Apartheid, Notes and Documents No. 23/78 (August 1978).

Dan O'Meara, 'Muldergate and the Politics of Afrikaner Nationalism', *Work In Progress*, No. 22 (April 1982), supplement pp. 1–19.

Dan O'Meara, *Forty Lost Years: The Apartheid State and the Politics of the National Party, 1948–1994*, Ravan Press, Johannesburg, 1996.

Patrick O'Meara, *American Universities Field Staff Reports, No. 43: South Africa's Watergate: The Muldergate Scandals*, American Universities Field Staff, New Hampshire, 1979.

David Owen, *Time to Declare*, Michael Joseph, London, 1991.

Alan Paton, *Cry, The Beloved Country*, Jonathan Cape, London, 1948.

Mark Pedelty, *War Stories: The Culture of Foreign Correspondents*, Routledge, New York, 1995.

Barrie Penrose and Roger Courtiour, *The Pencourt File*, Harper &

Row, New York, 1978.

Greg Philo, John Hewitt, Peter Beharrell and Howard Davis, *Really Bad News*, Writers and Readers Publishing Co-operative Society, London, 1982.

Chapman Pincher, *Inside Story: A Documentary of the Pursuit of Power*, Sidgwick & Jackson, London, 1978.

'Playboy Interview: Jimmy Carter', *Playboy*, Vol. 23, No. 11 (November 1976), pp. 63–86.

'Playboy Interview: Andrew Young', *Playboy*, Vol. 22, No. 7 (July 1977), pp. 61–83.

Gary Player, *Grand Slam Golf*, Cassell, London, 1966.

Benjamin Pogrund, 'United States Interests in Southern Africa', *Nieman Reports* (Summer 1976), pp. 3–7.

Benjamin Pogrund, 'The South African Press', *Index on Censorship*, Vol. 5, No. 3, Autumn 1976, pp. 10–16.

Political Imprisonment in South Africa: An Amnesty International Report, Amnesty International Publications, London, 1978.

Richard Pollak, *Up Against Apartheid: The Role and Plight of the Press in South Africa*, Southern Illinois University Press, Carbondale and Edwardsville, 1981.

Christian P. Potholm and Richard Dale (eds), *Southern Africa in Perspective*, The Free Press, New York, 1972.

Elaine Potter, *The Press as Opposition: The Political Role of South African Newspapers*, Chatto & Windus, London, 1975.

Richard A. Pride and Daniel H. Clarke, 'Race Relations in Television News: a Content Analysis of the Networks', *Journalism Quarterly*, Vol. 50 (Summer 1973), pp. 319–28.

Daan Prinsloo, *United States Foreign Policy and the Republic of South Africa*, Foreign Affairs Association, Pretoria, 1978.

Chris Pritchard and Mike Wharton (Mike Popham), 'The Spy in the Newsroom', *Playboy* [Australian edition], June 1982, pp. 111–16.

Adam Raphael, *Grotesque Libels*, Corgi, London, 1993.

Charles Raw, *A Financial Phenomenon: An Investigation of the Rise and Fall of the Slater–Walker Empire*, Harper & Row, New York, 1977.

Donald Read, *The Power of News: The History of Reuters, 1849–1989*, Oxford University Press, Oxford, 1994.

E.S. Reddy (ed.), *The Struggle for Liberation in South Africa and International Solidarity: A Selection of Papers published by the United Nations Centre Against Apartheid*, Sterling Publishers Private Limited, New Delhi, 1992.

Mervyn Rees and Chris Day, *Muldergate: The Story of the Info Scandal*, Macmillan, Johannesburg, 1980.

Michael Reisman, 'Polaroid Power: Taxing Business for Human Rights', *Foreign Policy*, No. 4 (Fall 1971), pp. 101–10.

Report of the Commission of Inquiry into Alleged Irregularities in the Former Department of Information, Government Printer, Pretoria, December 1978.

Eschel Rhoodie, *South West: The Last Frontier in Africa*, Voortrekkerpers, Johannesburg, 1967.

Eschel Rhoodie, *The Third Africa*, Nasionale Boekhandel, Cape Town, 1968.

Eschel Rhoodie, *The Paper Curtain*, Voortrekkerpers, Johannesburg, 1969.

Eschel Rhoodie, *The Real Information Scandal*, Orbis SA, Pretoria, 1983.

Eschel Rhoodie, *P.W. Botha: The Last Betrayal*, SA Politics, Melville, 1989.

Churchill Roberts, 'The Presentation of Blacks in Television Network Newscasts', *Journalism Quarterly*, Vol. 52 (Spring 1975), pp. 50–55.

Charles L. Robertson, *The International Herald Tribune: The First Hundred Years*, Columbia University Press, New York, 1987.

Barbara Rogers, *South Africa's Stake in Britain*, Africa Bureau, London, 1971.

Barbara Rogers, *White Wealth and Black Poverty: American Investments in Southern Africa*, Greenwood Press, CT, 1976.

Barbara Rogers, *Divide and Rule: South Africa's Bantustans*, International Defence and Aid Fund, London, 1986.

Barbara Rogers, *The Image Reflected by Mass Media: Manipulations. The Nuclear Axis: A Case Study in the Field of Investigative Reporting*, UNESCO International Commission for the Study of Communication Problems, No. 58, New York, 1980.

Paul Rose, *The Backbencher's Dilemma*, Frederick Muller Limited, London, 1981.

Mort Rosenblum, 'Reporting from the Third World', *Foreign Affairs*, Vol. 55, No. 4 (July 1977), pp. 815–35.

Mort Rosenblum, *Coups and Earthquakes: Reporting the World for America*, Harper Colophon Books, New York, 1981.

Karen Rothmyer, 'What Really Happened in Biafra?', *Columbia Journalism Review*, Fall 1970, pp. 43–47.

Karen Rothmyer, 'The McGoff Grab', *Columbia Journalism Review*, November/December 1979, pp. 33–9.

Karen Rothmyer, 'Citizen Scaife', *Columbia Journalism Review*, July/August 1981, pp. 41–50.

Kimberley Safford, 'Peter Davis' Film View of South Africa: An

American Review', *Critical Arts*, Vol. 1, No. 2 (June 1980).

Edward Said, *Orientalism*, Penguin Books, London, 1978.

Edward Said, *Covering Islam: How the Media and the Experts Determine How We See the Rest of the World*, Pantheon Books, New York, 1981.

Harrison E. Salisbury, *Without Fear or Favor: The New York Times and its Times*, Times Books, New York, 1980.

Anthony Sampson, *Black and Gold: Tycoons, Revolutionaries and Apartheid*, Hodder & Stoughton, London, 1987.

David Scott, *Ambassador in Black and White: Thirty Years of Changing Africa*, Weidenfeld & Nicolson, London, 1981.

Second Portion of the Report of the Commission of Inquiry into the Press, Government Printer, Pretoria, 1964.

Aaron Segal, 'Africa and the United States Media', *Issue*, Vol. 6, No. 2/3 (Summer/Fall 1976), pp. 49–56.

John Seiler, 'South African Perspectives and Responses to External Pressures', *Journal of Modern African Studies*, Vol. 3, (1975), pp. 447–68.

J.H.P. Serfontein, *Brotherhood of Power: An Exposé of the Secret Afrikaner Broederbond*, Rex Collings Ltd, London, 1979.

George W. Shepherd Jr, *Anti-Apartheid: Transnational Conflict and Western Policy in the Liberation of South Africa*, Greenwood Press Inc., CT, 1977.

Robert Sherrill, 'The New Regime at The New Republic', *Columbia Journalism Review*, March/April 1976, pp. 23–29.

Leon V. Sigal, *Reporters and Officials: The Organization and Politics of Newsmaking*, D.C. Heath and Company, Massachusetts, 1973.

Andrew Silk, *A Shanty Town in South Africa: The Story of Modderdam*, Ravan Press, Johannesburg, 1981.

John Simpson, *Strange Places, Questionable People*, Macmillan, London, 1998.

Jim Slater, *Return To Go: My Autobiography*, Weidenfeld & Nicolson, London, 1977.

Howard Smith, 'Apartheid, Sharpeville and "Impartiality": The Reporting of South Africa on BBC Television 1948–1961', *Historical Journal of Film, Radio and Television*, Vol. 13, No. 3 (1993), pp. 251–98.

Timothy H. Smith, *The American Corporation in South Africa: An Analysis*, United Church Of Christ, New York, 1970.

South Africa 1974: Official Yearbook of the Republic of South Africa, First Edition, Perskor, Johannesburg, 1974.

South African Broadcasting Corporation, *Fortieth Annual Report of the South African Broadcasting Corporation: 1976*, SABC,

Johannesburg, 1977.

South African Conference on the Survival of the Press and Education for Journalism, 4–6 October 1979, Department of Journalism, Rhodes University, Grahamstown, 1979.

South Africa Foundation, *Annual Reports: 1972–80*, SAF, Johannesburg, 1973–80.

Gerald Sparrow, *Invitation to South Africa*, Neville Spearman, London, 1974.

Martin Spring, *Confrontation: The Approaching Crisis between the United States and South Africa*, Valiant, South Africa, 1977.

Fred St Leger, 'The World Newspaper, 1968–1976', *Critical Arts: A Journal for Media Studies*, Vol. 2, No. 2 (1981), pp. 27–37.

Willem Steenkamp, *South Africa's Border War, 1966–1989*, Ashanti Publishing Ltd, Gibraltar, 1989.

Stepping into the Future: Education for South Africa's Black, Coloured and Indian Peoples, Erudita Publications, Johannesburg, 1975.

Alexander Steward, *The World, the West and Pretoria*, David McKay Company Inc, New York, 1977.

John Stockwell, *In Search of Enemies: A CIA Story*, W.W. Norton & Co. Inc, New York, 1978.

Patience Strong, *The Other Side of the Coin: Thoughts and Afterthoughts on a Visit to South Africa*, Bachman & Turner, London, 1976.

Newell M. Stultz, 'The Apartheid Issue at the General Assembly: Stalemate or Gathering Storm', *African Affairs*, Vol. 86, No. 342 (1987), pp. 25–45.

Supplementary Report of the Commission of Inquiry into Alleged Irregularities in the Former Department of Information, Government Printer, Pretoria, June 1979.

Les Switzer and Donna Switzer, *The Black Press in South Africa and Lesotho: A Descriptive Bibliographic Guide to African, Coloured and Indian Newspapers, Newsletters and Magazines, 1836–1976*, G.K. Hall & Co., Boston, 1979.

Mokhtar Taleb-Bendiab, *South African Propaganda*, United Nations Centre against Apartheid, Notes and Documents, SEM/12, June 1976.

Gay Talese, *The Kingdom and the Power*, Caldar & Boyars, London, 1971.

Geoffrey Taylor, *Changing Faces: A History of The Guardian, 1956–88*, Fourth Estate, London, 1993.

Scott Thomas, *The Diplomacy of Liberation: The Foreign Relations of the African National Congress since 1960*, Tauris Academic Studies, London, 1996.

James Thomson, Benjamin Pogrund, John Corr, Gatsha Buthelezi and

Percy Qoboza, 'Focus on South Africa', *Nieman Reports*, Autumn & Winter 1975, pp. 2–61.

James C. Thomson Jr, 'African Nemesis', *Nieman Reports*, Summer and Autumn 1977, pp. 27–31.

Keyan Tomaselli, 'Review Article – Up Against Apartheid: The Role and Plight of the Press in South Africa', *Critical Arts: A Journal for Media Studies*, Vol. 2, No. 3 (1982), pp. 39–44.

Keyan Tomaselli, Ruth Tomaselli and Johan Muller, *Studies on the South African Media: The Press in South Africa*, James Currey, London, 1987.

Keyan Tomaselli and P. Eric Louw, *Studies on the South African Media: The Alternative Press in South Africa*, James Currey, London, 1991.

Andrew Torchia, 'Assignment Africa', *Columbia Journalism Review*, May/June 1981, p. 41.

John Train, 'South Africa: US, Don't Go Home', *Forbes*, 27 November 1978, pp. 33–35.

Humphrey Tyler, *Life in the Time of Sharpeville – and Wayward Seeds of a New South Africa*, Kwela Books, Cape Town, 1995.

Harvey Tyson (ed.), *Conflict and the Press: Proceedings of The Star's Centennial Conference on the Role of the Press in a Divided Society – Johannesburg, October 7–9 1987*, Argus Printing & Publishing Company, Johannesburg, 1987.

Sanford J. Ungar, *The Papers and The Papers: An Account of the Legal and Political Battle over the Pentagon Papers*, Columbia University Press, New York, 1989.

Sanford J. Ungar, *Africa: The People and Politics of an Emerging Continent*, Simon & Schuster, New York, 1986.

The United Nations and Apartheid, 1948–1994, Department of Public Information United Nations, New York, 1994.

US Business Involvement in Southern Africa: Hearings before the Subcommittee on Africa of the Committee on Foreign Affairs, Ninety-Second Congress, First Session, part one, US Government Printing Office, Washington DC, 1972.

US Business Involvement in Southern Africa: Hearings before the Subcommittee on Africa of The Committee on Foreign Affairs, Ninety-Second Congress, First Session, part two, US Government Printing Office, Washington DC, 1972.

Cyrus Vance, *Hard Choices: Critical Years in America's Foreign Policy*, Simon & Schuster, New York, 1983.

Les de Villiers, *South Africa: A Skunk Among Nations*, International Books, London, 1975.

Les de Villiers, *South Africa Drawn In Colour: The Smuts Years,*

1945–46, Gordon Publishing, Sandton, 1979.

Les de Villiers, *Secret Information*, Tafelberg, Cape Town, 1980.

Les de Villiers, *In Sight of Surrender: The US Sanctions Campaign Against South Africa, 1946–1993*, Praeger, Connecticut, 1995.

Martin Walker, *The Powers of the Press: The World's Great Newspapers*, Quartet Books, London, 1982.

Patrick Wall, *Prelude to Détente: An In-depth Report on South Africa*, Stacey International, London, 1975.

Neil Wates, *A Businessman Looks at Apartheid*, United Nations Unit on Apartheid, October 1970.

Carol H. Weiss, 'What America's Leaders Read', *The Public Opinion Quarterly*, Vol. 38, No. 1 (Spring 1974), pp. 1–22.

Lloyd Wendt, *Chicago Tribune: The Rise of a Great American Newspaper*, Rand McNally & Co., Chicago, 1979.

Lloyd Wendt, *The Wall Street Journal: The Story of Dow Jones and the Nation's Business Newspaper*, Rand McNally & Co., Chicago, 1982.

Arnold Wesker, *Journey into Journalism: A Very Personal Account in Four Parts*, Writers & Readers Publishing Co-operative, London, 1977.

Odd Arne Westad, 'Moscow and the Angolan Crisis, 1974–1976: A New Pattern of Intervention', *Cold War International History Project Bulletin*, No. 8/9 (1997), pp. 21–37.

Tom Wicker, 'The Greening of the Press', *Columbia Journalism Review*, May/June 1971, pp. 7–12.

David Wiley, 'Anti-Apartheid Movements versus Government Policy in US and UK', *Africa Today*, Vol. 26, No. 1 (1979), pp. 61–63.

Peter Willetts (ed.), *Pressure Groups in the Global System: The Transnational Relations of Issue-Orientated Non-Governmental Organizations*, Frances Pinter Ltd, London, 1982.

Ivor Wilkins and Hans Strydom, *The Super-Afrikaners*, Jonathan Ball Publishers, Houghton, 1978.

Edwin N. Wilmsen, 'Primitive Politics in Sanctified Landscapes: The Ethnographic Fictions of Laurens van der Post', *Journal of Southern African Studies*, Vol. 21, No. 2 (June 1995), pp. 201–23.

Elaine Windrich, *The Cold War Guerrilla: Jonas Savimbi, the US Media and the Angolan War*, Greenwood Press, New York, 1992.

Gordon Winter, *Inside BOSS: South Africa's Secret Police*, Penguin, Middlesex, 1981.

Gordon Winter, 'Inside BOSS and After', *Lobster*, No. 18 (1989), pp. 26–30.

Michael Wolfers and Jane Bergerol, *Angola in the Frontline*, Zed Books, London, 1983.

Donald Woods, *Biko*, Paddington Press, London, 1978.

Donald Woods, 'South Africa's Face to the World', *Foreign Affairs*, Vol. 56, No. 3 (April 1978), pp. 521–28.

Donald Woods, 'South Africa: Black Editors Out', *Index on Censorship*, Vol. 10, No. 3 (June 1981), pp. 32–34.

Donald Woods, *Asking For Trouble*, Gollancz, London, 1980.

Donald Woods, *South African Dispatches: Letters to my Countrymen*, Penguin Books, Middlesex, 1986.

Hugo Young, 'Rupert Murdoch and The Sunday Times: A Lamp Goes Out', the *Political Quarterly*, Vol. 55, No. 4 (1984), pp. 382–90.

Peter Younghusband, 'How Eschel Rhoodie Fought the Paper Curtain', the *Capetonian*, Vol. 1, No. 3 (February 1979), pp. 7–11.

UNPUBLISHED SOURCES

Oral interviews in Great Britain and Europe

David Adamson, 24 March 1995; Guy Arnold, 5 March 1996; Neil Behrmann, 15 March 1996; Hilda Bernstein, 15 July 1996; Bridget Bloom, 21 March 1995, 28 June 1996; Lord Chalfont, 12 March 1996; Len Clarke (John Laurence), 22 June and 7 July 1995; Stewart Dalby, 17 October 1995; Lord Deedes, 16 November 1995; Ethel de Keyser, 9 and 21 November 1995; Will Ellsworth-Jones, 8 March 1996; Richard Gott, 14 May 1996; John Grimond, 29 January 1996; Christabel Gurney, 6 August 1996; Brian Hackland, 13 November 1995; Peter Hain MP, 4 March 1996; David Harrison, 8 December 1995; Graham Hatton, 2 October 1995; Denis Herbstein, 17 November 1994, 9 March 1995, 7 February 1996; Barry Hillenbrand, 12 March 1996; Tony Hodges, 23 January 1995; Michael Holman, 10 January and 28 February 1995; John Humphrys, 26 February 1996; Derek Ingram, 16 January 1996; J.D.F. Jones, 3 November 1995; Henry Kamm, 15 January 1996; Robin Knight, 9 November 1995; Michael Knipe, 12 April 1995; Graham Leach, 24 October 1995; Colin Legum, 15 June 1995; Joan Lestor MP, 14 August 1996; Inge Lippman, 14 August 1996; David Loshak, 23 January 1996; Kenneth Mackenzie, 30 January 1996; James MacManus, 16 October 1995; Roy Macnab, 26 October 1996; Eric Marsden, 20 February 1997; Michael Nicholson, 13 February 1995; Roger Omond, 23 March 1995; Bruce Page, 17 May 1996; Quentin Peel, 7 July 1995; Mike Popham, 2 March 1995; Adam Raphael, 30 September 1994, 13 October 1995; William Raynor, 5 December 1995; Joe Rogaly, 22 November 1995; Barbara Rogers, 5 and 15 December 1995; Anthony Sampson, 24 October 1995; Xan Smiley, 6 February 1996; Jonathan

Steele, 15 November 1994; Geoffrey Taylor, 24 March 1996; Mike Terry, 14 December 1995; Antony Thomas, 26 July 1996; Stanley Uys, 22 September 1994, 5 January and 24 March 1995, 19 January 1996; Dan van der Vat, 31 October 1995; Ian Waller, 15 July 1996; Richard West, 28 November 1995; Robin White, 19 February 1997; Ray Wilkinson, 7 March 1996; Donald Woods, 19 June 1995; Sir Peregrine Worsthorne, 15 January 1996; Ian Wright, 26 October 1994; Hugo Young, 21 November 1995.

Oral interviews in North America

Heather Allen, 15–16 April 1996; Arnaud de Borchgrave, 14 November 1996; John Chettle, 23 May 1996; Jennifer Davis, 8 November 1996; Donald deKieffer, 12 April 1996; Jack Foisie, 16 April 1996; Paula Giddings, 19 April 1996; June Goodwin, 5 April 1996; Jimmy Greenfield, 29 March 1996; Lee Griggs, 16 September 1995; Henry S. Hayward, 21 September 1995; Larry Heinzerling, 19 September 1995, 19 April 1996; Christopher Hitchens, 15 April 1996; Jim Hoagland, 10 April 1996; George Houser, 17 April 1996; Graham Hovey, 17 April 1996; Tami Hultman, 8 April 1996; Frederic Hunter, 16 April 1996; Andrew Jaffe, 18 April 1996; Michael Kaufman, 9 September 1995; Reed Kramer, 8 April 1996; David Lamb, 10 April 1996; Joseph Lelyveld, 22 September 1995; Anthony Lewis, 12 September 1995; Tiuu Lukk (Litwik), 6 November 1996; William McWhirter, 6 April 1996; Bill Minter, 11 April 1996; Caryle Murphy, 9 September 1995; Bill Nicholson, 9 April 1996; David Ottaway, 15 September 1995; Les Payne, 8 November 1996; Benjamin Pogrund, 12 and 27 September 1995, 1 April and 23 July 1996; Stephen Rosenfeld, 1 November 1996; Karen Rothmyer, 16 April 1996; Danny Schechter, 19 April 1996; Bernard Simon, 4 April 1996; James Srodes (Lewis James), 11 April 1996; Dan Swanson (James North), 28 March 1996; James Thomson, 12 September 1995; Les de Villiers, 18 April 1996; Martin Walker, 9 April 1996; Tom Wicker, 19 September 1995; Robin Wright, 9 April 1996.

Oral interviews in South Africa and elsewhere

David Beresford, 21 May 1995; Jane Bergerol (Wilford), 22 May 1995; Fred Bridgland, 9 May 1995; John Burns, 19 November 1996; John Carlin, 21 April 1994; Rex Gibson, 24 May 1995; Peter Gregson, 26 May 1995; Cresley Gumede, 20 September 1996; Peter Hawthorne, 16 May 1995; Tony Heard, 23 September 1996; R.W. Johnson, 3 October 1996; Ray Kennedy, 11 May 1995; Alf Kumalo,

12 May 1995; Patrick Laurence, 12 May 1995; Raymond Louw, 20 September 1996; Peter Magubane, 20 May 1995; Francois Marais, 24 May 1995; David Martin, 4 September 1996; Harry Mashabela, 24 May 1995; Don Mattera, 20 September 1996; Sendiso Mfenyana, 18 May 1995; Abdul Minty, 3 October 1996; Chris More, 27 May 1995; Stephen Mulholland, 30 September 1996; Chris Munnion, 10 and 22 May 1995; Carl Noffke, 12 May 1995; John Platter, 15 May 1995; Dr John Poorter, 22 and 26 May 1995; Mervyn Rees, 25 April 1994, 9 May 1995; Reg September, 17 May 1995; Nat Serache, 4 October 1996; Hennie Serfontein, 3 October 1996; Gerald Shaw, 15 May 1995, 23 September 1996; Keith Shaw, 26 May 1995; Allister Sparks, 25 May 1995; Gerry Suckley, 11 May 1995; Gabu (Jan) Tugwana, 20 September 1996; Humphrey Tyler, 3 October 1996; Eric Van Ees, 22 May 1995; Tony Wasserman, 4 October 1996; Martin Welz, 4 October 1996; Peter Younghusband, 15 May 1995.

Graeme Norris Addison, 'Censorship of the Press in South Africa during the Angolan War: A Case Study of News Manipulation and Suppression', unpublished MA dissertation, Rhodes University, Grahamstown, 1980.

Howard Barrell, 'Conscripts to their Age: African National Congress Operational Strategy, 1976–1986', unpublished DPhil dissertation, Oxford University, 1993.

BBC, telegram to Peter Hawthorne, 16 June 1976.

Len Clarke, letter to author, 21 May 1997.

Marsha Lynne Coleman, 'Prestigious American Newspapers' Coverage of African Political Crises Events', unpublished PhD dissertation, Massachusetts Institute Of Technology, 1982.

David Everatt, 'The Politics of Non-racialism: White Opposition to Apartheid, 1945–1960', unpublished DPhil dissertation, Oxford University, 1990.

The Foreign Correspondents' Association of South Africa, complete archive, Institute of Commonwealth Studies, University of London.

'From the Afrikaans Press' 1978–1979, archive, University of the Witwatersrand.

June Goodwin and Ben Schiff, *The Heart of Whiteness*, unpublished extracts from interviews.

Galen Hall, 'South African Lobbies', May 1977, draft chapter of an unpublished book.

Graham Hovey, letter to author, 18 October 1997.

John Humphrys, letter to author, November 1995.

Bernard Levin, letter to author, 10 July 1996.

Mike Murphy, letter to author, 25 July 1995.

Benjamin Pogrund, letter to author, 25 May 1996.

John Poorter, letter to author, 20 November 1997.

Llewellyn Raubenheimer, 'A Study of Black Journalists and Black Media Workers in Union Organisation, 1971 to 1981', unpublished BA (Hons) dissertation, University of Cape Town, 1982.

William Raynor and Geoffrey Allen, 'Smear: The Thorpe Affair', unpublished book, 1978.

Mervyn Rees interview with Eschel Rhoodie, transcript, 1979.

The secret projects list, 1978.

John Seiler, 'The Formulation of US Policy toward Southern Africa, 1957–1976: The Failure of Good Intentions', unpublished PhD thesis, University of Connecticut, 1976.

Gerald Shaw, 'The *Cape Times* and The Angola War: August 1975– March 1976', unpublished essay.

Scott Thomas, 'The Diplomacy of Liberation: The International Relations of the African National Congress of South Africa, 1960–1985', PhD dissertation, London School of Economics, 1990.

Les de Villiers, 'US Sanctions Against South Africa: A Historical Analysis of the Sanctions Campaign and its Political Implications', DPhil dissertation, University of Stellenbosch, 1994.

Lynne Watson, letter to Julian Ross (*Washington Post*), 9 April 1977.

Marion Whitehead, 'The Black Gatekeepers: A Study of Black Journalists on Three Daily Newspapers which Covered the Soweto Uprising of 1976', unpublished BA (Hons) dissertation, Rhodes University, Grahamstown, 1978.

Oliver Wright, Confidential memo to P.W. Carey, Board of Trade, 17 October 1964 (Public Records Office: PREM 13/092).

Index

Publications (newspapers, books) are shown in *italics*